BROOKLANDS
BOOKS

# ALLARD

## *Gold Portfolio*

## 1937-1959

Compiled by
R.M. Clarke

ISBN 1 870642 481

Distributed by
Brooklands Book Distribution Ltd.
'Holmerise', Seven Hills Road,
Cobham, Surrey, England
Printed in Hong Kong

**BROOKLANDS BOOKS**

## BROOKLANDS BOOKS SERIES
AC Ace & Aceca 1953-1983
AC Cobra 1962-1969
Alfa Romeo Alfasud 1972-1984
Alfa Romeo Alfetta Coupes GT.GTV.GTV6 1974-1987
Alfa Romeo Guilias Berlinettas
Alfa Romeo Giulia Berlinas 1962-1976
Alfa Romeo Giulia Coupés 1963-1976
Alfa Romeo Spider 1966-1987
Allard Gold Portfolio 1937-1958
Aston Martin Gold Portfolio 1972-1985
Austin Seven 1922-1982
Austin A30 & A35 1951-1962
Austin Healey 100 1952-1959
Austin Healey 3000 1959-1967
Austin Healey 100 & 3000 Collection No. 1
Austin Healey 'Frogeye' Sprite Collection No. 1
Austin Healey Sprite 1958-1971
Avanti 1962-1983
BMW Six Cylinder Coupés 1969-1975
BMW 1600 Collection No. 1
BMW 2002 1968-1976
Bristol Cars Gold Portfolio 1946-1985
Buick Automobiles 1947-1960
Buick Riviera 1963-1978
Cadillac Automobiles 1949-1959
Cadillac Automobiles 1960-1969
Cadillac Eldorado 1967-1978
Camaro 1966-1970
Chevrolet Camaro & Z-28 1973-1981
High Performance Camaros 1982-1988
Chevrolet Camaro Collection No. 1
Chevrolet 1955-1957
Chevrolet Impala & SS 1958-1971
Chevelle & SS 1964-1972
Chevy II Nova & SS 1962-1973
Chrysler 300 1955-1970
Citroen Traction Avant 1934-1957
Citroen DS & ID 1955-1875
Citroen 2CV 1948-1988
Cobras & Replicas 1962-1983
Cortina 1600E & GT 1967-1970
Corvair 1959-1968
Daimler Dart & V-8 250 1959-1969
Datsun 240z 1970-1973
Datsun 280Z & ZX 1975-1983
De Tomaso Collection No. 1
Dodge Charger 1966-1974
Excalibur Collection No. 1
Ferrari Cars 1946-1956
Ferrari Cars 1962-1966
Ferrari Cars 1969-1973
Ferrari Dino 1965-1974
Ferrari Dino 308 1974-1979
Ferrari 308 & Mondial 1980-1984
Ferrari Collection No. 1
Fiat-Bertone X1/9 1973-1988
Fiat Pininfarina 124+2000 Spider 1968-1985
Ford Falcon 1960-1970
Ford Mustang 1964-1967
Ford Mustang 1967-1973
High Performance Mustangs 1982-1988
Ford RS Escort 1968-1980
Honda CRX 1983-1987
High Performance Escorts MkI 1968-1974
High Performance Escorts MkII 1975-1980
Hudson & Railton Cars 1936-1940
Jaguar XK120 XK140 XK150 Gold Portfolio 1948-1960
Jaguar Cars 1957-1961
Jaguar Cars 1961-1964
Jaguar MK2 1959-1969
Jaguar E-Type 1961-1966
Jaguar E-Type 1966-1971
Jaguar E-Type V12 1971-1975
Jaguar XKE Collection No. 1
Jaguar XJ6 1968-1972
Jaguar XJ6 Series II 1973-1979
Jaguar XJ6 & XJ12 Series III 1979-1985
Jaguar XJ12 1972-1980
Jaguar XJS Gold Portfolio 1975-1988
Jensen Cars 1946-1967
Jensen Cars 1967-1979
Jensen Interceptor Gold Portfolio 1966-1986
Lamborghini Cars 1964-1970
Lamborghini Cars 1970-1975
Lamborghini Countach Collection No. 1
Lamborghini Countach & Urraco 1974-1980
Lamborghini Countach & Jalpa 1980-1985
Lancia Stratos 1972-1985
Land Rover 1948-1973
Land Rover Series II & IIa 1958-1971
Land Rover Series III 1971-1985
Land Rover 90 & 110 1983-1989
Lotus Cortina 1963-1970
Lotur Elan Gold Portfolio 1962-1974
Lotus Elan Collection No. 2
Lotus Elite 1957-1964
Lotus Elite & Eclat 1974-1981
Lotus Turbo Esprit 1980-1986
Lotus Europa 1966-1975
Lotus Europa Collection No. 1
Lotus Seven 1957-1980
Lotus Seven Collection No. 1
Maserati 1965-1970
Maserati 1970-1975
Marcos Cars 1960-1988
Mazda RX-7 Collection No. 1
Mercedes 190 & 300SL 1954-1963
Mercedes 230/250/280SL 1963-1971
Mercedes 350/450SL & SLC 1971-1980
Mercedes Benz Cars 1949-1954
Mercedes Benz Cars 1954-1957
Mercedes Benz Cars 1957-1961
Mercedes Benz Competition Cars 1950-1957

Metropolitan 1954-1962
MG Cars 1929-1934
MG TC 1945-1949
MG TD 1949-1953
MG TF 1953-1955
MG Cars 1957-1959
MG Cars 1959-1962
MG Midget 1961-1980
MGA Collection No. 1
MGA Roadsters 1955-1962
MGB Roadsters 1962-1980
MGB GT 1965-1980
Mini Cooper 1961-1971
Morgan Cars 1960-1970
Morgan Cars 1969-1979
Morris Minor Collection No. 1
Old's Cutlass & 4-4-2 1964-1972
Oldsmobile Toronado 1966-1978
Opel GT 1968-1973
Packard Gold Portfolio 1946-1958
Pantera 1969-1973
Pantera & Mangusta 1969-1974
Plymouth Barracuda 1964-1974
Pontiac Fiero 1984-1988
Pontiac GTO 1964-1970
Pontiac Firebird 1967-1973
Pontiac Firebird and Trans-Am 1973-1981
High Performance Firebirds 1982-1988
Pontiac Tempest & GTO 1961-1965
Porsche Cars 1960-1964
Porsche Cars 1964-1968
Porsche Cars 1968-1972
Porsche Cars in the Sixties
Porsche Cars 1972-1975
Porsche 356 1952-1965
Porsche 911 Collection No. 1
Porsche 911 Collection No. 2
Porsche 911 1965-1969
Porsche 911 1970-1972
Porsche 911 1973-1977
Porsche 911 Carrera 1973-1977
Porsche 911 SC 1978-1983
Porsche 911 Turbo 1975-1984
Porsche 914 Gold Portfolio 1969-1988
Porsche 914 Collection No. 1
Porsche 924 1975-1981
Porsche 928 Collection No. 1
Porsche 944 1981-1985
Porsche Turbo Collection No. 1
Reliant Scimitar 1964-1986
Riley 1½ & 2½ Litre Gold Portfolio 1945-1955
Rolls Royce Silver Cloud 1955-1965
Rolls Royce Silver Shadow 1965-1980
Range Rover Gold Portfolio 1970-1988
Rover 3 & 3.5 Litre 1958-1973
Rover P4 1949-1959
Rover P4 1955-1964
Rover 2000 + 2200 1963-1977
Rover 3500 1968-1977
Rover 3500 & Vitesse 1976-1986
Saab Sonett Collection No. 1
Saab Turbo 1976-1983
Studebaker Hawks & Larks 1956-1963
Sunbeam Tiger And Alpine Gold Portfolio 1959-1967
Thunderbird 1955-1957
Thunderbird 1958-1963
Thunderbird 1964-1976
Toyota MR2 1984-1988
Triumph 2000-2.5-2500 1963-1977
Triumph Spitfire 1962-1980
Triumph Spitfire Collection No. 1
Triumph Stag 1970-1980
Triumph Stag Collection No. 1
Triumph TR2 & TR3 1952-1960
Triumph TR4.TR5.TR250 1961-1968
Triumph TR6 1969-1976
Triumph TR6 Collection No. 1
Triumph TR7 & TR8 1975-1982
Triumph GT6 1966-1974
Triumph Vitesse & Herald 1959-1971
TVR Gold Portfolio 1959-1988
Volkswagen Cars 1936-1956
VW Beetle 1956-1977
VW Beetle Collection No. 1
VW Golf GTi 1976-1986
VW Karmann Ghia 1955-1982
VW Scirocco 1974-1981
VW Bus-Camper-Van 1954-1967
VW Bus-Camper-Van 1968-1979
Volvo 1800 1960-1973
Volvo 120 Series 1956-1970

## BROOKLANDS MUSCLE CARS SERIES
American Motors Muscle Cars 1966-1970
Buick Muscle Cars 1965-1970
Camaro Muscle Cars 1966-1972
Capri Muscle Cars 1969-1983
Chevrolet Muscle Cars 1966-1972
Dodge Muscle Cars 1967-1970
Mercury Muscle Cars 1966-1971
Mini Muscle Cars 1961-1979
Mopar Muscle Cars 1964-1967
Mopar Muscle Cars 1968-1971
Mustang Muscle Cars 1967-1971
Shelby Mustang Muscle Cars 1965-1970
Oldsmobile Muscle Cars 1964-1970
Plymouth Muscle Cars 1966-1971
Pontiac Muscle Cars 1966-1972
Muscle Cars Compared 1966-1971
Muscle Cars Compared Book 2 1965-1971

## BROOKLANDS ROAD & TRACK SERIES
Road & Track on Alfa Romeo 1949-1963
Road & Track on Alfa Romeo 1964-1970
Road & Track on Alfa Romeo 1971-1976

Road & Track on Alfa Romeo 1977-1984
Road & Track on Aston Martin 1962-1984
Road & Track on Auburn Cord & Duesenberg 1952-1984
Road & Track on Audi 1952-1980
Road & Track on Audi 1980-1986
Road & Track on Austin Healey 1953-1970
Road & Track on BMW Cars 1966-1974
Road & Track on BMW Cars 1975-1978
Road & Track on BMW Cars 1979-1983
Road & Track on Cobra, Shelby &
  Ford GT40 1962-1983
Road & Track on Corvette 1953-1967
Road & Track on Corvette 1968-1982
Road & Track on Corvette 1982-1986
Road & Track on Datsun Z 1970-1983
Road & Track on Ferrari 1950-1968
Road & Track on Ferrari 1968-1974
Road & Track on Ferrari 1975-1981
Road & Track on Ferrari 1981-1984
Road & Track on Fiat Sports Cars 1968-1987
Road & Track on Jaguar 1950-1960
Road & Track on Jaguar 1961-1968
Road & Track on Jaguar 1968-1974
Road & Track on Jaguar 1974-1982
Road & Track on Jaguar 1983-1989
Road & Track on Lamborghini 1964-1985
Road & Track on Lotus 1972-1981
Road & Track on Maserati 1952-1974
Road & Track on Maserati 1975-1983
Road & Track on Mazda RX7 1978-1986
Road & Track on Mercedes 1952-1962
Road & Track on Mercedes 1963-1970
Road & Track on Mercedes 1971-1979
Road & Track on Mercedes 1980-1987
Road & Track on MG Sports Cars 1949-1961
Road & Track on MG Sports Cars 1962-1980
Road & Track on Mustang 1964-1977
Road & Track on Peugeot 1955-1986
Road & Track on Pontiac 1960-1983
Road & Track on Porsche 1951-1967
Road & Track on Porsche 1968-1971
Road & Track on Porsche 1972-1975
Road & Track on Porsche 1975-1978
Road & Track on Porsche 1979-1982
Road & Track on Porsche 1982-1985
Road & Track on Rolls Royce & Bentley 1950-1965
Road & Track on Rolls Royce & Bentley 1966-1984
Road & Track on Saab 1955-1985
Road & Track on Toyota Sports & G T Cars 1966-1986
Road & Track on Triumph Sports Cars 1953-1967
Road & Track on Triumph Sports Cars 1967-1974
Road & Track on Triumph Sports Cars 1974-1982
Road & Track on Volkswagen 1951-1968
Road & Track on Volkswagen 1968-1978
Road & Track on Volkswagen 1978-1985
Road & Track on Volvo 1957-1974
Road & Track on Volvo 1975-1985
Road & Track Henry Manney At Large & Abroad

## BROOKLANDS CAR AND DRIVER SERIES
Car and Driver on BMW 1955-1977
Car and Driver on BMW 1977-1985
Car and Driver on Cobra, Shelby & Ford GT40
  1963-1984
Car and Driver on Datsun Z 1600 & 2000
  1966-1984
Car and Driver on Corvette 1956-1967
Car and Driver on Corvette 1968-1977
Car and Driver on Corvette 1978-1982
Car and Driver on Corvette 1983-1988
Car and Driver on Ferrari 1955-1962
Car and Driver on Ferrari 1963-1975
Car and Driver on Ferrari 1976-1983
Car and Driver on Mopar 1956-1967
Car and Driver on Mopar 1968-1975
Car and Driver on Mustang 1964-1972
Car and Driver on Pontiac 1961-1975
Car and Driver on Porsche 1955-1962
Car and Driver on Porsche 1963-1970
Car and Driver on Porsche 1970-1976
Car and Driver on Porsche 1977-1981
Car and Driver on Porsche 1982-1986
Car and Driver on Saab 1956-1985
Car and Driver on Volvo 1955-1986

## BROOKLANDS MOTOR & THOROUGHBRED & CLASSIC CAR SERIES
Motor & T & CC on Ferrari 1966-1976
Motor & T & CC on Ferrari 1976-1984
Motor & T & CC on Lotus 1979-1983
Motor & T & CC on Morris Minor 1948-1983

## BROOKLANDS PRACTICAL CLASSICS SERIES
Practical Classics on Austin A 40 Restoration
Practical Classics on Land Rover Restoration
Practical Classics on Metalworking in Restoration
Practical Classics on Midget/Sprite Restoration
Practical Classics on Mini Cooper Restoration
Practical Classics on MGB Restoration
Practical Classics on Morris Minor Restoration
Practical Classics on Triumph Herald/Vitesse
Practical Classics on Triumph Spitfire Restoration
Practical Classics on VW Beetle Restoration
Practical Classics on 1930S Car Restoration

## BROOKLANDS MILITARY VEHICLES SERIES
Allied Military Vehicles Collection No. 1
Allied Military Vehicles Collection No. 2
Dodge Military Vehicles Collection No. 1
Military Jeeps 1941-1945
Off Road Jeeps 1944-1971
V W Kubelwagen 1940-1975

**BROOKLANDS BOOKS**

CONTENTS

**BROOKLANDS BOOKS**

## *ACKNOWLEDGEMENTS*

Some of the most popular titles in our series cover cars that have European bodywork and American engines. These include the AC Cobra, Sunbeam Tiger, Jensen Interceptor and of course the Panteras. Sydney Allard was one of the first to recognise the value of this dynamic combination, as will be seen from the pages that follow.

We have received much help in producing this book firstly from Tom Turner and Syd Silverman in the US. The former generously lending us some excellent colour slides of an Allard in action one of which we have included on the back cover. Help was also forthcoming from Tom Lush in England. Tom joined Sydney Allard before the war and was his competition manager and personal assistant. In 1977 he wrote the very readable and informative "Allard — The Inside Story" which is sadly out-of-print. He kindly agreed to pen a short introduction to this anthology which can be found below.

We are also indebted to the publishers of Autocar, Automobile Engineer, Autosport, Car and Driver, Classic and Sportscar, Motor, Motor Sport, Motor Trend, Road & Track, Speed Age, Sports Cars Illustrated, Thoroughbred & Classic Cars and Wheels for allowing us once again to include their copyright road tests and other stories in the compilation of this book.

R.M. Clarke

When Sydney Allard built his first special from the remains of a crashed V8 Ford in 1936 his intention was simply to create a suitable vehicle for use in motoring events and certainly had no thoughts of starting a manufacturing business. However the car proved so successful that he began to receive requests to build replicas for other enthusiasts and accordingly built another eleven before the outbreak of war in 1939, with the twelfth designated as an exhibit in the Earls Court Motor Show of that year. The show abandoned, and the partially built car stored until 1945 and then hurriedly completed in time for Allard to compete in the Bristol Club Hillclimb in July. In view of this unexpected demand, and forseeing a shortage of all types of vehicles after the war, plans were made during this time to set up a company to build a range of cars suitable for general use and not solely for competition.

In 1946 the Allard Motor Company was formed for this purpose, but as the substantial financial outlay required to design and build the major components would not be available Ford units would be incorporated in a chassis of Allard design and the first two cars built to this specification were seen by the public in the SMMT/RAC Cavalcade through London in July 1946.

Following this introduction, some 1,900 cars were built, until the changing economic climate of 1958 made production no longer viable and 1957 Motor Show was the last at which Allard cars were represented. During this life span the name became known world-wide, particularly in America where the J2 series cars played a major role in the revival of sports car racing.

The following pages sum up the achievements of a small private company with the unique distinction of being controlled by a man who regularly competed in motor sport with cars bearing his own name and who once said he had no wish to become a millionaire and only wanted his Company to support his personal interests and to provide employment for others.

Tom Lush
Stoke Prior
Worcs

# A SPECIAL TRIALS FORD V8

## A VERY HIGH-PERFORMANCE CAR BUILT FOR A CLIENT BY S. H. ALLARD

No trials car has caused quite such a sensation of recent years by reason of consistently successful " pot " lifting as S. H. Allard's Special 30 h.p. Ford V8. This car, has, we believe, never gained lower than a second class award, and usually a " premier," in all the trials in which it has run, besides winning very many special prices in addition. Indeed, we understand that the only mechanical trouble ever experienced in connection with trials was a cracked head on a re-placement engine when going to the start, and that only once, during a two-day Scottish trial, has oil been added to the engine away from the home garage. That is a highly commendable record for any car and quite astonishing from one of such potent performance. In racing, something like 105 m.p.h. was attained in the Relay Race at Brooklands, but the fibre timing wheels gave trouble, pre-sumably because at high revs. the small head of oil is insufficient to feed the drive. As the V8 exhaust system is prone to cause general overheating under racing conditions Allard never experimented with steel pinions, which would probably have cured the other trouble.

This special has a 1935 engine, with raised compression-ratio, and Scintilla magneto ignition, and is otherwise prac-tically standard. The chassis is of 1933 type, cut down to give a wheelbase of 8 ft. 4 in., a front track of 4 ft. 8 in. and a rear track of 3 ft. 10 in. The body came from a 2.3-litre G.P. Bugatti and Bugatti very high-geared steering is used. The bottom gear ratio is 10 to 1 and top 3.56 to 1, second being around 5½ to 1. The rear axle incorporates a novel form of clutch, lever controlled, for locking the rear axle, and the front assembly incor-porates L.M.B. independent suspension. In the form in which it ran in the recent Lawrence Cup Trial, minus screen and spare wheels, it weighed exactly one ton, and with equipment probably weighs 21 cwt. This is with fuel aboard, which accounts for some 2½ cwt., as the rear Bugatti tank holds forty gallons and is filled to the brim to aid wheel adhesion. As is well known, this remarkable Ford has climbed the worst of our trials gradients and it does 0 to 50 m.p.h. in something under 7 secs., and gives 18 to 20 m.p.g. The tyre sizes are varied for different events.

It was experimentation with this car that enabled Allard to construct a very interesting Ford for a client, Mr. Gilson, who has driven an M.G. in recent trials. As these cars will probably go into small scale production, with certain bodywork modifications, we were interested to examine Mr. Gilson's car at the Ranalah coachworks, where the body was being built.

The chassis is specially constructed from a combination of 1933 and 1937 parts, united at major points by welding. The aim has been to provide a very high-performance car for competition and touring, with the majority of parts readily interchangeable with standard Ford spares, and Allard has succeeded remarkably well.

The only cut-down parts are rear-axle half-shafts and the propeller-shaft and torque-tube. The wheelbase is now 8 ft. 6½ in., the front track 4 ft. 8 in. and the rear track 4 ft. 2½ in., resulting in a very compact construction. There is about 8 to 9 in. ground clearance everywhere.

At the front L.M.B. independent sus-pension is fitted, with the Ford axle-radius arms linked to the frame side-members to improve the ground clear-ance. At the rear the axle has the standard ratio and incorporates an ingenious diff-erential lock similar to that on the Allard-Special. It takes the form of a friction clutch with Ford plates, which can be adjusted so that the differential is nor-mally locked but enabling slip to take place under excessive loadings to obviate sheared axle-keys. To lock the axle for those trials where this is permissible, a cover-plate on the housing is removed, and bolts tightened with a box spanner. André Telecontrol shock-absorbers are fitted to the rear axle. The gearbox has a short lever of remote control type, working in a long tunnel and retaining the conventional gear-positions. The hand-brake is of M.G. pattern, racing-type, set almost horizontally, the chassis cross-member, and brake-gear thereon, being of 1933 type. The steering wheel is an Ashby spring-spoke.

The 1937 30 h.p. V8 engine is mounted well behind the front axle on standard, but rather more rigid, mountings It is standard except for thinner cylinder-head gaskets, a Scintilla Vertex horizon-tally-placed magneto to aid high-revving on the lower ratios, and double-branch exhaust off-takes. The silencers are standard. Fuel feed is by twin Auto-pulses, one arranged as a spare and the air-cleaner on the carburetter is retained. There is an 18 gallon slab-shape fuel tank at the rear, with provision for mounting twin comp. shod wheel behind it. The fuel lines enter the tank from the

*The Special Trials Ford V8 in Chassis form*

top, running down within, to obviate any chance of fracture in trials conditions. The radiator is a Ford unit cut down by 2 in. to lower it, and fitted with the com-bined " Allard-Special " cowl and stone-guard and a quick-action filler cap. The Ranalah body has a wood frame covered with aluminium panels, finished cream and black. It is a two-door, two-three-seater with front bucket seats and ample room for the rear-seat occupant. The doors slope away and the single-pane screen folds forward. The 6-volt battery sits on a tray beside the rear seat on the off side. Equipment includes standard wheels and tyres, Lucas P100 headlamps, and radio. The instrument panel carries a Cooper-Stewart rev.-counter that matches the Ford speedometer and is driven from a gear-head on the off-side water-pump assembly. A Marles high-geared steering-box is used. The com-plete car is expected to turn the scales at 20 cwt., or less with Bosch headlamps and the radio removed.

It has almost every part easily replace-able and is expected to be even faster than the Allard-Special. The acceleration is expected to be in the order of 7 secs. from 0 to 50 m.p.h. and 10 to 11 secs. from 0 to 60 m.p.h. and we hope to be able to take test figures when the car is run in. It has cycle-type wings and no running-boards, but Allard anticipates wings and bodies similar to those of the H.R.G. for future cars on these lines, the price of which would work out at about £475. Particulars are available from Messrs. Adlards Motors, 3, Keswick Road, Putney, S.W.

---

## ON THE OPENING OF THE SOUTHERN ROAD CIRCUITS

When this article was written for the May issue the author stated that the attendance figures at Brooklands on May 1st had not been issued. The official figure is 18,000.

# Built for Performance—The Allard Special

## Replicas of Famous Trials Car Now Available to the Public. Independent Front-wheel Springing

*A speedy character is suggested in the very lines of the Allard Special which is fitted with the L.M.B. independent front-wheel suspension system and is tuned for performance.*

THE first production model of the Allard Special has just been completed. The trials successes of S. H. Allard are so well known as to need no special comment and they have led to repeated requests that replicas of the car should be made available for sale. Production has now been started by Adlard Motors, Ltd., 3, Keswick Road, Putney, London, S.W., and, as can be seen from the photographs, a very useful vehicle for competitions and high-speed road work has been produced.

The engine is a standard V-8 Ford unit with the addition of a supplementary electric fuel feed, Scintilla magneto and a high-compression gasket. It is, however, set back 12 ins. into the chassis and this, in combination with the revised driving position, has effected a transfer of 3 cwt. from the front to the rear axle.

The latest type engine has twin water pumps with a delivery of 90 gallons per minute. High maximum speeds can, in consequence, be safely maintained with no fear of overheating. It is, indeed, possible to use normal soft plugs for competition work.

The chassis itself is entirely "special" with parallel torque arms from the front axle which have resulted in the minimum ground clearance of 9½ ins. L.M.B. independent front suspension is used and all springs are damped by large Andre telecontrol shock absorbers. Marles steering is fitted, giving four turns from lock to lock and the rear track is narrowed to 50½ ins.

The gearbox has remote control and

Columbia two-speed overdrive is an optional extra. As standard equipment there is a special friction clutch mechanism designed by Mr. Allard to enable the differential to be locked when climbing steep hills with poor surfaces.

Another unusual feature is the use of a fixed starting handle. This enables the car to be stripped of electrical equipment (except magneto) yet to be rapidly started in any special test.

The instruments are mounted on a high and inclined facia. They are, therefore, easy to read and include both speedometer and rev. counter. A four-spoke spring steering wheel is

fitted and the light cycle-type wings are both in view from the driving seat.

The standard body is a two-seater with a 20-gallon tank having twin fillers. Two competition tyres are fitted at the back; there are Bosch lamps and screen wiper and a fold-flat windscreen. The radiator is lowered and has an outside quick filler. The total weight of this very interesting car is only 22 cwt., or under 0.70 lb. per c.c. It should, therefore, have outstanding acceleration and, in view of its low frontal area, the claim made for a maximum of over 90 m.p.h. is not unreasonable. The price at which it is offered is £475.

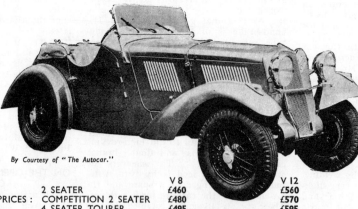

# THE FOUR-SEATER PRODUCTION-MODEL ALLARD-SPECIAL

THE V8 Allard-Specials of Sydney Allard, Guy Warburton and F. D. Gilson, together with the amazing V12 Allard-Special driven by K. N. Hutchison, are universally recognised as amongst the most potent trials and sprint motors of the present era. Messrs. Adlards Motors Ltd. have been in a position to supply replicas of these cars to private owners for some time past, quick completion of orders being accomplished. Recently they have embarked very seriously on a proper production programme and have introduced a full four-seater edition of the Allard-Special.

The familiar and imposing radiator-guard, dumb-iron apron and bonnet are retained, likewise the slab-pattern sixteen gallon rear fuel tank with dual feed, flexible pipe-lines and facia-reserve. The chassis details follow the same specification as that of the competition two-seaters, and it is notable that the weight has only been increased by a small amount, so that the remarkable acceleration is not materially impaired. But the new body has full touring equipment and graceful flowing wings and running boards of full size. The spare wheel is mounted at the rear and the hood is accommodated when folded in a well behind the rear seat. The front seats are of bucket type, there are cut-away doors on both sides, and the rear seat occupants have adequate leg room.

This body is constructed of seasoned ash, strengthened when necessary by steel plates, and panelled in 18 gauge aluminium. The rigid side curtains are carried in the rear locker. The wings are of 20 gauge steel and the bonnet, which has a spring loaded strap, is of 16 gauge

aluminium. The seats have leather-upholstered Dunlopillo cushions, and any colour cellulose may be specified. The demonstration car which we inspected looked extremely well, finished entirely in cream. The equipment includes Dunlop tyres, Burgess silencers, Hartford shock-absorbers, Marles steering and Bosch electrical equipment, while numerous extras are listed to meet competition requirements. A two-speed rear axle and Telecontrol shock-absorber control is standardised on the four-seater. The modern Allard-Special is no longer a Ford conversion. It is a reliable, practical job built throughout for hard work at high performance. The chassis was described in MOTOR SPORT, July 1937.

This new tourer should be a quite exceptional car for fast travel, rallies and trials, and it combines very happily an air of dignity and speed. The maximum speed is stated to be in the neighbourhood of 90 to 95 m.p.h. and the acceleration should be almost unbeatable. The price is £495, or £595 with the V12 Lincoln motor. The chassis price is £380 and replicas of the famous V8 and V12 trials cars are listed at £480 and £570 respectively. The four-seater has a wheelbase of 8 ft. 6½ in. with V8 engine and 9 ft. 0 in. with the V12 engine. Full details and a catalogue will be forwarded on request by Adlards Motors, Ltd., 3, Keswick Road, Putney, London, S.W.15 (Putney 2333).

*An imposing three-quarter front view photograph of the Allard-Special.*

# THE TWO-SEATER PRODUCTION MODEL ALLARD SPECIAL

Last month we announced exclusively the introduction of a production four-seater version of the Allard-Special. We are now able to add that S. H. Allard will shortly open extensive new works at Putney for the manufacture of these cars. The production model two-seater is a very smart car, equipped for fast road work, with more suitable wings and body layout than those of the Competition two-seater. A straight bonnet line has been achieved and the ugly gap between dumb-irons and front axle eliminated. Great care has been taken to secure a good driving position, the wing treatment is particularly neat, and knock-off wire wheels are standard. A short run in heavy traffic showed up the extremely smooth, silent flow of power from the V8 engine, the astonishing acceleration and complete tractability, while we observed with satisfaction the rigidity of the bodywork and " front works," a feature all too rare in modern light-weight high-performance cars. The instrument board carries a simple and effective array of dials, and a sprung steering wheel, Marles high-geared steering, racing-pattern hand-brake, remote gear control, Bosch lighting, twin pump fuel feed, Burgess silencers, disappearing hood,

side screens, and Dunlop tyres are standardised. The price is £460, or £560 with the V12 Lincoln engine. Replicas of the Competition models are also available, at £480 and £570 respectively. Naturally, the specifications and equipment can be considerably adapted to

suit individual requirements. The bodywork of the first production four-seater was made by Messrs. Coachcraft Ltd., and that of the two-seater by Whittingham and Mitchell. Full details are available from Messrs. Adlards Motors, 3, Keswick Road, Putney, S.W.15.

*The two-seater Allard Special.*

# THROUGH THE EXPERTS' TRIAL IN K. N. HUTCHISON'S NEW V8 ALLARD SPECIAL

WHEN K. N. Hutchison, well known trials driver in the now famous Allard-Special "Tail-waggers" team, rang up and asked me to ride with him through the Experts' Trial I accepted readily, for two very sound reasons. In the first place it is extremely instructive to ride through a classic trial beside someone who has an unrivalled reputation as a skilful slime stormer. Secondly, I was anxious to gain experience of the latest Allard-Special, a car which is the Allard answer to next season's plain-tyre enforcement, and as yet in decidedly experimental trim, having left the coachbuilders only a few days before the event. It is true that "Hutch." explained, rather hurriedly, I thought, as if trying to seem more than usually matter of fact, that this new car had no screen before the passenger, not even a scuttle cowl, nor had it a hood, while if I required a change of clothes I must needs pack a very small parcel, luggage accommodation being at a distinct premium.

Mrs. Hutchison, who regularly rides on her husband's left, had, it was only too evident, given the new "Tailwagger" one rapid, thorough glance and firmly announced that she would go *to* the trial but not *on* it—in the security of the Railton saloon. I like to pose as an enthusiast, so, bar praying for fine days when I thought of it, I made no bones about this lack of protection—borrowing a decent flying hat and a pair of waterproof goggles was far more to the point.

The new car, it should be explained, is based on Sydney Allard's highly successful, not to say potent, original V8 Allard-Special, now meritoriously motored in competition by Guy Warburton. In dimensions and specification it is the catalogue £450 Allard. Actually, the engine, at present a V8, is set further back than ever before, while weight has been saved wherever possible by judicious simplification, so that it is a mere 17½ cwt., or some 3 cwt. lighter than Warburton's car. The engine has Vertex magneto ignition, raised compression ratio, and special water off-takes and exhaust system. This tail is a replica of that used for the G.P. "2.3" Bugatti bodies and accommodates a big fuel tank well clear of the axle. Not only does it contribute towards one of the best-balanced starkest-looking cars ever constructed, but it must be of considerable help at high knots—and "Hutch." intends to do much sprint work in 1939, probably with a V12 Lincoln engine slipped in. In addition, the pointed tail makes it possible for the passenger to drape the right arm behind the driver—essential on a trials hill in the narrow cockpit—without experiencing cramped muscles. The body-builders, Messrs. Whittingham and Mitchell, really do deserve great credit for turning out an intensely attractive body in the space of a fortnight. The construction is of very light gauge aluminium, and in spite of the great length of bonnet and its dispensation of heavy cross-stays there is not a trace of flexion or ripple over the roughest surfaces—and you certainly encounter rough stuff in Exmoor. The spare wheel-mounting problem is nicely met by a very rigid bracket on the near side and the use of fixed bonnet-sides, the engine being perfectly accessible through the medium of the opening top bonnet-panels, mounted with hinge off-set.

These Allards are certainly the outstanding version of the modern style of truly potent sports-car. And few old-school motors look as stark, as does the latest of the breed. After lunch with "Hutch." and his Siamese cats at his London flat I was taken swiftly and easily West. The Allard demands no special plugs and masses of "in-case" extras. It is flexible down to a crawl in top, yet accelerates like a racing-car. It is very stable and rides solidly, yet without much pitching and tossing at touring gaits. As to speed, "Hutch." wasn't hurrying, but seventy was comfortable cruising. Incidentally, the normal Ford combined dial, incorporating oil-gauge, water thermometer, oil thermometer and ammeter, is the only dial on the dash and, as "Hutch." drily observed, you do not need a bevy of confusing needles when Dagenham can dish all the necessary readings up in one.

The flip down was exhilarating, but uneventful, save for the breakage of the near side main wing stay—did I say the car is experimental, as yet ?—and consequent fusing of all lights, a matter efficiently coped with from the emergency aspect by Hutchison and from the repair aspect of a Langport garage proprietor who used to ride Cotton and Sunbeam motor-cycles and Aston-Martin and other cars in trials some years ago. The ragged October sunset over the Plain, fiery sunrays reflected in our long bonnet, was an incident not readily to be forgotten.

At the Beach Hotel at Minehead we found Guy Warburton, cheery as ever, with Mrs. Warburton simply exuding enthusiasm, awaiting us, anxious to compare this latest Allard with the original car which it resembles. Late that night Michael Soames came in on the V12 Allard-Special which Sydney Allard was to handle, and the Allard team for the morrow was complete. Until then, sherry, table-tennis and more sherry and a spot more table-tennis . . . .

Our luck, mine especially, was "in," for the day dawned dry. Dunster was full of good trials motors and their literally expert pilots, with a D.K.W. as official car. Of the trial I could write reams but, the Experts, being held at the close of the month, this is in the nature of a stop-press report, so the limitations of space must curb my enthusiasm. Well-blistered hands, from clinging grimly to hand-grip and tank-filler on all observed and many unobserved sections, will in any case make it a relief to lay aside the pen. Truly, there were times when one came very near to parting company with the car and it was difficult enough to retain the flimsy route-card, Hutchison's goggle-case and our bottle (containing water, *not* beer, though a legend was soon about that we ran on spirit other than petrol !

The Allard boiled a deal, possibly because twin headlamps sit coyly inside the radiator cowl and wind does queer things over big surfaces). About the route . . . Care at the first brake test gave a time of 6½ secs., confirmed by Lionel Martin from his bush. In the next timed test Allard-urge came into play very nicely, but our wheels (standard Ford discs. comp. shod all round, as for the run down), spun dangerously up Kersham. Ditch Lane, where Allard inverted last year, is ghastly, but "Hutch." picked a praiseworthy way and we got up bruised but not battered. Here Warburton did yeoman work with some steering wheel spokes loose in his hand. Congratulations to Mrs. Allard, too, for her contempt of Colley—which is the hill's better known name. Incidentally, you really can get purchase on the metal floorboards of "Hutch's" motor, which in other cars so often you wish to do, but cannot. "Hutch." was measured for his seating position. Our wing stay hereafter demanded frequent attention and string proved stouter than steel. Widlake was in curious condition and our Waterloo, for we ceased momentarily, all the more disappointing as the Allard at once built away well. Clousham was very rough going but did not worry the V8 or rear axle departments. The Pennycombe triangle test demonstrated real Allard acceleration after initial spin from the final hazard was stifled, Cowcastle was muddy and Picked Stones, where Fotheringham Parker's Ford coupé was nicely stuck, was extremely rock-strewn and had a nasty drop at one section. Moreover, it was approached by an unbelievably deep splash in the observed section. All of which the Allard regarded as its natural habitat. Stokemill, unused before, very long, with deep mould trapped between high banks, proved the finest hill of all, and up we got triumphantly only by dint of thirty willing horses (plus those the R.A.C. doesn't count), immense and exhausting bouncing, and Hutchison's right-footwork. It was truly magnificent going. All praise to Mid-Surrey ! Yeovale One gave no bother and Yeovale Two was child's play save for the disrespect for one's personal beauty of the bushes and young trees bordering the track. We now had only to finish, which No. 27 did well ahead of most of the others. The sections between hills were horrid in the extreme, but, back on sane going, the Allard showed again its other aspect, that of a thoroughly fierce, beautifully controllable road-motor, possessed of splendid top-gear pulling powers and devouring hills with an enthralling patter of comps. and hiss of air through the intake. The Experts is a first-class trial and will be extremely interesting under next year's ruling. To ride through it beside Hutchison is a valuable experience. And, in spite of bruises and blisters, I would do it again if the opportunity arose, for here is a driver who drives with his head, although his hands do a mighty lot of the work. I am happy to conclude that the Allard-Special team netted the Team Prize.

# The Allard Special V12

## *THREE-SEATER*

FLX 650

## A Versatile Sports Model for Fast Road Work and Competition Motoring

THE V12 Allard Special, now being delivered to private owners, is a very different vehicle from the first of the type which we tried over a year ago. The stark, strictly-business competition body and sketchy cycle-type wings have given place to a comfortable two-three-seater body by Whittingham and Mitchell and deeply valanced wings of pleasing proportions with countersunk head lamps. This new Allard is a smart and well-finished sports car but it retains the exceptional performance which has always been associated with these cars.

Indeed this latest model is even quicker than the first car of the type. Its acceleration is something quite outside the experience of the vast majority of motorists. One moment the car is standing still, the next there is a rumble from the twin tail pipes and it has just leapt away more as though propelled by a rocket than as a car driven by an engine. Once passengers have got over their own surprise they wedge themselves in position and sit continually laughing at the antics of onlookers who literally cannot believe the evidence of their own eyes.

### Acceleration

For the first part of our test the car happened to be running with the 6-in. section tyres and thus equipped it recorded the fastest standing quarter-mile figure so far achieved in these road tests—16.8 secs. Later, however, the 7.50-in. tyres were substituted with a corresponding improvement in maximum speed and also in certain of the acceleration figures owing to the reduction in wheelspin. The standing quarter-mile figure then became 17.4 secs., but even this has only been beaten on one occasion. A mean maximum speed of 94 m.p.h. was recorded with the screen erected and with the screen down we just touched 100 m.p.h

From a standstill the car is doing 30 m.p.h. in 3.2 secs. It leaps up to 50 in 7 secs., and to 80 in less than 20 secs. The equipment includes a combined clock and stopwatch on the dash which assists in obtaining some interesting figures. For example, from cruising behind the average 25 m.p.h. dawdler in built-up areas one is out and past him in precisely 2½ secs. All this is accomplished without any sensation of effort, without appreciable noise from under the bonnet and without more than a discreet rumble from the twin tail pipes.

Such performance obviously demands the utmost concentration from the driver and the driving position is well

---

## "The Motor" Data Panel (Allard Special V12)

Price, £625 ; 16 m.p.g. ; tax, £27 15s. ; weight (unladen), 22¾ cwt. turning circle, 32 ft. (2½ turns steering wheel).

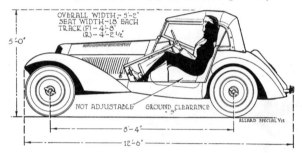

OVERALL WIDTH – 5'-8"
SEAT WIDTH – 18" EACH
TRACK (F) – 4'-8"
(R) – 4'-2½"
5'-0"
NOT ADJUSTABLE    GROUND CLEARANCE
ALLARD SPECIAL V12
8'-4"
12'-6"

### ENGINE

| | | |
|---|---|---|
| No. of cyls. | .. | 12 |
| Bore and stroke | .. | 69.85 × 95.25 mm. |
| Capacity | .. | 4,379 c.c. |
| Valves | .. | Side |
| Rating | .. | 36.3 h.p. |
| B.H.P. | .. | 112 at 3,900 r.p.m. |

### PERFORMANCE

| m.p.h. | Top secs. | 2nd secs. |
|---|---|---|
| 10-30 | 7.1 | 4.2 |
| 20-40 | 7.2 | 4.1 |
| 30-50 | 7.0 | 4.2 |
| 40-60 | 7.0 | 4.6 |
| 50-70 | 8.5 | |

| | m.p.h. | |
|---|---|---|
| Mean Max. | 94 | 70 |

| | |
|---|---|
| 0-30 m.p.h. | 3.2 secs. |
| 0-50 m.p.h. | 7.0 secs. |
| 0-60 m.p.h. | 9.5 secs. |
| 0-70 m.p.h. | 13.3 secs. |
| 0-80 m.p.h. | 19.4 secs. |
| Standing ¼-mile | 17.4 secs. |

### CHASSIS

| | | |
|---|---|---|
| Frame | .. | Channel section, box braced |
| Springs | .. | Transverse I.F.S. ; transverse rear |
| Brakes | .. | Mechanical cable operated |
| Tyres | .. | 7.50 × 16 ins. rear ; 6.00 × 16 ins. front |
| Tank | .. | 16 galls. rear |
| Glass | .. | Triplex toughened |

### GEARS    HILLS

| | | | |
|---|---|---|---|
| Top | .. | 3.5 | Max. grdnt. 1 in 6.7 |
| 2nd | .. | 5.5 | Max. grdnt. 1 in 4.2 |
| 1st | .. | 10.0 | Max. grdnt. 1 in 2.3 |

Engine speed, 1,880 r.p.m. at 50 m.p.h.    PULL, Tapley Q figure, 320

### BRAKES

| 30 m.p.h. to stop | | lb. on pedal |
|---|---|---|
| 120 ft. | .. | 50 |
| 60 ft. | .. | 80 |
| Best 35½ ft. (85%) | .. | 160 |

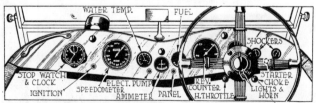

WATER TEMP.    FUEL
STOP WATCH & CLOCK    SPEEDOMETER    ELECT. PUMP    PANEL    REV. COUNTER    SHOCKERS    STARTER CHOKE LIGHTS & HORN
IGNITION    AMMETER    H.THROTTLE

**SEATING.**—Black figure portrays woman 5 ft. 5 ins. high, 26 ins. from hips. White figure shows 6-ft. man, 30 ins. from hips. Scale of drawing 1/30 actual size.
**HILL-CLIMBING.**—Maximum gradients for each gear are shown. Where 1 in 6.5 is recorded the car will climb Edge, South Harting, Kirkstone and Rest and Be Thankful Hills.
**BRAKES.**—Scale gives distance in feet from 30 m.p.h. as determined by a Ferodo-Tapley meter. Pressures needed to stop in shortest distance, in 60 ft. (normal short stop) and in 120 ft. or "slow up" are also shown. Average figures are 50 lb. for 60 ft., and about double for shortest; 100 lb. is the maximum pressure for average woman. If the 60-ft. and shortest-stop pressures are close together (e.g., 60 ft., 50 lb.—shortest, 72 lb.), the brake tends to fierceness.    August 1, 1939.

planned to give the maximum sense of control. Purchasers of the Allard naturally have an eye on sporting events and the vehicle bears the stamp of the expert competition drivers who designed it. The hand-brake is well placed and powerful, giving an efficiency of 30 per cent., acting only on the rear wheels. As a result we cannot recall a more controllable vehicle for the type of driving demanded in eliminating tests. A driver strange to it can skid the car round in its own length and place it to a foot or so almost immediately.

The steering is very light and requires 2½ turns of the wheel from lock to lock. The combination of terrific acceleration and extreme lightness in the steering may be disconcerting to some drivers at first, but it makes the car a sheer joy to handle when the driver is familiar with it. Cruising speeds of 75-80 m.p.h. are held without effort regardless of all except the steeper hills, and at this pace the car can be rushed through fast bends with

great precision. At speeds of 85 and over a certain amount of discretion is required and shock absorber adjustment needs to be correct. It must be borne in mind that the car is designed with

the requirements of standard-tyre trials in mind and the engine is set fairly well back in the frame. In our opinion it represents an excellent effort to achieve a compromise between the requirements of a fast road car and those of a trials machine where maximum adhesion is essential on the rear wheels.

On the road the independent front suspension gives a standard of riding comfort superior to that of the average stiffly sprung sports car but it is on bumpy trials hills that the suspension really comes into its own. Through mud, ruts and over rocky tracks the front wheels remain on the ground. As uneasiness at the front end is one of the factors which start wheelspin the value of this suspension in trials is **obvious**.

Among the points which will be appreciated by competition drivers are duplicated fuel leads with both mechanical and electrical pumps, with separate leads from the rear tank. A certain amount of trouble was experienced owing to the substitution of a T-piece on one pipe for the separate lines but performances in countless trials show that the normal arrangement works adequately.

The clutch is pleasantly light in action and centrifugal weights ensure maximum grip at high revolutions. The brake pedal on the other hand requires fairly heavy pressure for maximum results. Telecontrol hydraulic shock absorbers are an optional extra fitted to the car tested and they give a range of damping suitable for all conditions.

To a great extent the specification is variable to suit the requirements of the purchaser and variations listed in the catalogue include such items as magneto ignition, a 30-gallon tank in place of the normal 16-gallon receptacle, and revolution counter. On the four-seater tourer a two-speed rear axle is fitted as standard, giving a high-ratio overdrive when required and this is also available on other models at an extra cost of £12. The electrical system is 6-volt throughout, with Bosch head lamps.

This Allard is one of the most versatile machines produced to-day. For the enthusiast who requires a fast road car at a reasonable price and a car which has at the same time extraordinary cross-country abilities it is an obvious choice. There are very few cars indeed which can compete, without modification, in trials, rallies and sprint events with such hopes of success.

The model tested is listed at £625 and the four-seater on a slightly longer chassis, is available at the same figure. For those who scorn any concessions to creature comfort the stripped two-seater, similar in appearance to the V8 run by S. H. Allard himself, is available at £525.

In the V8 range the same body styles are supplied, the prices being £520 for the three-seater, £535 for the tourer, and £480 for the competition two-seater.

Side lamps and head lamps faired into the wings add to the neat appearance. The transverse seat is for occasional use, but has adequate headroom with hood and side curtains erected.

Normally a tonneau cover conceals the third seat.

# Detroit Magic

**H. L. Biggs describes a run in K. N. Hutchison's Light Trials Allard-Special**

OF the many basic Ford V8 sports cars which were built in this country up to the outbreak of war, undoubtedly the best known, and by far the most successful, was the Allard. Originally intended as a trials car pure and simple, the Allard had developed into a sports car of unequalled performance in speed events and hill-climbs.

The particular Allard to found the marque's reputation as a sprint car was FGP750, the light trials job owned and driven by Sydney Allard himself.

This car was built towards the end of 1938, together with a duplicate for K. N. Hutchison, a fellow " Tailwagger," and made its first appearance in the North-West London–Gloucester trial, driven by the late Martin Soames. How well I remember that night, the colourful scene at the Anchor Hotel at Shepperton, lit with fairy lights and surrounded with the cream of trials entries. I can hardly do better than quote verbatim from my own diary : " Allard's new light Allard, driven by Soames. A beautiful job, very narrow, about two ' hips width ' (actually it is 2′ 10″ across the body), latex seats, enormous rear tyres (7.50″ × 16″), scuttle cowl and aero screen, much wider open grille for increased cooling, plywood flooring, small flaired front wings with tubular stays, car unpainted." That brief description will give an impression of the car as it appeared in its maiden trial, and it is a matter of history that it, and Guy Warburton's CLK5 (the original Allard), were the only two out of the huge entry to get through clean.

To enlarge on this brief description of its technical details, the wheelbase was 8′ 4″ and the rear track 4′ 2″, with a front track of 4′ 8″. In trials trim, using the standard 4.11-to-1 axle ratio, with no passenger and the screen down, it covered the standing quarter-mile at the Track in 17.5 secs., and the half-mile in 28.9 secs.

Its successes in trials are too well known to enumerate, but it is of interest that, out of 12 trials in which FGP750 started in 1938/9 season, it secured seven consecutive premiers, two cups, one first-class award, one second, and ten team awards. In one trial only it secured no award, and even then it made the second-best performance.

During early 1939 much experimental work was done on carburation, and sweeping exhaust manifolds were fitted, and in June the whole car was rebuilt. The block was bored out to 80 mm., giving a capacity of 4.8 litres, the same as the well-known Ford " Mercury " unit, the crank was modified to the 91A type which carries the fan (this enabled the whole radiator to be lowered and the new and pleasing vee-fronted grille used), the generator, now an 8-h.p. type, nestled in a cut-away in the header tank, and a special induction manifold, bearing two double-choke Stromberg carburetters, was

fitted. The fuel feed was boosted by the addition of an Autopulse, run in conjunction with the standard Ford mechanical pump to cope with the demands of four chokes ; in addition, the flywheel was lightened by some 13 lb., and the ports ground out dead smooth. Using a 3.56-to-1 axle ratio, with 6.50″ tyres, a 7.2-to-1 compression ratio, and carrying a 15-stone passenger, the standing quarter was improved to 16.8 secs., and the half to 27.2 secs. The best speed, at this time, was about 98 m.p.h.

In August, 1938, the compression was raised to 8 to 1, using new heads with 14 mm. plugs, and, on the standard gear ratio of 4.11 to 1 with 7.00″ tyres and a 17-stone passenger, the standing start figures were again improved to 16.2 secs. for the quarter and 27 secs. for the half-mile.

About this time the frame was boxed and undershielded, and the total unladen weight stood at 16½ cwt. the addition of lead ballast to proportion the weight distribution, which varied with the course used, altered this weight by some 2 cwt.

At this juncture a list of the awards gained in hill-climbs may prove of interest. The year is 1939 ; in May, at Prescott, it was the fastest unsupercharged car, and made fastest sports-car time, and the fifth best time of the day. In July, at Wetherby, it was first in class four, a new class record and new sports-car record ; at Backwell, in July, it made fastest time for sports and racing cars ; again, at Prescott, it took the sports-car record. At Lewes, in August, it was third in the unlimited class, and at the Vintage S.C.C. meeting at Prescott, fastest in the racing class and second fastest in the all-comers class. Truly imposing !

Here are some ultimate acceleration figures which make one gasp, especially when a passenger : 0 to 60 in eight secs., 0 to 83 in 16.4 secs., and 0 to 96 in 27 secs. The ultimate maximum speeds on the 3.56-to-1 ratio were : flying lap at 100 and the standing lap at 90. The flying half-mile at 105 is pretty astonishing for a completely equipped car in trials trim.

Shortly after the outbreak of war this car was sold to Clarkson, of the Scottish Sports Car Club, and Hutchison sold his more or less similar job to C. Ian Craig, well known to Bugatti folk. During 1942

*The Allard, photographed by Hutchison, immediately after its arrival at Farnham, as described by H. L. Biggs in this article.*

Hutchison purchased FGP750 from Clarkson and proceeded to beautify it. The car had always appeared naked and unashamed in its bare aluminium panelling. This was sprayed a particularly pleasing opalescent blue, by Abbots, of Farnham, and the engine ancillaries were chromiumplated, giving the Ford unit, always so compact, a most workmanlike appearance. At this stage it came up to the works for attention by the trimmers and electricians. Owing to the width of the body it was impossible to fit two bucket seats, and a single bench-type seat was built up, covered with a matching blue hide ; the back squab was slightly raised in the centre to prevent the driver sliding sideways on fast corners, and the edges of the cut-away sides were covered with rubber tubing and finished with the same blue hide. Blue floor mats finished the ensemble, and the car looked quite " concours." Individual switches were fitted for all electrical equipment, and it was at about this time that I felt the urge to experience, first hand, some of the " Detroit Magic " in this car. Hutchison was, therefore, approached, and it was suggested that I meet him with the finished article at Surbiton and drive down to Farnham.

It was one of the coldest days of the year when I arrived at the works (complete with as many clothes as I could conveniently wear, including the famous cap, now some 20 years old), and settled myself in the Allard with the aid of a cushion as the seat is non-adjustable, and these " Tailwaggers " are a lengthy crowd. Thanks to the Autopulse, Scintilla magneto and pump carburetters, the car started up straight away and, after a few minutes warming up, was on its way. Coming straight off my Fiat 500 it was astonishing how quickly I accustomed myself to an entirely different type of car. The terrific acceleration is of paramount value under traffic conditions and, at the same time, 25 to 30 miles an hour can be maintained with no inconvenient sounds from the engine. The brakes, whilst being immensely powerful, are of the mechanical, cable-operated pattern and require considerable physical effort, in addition to which one's toe is apt to foul the steering column when braking hard. This is of minor importance, as the racing-type outside hand-brake can be used additionally to effect a rapid pull up.

Having attained the Kingston By-Pass, the right foot was depressed a little ; the result was astonishing, 80 m.p.h. appearing like magic and the finger-light, high-geared Marles steering enabled one to put the car just where one wanted, and hold it there. All too soon the " Ace of Spades " was reached, and the roundabout taken in one's stride, aided by the Allard remote-control gear lever, and the car once more idled along at 30 to Surbiton station. Whilst waiting for Hutchison I had to answer questions from the most unlikely persons, who turned out to be B.M.W. and Lagonda " Rapier " owners, who were most intrigued with the appearance of the Allard, which none of them recognised. Upon the arrival, somewhat late, of Hutchison, it was decided that he should drive the car, and a return was made to the By-Pass, where once more Allard urge was brought into play. A halt was made in Esher, at Hugh Hunter's, as " Hutch " wished to show him the car. Unfortunately, we were told that he was in Weybridge Hospital for an appendix removal ; can this be to improve the power/weight ratio ? Once more on our way, " Hutch," becoming accustomed to the car after a long period of 50 m.p.h. travel in his gas-producer V8, proceeded to give the motor the gun, and 80 appeared commonplace. After the silent speed one is disturbed by the terrific reports on the overrun, due to the fact that no tail pipes are fitted. On more than one occasion 90 was held, very often on long bends with one front wheel in the gutter, giving the characteristic " flickering " of the Ballamy front suspension. As FGP750 now has

the 4.1-to-1 axle, that would be about the maximum permissible. This speed is not so impressive and not so important on English roads as the manner of its attaining it. Over roads with a light covering of snow we streaked across the Hog's Back to the astonished gaze of the military, and were soon in Farnham, where we stopped at Hawthorn's Tourist Trophy Garage to give the proprietor a short run in the car. Meanwhile, I was pleased to see some three or four Fiat 500s in the workshop and to hear that Hawthorn has a great respect for these amazing little cars. A brief glance round his showrooms revealed a very fine "2.3" "Mille Miglia" Alfa-Romeo, lately the property of Russell Roberts, the M.G. and Hudson driver ; Dobbs's second string 2-litre Riley with six Amals, Lucas vertical magneto, and many electron parts (an ideal purchase this for the beginner), and a somewhat shabby-looking o.h.c. Norton, which Hawthorn told me was a Gold Star winner, and was ex-Ron Harris and Francis Beart, thus commanding respect.

Hutchison, having made arrangements for the collection of a Railton " Cobham " saloon that he had just purchased, we continued to his fascinating home at Frensham Vale. There I was introduced to Mrs. Hutchison, whose delightful and spontaneous articles in MOTOR SPORT we have all read with such pleasure ; many photographs were taken of the car, a few feet of cinematograph film exposed, and the car put away in its garage alongside a colossal Buick, circa 1940, about two cars long and fitted up internally with every conceivable luxury, though an under-bonnet view displayed a radiator filler cap which would have disgraced the cheapest British pickle bottle. Incidentally this car, weighing a few tons it would seem, achieves an effortless 90 !

Back at the house I was delighted to be introduced to Hutchison's Siamese cats, and more than a little intrigued to hear that one bore the name, registered at the Siamese Cat Club, of Mr. George Biggs. He seemed strangely indifferent to the admiration of his human namesake ! It was extremely interesting to talk cars, and to see Hutchison's collection of awards and his coloured portraits of some of his cars, the blue fabric Anzani-engined and the red Meadows roller-bearinged Frazer-Nashes, which I knew so well, the white Bainshaw-built Ford Special, and the green Jensen, and to look through his collection of books containing cuttings and Press photographs of successes. After lunch, more talking of the Sport, when I obtained confirmation that Warburton did build a light Railton from a saloon and used it in trials, that the chassis dimensions of Symmons L.M.B. V8 were taken from the white Ford Special, and that Hutchison intended obtaining Crozier's double Marshall-blown Ford V8 unit.

However, all good things come to an end, and I was very kindly taken down to Farnham station in Hutchison's comp-shod 8-h.p. Ford saloon, to begin a seemingly interminable journey back to town. I shall never become reconciled to railways for these mid-distance journeys, but it gave me time to ponder on matters motoring. What other car would you find, with such a performance, that you could get serviced in any town in the world where there was a Ford agent ?

Thank you, Mr. Hutchison, thank you, Mr. Allard, thank you, Henry Ford !

[I have allowed Harold Biggs to call this article " Detroit Magic," but I hope it will not incur heated discussion as to which is more mystic, the magic brewed at Molsheim or that gotten from Detroit. —ED.]

# The New Allard 3.6 Litre

The three new styles of Allard coachwork.

## Preliminary details of an Entirely New High Performance Model With Three Body Styles

A NEW company, the Allard Motor Co., Ltd., Hugon Road, Fulham, has recently been formed to make and market the Allard sports car.

It may be recalled that the prototype Allard was built in 1936, and comprised a Ford V8 chassis very much modified, with, inter alia, independent springing, modified engine position and weight distribution, with a sports-car body.

Driven by S. H. Allard, the best performance was obtained in four big trials in that year. In the following three years a considerable number of cars were built for private owners, and the best performance of the day was put up in 30 reliability trials and the sports-car records obtained for Poole, Backwell, Prescott, and Wetherby courses.

Tested by "The Motor" in 1939, the 12-cylinder 2-seater version of the Allard made the quickest standing quarter-mile ever made in a road test, recording the outstanding time of 16.8 secs. During the war years a considerable user mileage and the lessons of past competition experience form the basis of an entirely new design, which has been laid out for the present company. The principals of this concern are S. H. Allard as managing director, and R. J. Cann, general manager. Design has been in the hands of L. Hill and H. L. Biggs, and the well-known trials and rally driver, Geoffrey Imhoff, has been consulted in respect of body design. The car will be fully described at a later date, but, meanwhile, the principal features can be disclosed.

The V.8 engine has a capacity of 3.6 litres, and is rated at 30 h.p., R.A.C. rating, the bore and stroke being 77.79 by 95.25 mm. Developing 90 b.h.p., the power is transmitted through a single-plate clutch, with centrifugal assistance to gearbox, giving ratios of 3.5, 6.61, and 12.3:1, the road speed being approximately 90, 55, and 25 m.p.h. at maximum r.p.m. The gear-change lever is of the normal remote-control type.

This engine and gearbox unit is fitted into an entirely new box-section frame, having box-section cross-members and carrying transverse springs front and rear. At the back the conventional rear axle, which gives a track of 4 ft. 2 ins., is located fore and aft by a torque tube which provides the drive, and sideways by a Panhard rod. Damping is by the new Luvax-Girling device, with pressure recuperation.

### Revised Suspension

At the front end the independent springing system has been considerably revised. The single transverse spring is retained as previously, and forms one locating member for the front wheels. The other comprises a single wishbone running above the spring, together with a further arm extended some way backwards on to the frame, so that it can act as a torque member under braking loads. The pivot axes of both short and long wishbone arms are in line, and in this respect the system resembles the layout used on the Packard and Bentley V.

The track at the front is 4 ft. 8 ins. The wheelbase of the car varies according to the body type, being 9 ft. 4 ins. for the closed coachwork and 8 ft. 10 ins. for the competition two-seater. In both cases the ground clearance is 9 ins.

Steering is by a Marles cam gear, with an extensile steering column to give adjustment to a spring-type wheel, the column also being adjustable for rake. Every effort has been made to reduce the number of joints in the steering linkage, as it is felt that friction at these joints is responsible for the "dead" feeling of a number of cars which have independent suspension, offering almost impeccable geometry.

Braking on the Allard is by Lockheed in ribbed drums, the hand-brake, operating by cable on the rear wheels alone, being of the racing quick-release type.

An item of equipment which is of particular interest is the 12-volt electric system, this being the Lucas special type which was introduced a year or two before the war for cars where quality was placed before cost of production.

The chassis weight, varying according to wheelbase and type, is between 17½ and 18½ cwt., and the estimated weights for complete cars vary between 19½ cwt. for the open two-seater to 22½ cwt. for the saloon.

The provisional prices for the four models which will be offered are:—Competition 2-seater, £750; four-seater sports, £765; two-door coupé (four-seater), £850; and two-door saloon, £925—plus purchase tax.

Although the Allard has previously excelled in the sports-car field, the post-war models have been designed for the needs of the high-speed traveller (on business as well as pleasure) particularly in mind.

The large ground clearance and the use of many proprietary parts (which appreciably eases the spares situation in districts remote from the manufacturers) make the Allard particularly suitable for use abroad. In this respect a large engine of low specific output, capable of running for long distances without attention, is of great value. At the same time, the lightweight chassis and the care given to the steering gear and suspension are points which will be especially valued by Continental users. To these qualities are added the acknowledged excellence of British bodywork, brakes which are well up to the job and the convenience and efficiency of a 12-volt electrical system.

It is hoped to publish a full chassis description, together with some comments on the coachwork and handling of this interesting high-performance car, at an early date.

# V Twelv

### First of Its Kind.

The versatile twelve-cylinder Allard as a track machine. It is seen in the Light Car Club's three-hour sports car race over the Brooklands Campbell Circuit in July, 1938. Delayed by losing the fan belt, and thus its water pumps, the car finished ninth at 56.41 m.p.h. average.

THIS week a machine that many trials and speed trials competitors will remember, K. Hutchison's twelve-cylinder Allard, "Tailwagger the First." He previously had the original V8 Allard Special, and after his highly successful experiences in competitions and general motoring with that car decided that the extra power to be obtained by fitting a Lincoln Zephyr engine would be a good thing to have. Thus he became the first owner of the twelve-cylinder version. Naturally it possessed a remarkably good power-weight ratio and terrific acceleration and climbing power.

During the 1938 season Hutchison appeared with this car in the majority of the more important trials, as well as in quite a few speed trials, hill-climbs, and a Campbell Circuit race, a variety of events which speaks for its successful versatility. It was the expected thing to see it rocket up any trials hill, and the list of "terrors" of the stickiest sort vanquished by this machine is one of which any car—and driver—might feel proud.

#### " Specials "

The Allard Special was representative of a type of car that appeared in increasing, though necessarily restricted, numbers during the last year or two before the war. The general recipe was a lot of engine and comparatively little body. To a lesser extent the big Atalanta was another example, also using the Zephyr engine; the production Railton was yet another, of longer standing and not by any means built primarily as a trials car, of course. Still others come to mind: the Leidart, a "special" more akin again to the Allard, with a V8 engine; and even the luxurious Jensen, a fully "finished" car, with fine bodywork and fitted with a V8 engine, or, later, with a 4½-litre straight eight of American make. Should this catch the eye of an owner of one of the open Jensens, I would like to say that his experiences would be interesting to others.

The Allard was put on a small-production basis in 1938. Previously it had been more a question of the Allard brothers, Sidney in particular, demonstrating the car and amusing themselves with it in trials, and building a number of replicas to order as the car's fame spread among enthusiasts, as it rapidly did. The 30 h.p. V8-engined two-seater was priced at £460, by the way, in 1938, and £560 with the twelve-cylinder engine, and the competition model two-seater with appropriate equipment, including knock-off wire wheels, fly-off hand-brake lever and spring steering wheel, at £480 and £570, according to which engine was fitted.

#### Not " On the List "

Unfortunately, I never had an opportunity of sampling the twelve-cylinder model, though I had some fine motoring, taking in a lot of mud work across the Berkshire and Wiltshire downs, in a V8 edition. Some idea of the potentialities of the type of engine used was given by testing the similarly equipped, but, of course, quite distinct, Atalanta, though a saloon which weighed 27-odd cwt.

Later, K. Hutchison acquired a newer twelve-cylinder Allard, which automatically became "Tailwagger the Second." An illustration is included of this car, to supplement the action pictures of his first twelve-cylinder. He tells me that he has had the more recent car repainted and reupholstered, and that it looks very nice indeed, as I can well believe. Here are Hutchison's own words on the original twelve-cylinder. "V."

••••••••••••••••••

"The twelve-cylinder Allard Special" (he writes) "was built as the logical outcome of the success that Sidney Allard had been having from a full trials season with his very stripped V8 'special,' CLK 5, which has already been described in this series (November

28th, 1941) and which is now the pride and joy of Guy Warburton.

"As the new car was intended to have some refinements that the original Allard Special did not possess, it was felt that a slightly larger engine than the 30 h.p. Ford V8 was needed to cope with the extra weight of a more robust body with doors, hood, better mudguards and the general fittings of a touring car. After considering ways and means of installation, a twelve-cylinder Lincoln Zephyr engine with Ford V8 gear box was fitted. This engine has a bore and stroke of 69.85 by 95.25 mm. and the capacity is 4,379 c.c. Nominal h.p. is 36.3 and b.h.p. is 115. Using this engine in such a short chassis meant more weight forward (a bad trials feature) than if the shorter V8 unit had been used, though this was not too serious a drawback, since competition tyres were permitted at the time. Also the power-weight ratio of the V12 unit is not quite so good as that of the Ford V8 engine.

#### 40-gallon Tank !

"In spite of the inevitable extra weight of this car, it turned the scales at only just over 22 cwt. with full equipment but without a passenger or full petrol tank. All this machinery was compressed into a wheelbase of 8ft. 4in. I would add that the petrol tank held close on 40 gallons, and this, being behind the rear axle, provided ballast in just the right place for steep and muddy sections.

"For those who are not familiar with the Allard Special the following constructional details may be of interest. These cars were all made up from new and, in 99 cases out of 100,

# Allard

## cessful Trials Car

from standard Ford parts, and this fact undoubtedly contributed largely towards their amazing reliability and economical maintenance costs. The twelve-cylinder car, like all the other Allards, had an L.M.B. divided front axle and a cut-down but otherwise standard Ford V8 rear axle. The chassis frame was shortened and narrowed, with the resulting wheelbase of 8ft. 4in., and front and rear tracks of 4ft. 8in. and 4ft. 2½in. respectively.

### Alternative Ratios

The rear axle ratio was 4.11 to 1, and the standard Ford gear box gave 11.59 bottom, 6.59 second, and 4.11 to 1 top. I occasionally ran the V12 with an axle ratio of 3.5 to 1 with, of course, resultant higher gear ratios all round. In fact, with a 3.5 to 1 top and 7.50in. section tyres on the rear wheels one could cruise at 60 m.p.h. with the engine hardly turning over, and with the knowledge that a quick change down to second would take you up to over 80 on that gear in a very few seconds, all of which contributed towards very nice motoring.

"The only non-Ford parts on the mechanical side were Marles steering, Hartford shock absorbers, S.U. petrol pumps, and the L.M.B. front axle system. The steering, incidentally, was quite high geared, and the turning circle was 30ft.

"At all times I ran this car with standard compression ratio and coil ignition system and with no special tuning of the engine. Throughout twelve months of very strenuous competition work, during which the car did over 30,000 miles of only week-end motoring, it had but two breakdowns, and those were the only occasions when it

The later twelve-cylinder Allard which Hutchison acquired to replace " Tail-wagger I." Though well equipped and comfortable, it has much of the good " vintage " starkness of outline. Note the built-in head lamps.

failed to finish an event. Once it was a sheared key in a half-shaft, and the other failure was a stripped gear pinion during a speed trial. Both times it returned home under its own power in spite of broken parts.

"As regards road performance the greatest feature was the remarkable acceleration, and although a high maximum speed was never sought, an all-out speed of between 90 and 96 m.p.h. was available. On the few occasions when I personally took it up to over 90 I found the car very comfortable and controllable and not in the least bit alarming, but, strangely enough, through having such a fine range of performance from a standstill up to 70 m.p.h., one never seemed to need or want to drive flat out. Top gear used in conjunction with 6.00 × 16in. rear covers and the comparatively low axle ratio of 4.11 to 1 gave a performance remarkable in itself. Others besides myself on several occasions climbed the Brooklands test hill from a standing start using only top gear, and this ratio was easily capable of dealing with almost any main road hill.

### Performance Data

"The following acceleration figures, using all the gears needed, were professionally compiled for a road test, and illustrate the performance available lower down the speed range.

> 0-50 m.p.h., 7.5 sec.
> 0-60 m.p.h., 10.2 sec.
> 0-70 m.p.h., 14.2 sec.

Standing quarter-mile (average of two runs in opposite directions), 17.8 sec.

| M.p.h. | Top gear. Sec. | Second. Sec. | First. Sec. |
|---|---|---|---|
| 10-30 | 4.5 | 2.7 | 1.8 |
| 10-50 | 9.5 | 7.1 | — |
| 10-60 | 12.4 | — | — |

"These were averages taken over several runs.

"I never kept a detailed log of the running costs or petrol consumption, but over any give-and-take main road journey the petrol consumption nearly always ranged pretty close to 18 m.p.g. With 40 gallons in the rear tank this gave a cruising range from base, so to speak, of rather more than 700 miles.

"As competition tyres were allowed as part of all trials competitors' equipment during the season I ran this V12 Allard,

it was usually fitted with ' knobbly ' covers both fore and aft. Under these conditions almost every well-known trials hill in the country was climbed at one time or another, and also many other sections which up till then had not been used in a trial. Such hills and sections included Juniper, Breakheart, Colly, Leckhampton, Widlake, Tin Pan Alley, Cloutsham and many others that will be remembered by competitors who, like myself, are no doubt longing for the days when we may tackle these sections once more.

### Successful Variety

"Although it was intended primarily as a trials car, it was extremely versatile and performed well in various speed trials and hill-climbs. Amongst the better performances were class wins at both the 1938 Lewes speed trials, Prescott hill-climb, Wetherby speed trials, and fastest sports car time at Poole speed trials. The car also ran in the Light Car Club's three-hour sports car race and finished ninth at an average of 56.41 m.p.h. This event was run over the Campbell Circuit at Brooklands, and the only trouble experienced was a broken fan belt, a rather tiresome little breakdown that delayed the car for about ten minutes. Later it ran in the 50-mile race at Southport and finished the course without trouble, driven by Sidney Allard.

"During the 1938 season G. Warburton, Allard and myself were running in most of the reliability trials as a team of three, calling ourselves 'The Tailwaggers,' but that is another story. Needless to say, the white twelve-cylinder gave me thousands of miles of delightful and trouble-free motoring, and in many ways I was sorry when it was finally retired to give place to a newer and lighter, but more Spartan, two-seater, which became my mount for the 1939 season."

•••••••••••••••••

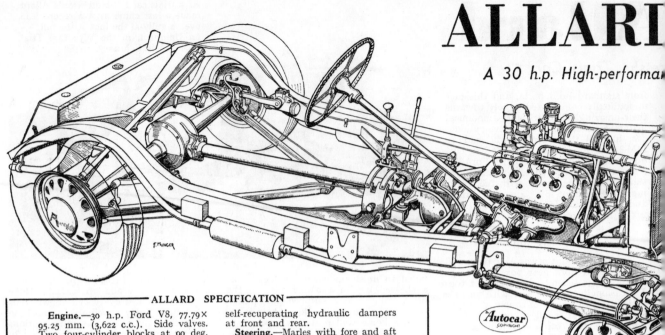

## ALLARD SPECIFICATION

**Engine.**—30 h.p. Ford V8, 77.79 × 95.25 mm. (3,622 c.c.). Side valves. Two four-cylinder blocks at 90 deg. cast integrally with the crankcase. Cast alloy crankshaft in three bearings. Dual downdraught carburettor. Special coil and distributor. Dual exhaust manifolds with large-capacity pipes and straight-through silencers.

**Transmission.**—Centrifugally assisted dry single-plate clutch. Three-speed remote control gear box; synchromesh on top and second. Overall ratios: Top 3.5, second 6.61, first 12.3 to 1. Enclosed propellershaft and spiral bevel rear axle.

**Frame.**—Deep box section of great stiffness, well braced with crossmembers.

**Suspension.**—Independent front suspension of swinging half-axle type with transverse leaf spring. Transverse rear spring with stabilising rod. Luvax-Girling double-acting

self-recuperating hydraulic dampers at front and rear.

**Steering.**—Marles with fore and aft drag link and divided track rod. Steering column adjustable for length and height.

**Brakes.**—Lockheed hydraulic with special ribbed drums. Fly-off hand brake.

**Fuel Capacity.**—16-gallon rear tank with reserve.

**Wheels and Tyres.**—Easy-clean wheels with 6.25 × 16in. tyres.

**Electrical Equipment.**—Lucas 12-volt with large-capacity battery and compensated voltage control.

**Main Dimensions.**—Long chassis: Wheelbase 9ft. 4in. Track: (front) 4ft. 8in.; (rear) 4ft. 2in. Short chassis: Wheelbase 8ft. 10in. Track: (front) 4ft. 8in.; (rear) 4ft. 2in. Ground clearance 9in. Weight: Saloon 22½ cwt.; coupé 22½ cwt.; two-seater 19½ cwt.

THE first Allard was produced just on ten years ago as a trials "special" and it was so outstandingly successful that it was later put into limited production. The new Allard has changed its sporting tweeds for a lounge suit and has been designed for the driver who wants a high-performance road car rather than an out-and-out competitions machine. Much lower and with streamlined bodywork, the new car has a Continental appearance; but beneath all its refinement it still retains that flashing performance, combined with great reliability.

Two different chassis will be sold, one with a 9ft. 4in. wheelbase and the other a short-chassis competition model with an 8ft. 10in. wheelbase. The long chassis may be obtained with a fourseater sports body, price £765, plus £210 7s. 6d. purchase tax; a two-door four-seater coupé, price £850, plus £233 15s. purchase tax; and a two-door four-seater saloon costing £925, plus £254 7s. 6d. purchase tax. The short chassis will be obtainable with an open two-seater body for £750, plus £206 5s. purchase tax. These prices are provisional.

To turn now to a detailed examination of the specification, a practically standard 30 h.p. Ford V8 engine is used. This is a tried and tested unit whose reliability over a long period was amply proved before the war in many a tough trial. Moreover, spares are available for it all over the world, an important point now that the export market looms large on the horizon of all car manufacturers. This unit is so well known that little additional description is called for. Departures from standard are a special coil and distributor to look after the ignition side of things during long periods of

Artist's impressions of three of the styles of coachwork that will eventually be available. The smooth front end with the head lamps sunk into the wings should improve both the performance and the fuel consumption. An open four-seater will also be included in the range of models.

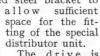

high-speed running and the mounting of the fan on a pressed steel bracket to allow sufficient space for the fitting of the special distributor unit.

The drive is taken to the three-speed gear box by a single-plate clutch, which is centrifugally assisted. The gear box is fitted with a neat remote control for the gear lever and its ratios are 3.5, 6.61 and 12.3 to 1. The high top gear ratio

----

The engine is set well back in the chassis which now has box-section side members. The deep front cross-member carrying the front axle and the neat simplicity of the remote control gear change are points that will be noticed. The bracket for mounting the fan at mid height is also visible.

----

plays a large part in giving that effortless performance for which the car is so notable and yet, owing to the good power-to-weight ratio, the acceleration does not suffer.

The new frame has box-section side-members upswept over the front and

rear axles and is braced by sturdy cross-members. A rigid frame is essential if any system of independent front suspension is to operate successfully, and special attention has been paid to making the front of the chassis as stiff as possible, an exceptionally sturdy cross-member spanning it beneath the radiator and carrying the central linkage for the divided front axle. A large-diameter tubular cross-member at the rear of the gear box also helps to make the structure rigid. Much attention has been paid to the retention of an adequate ground clearance in spite of the lowering of the chassis, for it is felt that this is often a weak point on British cars when they are exported. The actual figure of nine inches is certainly very creditable.

The independent front suspension is of the swinging half-axle type with a single transverse spring mounted above the divided axle beam, radius arms being used to position the beam and to take the braking torque. The latest Luvax-Girling double-acting self-recuperating hydraulic dampers are employed at both front and rear. The Marles steering box is con-

nected by a fore and a. to the divided track rod a Silentbloc bushes are fitted to a

A tubular propeller-shaft, enc. a torque tube, takes the drive i three-quarter floating rear axle, whic suspended by means of a transve. spring aided by a stabiliser rod. Lock heed brakes with specially ribbed drums are employed, the hand brake being of the fly-off type. Wheels of the easy-clean pattern carry 6.25 × 16in. tyres.

A 12-volt lighting system with compensated voltage control and a large-capacity battery provides sufficient illumination for rapid night motoring, the dipper switch being hand operated.

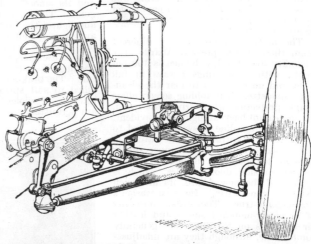

Details of the independent front wheel suspension, showing the divided axle with the transverse spring above it, the linkage for the divided track rod and the fore and aft drag link.

# HE SPECIAL SHORT-CHASSIS ALLARD "COMPETITION" 2-SEATER

THE post-war Allard, product of an enthusiast whose trials reputation up to 1939 was second to none, has aroused the greatest interest and speculation in motoring circles. Consequently, we are glad to be able to present a test report on one of these cars, with the proviso that the particular Allard tested was Sydney Allard's personal car, and as such has a wheelbase 6 in. shorter than the production "Competition" 2-seater, (*i.e.*, 8 ft. 4 in.) and a Ford V8 engine bored-out to Mercury capacity, giving about five additional b.h.p. It also has the 4.1-to-1 axle ratio of the long-chassis cars, but otherwise was in standard trim. It ran, of course, on Pool petrol and can claim to be a hard-used car, having won this year's Experts' Trial and having got back from a fast run to Devon on the day before we took it over.

The body lines are entirely different from those of the pre-war Allard. The visibility over the low bonnet is 100 per cent., with both wings always in full view and no filler cap to mar the clean-cut silhouette. The folding screen offers ample protection when driving at speed, no unpleasant back-draught being evident. The door hinge line is swept forward to provide easy entrance; the catch on the passenger's door proved unnecessarily difficult to operate. Incidentally, there are no outside door handles, which is typical of the new Allard, its unbroken exterior constituting the car-washer's dream-come-true. The seats, consisting of a nicely-moulded squab and leather air cushions on the floor, are generally comfortable, although they are unadjustable, and some people might prefer a little more support under the legs. The driving position is well suited to a medium-height driver who likes to sit close up to the wheel. The remote-control gear-lever and central, fly-off-type handbrake are very nicely placed, as is the spring-spoke steering wheel, and the door cut-away never impedes the right elbow. There is a footwell for the driver's feet, but the throttle pedal might be better placed in relation thereto.

The instrument board carries, left to right: lamp switch and main ignition key; reversing-lamp switch; combined water thermometer and oil gauge above; choke; "reserve" fuel-pump switch; rev.-counter; ignition light; speedometer; starter button; hand-throttle; ammeter; fuel gauge; additional ignition switch above; combined horn button and headlamp dipper. The rev.-counter was inoperative on the car tested; it is an Allard-Cooper-Stewart reading to 5,000 r.p.m. The 100 m.p.h. speedometer, of the same breed, read commendably steadily. The normal water temperature is 185° F. and the oil pressure stays at 45 lb./sq. in. at road r.p.m. We suggest that considerable improvement could be effected were the horn and lamp-dipper accessible without having to dive through, or feel behind, the steering wheel, and if fuel gauge and oil gauge were transposed. There is also the possibility of driving with the reversing light on when this is

**Brilliant top-gear flexibility and traditional acceleration. A silent, smooth-running car capable of high cross-country average speeds.**

controlled by switch and not by the gear-lever, while to use the light switch it was necessary to reach to the near side. The wiper-box is very well placed, and the dynamo gave a ready charge. Apparently no dashlamp is considered necessary.

First impressions in driving an Allard are its immense "step-off," the lightness of its controls, its very "useable" speed, and its smooth, silent, easy manner of going. The clutch action is excellent, and light; the brake pedal asks no effort and gives splendidly progressive, straight-line braking. The accelerator is also light to use except, perhaps, when delicate opening is called for from the over-run. The braking effect of the big engine, allied to soft springing, results in some pitching if violent throttle movements are permitted.

The V8 engine pours out its power in almost complete silence, so far as the car's occupants are concerned, and without any trace of flat-spot or vibration. To a large extent flexible engine mounting is responsible, but in some ways it is a mixed blessing, because the rigidly-mounted, remote gear-lever is unable to cope properly with gearbox movement, and this results in the lever becoming increasingly stiff to move under load, which slows the gear change and makes it necessary to "crash" *fast* upward and downward changes. However, clutch and transmission seem unruffled by such gear-changing, and for normal use it is quite a pleasing action. When opening up, the gear-lever can be felt to move if one's hand is resting on it. No gear noise is evident. There is no reverse stop.

The steering is generally light but gets somewhat heavier towards full lock, the wheel asking 2¼ turns from one lock to the other. Some return movement from the i.f.s. is felt over bad surfaces; a short, "Lambda"-like kick-back over rough roads and a very slight snatch when the front suspension is working hard with the

*The Allard production-model "Competition" 2-seater.*

wheels on appreciable lock. Normally, however, this return motion is negligible, while column judder is never excessive, which fits in with the general impression that the front of the car is adequately rigid, wings and facia included. There is excellent balance between over- and under-steer, and strong castor action. For rapid cross-country motoring the steering is sufficiently accurate and the car can be swung round open bends in a beautifully balanced fashion, while it " holds-in " splendidly, and break-away is almost impossible to promote. Nor is any trace of roll apparent, unless the car is thrown about in " rally-test " style. Incidentally, the tyres *can* be made to howl, and loudly, but in ordinary fast cornering no noise whatsoever comes from them, fairly modest tyre-pressures notwithstanding. The car holds a straight course at speed ; in reverse the steering becomes light and less decisive. The lock is exceptionally good and the steering ratio a nice compromise between low and high gearing.

Across country the Allard is very rapid indeed, and its smooth, entirely silent progression enhances its value in this respect. The acceleration, for which this make has always been famous, is especially useable in traffic and out of slow corners, etc. The difficult gear-lever action aforementioned is largely excused because the car has such excellent top-gear performance. There is little necessity to change down over the usual give-and-take motoring which British secondary roads entail. The Allard is, in effect, game for anything in its highest ratio and still out-performs most so-called fast cars. From a standstill 30 m.p.h. is reached almost instantaneously in bottom, in which gear a maximum of just over 34 m.p.h. is possible. Second-gear gives strong pick-up to about 55 m.p.h., with a maximum of over 58 m.p.h. On main roads 80 m.p.h. comes up very easily, and 65 m.p.h. is a commonplace cruising speed on by-roads.

When sheer performance is under discussion, timed tests tell the most convincing story. We were able to carry out a number of such tests on a private road and the results are given in the accompanying table. The high-lights of these figures can be stated concisely as a mean maximum speed of 79.32 m.p.h. over the flying ¼ mile, screen down, a standing ¼ mile in 20.05 sec., and acceleration from a standing start to 50 m.p.h. in 10 sec. and to 70 m.p.h. in 23.7 sec. These figures are the result of a number of runs in both directions, and as the axle ratio in use had rendered the speedometer inaccurate, this was re-calibrated carefully prior to timing the car. It is significant that exactly the same times were obtained on several occasions. Erecting the screen affected maximum speed by approximately 1½ m.p.h. In top gear it was possible to motor at a brisk walking pace without transmission snatch. The brakes were out of adjustment and we decided not to proceed with measured stopping distances, but can say that the car stopped in a straight line with locked wheels from 60 m.p.h. and that, bar very slight noise from one drum at the end of the day, did not suffer from brake squeal. After some 300 miles' hard driving the brake power had not diminished to any

extent, and for road motoring the car possessed adequate retardation. As the mileometer was inaccurate, fuel consumption tests were not undertaken, but rather better than 16 m.p.g. is obtainable without in any way restraining one's throttle foot. For the tests the road surface was dry ; the wind strength about 20 m.p.h. The fuel tank was half to three-quarters full and a lightweight passenger was carried.

Full marks were earned by the comfort of the car over poor surfaces. Clearly, this is achieved by soft springing in the modern tradition, and the wheels move quite an appreciable distance on occasion without affecting the rigid feel of the car. Humpback bridges can be negotiated at high speed without apprehension or unpleasant aftermath, and trials sections can be explored in comparative comfort.

Really fast cornering, entailing rapid change from one steering lock to the

---

**ALLARD SPECIAL SHORT-CHASSIS " COMPETITION " 2-SEATER**

*Engine :* V8, 80.96 by 95.25 mm. (3,917 c.c.), 32 R.A.C. h.p.

*Gear-ratios :* 1st, 14.4 to 1 ; 2nd, 6.5 to 1 ; Top, 4.1 to 1.

*Tyre size :* 6.25 in. by 16 in. Dunlop E.L.P.

*Weight* (in road trim with approx. 2 gall. of fuel, but less occupants) : 22½ cwt.

*Turning circle :* 34 ft. (right-hand).

*Steering ratio :* 2⅓rd turns, lock to lock.

*Fuel capacity :* 17 gall. (one in reserve).

PERFORMANCE DATA.

*Acceleration :—*
0–50 m.p.h., 10.0 sec. ⎫ Mean of
0–60 m.p.h., 14.25 sec. ⎬ two-way
0–70 m.p.h., 23.70 sec. ⎭ runs.
s.s. ¼ mile : 20.05 sec. (mean), 20.0 sec. (best run).

*Speed :* f.s. ¼ mile : 79.32 m.p.h. (mean), 80.40 m.p.h. (best run).

---

other, can result in some vagueness of control until the suspension copes with the transference of weight, but this is but a small penalty to pay for otherwise highly-effective springing. The outward appearance of the Allard belies the fact that the engine is well back in the chassis and that there is plenty of avoirdupois over the rear axle, which, however, the car's trials successes emphasise.

The lamp power was moderate, but some adjustment of beam from the head-lamps was called for, immediate attention to which was defeated by the inbuilt construction.

Behind the seats there is storage for hood (side screens are not supplied), tools, jack, etc., reached *via* the squab. The rear number plate is fully illuminated ; the bonnet has a safety catch to prevent it hinging upwards involuntarily, fits really snugly, and has practical fasteners. The hood is very effectively held taut

round the screen by special catches, and it is interesting that the front wings are of welded sheet-metal construction. Engine accessibility is a strong feature of the bonnet construction. A few quite minor body-noises were noticed. It is hardly necessary to say that the car attracted a crowd of admiring onlookers whenever it was parked in populated places.

On Pool petrol rather pronounced pinking occurred unless the throttle was opened very carefully (there is no hand ignition control), but this pinking did not appear to impair performance, and the engine stopped at once when switched off. The ignition switch rendered horn and other electrics dead when in the " off " position—a good point—and the reversing light was useful. The sidelamps could not be checked as " on " when in the car. The fuse boxes and cut-out are instantly accessible on lifting the bonnet. Starting from cold was instantaneous with very little choke. The spare wheel is partially concealed by a metal cover, and the tail treatment is very neat. The front number plate can be hinged flat for negotiation of " observed sections." The racing-type handbrake is very handy, if somewhat hard to lock. Each door has a zip-fastened pocket, and an effective umbrella-type hood is provided. The screen sealing-rubber emitted a " gobble " when it reached 75 m.p.h. In approximately 300 miles we added half-a-gallon of water and three pints of engine oil. The engine ticked-over correctly and never boiled ; it started as easily hot as cold. The suction-secured central mirror is reasonably useable.

That, then, is a critical analysis of the 1947 Allard. All the foregoing characteristics combine to form an essentially likeable car, which is as at home in town as on the open road or up trials hills. The Allard is very easy to drive and completely docile ; its acceleration from the bottom-end makes negotiation of even London's city traffic almost a pleasure. The way in which the car gets round bends, its immense performance, unaffected by main-road gradients, and its high degree of refinement, render it one of the most attractive day-to-day sports cars we have experienced. Further details of this intriguing car can be had from the Allard Motor Co., Ltd., 43, Acre Lane, London, S.W.2 (Brixton 6431). The price of the 8 ft. 10 in. wheelbase 2-seater is £750, *not* including purchase tax.—W. B.

✳ ✳ ✳ ✳ ✳ ✳ ✳ ✳ ✳

# FAST

TESTING new cars is not all steer and victuals, as some may think. A road test for "The Motor" involves long hours of running up and down the same dull stretch of concrete, first to calibrate the speedometer, and then to collect speed, acceleration, and m.p.g. figures. So when picking up a blue competition two-seater Allard from Brixton, it was rather pleasant in one way to hear that this was Sydney Allard's personal car, and so, being to some extent non-standard, was not eligible for a road test as such. That will have to come later. What follows now may be called a fast, light interlude, for a large, lazy engine in a smallish, rugged car is as good a recipe for the Fast Light Tourer now as it was when the 30/98 was born; and to judge by the season's results, the Allard, like the famous Vauxhall, is a useful all-rounder. So we decided to make the week-end a dual test—a fast trip into Dorset by Douglas Tubbs, and a hill-hunt in Somerset by Joseph Lowrey. Tubbs had the car first, so he leads off.

### American Flexibility

Lower built than pre-war models, and carrying the body designed by Godfrey Imhof, HLB 430 looks more Mayfair than mudlark, and proved a quick car for town, although too exotic for pace in the Dirty Thirties. Aluminium heads and an increased bore, which seem the main departures from standard, have not impaired the tractability of the Ford V8 engine. The trickle-factor remains high, so that one can either waffle along behind the trams or waft Detroitly past. The exhaust is quiet enough not to excite remark, although comments on the car as a whole overheard in passing through London ranged all the way from, "Cor, ain't she a smasher!" and "When d'yer take off, mate?" to "Why don't yer buy a real one?"—the last coming from an earnest character outside Waterloo, who evidently doesn't like jam on it.

I confess, now, that I had hoped for fine weather during my tenancy, expecting pronounced over - steer characteristics from the Allard, with incessant rear-wheel skids; and I fancy that Lowrey felt the same when rain started at lunch time on Friday. We discovered our mistake within a street or two. The car does not wag its tail unbidden, and holds the road well in the wet. The hood I cannot speak for; it lives in the boot, and we did not disturb it, although going home on Friday night I wished I had. One keeps dry enough at speed even in a downpour, but crawling behind unlighted lorries in the dark, with dazzlers coming towards one, no. Per Allardua ad Aquascutum.

Saturday morning was better, and an accelerating 60 m.p.h. in top gear up Polhill, between Riverhead and Bromley, set me well in the groove. Corkscrew Hill, out of West Wickham, usually rather a chore, fell behind in three taps of the throttle, despite other traffic, and we were almost in London again when we sighted a high familiar form. "Is that 'Old Bill'?" I asked a bus conductor. "That's him, all right," he replied. "Don't cut him up, mate." We formated with the old bus (survivor of the 1914-18 war) for the length of Tooting Bec, before sweeping across to the North Circular Road.

At the Ace Service Station John Wyer climbed in, to navigate me westwards. He looked behind as we exuberated off. "Black marks right the way up," he remarked, "with just a small break for the gear-change." But I doubt if anyone outside the car noticed. An Allard can leave streaks without putting up a black.

It was while threading through the Great West Road that John con-

# AND

firmed my suspicions about the speedo. "Have you noticed," he inquired, "how everything is going faster than usual?" I had. So we tested the instrument and found an error of 17 per cent., which tied in with another impression we had formed, viz., that the car was undergeared.

### Alternative Axle Ratios

Now the competition two-seater is offered with alternative axle ratios—4.1 for trials and sprints or 3.5 for open-road work. Clearly they had given this car the lower ratio, but without letting the speedometer into the secret. True readings of 75 m.p.h. came up more often than was kind to a newish engine as we pulled clear of London-based traffic and stopped for lunch at The Venture, that welcoming and fully licensed road house on the Basingstoke by-pass.

When we came out it was raining hard, and we were behind schedule. So we looked at watches and set the trip. The car sits down nicely to the open, shiny bend. Being designed primarily for trials, the Allard has most of its weight on the rear wheels—in fact, Wyer and I were sitting practically over the back axle, with a curved, jutting prow and two wing-humps as our front horizon. Seated like this, one recalls long-

## D. B. Tubbs and Joseph Lowrey take the rough with the smooth during a week-end with a new 4-litre Allard

fronted cars of the past—Mercedes-Benz in particular—but one thinks also of the modern racing car, which combines a long bonnet with independent springing at the front. As a matter of fact, there is a bit of both schools in the way the Allard behaves, and soon one is aiming the car as a whole through the bends and taking them in a pleasant four-wheeled drift. It under-steers, in fact, and although there is no feeling of the dreaded side-slip, it is the front wheels that break away first.

Barrelling down A30, we enjoyed the long switchbacks of Salisbury Plain, showing a genuine but unpressed 80 m.p.h. on the down grades and sweeping up the following rise as though it were flat. Arrived at Salisbury, we punted round the town for a little while seeking a good view of the Cathedral and then left for Blandford, in Dorset. En route, we consulted the watch again: despite the delay in Sarum and the sober maximum used, 51 miles (corrected) went into the hour, which is not so tardy, at that.

At Tarrant Hinton we paused to seek friends at the Eastbury Park Country Club—but they were in Town, so Wyer took topographical

# LOOSE

charge. He wanted to revisit Zig-Zag hill, which rises out of the village of Melbury.

So far as I know, Zig-Zag has never been used as a speed hill-climb course, although it would have made an even better venue than its near neighbour, Spreadeagle, where Humphrey Cook's Vauxhall, Mays's Bugattis and Frazer-Nash's " Kim " used to make history 20 years ago, before speed meetings were ruled off the public roads. Zig-Zag climbs the same escarpment as Spreadeagle (which is part of the old road from Shaftesbury to Blandford), but is much less steep, having probably been made as a by-pass in the equine days. It is an alpine pass in miniature, with four hairpins and another very sharp bend, but a very easy gradient

### Upward and Onward

No old man cried " Try not the pass " as we headed the Allard at the slope, but John Wyer seemed amused about something as we changed into second and poured on the coals. The bends come up pretty fast when you don't know them—and the better you know them the faster they come up. So either way you are kept busy. The Allard is a wide car and Zig-Zag was covered in damp leaves.

Until then we had not realized what a good lock the machine had—evidently better than most, because the banks of the hairpin bends are scored with the tyre marks of less handy cars and those lacking the surplus power with which to slide the tail.

Despite experience of the car on open bends in the wet, we were still half expecting the tail of the Allard to chase itself, but it proved just as much an under-steerer on Zig-Zag as it had elsewhere. Holding the car close in to the inside of the first corner, we found that the front would run wide; but a tap of throttle brought the after end round as well and one power-slid out of the corner and on up the hill in a way that felt professional—but probably looked most untidy.

The second and third hairpins come almost together and seem complementary. Caster action unwinds one from left lock, and right-hand tiller follows at once, with the car seeming to place itself. Very pleasant. Too bad we cannot have official hill-climbs on Zig-Zag any more!

From Melbury, after one or two more tries at Zig-Zag, we motored through wonderful autumn colouring to Fonthill, where Beckford built his fake " Gothick " abbey in the 18th century, and where he planted no fewer than 20,000 varieties of trees. There never were such colours. At Wylie, where we refilled tank and sump, we assured a mechanic that the Allard really was " a British job," and then made all convenient haste across the Plain, to hand over to Lowrey and collect our own car from him.

An Allard is a pleasant device for the main road, as Wyer and I discovered, we should both like to try one with a four-speed box if such a thing were made, giving 80 or so on the highest indirect, and 105 down hills without over-revving—say a 3 to 1 top and 4 to 1 third. But perhaps that would spoil the vehicle for trials. As Lowrey says, you have to take

HIGHSPOT.—Reached over soft turf tracks, this ruined beacon tower surmounts Cothelstone Hill.

## Fast and Loose—Contd.

the rough with the smooth. Over to him.

### Punishment Without Crime

The Gilbertian desire "to make the punishment fit the crime" is one with which I always sympathize. Now, the Allard V8 is no crime whichever way you look at it, but it was ours to punish nevertheless, and the right place to punish it seemed to me to be out in the wide open spaces. A quick look at the map of England settled the route problem, and, averting my gaze from the fuel contents gauge, I decided on the Quantock Hills.

My taste for this particular piece of Somerset springs from aerial views of it, when the rolling bracken-covered hills, so near the Bristol Channel and apparently traversed by a multitude of unfenced tracks, cried out for exploration. I paid one visit to the Quantocks in 1941, glimpsing them briefly when taking my own

H.R.G. over the top, and now I had just the car in which to revisit their wide open spaces.

The run west was uneventful, apart from a halt to measure out a quarter-mile stretch on the Shrewton to Heytesbury road. A cold task in November, completed as a rain squall arrived, and the wind was such as to blow the Allard up the considerable slope at precisely the same speed as it descended with gravity's aid. The Castle Hotel, Taunton, produced the roast beef one expects on an English sabbath, in quick time, but although we washed the lunch down with Somerset cider, the waiter's accent was unquestionably London.

The afternoon was finer than the morning, and as we headed north through Kingston village a wintry sun was shining. Entering the hills by a wooded valley, we essayed a muddy lane down which timber had been brought from the hilltop woods. An Allard has an amazing amount of wheel grip, and contrives to dig through mud where other cars would

spin their wheels helplessly; but from a leisurely start we found that there are limits to what can be done with normal tyre pressures. Retiring down the lane, we noted with relief that the brakes worked well in reverse and did not eliminate directional control.

### Turf Motoring

Reaching the crest of Buncombe Hill by the metalled road, an easy top-gear climb with our 33 horses, we curved sharply to the left, then headed on to an unmade track across the common. Soon we found ourselves motoring over soft green turf, and eventually reached the ruined beacon tower which marks the summit of Cothelstone Hill. Visitors to this particular hilltop may be puzzled to find strange markings on the ground not far from a circular earthwork; there are other ring-shaped markings on the ground. Let me confess that these have no archæological significance, but result from my wickedly succumbing to temptation, using the smooth grass to experiment with the mutual interaction of steering and throttle.

The southern end of the Quantock ridge is comparatively civilized, and we had to return to the tarred road for a mile or so before an "unsuitable for motors" sign pointed our route to the next crest, Lydeard Hill. There was not much space between the stone walls, but that little just sufficed to pass the Allard out on to the open hilltop. A couple of miles of tracks across the heather, with a clear view eastwards down a coombe towards Bridgewater replacing the mistier outlook to the south-west, and we found ourselves between banks

LONESOME PINE.—This caption may be botanically inaccurate, but we prefer it to "Cupressus Incognitus Isolatus."

SOMERSET.—This photograph of Lydeard Hill should show half the county. The fact that it does not is attributed by the photographer to poor weather, by the Temple Press photographic dept. to incompetent amateur shutter clicking.

## Fast and Loose

once more, temporarily deserting the 1,000-ft. contour.

Crossing something which closely resembled a road, we headed the Allard into a really overgrown track, forcing the way through long grass and brambles and running the gauntlet of mud and fallen branches. For nearly two miles the going remained sticky, with the Allard crew frequently ducking to avoid the whiplash blows of branches, and yet the car pottered gently along, in top gear most of the time or occasionally in second when the speed was reduced to a genuine walking pace by lack of a visible track. The problem of a closed gate in a muddy hollow proved to be no problem at all, and soon we came to a lane which crosses the open grassy track, a track on which the Allard leapt ahead with the wheels spinning merrily. After one more sticky patch we joined the ridge road and, finding even our astonishing steering lock unequal to the required left-hand hairpin, turned right and then reversed briskly along the ridgeway until a gap in the gorse bushes gave us room to turn round.

### 1,000 Feet Up

At Beacon Hill we reached the 1,000 ft. altitude again, and with it a view of the Bristol Channel. A solitary hiker, strangely unmoved at meeting a 1946 car miles from any road, directed us on to the track towards West Quantoxhead, and over the rough, open heath we began to hustle once more, eventually finding a Hills are in any case among the most unspoilt and attractive districts in southern England. They offer in a modest area anything from bare moorland to thick woods or rich farmland, and they are well served by a few tarred lanes and multitudinous rocky and overgrown byways.

The run home was as uneventful as the outward run, and no less brisk. The top-gear ratio which had served for most of the hill-top tracks whisked us past everything we met on the road, and after fortifying ourselves with bacon and chips at an Andover café we even detoured in search of a proposed Hants and Berks M.C. night trial section—a detour, incidentally, which caused us to go round in circles, the driver cursing the navigator, the navigator

WHERE DO WE GO FROM HERE?—Having piloted the expedition into a large mudhole entirely surrounded by gorse bushes, the navigator seeks the track he was supposed to be following.

ridge from Nether Stowey to Crowcombe.

A signpost warning that there was a one-in-four gradient tempted us to abandon the ridge road and descend into Crowcombe village, a colourful descent through trees which still showed their autumn colours, and we then began to seek a way back to the hill tops once more. An attempt to reach Hurley Beacon was abandoned in a quarry, solely out of respect for the Allard's glistening (though now mud-stained!) paintwork, so we took a muddy way along the hillside to Bicknoller village and tried again.

### Forcing a Pass

Once more we found the track overgrown, the gorse bushes providing barely room for cattle in single file, but this time we decided to force our way through. A rush crossing of the stream bottomed the rear springs loudly, but soon we reached a fairly tarred road again and finally dropping down from the deserted hilltops into inhabited country.

The Allard is a car which is designed to go anywhere, on the road or off it. Our little try-out had covered only about 15 off-the-road miles, but they had been really rough miles and had been interspersed with less than five miles of road. Despite the flowing body lines, and the fact that we had not bothered to replace all-enveloping wings with the scantier trials pattern, the only damage was a slight dent on the off-side rear wheel cover. True, soon after we had regained main roads and set off on a fast run home, the bracket securing the "Panhard rod" to the chassis broke, but this was not a standard car and it still cornered fast and happily without this rear axle steadying member.

Apart from our ostensible purpose of trying out the car, the Quantock cursing the driver, and both cursing low-mounted head lamps which will not shine over hilltops! The particular piece of highway concerned carries rather less traffic now than it did a couple of thousand years ago, and finding it at night is quite a problem, even to folk who should know the district.

Nipping quietly through the traffic as we entered London' on Monday morning, reluctantly taking the Allard back to its owner, with no noise save slight carburetter roar and a faint, uneven beat from the twin exhaust systems, we found that a thick layer of mud virtually silenced public comments on the car's striking lines—or can it be that even Cockney humour is at a low ebb on Monday morning? The speed over the flying quarter-mile —— Sorry, but until we can have the promised standard model for proper road test it must remain untold.

# THE STEYR-ALLARD

**The first published description of Sydney Allard's new air-cooled V8 sprint car, which is competing for the British Hill-Climb Championship.**

ONE of the sensations of this year's sprint events has been the debut of S. H. Allard's new sprint car, his air-cooled V8 single-seater Steyr-Allard. Allard commenced motoring fast many years ago with a Morgan 3-wheeler and later with a very ingenious four-wheeler conversion of that car. His subsequent highly successful and at times hectic career with the white T.T. Ford V8 and Allard cars, is well known to all followers of the Sport. Last season Allard built a special 2-seater sprint car and experimented with an o.h.-exhaust valve head to obviate the overheating to which Ford V8 engines are so prone at prolonged full-throttle. That car went very well indeed, but someone had brought to "S. H.'s" notice a certain German air-cooled V8 lorry engine of the same capacity as a V8 Ford, but some 100 lb. lighter and giving rather more b.h.p.—91 at 3,600 r.p.m. Allard did not rest until he had acquired one of those engines and a reasonable stock of spares. Then, employing his own team of selected mechanics and working after business hours himself, he commenced construction of the Steyr-Allard single-seater sprint car, which made its debut at Prescott last May and established f.t.d. in 47.25 sec., beating Abecassis' Bugatti. The car has been built as a private venture, quite independent of Adlards Motors, Ltd. and the Allard Motor Co., Ltd., of both of which S. H. Allard is a director. Since its sensational debut at the first Prescott meeting, it has made 6th fastest time, tying with Mrs. Darbieshire's Riley, at Bo'ness, finished 2nd in its class and made 10th fastest time at Shelsley Walsh, and tied for 2nd fastest time with Ansell's E.R.A. to win its class at the B.O.C. Club Prescott meeting, when Gerard's E.R.A. made fastest time. Being a sprint

car pure and simple it did not run at Gransden.

So well has this new Allard performed while still largely experimental, and so interesting is it technically, that we invited ourselves to inspect it and were privileged to do so when it was stripped down in the racing workshops beneath Allard Motors' Clapham Road showrooms, preparatory to the July Prescott and Bouley Bay hill-climbs.

The engine is, as we have said, a normal Steyr lorry engine, as used in German transports during the war. In a lorry it is fan-cooled through an elaborate ducting system, but Allard has dispensed with all that, trusting the alloy heads and well-finned cylinder barrels to keep cool enough for those brief periods during which the car is extended. The cast-iron crankcase has been mounted in the narrow chassis on two girder-brackets, one each side at the front, and on an alloy bell-housing at the rear, giving 3-point mounting. The cylinders are separate barrels, inclined in V-formation to constitute a 60 degree V8. Each cylinder head is a separate well-finned light-alloy casting carrying two inclined o.h. KE965 valves, the inlet valve having a diameter of 1¼ in., the exhaust valve a diameter of 1⅜ in., and both valves seating on steel inserts. The crankshaft runs in five plain bearings of the thin-shell variety and there are two connecting rods per crankpin. Above it is the chain-driven camshaft, which is thus enabled to actuate the valves *via*

short push-rods and the usual rockers. Cast-alloy covers hide the valve gear and each valve has two springs. Originally coil ignition was used, with the distributor set vertically above the engine, but this drive is now used for the rev.-counter and an 8-cylinder Scintilla "Vertex" magneto is driven-direct from the nose of the camshaft, it being mounted horizontal thereto. The ignition leads protrude from the bonnet sides and are led backwards through tubes above the outer valve covers, these tubes being concealed by streamline fairings when the bonnet is in place. The sump holds two gallons of oil, which is circulated by a gear-type pump driven from an extension of what was the distributor-drive shaft. One Amal carburetter is used per cylinder, mounted so that all eight are inside the V formed by the cylinders. Flanges, four each side, bolted beside the leading edge of each of the inner valve covers, form bearings for long rods which operate the throttle slides. A separate exhaust pipe runs vertically downwards from each exhaust port and these pipes are united by a horizontal, flexible-pipe exhaust system on each side of the car, which gives a distinctly "V8" exhaust beat. An improved layout of piping is now in hand.

This Steyr engine has the usefully short stroke of 92 mm., compared with 95.25 mm. of the Ford V8 "30," and, with a bore of 79 mm., its capacity is 3,600 c.c. Not only was this unit some 100 lb. lighter than the Ford to commence with, but, naturally, the fact that no radiator or coolant is required further reduces the weight of any car in which it is used. The main reason for its adoption, however, is the very good power-output which it gives low down the speed range. Something like 80 b.h.p. is developed at 2,000 r.p.m. and Allard thus finds he

*In action!*

[*Photo by Louis Klemantaski, A.I.B.P., A.R.P.S.*

*The Steyr-Allard and some of those responsible for it—Sydney Allard at the wheel, and behind, l. to r., J. McCallan, B. Arthur, ————, Alan May, (a friend of Sydney Allard) and Tom Lush.*

can let in the clutch at this speed and accelerate hard with little or no wheelspin, whereas with most racing cars the engine speed at which the car is taken off has to be far higher and the throttle has then to be eased as the car moves off to control wheel-spin. So far as maximum power is concerned, after special Martlet pistons, with slight cut-aways in the crown to clear the valves, had been acquired from the Brooklands Eng. Co., Ltd., the compression ratio went up to 12 to 1, and it is estimated that the b.h.p. is now between 140 and 150 at 4,000 r.p.m. The engine is started on benzole by pushing the car, as hand-cranking is impractical, and is then run on methanol-base J.A.P. fuel. No trouble has been experienced with the Lodge R49 plugs.

Turning to the car in which this interesting engine is installed, light weight was the obvious criterion and Allard is to be congratulated on having kept the weight of the complete car down to just under 13 cwt. This is an astonishing figure for a 3.8-litre car built, as we shall see, largely of standard Allard components.

The chassis side-members are those used for the "Competition" model Allard, united by the standard Allard girder cross-member, which carries the i.f.s., at the front, and thereafter by a substantial tubular cross-member ahead of the engine and two more of these tubular members aft. Front suspension is by the normal Allard divided front axle and transverse leaf spring, the axle having a track of 4 ft. 4 in. The rear suspension is most ingeniously simple, for a normal Allard rear axle, giving a slight crab-track of 4 ft. 2 in. with single rear wheels, is merely separated from the frame by a single Terry coil spring on each side. These springs are positioned in

cup abutments on axle and · chassis, respectively, and the axle is located by a ball mounted on the differential case, sliding in a guide on the chassis cross-member. Hartford double-arm friction shock-absorbers are used front and back and normally the suspension is used quite soft, in the modern manner. The steering column extends from the spring steering wheel right along above the engine to the nose of the car, where it terminates in a small rubber universal-joint coupling, which actuates a cut-down Allard-Marles steering box with the extended drop-arm shaft vertical, mounted on a bracket which is welded to the chassis frame. A divided track-rod connects with the steering arm.

The clutch is normal Ford and has stood up extremely well. The gearbox, in unit with the engine, is, again, standard Allard-Ford, giving ratios of 12 to 1, 6.5 to 1, and 4.1 to 1 with a 4.11 to 1 rear axle. These ratios are used for Prescott and it is both interesting and significant that " S. H." starts in 2nd gear—in fact, he has never yet used the lowest ratio. Second is held all the way up Prescott, yet something approaching 80 m.p.h. is reached before cutting for the first corner. Naturally, Bo'ness permitted a change into top, and about 100 m.p.h. over the line. If required, axle ratios of 3.5 to 1, or 4.55 to 1 can be substituted for the 4.11 to 1 axle, and with the former alternative the second-gear ratio then becomes 5.6 to 1. This is with twin 5.00 in. by 18 in. rear tyres, although 6.50 in. by 16 in. single rear tyres are another possibility. The gearbox is the side-control type and a short gear-lever, emerging through the r.h. side of the cockpit, now links directly to this control *via* a long rod and gives

very positive, if rather tricky, gear selection. Formerly a steering-column gear lever location was employed, but Allard knocked the lever into neutral at Bo'ness on one run and now prefers the more-positive normally-placed control. The rear-tyre size has already been given, and it may be remarked that Ford pressed steel wheels are used, those carrying the twin rear tyres being a clever job of welding together two standard rims. The front tyre size is 5.50 by 16 in.

The brakes are Lockheed hydraulic and two brake pedals are used, the additional one being to the left of the clutch pedal and used to steady the car while the throttle is still being operated. An external hand-lever operates on the rear wheels only. The body is a light alloy shell of very pleasing aspect, made for Allard by Woodward of Putney. The long bonnet is no more than a detachable cover over the engine and the narrow front grille is of Allard formation. Taking a page from Alfa-Romeo's book, the facia carries a minimum of instruments—a Smith's rev.-counter (replacing a former, inaccurate instrument), an aircraft air-pressure gauge and tiny ignition switch. The fuel tank lives in the tail and has a capacity of 2 to 3 gallons, but normally only a gallon is carried. The driver's seat is a metal bucket. That then, is the Steyr-Allard, one of 1947's most interesting and successful sprint cars. It is no secret that some trouble has been experienced, chiefly from stretched valves, but Allard and his racing staff are rapidly becoming acquainted with the temperament of the specialised Steyr engine and we are indebted to them for letting us examine what is likely to become one of the fastest sprint cars in this country.

Beside the Steyr-Allard at the time of our visit stood Sydney Allard's latest road-equipped Allard, which ran in a sports-car race at Gransden, for which it was finished only at the very last minute. This is a most intriguing car. Its dimensions are the same as those of the " Competition "-model Allard, which was recently withdrawn from the production range because these cars offer comparatively cramped accommodation, and are so little lighter than the normal 8 ft. 10 in.-wheelbase cars that there was no point in retaining them in production. They are, of course, still used most effectively in competition, notably by Imhof, Burgess and Appleton. Allard's latest sports car is like one of these, but has a low light-shell 2-seater body, its side panels merging into the centre of light rear mudguards, to give a very wide cockpit. At Gransden the o.h.-exhaust heads were used, in an attempt to make the engine last the 5 laps, which was unsuccessful, as the gaskets protested, but this typically " S. H." sports Allard is likely to be run in future with a normal Mercury· V8 engine. As it weighs in the region of 18¼ cwt., it should be well worth seeing. In conclusion, plenty of production-model Allards and Allard chassis are on view at the new Clapham Road showrooms (by Clapham North Underground Station) if you are interested in one of Britain's most potent and practical high-performance cars.—W. B.

**Make:** Allard.  **Type:** Coupe.  **Makers:** Allard Motor Co. Ltd.,
24/28 High Street, Clapham, London, S.W.4

## Dimensions and Seating

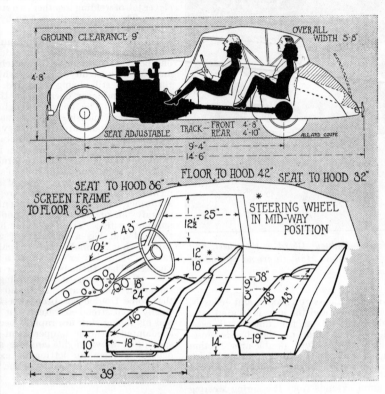

## In Brief

Price: £999. Plus purchase tax £278 5s. 0d.
= £1,277 5s. 0d.

| | |
|---|---|
| Capacity .. .. .. | 3,622 c.c. |
| Road weight unladen .. | 26 cwt. |
| Front/rear weight distribution | 46/54 |
| Laden weight as tested .. | 30 cwt. |
| Fuel consumption .. .. | 17 m.p.g. |
| Maximum speed .. | .81.5 m.p.h. |
| Maximum speed on 1 in 20 gradient .. .. | .72 m.p.h. |
| Maximum top-gear gradient | 1 in 7½ |
| Acceleration 10-30 on top .. | 7.0 secs. |
| 0-50 through gears | 10.6 secs. |

Gearing, 19.8 m.p.h. in top at 1,000 r.p.m.
79 m.p.h. at 2,500 feet per
minute piston speed.

## Specification

**Engine**

| | | |
|---|---|---|
| Cylinders .. .. | .. | V-8 |
| Bore .. .. | .. | 78 mm. |
| Stroke .. .. | .. | 95.2 mm. |
| Cubic capacity .. | .. | 3,622 c.c. |
| Piston area .. | .. | 58.9 sq. in. |
| Valves .. .. | .. | Side |
| Compression ratio | .. | 6.12 |
| Max. b.h.p. .. | .. | 85 |
| at .. .. | .. | 3,800 r.p.m. |
| B.h.p. per sq. in. piston area | .. | 1.44 |
| Piston speed at max. b.h.p. | | 2,375 ft./min. |
| Carburetter .. | .. | Double-choke Down-draught |
| Ignition .. | .. | Lucas Coil |
| Sparking plugs .. | ..Champion C7 (18 mm.) | |
| Fuel pump.. | .. | Mechanical |
| Oil filter .. | .. | Gauze at oil pump |

**Transmission**

| | | |
|---|---|---|
| Clutch.. .. | .. | Single-plate, centrifugally assisted |
| Top gear .. | .. | 4.11 |
| 2nd gear .. | .. | 6.95 |
| 1st gear .. | .. | 14.4 |
| Propeller shaft .. | .. | Enclosed Hardy Spicer in torque tube |
| Final drive .. | .. | Spiral bevel |

**Chassis**

| | | |
|---|---|---|
| Brakes .. | .. | Lockheed hydraulic |
| Brake drum diameter .. | | 12 ins. |
| Friction lining area .. | | 164 sq. ins. |
| Tyres .. | .. | Dunlop, 6.25/16 |
| Steering gear .. | .. | Marles, |

**Performance Factors** (at laden weight as tested)

| | |
|---|---|
| Piston area, sq. ins. per ton | 39.2 sq. ins. |
| Brake lining area, sq. ins. per ton .. .. | 109 sq. ins. |
| Litres per ton-mile .. | 3,660 |

Originally described in "The Motor," February 6th, 1946.

## Test Conditions

Mild, moderate wind, damp concrete surface, British pool petrol. Tested on Jabbeke motor road, Belgium, with two people and luggage in the car.

## Test Data

**ACCELERATION TIMES on Two Upper Ratios**

| | Top | 2nd |
|---|---|---|
| 10–30 m.p.h. .. .. .. .. .. | 7.0 secs. | 4.6 secs. |
| 20–40 m.p.h. .. .. .. .. .. | 7.2 secs. | 4.7 secs. |
| 30–50 m.p.h. .. .. .. .. .. | 7.9 secs. | 5.7 secs. |
| 40–60 m.p.h. .. .. .. .. .. | 9.7 secs. | 8.8 secs. |
| 50–70 m.p.h. .. .. .. .. .. | 12.8 secs. | — |

**ACCELERATION TIMES Through Gears**

| | |
|---|---|
| 0–30 m.p.h. .. .. .. | 4.4 secs. |
| 0–40 m.p.h. .. .. .. | 7.0 secs. |
| 0–50 m.p.h. .. .. .. | 10.6 secs. |
| 0–60 m.p.h. .. .. .. | 15.2 secs. |
| 0–70 m.p.h. .. .. .. | 22.8 secs. |
| Standing ¼-mile .. .. | 20.5 secs. |

**MAXIMUM SPEEDS**
**Flying Quarter-mile**

| | |
|---|---|
| Mean of four opposite runs .. | 81.5 m.p.h. |
| Best time equals .. .. | 84.9 m.p.h. |

**Speeds in Gears**

| | |
|---|---|
| Max. speed in 2nd gear .. | 61 m.p.h. |
| Max. speed in 1st gear .. .. | 32 m.p.h. |

**BRAKES AT 30 m.p.h.** (Tested on dry tarmacadam.)
0.93 g. (=32½ ft. stopping distance) with 85 lb. pedal pressure.
0.88 g. (=34 ft. stopping distance) with 75 lb. pedal pressure.
0.64 g. (=47 ft. stopping distance) with 50 lb. pedal pressure.
0.40 g. (=75 ft. stopping distance) with 25 lb. pedal pressure.

**FUEL CONSUMPTION**
Overall consumption for 469 miles, 27¾ gallons, equals 16.9 m.p.g.
21.5 m.p.g. at constant 30 m.p.h.
21.5 m.p.g. at constant 40 m.p.h.
20.0 m.p.g. at constant 50 m.p.h.
17.0 m.p.g. at constant 60 m.p.h.
15.5 m.p.g. at constant 70 m.p.h.
11.0 m.p.g. at constant 80 m.p.h.

**HILL CLIMBING**
Max. top-gear speed on 1 in 20 .. 72 m.p.h.
Max. top-gear speed on 1 in 15 .. 68 m.p.h.
Max. top-gear speed on 1 in 10 .. 58 m.p.h.
Max. gradient climbable on top gear, 1 in 7½
(Tapley 290 lb. per ton.)
Max. gradient climbable on 2nd gear, 1 in 5
(Tapley 455 lb. per ton).

**STEERING**
Left- and right-hand lock .. .. 41 ft.
2¼ turns of steering wheel, lock to lock.

## Maintenance

**Fuel tank:** 17 gallons (including 2 gallons reserve). **Sump:** 8 pints, S.A.E. 30. **Gearbox:** 2 pints, S.A.E. 140 E.P. gear oil. **Rear axle:** 2 pints S.A.E. 140 E.P. gear oil. **Radiator:** 36 pints. **Chassis lubrication:** 16 grease-gun points. **Ignition timing:** 4 degrees B.T.D.C. **Spark-plug gap:** 0.022 in. **Contact-breaker gap:** 0.014-0.016 in. **Tappets:** inlet and exhaust, 0.0125 in. **Valve timing:** I.O., T.D.C., E.C., 6° A.T.D.C. **Front-wheel toe-in:** 3/16 in. **Castor angle:** 6°. **Tyre Pressures:** Front 25 lb.: Rear 25 lb. **Brake fluid:** Lockheed. **Shock-absorber fluid:** Luvax Girling piston type. **Battery:** 12 v., 60 a.h. **Lamp bulbs:** 12 volts, headlamps, 36 watts double filament, side and rear lamps 6 watts, stop and reversing lamps, 24 watts.

Ref. B/37/48

# THE ALLARD DROPHEAD COUPE

### A Modern High-performance Car With Exceptional Road-holding Qualities

EXPRESS TO ANYWHERE.—
Strikingly modern lines mask
a ground clearance of 9 inches,
the greatest figure for any
British-production car.

IT is a paradox, but none the less true, that the post-war Allard combines in an altogether unprecedented degree modern appearance with old-fashioned characteristics. This statement is meant in a complimentary, and not a derogatory sense, and should, perhaps, be amplified.

The modern appearance of the car requires little comment, for it is self-evident from the photographs, and will be well known to many thousands of motorists who have attended motoring competitions in this country and abroad, in which the Allard has scored outstanding successes. It is rare in being a car produced in small numbers which has been styled by an expert, and the resultant long-curved nose and striking radiator grille are thus the conscious products of a skilled brain.

On entering the driving seat, one is, moreover, immediately impressed by the way in which appearance has been blended with the requirements of the fast driver. The bonnet falls away between the front mudguards, so as to give outstanding forward visibility, whilst at the same time the raised wings make excellent sights which are of material assistance in helping the driver accurately to place the car on the road.

This brings us at once to the leading feature of the car, which is the way in which it has retained the old-fashioned virtues of l i g h t precise steering, abnormal cornering power, and very easy correction if the skid point be overrun.

The modern trend of design has developed cars with the majority of weight on the front wheels, and this in turn gives inherent straight-running characteristics, but heavy steering unless this is countered by lower gearing. There is a marked reluctance to move from the straight, and this, in conjunction with low-geared steering, gives a slow response to the wheel. Additionally, due to lack of weight on the rear tyres, a back-end skid is comparatively easily provoked and, again due to the low-geared steering, is sometimes hard to control. Cars of this kind are excellent performers at high speeds on straight roads; they resist the effects of wind and road camber; they are also able to give a notably pitch-free ride, giving great comfort on rough surfaces. In the Allard, however, these

advantages are deliberately disclaimed in order to retain other virtues which many will think are of overriding importance. As can be seen from the cutaway drawing, the engine is mounted very far back in the frame, and this results in 54 per cent. of the weight being on the back wheels when the car is unladen, and probably 60 per cent. on the rear when driven with two up. It is certainly safe to say that the rear wheels of the Allard carry perhaps 30 per cent. more weight than is common practice to-day, and this results in handling characteristics which are of extraordinary interest.

#### Remarkable Road Adhesion

The first thing noticed by the driver when taking the car over is that, although only two turns of the wheel are required to pass from one extreme to the other of a very good lock, the effort required is small, while the feel is extremely positive. When accelerating over wet city roads in the lower gears it is quickly apparent that the car has extreme resistance to wheel spin, and the getaway is such that the struggles of many cars following the more modern trend appear pathetic. When open country is reached, it is additionally found that the Allard has remarkable tenacity in clinging to wet or dry road surfaces. Particularly on sharply radiused corners, what appear to be impossible speeds can be safely maintained without the slightest sign of skidding, and it must also be mentioned that if and when the skid point is reached, it is invariably the back which "breaks away." The high-geared steering, however, renders the driver completely master of the situation. In consequence, the Allard is a car which can be driven over winding roads with the utmost confidence in all weather conditions for it has a stability and certainty of gait which inspires the utmost confidence.

On rough roads, also, suspension, which is independent at the front by a form of split axle, performs adequately, although being, perhaps, a little on the hard side, compared with some types. Moreover, the gyroscopic effects associated with this design make their presence felt when really serious inequalities of road are reached, or on moderately bad roads at speeds of much over 70 m.p.h. The car is, however, reasonably free from pitch, and its poise is completely unaffected by heavy braking or fierce acceleration.

Reference to the Data Panel will show that the standing quarter-mile time on a wet road approaches 20 seconds, and there is reason to believe that, in favourable conditions, one could get below this figure. On the car tested the three-speed synchromesh gearbox objected to rapid gear changing, although it would doubtless have become better in this respect after it had put up a larger mileage.

For all practical purposes, the car can be treated as a single-speed model, and certainly there was no advantage to be derived from changing into an indirect gear above 40 miles per hour, although a mile a minute could be realized on the second ratio by taking the engine to its utmost r.p.m. On top, however, the car would convert 30 into 70 miles per hour in little over 20 seconds, a particularly creditable figure in view of the relatively high gearing that is used. Here again, one may call this an old-fashioned virtue, for there are few cars built to-day which are capable of 60 m.p.h. at 3,000 r.p.m., and in which the maximum piston speed in top gear is never more than 2,700 ft./min. Despite this high gearing, the car will climb a 1 in 20 gradient at 72 m.p.h., and a 1 in 10 hill at the remarkably high speed of 58 miles per hour, without changing gear.

The maximum speed is perhaps somewhat less than many might anticipate.

RETURN FROM DUNKIRK.—The Allard is driven onto the night boat for Dover, following the tests on Belgian and French roads.

It should, however, be remembered that the 3.6-litre Ford power unit used for this car is particularly notable for reliable running at full throttle, and no great effort has been made to achieve high power per litre.

Accepting, therefore, an output of 85 b.h.p., the relatively large frontal area, and air-drag characteristics which are inevitable with a drophead coupe body, the timed road speed is about according to expectations

Exceedingly high average speeds can be realized by reason of the outstanding top-gear acceleration and magnificent road-holding characteristics. These are reinforced by the very fine braking equipment provided by Lockheed. The 12-in diameter drums give over 100 sq. ins. per ton of laden car weight, and an efficiency of 93 per cent. with only 85 lb. pedal pressure. A mere 25 lb. suffices for the 40 per cent. efficiency which is the maximum used by any driver under normal conditions.

The fuel consumption curve is particularly flat, that is to say the difference between travelling with almost shut throttle at 30 m.p.h. and on the open road at 70 m.p.h. is not great. The overall result on the road is very reasonable, and the car can be driven really hard without ever bringing the consumption to an excessive level.

It should be mentioned that as is our usual practice with high-performance cars, this particular model was run for many hundreds of miles abroad. On the Autobahn section of the Brussels-Ostend road one could sustain 75 m.p.h. on the speedometer (which was equal to 75 m.p.h. on the road) continuously with no loss of oil pressure or noticeable rise in water temperature. The suspension system was severely tested on many miles of Belgian pavé, which

is probably the most severe surface over which cars have to run, for it combines severe inequalities with the possibility of travelling at high speeds. These conditions failed to find any weak point in the Allard chassis and proved the shock absorbers to be well up to their work.

**Concerning Coachwork.**

Turning now from the mechanical aspects of the car to the bodywork, we were particularly impressed by the driving position, and the excellent visibility, to which reference has already been made. The interior finish of the car is good, and the layout of the facia panel pleasing, whilst on the dash proper is a very wide parcel rack, which is of considerable value.

In view, however, of the very high lateral 'G' which can be developed by this car on corners, it might be desirable to have partitions along this shelf, to prevent small objects being continuously despatched from one side to the other. The good construction of the body is proved by the unusual freedom from draught, which gives warm travel even in the absence of an interior heater, and by the fact that a

large mileage on bad roads produced no fresh noises. The rear seats, however, are somewhat cramped, and although a third person and luggage can be carried on them, it would be unfair to regard the car as a full four-seater for long distance occasions. It is additionally unfortunate that the enclosed space for luggage at the back of the car should be so small, and that anything placed therein is not under lock and key. However, by using the lid as a platform, a considerable quantity of luggage can be carried externally. We had no opportunity of driving the car in open condition, but the top may be quickly changed from one position to the other.

As is so often the case on modern productions, the head lamps were in no way equal to the maximum speed of the car. Modern styling almost obliges designers to submerge the head lamps into the front wings and this obviously limits the diameter which can be used. We remain convinced, however, that small diameter lights can be built with adequate long range and we feel that this is an aspect of design which must be seriously tackled if high speed motoring at night is to remain safe.

The Allard appealed to us as being an extremely practical car, for the advantage of widespread use of Ford components in engine and transmission lines is obvious in so far as worldwide availability of spares and service is concerned. Although developed originally to carry open two-seater bodies of a somewhat stark sporting nature, the chassis makes a fine foundation for the close-coupled coupe, although further attention could profitably be given to the problems of exhaust and air intake silencing. The absence of an air silencer or filter results in noticeable power roar at full throttle between 50 and 70 miles per hour, and the rigid mounting of the exhaust pipes produces some boom inside the closed body at lower speeds. These, however, are criticisms of a minor order, whereas the car as a whole is possessed of marked virtues which are both major and, be it admitted, surprising.

AMENITIES FOR SPEED.—This view of the close-coupled drophead body reveals the individual front seats, spring steering wheel on telescopic column, and remote gear-change control.

STANDARD TWO SEATER

FOUR SEATER TOURER

DROPHEAD COUPÉ

COACHBUILT SALOON

# ALLARD

The New Allard is a truly modern car. It incorporates every up-to-minute feature called for by the discriminating motorist. Yet, in spite of its modern design, every part of the car has been thoroughly proved. Since 1936 the Allard has won a reputation as Britain's premier competition car, and now in addition to the short chassis sports two-seater there are offered the drophead coupe, the four-seater tourer and the coachbuilt saloon. The Allard cars have been designed to provide a reliable and fast car suitable both for roadwork and sporting events. The high power-weight ratio, coupled with correct weight distribution, gives a high performance without undue effort.

The results gained by these cars in sporting events since 1936 are sufficient proof of their reliability, and road tests by various motoring correspondents in every case stress the fine performance, smooth riding, efficient braking and good road-holding capabilities.

All models embody the same advanced engineering features which have won the Allard its outstanding reputation. Some of the outstanding Allard advantages :—

(1) New rigid box section chassis with independent front wheel suspension and correct weight distribution ensures exceptional road-holding and safety. (2) Large, smooth acting and powerful Lockheed 4-wheel hydraulic brakes. (3) Engine, made by Ford Motor Co. Ltd. (4) Excellent ground clearance (9 inches). (5) The famous Marles steering, light but positive. (6) Excellent visibility due to the curved radiator front and low bonnet with perfect driving position. (7) Latest type, double-acting self-recuperating shock absorbers. (8) Steering column adjusts for length and height, adjustable seats. (9) Low running costs in proportion to performance. (10) Service and parts readily available.

ALLARD MOTOR COMPANY LTD., 24-28 CLAPHAM HIGH STREET, LONDON, S.W.4

ALMOTCO, LONDON

MACAULAY 3201

# TEST REPORTS by the Press Experts
## on the New ALLARD

### "THE LIGHT CAR"
**April, 1948**

"The Allard coupe is top of the class as regards road-holding and all-round performance. Steering is superb. It has that true sports-car feeling—light and lively, but never sloppy. With the comfort of a completely draught-proof convertible body, well-planned seating, and a top-gear performance almost without parallel in a sporting car, the pilot can get down to the business of putting a remarkable number of miles into the hour. It is speed with perfect safety, too, for the powerful Lockheed brakes will always stop the car in a dead straight line."

### "THE AUTOCAR"
**March 26, 1948**

". . . has road holding and stability which allow an enthusiastic driver to throw it about as he pleases. That it should have such characteristics is to be expected when one remembers that the whole idea of this car has evolved in the minds of enthusiastic and hard-driving competitors in the trials and rallies which have done so much to develop the British sports car.

Perhaps the outstanding feature of the specification is the good ratio of power to weight, whereby without specially tuning or stressing the $3\frac{1}{2}$-litre V8 engine the car can provide exceptional acceleration on quite high gear ratios. The engine will run quite smoothly down to about 9 m.p.h. on top gear, and as soon as the throttle is depressed pull away strongly and smoothly.

On an average main road run in this country the acceleration is so good that 80 m.p.h. can frequently be seen if required. The highest reading obtained was 92-93 on level ground. . . . During the course of the testing perhaps the most impressive recording obtained in this direction was between 52 and 53 miles covered in an hour without exceeding 75 m.p.h.—a speed 15 m.p.h. within the car's maximum. The feeling of safety for fast cornering experienced in the Allard is exceptional among present-day cars and enables high average speeds to be maintained in safety even over winding roads. . . . and there is the admirable quality of the car almost steering itself on the straights and of following an accurate course on corners. The brakes are Lockheed hydraulic, and they behave admirably for purposes of a fast car, acting very smoothly indeed.

In petrol consumption the Allard proved commendably moderate considering its engine size and and the hard driving to which it was subjected during a long-distance test. An enthusiastic driver could hardly fail to be impressed by this car. An important point is that the fact of its embodying Ford components, notably the power unit, means that parts and service are available all over the world."

### "THE MOTOR"
**March 10, 1948**

"On entering the driving seat, one is, moreover, immediately impressed by the way in which appearance has been blended with the requirements of the fast driver. . . . Outstanding forward visibility. . . . light, precise steering, abnormal cornering power, and very easy correction if the skid point be overrun.

When accelerating over wet city roads in the lower gears it is quickly apparent that the car has extreme resistance to wheel spin, and the getaway is such that the struggles of many cars appear pathetic. . . . What appear to be impossible speeds can be safely maintained without the slightest sign of skidding. In consequence the Allard is a car which can be driven over winding roads with the utmost confidence in all weather conditions for it has a stability and certainty of gait which inspires the utmost confidence. . . . The standing quarter-mile time on a wet road approaches 20 seconds.

Exceedingly high average speeds can be realised by reason of the outstanding top-gear acceleration and magnificent road-holding characteristics. These are reinforced by the very fine braking equipment provided by Lockheed. . . . One could sustain 75 m.p.h. . . . continuously with no loss of oil pressure or noticeable rise in water temperature.

The Allard appealed to us as being an extremely practical car, for the widespread use of Ford components in engine and transmission lines is obvious in so far as world-wide availability of spares and service is concerned. . . . The car as a whole is possessed of marked virtues which are both major and, be it admitted, surprising."

### "MOTOR SPORT"
**April, 1948**

"The coupe model Allard—one of Britain's most popular high performance cars. It combines vivid acceleration, high speed and modern outline with the advantages of Ford's world wide service facilities.

I wistfully recall a run in one of these cars, and particularly its acceleration from rest, making even a drive along London's congested Oxford Street a grand experience."

**★**

**ALLARD MOTOR CO. LTD.**
24-28, Clapham High Street,
London, S.W.4. Tel. MACaulay 2431

INVULNERABLE.—Planned to be able to participate in tough reliability trials without suffering damage, the special-bodied Allard has generous ground clearance, the minimum of front or rear overhang, and stoneguarded inbuilt lamps.

epicyclic type with electro-magnetic control giving outstandingly quick gear changes. The two-speed rear axle enables a fairly low final drive ratio to be used for acceleration, or a higher ratio obtained at will for fast cruising at minimum fuel consumption.

Modifications to the chassis initially have been few. The most important of these have been the fitting of Telecontrol adjustable friction shock absorbers, to supplement the piston-type hydraulic shock absorbers, and the manufacture of a removable outside hand brake which can be used when needed for special tests.

The two-seater body has been designed to combine smartness and comfort with invulnerability under

# Competitions in Comfort
## Special Bodywork Fitted to an Allard to be used in Trials
### by Leonard Potter

ILLUSTRATED on this page is a short-wheelbase Allard with two-seater coachwork which is to make its competitions debut in the Rallye International Automobile des Alpes during July, driven by Leonard Potter of the Galibier Engineering Co., Ltd., Farnham.

The first of a trio of similar cars, the prospective drivers of the remaining two being Len Parker and Kenneth McAlpine, this model has been built with the idea that a properly designed car should be able to run in arduous trials without suffering damage, and if so designed can be as smartly turned-out as anything on the road.

In view of the insistence on a basically standard specification for cars competing in the Alpine Rally, this car has been built on a substantially unmodified Allard chassis with provision made for the incorporation of special features at a later date. There is the manufacturer's usual layout of independent front and transverse rear springing, but the engine is the 3.9-litre Mercury type of V8 in place of the 3.6-litre size fitted to most home-sale Allards.

Martlett pistons are fitted to the engine, which will normally be run with Offenhauser side-valve aluminium heads. There is provision for replacing the normal induction system by a twin carburetter layout, or by a supercharger installation, to suit particular competitions.

The transmission is at present by normal three-speed synchromesh gearbox, but a Columbia two-speed rear axle can be installed. Looking further into the future, a Cotal gearbox is being produced for the car, of the

conditions of abuse. As may be seen from the photograph, it is of classic appearance, with separate mudguards and carrying spare wheels and a fuel tank externally at the rear. A cowled radiator, and inbuilt lamps and trafficators, are practical modern features.

To facilitate changes in engine specification and general preparation for competitions or touring, all the front sections of the bodywork have been made conveniently removable. This applies to front mudguards, the radiator cowl, and the bonnet top and sides. The fixings for these parts have been carefully arranged to do without any woodscrews or inaccessible nuts.

All-weather equipment comprises hood, tonneau cover and sidescreens, the main windscreen being of the fold-flat variety. The cubby hole on the passenger's side of the instrument panel accommodates a car radio set, of a type which is easily removable and can then be run off A.C. mains instead of from the car electrical system. With twin spare tyres of 7.50 by 16 size, and a fuel tank having 35 gallons capacity in two distinct sections, the car has eminently trials-worthy weight distribution, yet it is suitable for everyday journeys.

SHE SHALL HAVE MUSIC.—A concession to passenger comfort is the provision on the generously instrumented facia panel of a cubby hole accommodating a removable radio receiver.

SLEEK SPORTS.—The open two-seat Allard is built on a shortened chassis but still retains some luggage space at the rear.

# THE V8 ALLARDS

## Detail Refinements in a Successful Range of Sporting Cars

THE range of Allard cars to be offered during 1949 will comprise three models, all powered by the same 3.6-litre V8 engine, comprising a drop-head coupé, an open four-seat tourer, and an open two-seat tourer on a short chassis. These models are all in full production.

Externally, the latest cars are recognizable by the adoption of pressed-steel wheels, rather simpler in style than those hitherto used, with an appearance more suited to the smooth lines of the current bodies. These wheels have inconspicuous slots formed in them, to provide a flow of cooling air over the brake drums.

Internally, the main innovation is the adoption of a steering-column-mounted gear lever on the coupé model.

The short, centrally located gear lever, giving remote control over a three-speed and reverse gearbox, is being retained on the open cars, as being probably more suited to the requirements of competition drivers.

The gearbox fitted to the coupé models is, in fact, a new design throughout, with selector mechanism located at the side to suit a steering column control.

Internally, it differs from the previous pattern in respect of incorporating a different synchromesh mechanism of the baulk-ring type on the two upper ratios, a system which gives substantially clash-proof engagement of the ratios.

### Sturdy and Well Sprung

The basis of the Allard is a sturdy box-section chassis frame braced amidships by a deep X member.

The front suspension is independent, by a transverse leaf spring working with hydraulic dampers, and approximates to what is known as the swinging half-axles layout. Each front wheel is controlled by a single built-up wishbone member, formed of a transverse forging braced by a rearwardly extending tubular arm This means that, on each side of the car, there are only two bearings, wear of which can affect the accuracy of front wheel location, plus a spring shackle and the usual steering ball joints.

A distinguishing feature of the Allard layout is that the widely spaced pivots, about which each wishbone member swings, have their axes set diagonally to the car frame—the axis about which a wishbone swings

intersects the centre of the front cross-member, and meets the chassis side-member slightly ahead of the scuttle. Geometrically precise steering is obtained by use of a divided track rod and a drag link swinging about an arc precisely matching that traced by one suspension member.

At the rear of the chassis, an hydraulically damped transverse leaf spring is also used. This gives a wide springbase with minimum unsprung weight and, in conjunction with a torque tube enclosing the propeller shaft, provides axle location.

Lockheed hydraulic brakes are fitted to all wheels, 12-in. diameter drums accommodating exceptionally generous areas of lining. The success of a two-seater model in completing the recent French Alpine Rally without loss of marks confirms that the brakes are not merely adequate for a fast car, but will withstand a quite exceptional amount of hard usage. The hand brake,

COUPÉ FASHION.—Although the standard gear lever is being retained on the open models, the new Allard coupés will have a steering-column gearshift. Draught excluders are a standard fitting.

operating on the rear wheels, is of cable type.

The engine of the Allard, like the majority of the wearing parts incorporated in the chassis, is a product of the Ford Motor Co., Ltd., for which spare parts and service are available throughout the world. A compact V8 design, with non-adjustable side valves and a twin-choke downdraught carburetter, its power output of 85 b.h.p. gives the heaviest model in the range a maximum speed (as confirmed by "The Motor" continental road test) substantially in excess of 80 m.p.h., but it is mainly notable for immense pulling power at low speeds which produces striking top gear acceleration.

Coachwork on all models is of strikingly modern appearance, but has been combined with generous ground clearance.

Perhaps the most popular model, the drop-head coupé, is a two-door two-light type, compact, but a genuine four-seater. There is some luggage capacity in the rear locker, which also contains the spare wheel. Leather upholstery and a polished wood facia are common to all models, and on the coupé scuttle ventilators can deliver air to ducts behind the facia panel to de-mist the windscreen and supplement the no-draught ventilation provided by hinged window flaps.

On the same wheelbase, there is also available an open four-seater tourer body. Finally, a two-seater body of notably sleek appearance is available on a chassis which, although shorter and with reduced rear track to suit competitive motoring conditions, allows for some enclosed luggage space within the tail.

**ALLARD PRICES**

Chassis, £670
2-seater, £968 plus tax £269 12 10 = £1,237 12 10
4-seater, £990 plus tax £275 15  0 = £1,265 15  0
Coupé. £999 plus tax £278  5  0 = £1,277  5  0

## ALLARD DATA

| MODEL | Coupé | 4-seater | 2-seater |
|---|---|---|---|
| **Engine Dimensions:** | | | |
| Cylinders | V8 | V8 | V8 |
| Bore | 77.8 | 77.8 | 77.8 |
| Stroke | 95.2 | 95.2 | 95.2 |
| Cubic capacity | 3,622 | 3,622 | 3,622 |
| Piston area | 58.9 | 58.9 | 58.9 |
| Valves | Side | Side | Side |
| Compression ratio | 6.1 | 6.1 | 6.1 |
| **Engine Performance:** | | | |
| Max. b.h.p. | 85 | 85 | 85 |
| at | 3,800 r.p.m. | 3,800 r.p.m. | 3,800 r.p.m. |
| Max. b.m.e.p. | 102 | 102 | 102 |
| at | 2,000 r.p.m. | 2,000 r.p.m. | 2,000 r.p.m. |
| B.H.P. per sq. in. piston area | 1.44 | 1.44 | 1.44 |
| Peak piston speed ft. per min. | 2,375 | 2,375 | 2,375 |
| **Engine Details:** | | | |
| Carburetter | Ford | Ford | Ford |
| Ignition | Lucas (coil and dist.) | Lucas (coil and dist.) | Lucas (coil and dist.) |
| Plugs : make and type | Champion 18 mm. C7 | Champion 18 mm. C7 | Champion 18 mm. C7 |
| Fuel Pump | Ford mech. diaphragm | Ford mech. diaphragm | Ford mech. diaphragm |
| Fuel capacity | 17 gals., inc. 2 in reserve | 17 gals., inc. 2 in reserve | 17 gals., inc. 2 in reserve |
| Oil filter (make, by-pass or full flow) | Ford, full flow | Ford, full flow | Ford, full flow |
| Oil capacity | 1 gallon | 1 gallon | 1 gallon |
| Cooling system | Thermo siphon with impellers and fan | Thermo siphon with impellers and fan | Thermo siphon with impellers and fan |
| Water capacity | 5 gallons | 5 gallons | 5 gallons |
| Electrical system | 12 volt, 2 pole | 12 volt, 2 pole | 12 volt, 2 pole |
| Battery capacity | 60 a.h. | 60 a.h. | 60 a.h. |
| **Transmission:** | | | |
| Clutch | Single dry plate | Single dry plate | Single dry plate |
| Gear ratios: Top | 4.11 | 4.11 | 4.11 |
| 2nd | 7.29 | 6.59 | 6.59 |
| 1st | 12.8 | 14.4 | 14.4 |
| Rev. | 16.46 | 18.52 | 18.52 |
| Prop. shaft | Torque tube | Torque tube | Torque tube |
| Final drive | Spiral bevel | Spiral bevel | Spiral bevel |
| **Chassis Details:** | | | |
| Brakes | Lockheed | Lockheed | Lockheed |
| Brake drum diameter | 12 ins. | 12 ins. | 12 ins. |
| Friction lining area | 164 sq. ins. | 164 sq. ins. | 164 sq. ins. |
| Suspension, front | Transverse leaf and divided axle I.F.S. | Transverse leaf and divided axle I.F.S. | Transverse leaf and divided axle I.F.S. |
| Suspension, rear | Transverse leaf | Transverse leaf | Transverse leaf |
| Shock absorbers | Girling-Luvax | Girling-Luvax | Girling-Luvax |
| Wheel type | Ventilated disc | Ventilated disc | Ventilated disc |
| Tyres | 6.25 x 16 Dunlop | 6.25 x 16 Dunlop | 6.25 x 16 Dunlop |
| Steering gear | Marles, cam and double roller | Marles, cam and double roller | Marles, cam and double roller |
| Steering wheel | 17-in. Bluemels Extensile | 17-in. Bluemels Extensile | 17-in. Bluemels Extensile |
| **Dimensions:** | | | |
| Wheelbase | 9 ft. 4 ins. | 9 ft. 4 ins. | 8 ft. 10 ins. |
| Track, front | 4 ft. 8 ins. | 4 ft. 8 ins. | 4 ft. 8 ins. |
| Track, rear | 4 ft. 10½ ins. | 4 ft. 10½ ins. | 4 ft. 4½ ins. |
| Overall length | 15 ft. 2 ins. | 15 ft. 2 ins. | 14 ft. |
| Overall width | 5 ft. 11 ins. | 5 ft. 9 ins. | 5 ft. 9 ins. |
| Overall height | 5 ft. 2 ins. | 5 ft. 2 ins. | 5 ft. 2 ins. |
| Ground clearance | 9 ins. | 9 ins. | 9 ins. |
| Turning circle | 41 ft. | 41 ft. | 39 ft. |
| Dry weight | 25¾ cwt. | 24¼ cwt. | 23½ cwt. |
| **Performance Data:** | | | |
| Piston area, sq. ins. per ton | 45.8 | 48.5 | 50.1 |
| Brake lining area, sq. ins. per ton | 127 | 135 | 140 |
| Top gear m.p.h. per 1,000 r.p.m. | 19.8 | 19.8 | 19.8 |
| Top gear m.p.h. at 2,500 ft./min. piston speed | 79.0 | 79.0 | 79.0 |
| Litres per ton-mile, dry | 4,300 | 4,550 | 4,700 |

ROOM FOR FOUR.—The Allard coupé has no-draught ventilation, windscreen de-misting, and is a genuine four-seater.

# *The Autocar* ROAD TESTS

## DATA FOR THE DRIVER

### V8 ALLARD

**PRICE,** with sports two-seater body, £968, plus £269 12s British purchase tax. Total (in Great Britain), £1,237 12s 10d.

**RATING :** 30 h.p., 8 cylinders, side valves, 77.99 × 95.25 mm, 3,622 c.c.

**TAX** (in Great Britain), £10.

**BRAKE HORSE-POWER:** 85 at 3,800 r.p.m.   **COMPRESSION RATIO:** 6.12 to 1.

**WEIGHT,** without passengers : 21 cwt 3 qr 21 lb.   **LB. per C.C. :** 0.68.

**TYRE SIZE :** 6.25 × 16in on bolt-on pressed steel wheels.

**LIGHTING SET :** 12-volt.   Automatic voltage control.

**TANK CAPACITY :** 20 gallons; approximate fuel consumption range, 17-21 m.p.g.

**TURNING CIRCLE :** 39ft (L and R).   **MIN. GROUND CLEARANCE :** 9½in.

**MAIN DIMENSIONS :** Wheelbase, 8ft 10in.   Track, 4ft 8in (front) ; 4ft 4in (rear).   Overall length, 14ft 0in ; width, 5ft 11in ; height, 4ft 11¼in.

| ACCELERATION | | | |
|---|---|---|---|
| Overall gear ratios | *From steady m.p.h. of* | | |
| | 10 to 30 | 20 to 40 | 30 to 50 |
| 4.11 to 1 | 7.4 sec. | 7.5 sec. | 8.3 sec. |
| 6.59 to 1 | 4.7 sec. | 4.8 sec. | 5.5 sec. |
| 14.40 to 1 | 3.3 sec. | — | — |

| From rest through gears to :— | | | sec. |
|---|---|---|---|
| 30 m.p.h. | .. | .. | 3.9 |
| 50 m.p.h. | .. | .. | 9.2 |
| 60 m.p.h. | .. | .. | 13.6 |
| 70 m.p.h. | .. | .. | 20.5 |
| 80 m.p.h. | .. | .. | 34.4 |

Steering wheel movement from lock to lock : 2¼ turns.

| Speedometer correction by Electric Speedometer :— | | | |
|---|---|---|---|
| Car Speed-ometer | Electric Speed-ometer | Car Speed-ometer | Electric Speed-ometer |
| 10 | = 10.5 | 50 | = 48.5 |
| 20 | = 20 | 60 | = 58 |
| 30 | = 29.5 | 70 | = 67.5 |
| 40 | = 39 | 80 | = 76.25 |

| Speeds attainable on indirect gears (by Electric Speed-ometer) | M.p.h. (normal and max.) |
|---|---|
| 1st .. .. .. | 21—35 |
| 2nd .. .. .. | 47—66 |
| Top .. .. .. | 86 |

**WEATHER :** Dry, warm ; wind light.

Acceleration figures are the means of several runs in opposite directions.

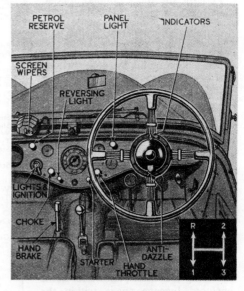

*Current model described in " The Autocar " of February 1, 1946.*

MODERN though the Allard is in appearance, it has many of the characteristics in road behaviour of the older type of sports car which are valued by enthusiastic drivers. The two-seater now tested is remarkably suitable for competition work, on which the make has built up its reputation by a string of successes in recent years, and to those who want at other times a car capable of covering long distances at a high average and one which has "interest" in full measure in its handling and running.

With its 3.6-litre Ford V8 power unit and a weight close to 22 cwt in running trim, the power-to-weight ratio is outstandingly good, and the acceleration phenomenal in consequence. Limited in seating accommodation strictly to two people with some enclosed luggage space, it would be an unpractical car in some eyes, but to the enthusiast is wholeheartedly a "real" car, full of life and capable of holding almost anything on the road up to speeds in the eighties.

Earlier in the year a high opinion from a somewhat similar standpoint was formed of the post-war Allard when a Road Test was carried out of the drop-head coupé. The open two-seater is 6 inches shorter in the wheelbase and has a narrower rear track, and is very considerably lighter, the result being that, whilst the conventional engine is not at all highly stressed, this car has almost 77.5 b.h.p. per ton, an altogether exceptional figure which is vividly reflected in the accompanying acceleration figures and in the whole road behaviour. It is able to run on high gear ratios, and yet be almost entirely a top-gear car when the driver chooses to handle it in that way, although the two indirect ratios, including first with its high maximum up to 35 m.p.h., can be used with great effect for lifting the speed really rapidly.

A practical indication of the benefits gained from the exceptional power-to-weight ratio is the way in which a hill of a maximum gradient of 1 in 6½ which has long been included in these Road Tests can be treated in the Allard. The gradient has a winding approach and about a 40-degree corner where it begins to steepen sharply. First this hill was taken on top gear throughout at a speed not falling below 36 m.p.h. from an approach speed of 50, slowing to 43 on the corner, an impressive performance which could be equalled by very few current cars. The same climb was then tackled by a different technique, with a change to second gear below the bend, and the summit was crested at 38 to 40 m.p.h. on that gear, the rear wheels spinning even over the steepest section on a slightly damp surface. By either method the car gave the impression of great power delivered in an easy manner.

The value of this car on a journey is not the possession of a very high maximum for its engine size, but the way in which it leaps up to 60 m.p.h. or so even when only short stretches of clear road are available, and under more favourable going the way in which it holds 70 m.p.h. as a cruising speed free from mechanical fuss. Without any particular attempt to hurry, averages of the 40 m.p.h. order are achieved, and on a route which gives any chance of fast cruising to put 50 miles into the hour is a gift. A quicker means of transport over, say, 400 miles between London and Scotland is not easily visualized. It is refreshing to find that the Allard company do not claim more than 85 m.p.h. in standard trim, and such a figure was seen with ease, the speedometer reaching a reading of 90, though there was the definite impression that speed remained in reserve had there been a longer stretch of road available.

## Weight Distribution

The handling is "old style"; that is to say, because the engine is carried farther back in the frame than is now usual the weight distribution is such as to bring more weight on to the rear wheels than is customary nowadays, and as a result the car handles much in the way that the sports cars of the early 'thirties handled. On corners one knows where one is without having to learn the habits of the car to the same extent as frequently applies to-day, and when enterprising cornering methods are employed the tail slides first to give ample warning, and not all four wheels together. This particular two-seater went through the Alpine Trial in July with success, winning a coveted Coupe des Alpes, so it had seen some hard service.

Again in the old style is the fact that there is some reaction through to the steering wheel from the road wheels, though this does not become tiring. With high-

This front view, apart from showing the modern treatment, gives an indication of the high ground clearance which is a feature of the car, making it highly suitable for trials work and some conditions overseas.

Spring-spoked steering wheel, which is telescopically adjustable, remote control gear lever, and fly-off type of hand brake lever are seen, as well as the instrument layout and such details as the zipp-fastened door pocket.

The " alligator " bonnet is spring-balanced to remain in the open position. Top accessibility of the V8 engine is good and the under-bonnet finish is pleasing.

geared steering, which is not heavy, the car can be placed exactly in a bend. The suspension is firm without being harsh and the car can take rough ground without any suggestion of being maltreated. It rides well over stone sett surfaces, and in general is comfortably sprung, considering its marked lateral stability, by a transverse spring at front and rear on the Ford principle, but with a divided front axle.

The brakes, hydraulically operated, at first give the impression of not being particularly powerful, but a driver strange to the car soon realizes that there is all the power required for rapid deceleration from speed and that a really quick pull up can be made from lower speeds in an emergency.

## Vertical Gear

For the open two-seater a vertical remote-control gear lever has been retained for the three-speed box, but a steering column gear lever has now been adopted for the Allard coupé. With synchromesh which is adequate for general purposes, fast changing can be made without clashing gears, though for the fastest work, as in competitions, and for making the through-the-gears tests which are a feature of these Tests, the synchromesh does not quite cope. The centrifugally loaded clutch is entirely up to the heavy work imposed by full-throttle getaways, and the power at the road wheels is such that black marks are left by the tyres under such exceptional conditions.

There are times when one wishes that a four-speed box were fitted, chiefly to enable one to drop to a close-ratio third gear for its steadying effect when taking bends really fast, but on the whole the car does not suffer in having only three speeds, for, as already indicated, the top-gear performance is outstandingly good, and even in traffic it is seldom necessary to drop below second, which is a quiet gear. The engine will throttle down to a smooth 6 m.p.h. on top, and pick up with a rush of power on

a snap depression of the throttle pedal and with only a mild degree of pinking.

The driving position proved rather "long" for a driver of average height, who also found the spring-spoked steering wheel, though telescopically adjustable on its column, a trifle high, and the bucket seat back rest inclined rearward more than he likes. A taller driver who sampled the car during the test was, however, perfectly happy with the position. The handbrake lever, of fly-off type, is placed a little far to the left for maximum convenience. In the latest production car improvements have been made in the interior of the body and to the driving position, and also a quick form of adjustment has been provided for the separate seats, which was lacking on the car tested. The driver has excellent visibility, with a full view of both front wings, which gives a feeling of confidence and which is a particularly good feature in view of the considerable overall width of the car.

### Reserve Petrol Provision

The instruments include a water thermometer. A clock is not fitted, nor has the speedometer a trip mileage recorder. Against these omissions there is the increasingly rare provision of a reserve petrol supply of two gallons, brought into use by means of a switch on the instrument panel. The fuel tank holds twenty gallons in all, giving an operating range around 400 miles, for the engine is economical for its size, another benefit deriving from low weight and high gear ratios.

The luggage space is reached by removal of a panel behind the driving seat, held by a carriage lock, and in this compartment are housed the tools, side screens, and the hood when this is not in use. It is easy to put the hood up and down, it being secured to the windscreen frame by quick-action clips, and it is a neat arrangement whereby both fabric and frame go out of sight when not in

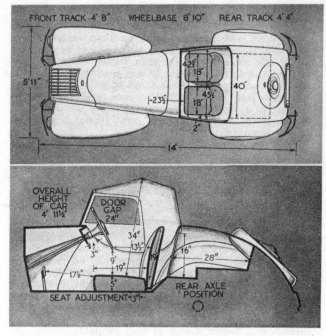

Measurements are taken with the driving seat at the central position of fore and aft adjustment. These body diagrams are to scale.

use. The hood fabric detaches entirely from the frame. Steel disc wheels are fitted on the latest cars in place of the perforated steel wheels on the car tested.

Occasion arose to use the jacking system, a puncture being caused in a rear tyre by a large nail. The jack is a portable hydraulic unit, of which a squared end is fitted in a socket at either side, the car being raised by a winding handle; a fairly quick lift is obtained.

Starting from cold is instantaneous, with a pleasing suggestion of subdued exhaust note, which is not at any time obtrusive on the road, and the engine operates almost at once with full efficiency with very little use of the choke. Some appreciable warmth is felt in the driving compartment, which would be comforting in cold weather. The windscreen can be folded flat on the scuttle. The beam given by the built-in lamps would not be adequate for the highest speeds on unfamiliar roads, but is reasonable up to about 70 m.p.h.

Owing to the use of a Ford engine and other components world-wide availability of major replacements for this London-built car is assured.

It is easy to put the hood up and, in conjunction with side screens, the car is enclosed snugly for bad weather. The hood fabric is removed entirely from the frame when not required and stowed, together with the side screens, in the space behind the seats which serves for luggage.

Valances partially enclosing the rear wheels are fitted to current Allard productions, but were not used on this particular car, which performed successfully in the international Alpine Trial in July. The spare wheel, carried externally, is enclosed by a light aluminium cover.

# ALLARD Extend Their Range of High-performance V-8 Cars

**FASTEST LINE.**—Known as the "J"-type, the latest Allard 2-seater chassis is especially designed for competitive speed events.

## Saloon and 4.4-litre Competition 2-seater Models in Production to Supplement Tourer and Convertible Types

A NEW model added to the Allard range for 1950 is a neat and businesslike competition two-seater, which incorporates all the lessons learnt from many years of regular and successful participation in speed events of all types. Effortlessly rapid acceleration and outstanding controllability have been the strong points of recent Allard productions, and the latest car should provide these qualities in increased measure.

Increased power output, reduced weight and improved chassis layout are offered by the "J"-type Allard, which, now standardized in place of a heavier two-seater model, and to be exhibited at the forthcoming Motor Show, is being offered with a wide range of optional items of equipment. The basic price is thus subject to some variation according to what standard of performance and comfort is required, but is normally within the limit of £1,000 beyond which British purchase tax is doubled.

The new chassis with 100-in. wheelbase uses channel-section side rails braced by tubular cross-members Closely resembling earlier models in general layout, the front suspension system is of the divided-axle type, but some weight and height have been saved by the use of coil springs in conjunction with direct-acting hydraulic shock absorbers. There has also been a detail revision of the steering layout to suit increased speed, a three-piece track rod eliminating slight variations of toe-in with spring deflection.

### Good Steering Geometry

Mechanically sturdy and with unusually few wearing parts, this independent front-wheel suspension system locates each wheel by means of two beams joined rigidly together to form a single wishbone member. Each of these wishbones swings about two co-axial pivots, one near the centre of the front cross-member and the other well back along the chassis side rail, and although this layout allows caster angle to increase slightly and camber angle to decrease as the springs deflect, good steering geometry and the absence of wheel tilting during fast cornering are valuable contributions to extremely responsive controllability over a wide range of speeds.

For some time past a regular and extremely successful competitor in speed events has been the racing single-seater Allard special driven by S. H. Allard, and this very light car was much improved last year by the incorporation of a De Dion rear suspension layout. A closely similar layout is now introduced on the "J"-type sports model, the first application of this well-proven racing feature to a modern British production car.

In this layout, the rear wheels are coupled by a dead axle beam in the form of a curved tube, power being transmitted to them by universally jointed shafts from a differential gear mounted on the chassis frame. The radius arms locating the hubs pivot about a common point on the chassis centreline, and lateral location of chassis relative to the axle tube

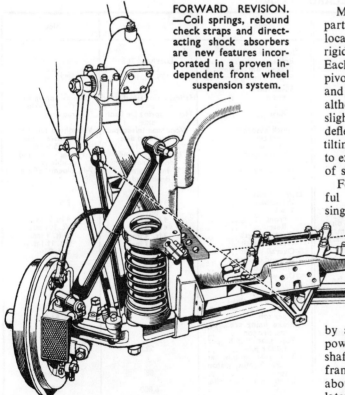

**FORWARD REVISION.**—Coil springs, rebound check straps and direct-acting shock absorbers are new features incorporated in a proven independent front wheel suspension system.

is maintained by a peg sliding in a vertical channel

Suspension modifications have not involved a complete departure from the Allard practice of using Ford parts wherever possible, a policy which keeps servicing costs low. Hubs continue to be of Ford type, as do steering joints, and the final drive assembly is also a modified Ford unit linked to the gearbox by a propeller shaft enclosed in the usual torque tube. Brakes, however, are Lockheed hydraulic with 12-in. drums, the front brakes of two-leading-shoe type, the rear of normal type but mounted in unit with the sprung differential assembly.

Bodywork on the " J "-type Allard is of neat two-seater form, comprising removable light-alloy panels mounted on a tubular steel framework integral with the chassis. A large fuel tank mounted at the rear of the frame carries a reserve supply, and customers will have the option of full-length or quickly detachable cycle-type mudguards according to the use they expect to make of the car.

Power unit details have been left until last, as it is anticipated that some of the cars to be built will be shipped across the Atlantic ocean without engines in readiness to be fitted with locally tuned " hot rod " power plants. The engine normally offered with the car is based on the Mercury V-8, but has increased bore and stroke, an external oil cooler, British-made aluminium-alloy cylinder heads, an Allard induction system carrying two dual-choke carburetters, and two free-flow exhaust manifolds feeding separate straight-through silencers. A three-speed gearbox with central remote control is mated to this engine.

A very useful range of alternative equipment is being

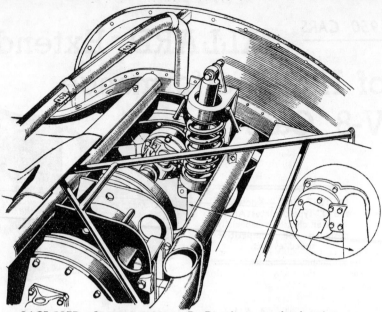

RACE BRED.—Rear suspension on De Dion lines was developed on a racing Allard and is now applied to the 2-seater. Lateral location of the axle tube relative to the chassis is by a peg sliding in a vertical slot.

made available for these cars, to enable owners to equip them for participation in particular types of motoring competition. Rear-axle ratios can be 3.78 or 4.11 as alternatives to the normal 3.5, and with the highest final-drive ratio alternative gears allow first and third gears to be raised from 10.9 and 6.19 to 6.2 and 4.58. A limited-slip cam differential can be used in place of the ordinary gear type, and light-alloy wheels are interchangeable with the steel-disc pattern. All these special items of equipment are, of course, extra to the basic price of the car.

For those who seek an open sports car but need more accommodation than the competition two-seater provides, the four-seater tourer continues unchanged with the leaf-spring I.F.S. layout.

## ALLARD DATA

| Model | " J " 2-seater | Saloon | Model | " J " 2-seater | Saloon |
|---|---|---|---|---|---|
| **Engine Dimensions :** | | | **Chassis details :** | | |
| Cylinders | V8 | V8 | Brakes | Lockheed 2LS | Lockheed 2LS |
| Bore | 84.13 mm. | 77.8 mm. | Brake drum diameter | 12 ins. | 12 ins. |
| Stroke | 98.42 mm. | 95.2 mm. | Friction lining area | 179 sq. ins. | 172 sq. ins |
| Cubic capacity | 4,375 c.c. | 3,622 c.c. | Suspension : | | |
| Piston area | 68.9 sq. ins. | 58.9 sq. ins. | Front | Helical spring and divided axle | Helical spring and divided axle |
| Valves | Side | Side | Rear | Helical spring De Dion axle | Transverse leaf |
| Compression ratio | 8 to 1 | 6.1 to 1 | Shock absorbers | Woodhead telescopic | Woodhead telescopic |
| **Engine Performance :** | | | Wheel type | Ventilated disc | Ventilated disc |
| Max. power | 120 b.h.p. | 85 b.h.p. | Tyre size | 6.00 × 16 | 6.25 × 16 |
| at | 3,800 | 3,800 | Steering gear | Marles cam and double roller | Marles cam and double roller |
| Max. b.m.e.p. | 125 | 102 | Steering wheel | 17-in. Bluemel's Brooklands | 17-in Bluemel's Extensile |
| at | 2,000 | 2,000 | | | |
| B.h.p. per sq. in. piston area | 1.74 | 1.44 | **Dimensions :** | | |
| Peak piston speed, ft. per min. | 2,450 | 2,375 | Wheelbase | 8 ft. 4 ins. | 9 ft. 4 ins. |
| **Engine Details :** | | | Track : | | |
| Carburetter | 2 Ford downdraught | Ford downdraught | Front | 4 ft. 8 ins. | 4 ft. 8 ins. |
| Ignition | Lucas coil and dist. | Lucas coil and dist. | Rear | 4 ft. 4 ins. | 4 ft. 10½ ins. |
| Plugs : Make and type | Lodge 14 mm. HM. | Champion 18 mm. C7 | Overall length | 12 ft. 4 ins. | 15 ft. 9 ins. |
| Fuel pump | Twin S.U. electrical | Ford mech. diaphragm | Overall width | 5 ft. 3 ins. | 5 ft. 11 ins. |
| Fuel capacity | 25 gal., inc. 2 reserve | 17 gal., inc. 2 reserve | Overall height | 2 ft. 10 ins. | 5 ft. 0 in. |
| Oil filter (make, by-pass or full flow) | Ford full flow | Ford full flow | Ground clearance | 6½ ins. | 9 ins. |
| Oil capacity | 2 gal. | 6½ pints | Turning circle | 42 ft. | 42 ft. |
| Cooling system | Impellors and fan | Impellors and fan | Dry weight | 17 cwt. | 27 cwt. |
| Water capacity | 4½ gal. | 5 gal. | | | |
| Electrical system | Lucas 12-volt 2-pole | Lucas 12-volt 2-pole | **Performance data :** | | |
| Battery capacity | 60 amp.-hrs. | 60 amp.-hrs. | Piston area, sq. ins. per ton | 76.6 | 43.6 |
| **Transmission :** | | | Brake lining area, sq. ins. per ton | 191 | 127 |
| Clutch | Single dry plate | Single dry plate | Top gear m.p.h. per 1,000 r.p.m. | 22.8 | 21.5 |
| Gear ratios : | | | Top gear m.p.h. at 2,500 ft./min. piston speed | 88 | 86 |
| Top | 3.54 | 3.78 | Litres per ton-mile, dry | 6,800 | 3,740 |
| 2nd | 6.19 | 6.68 | | | |
| 1st | 10.9 | 11.75 | | | |
| Rev. | 14.0 | 15.0 | | | |
| Prop. shaft | Enclosed in torque tube | Enclosed in torque tube | | | |
| Final drive | Spiral bevel | Spiral bevel | | | |

# THE NEW
# ALLARD SPRINT CAR
## by T. Lush

The recent announcement that the famous Steyr-Allard is for sale has aroused considerable speculation in British sprint and hill climb circles. Powered by an ex-German army Steyr air-cooled V-8 engine, this car was used by Sidney H. Allard in capturing the title of British Hill Climb Champion for 1949.

As has been rumored, Allard is building an entirely new car. The designing of this car was commenced in June, 1948, but progress has been slow due to the Competition Department's extensive program during the past season. Much of the machine work is completed, but assembly has not commenced, and it is doubtful whether the car will be ready for the early part of the 1950 season.

The new Allard sprint car is to be a four-wheel drive machine, constructed almost entirely of light alloys and having an estimated weight of between 1350 and 1450 pounds. The air-cooled V-8 engine of 4½ litre capacity will be used in conjunction with Clerk patent electrically controlled epicyclic gears so arranged that the torque to each wheel may be under the driver's control. The wheelbase will be 100 inches with front and rear track of 56 inches.

The frame will consist of two parallel tubes of oval section joined by five cross members, these being Dural tubes of 5 inch diameter. Front suspension will be by unequal length wishbones carrying fully floating hubs, and the rear axle of the de Dion type located by a central slide and radius arms to the center of the frame. Lockheed suspension struts will be used front and rear.

The original design called for an entirely new engine with a magnesium alloy crankcase, aluminum heads and cylinder barrels and duralumin connecting rods, which would have given an estimated saving in weight over the present Steyr engine of some 100 pounds. Manufacturing difficulties in the short time available, however, leave no alternative but to use a Steyr crankcase and crankshaft, with Wellworthy Al-Fin barrels, Specialloid pistons, and redesigned connecting rods and cylinder heads together with Lucas ignition and Amal carburetors. It is hoped to achieve a power output of 250 BHP at 6,000 RPM. This is not an impossible figure when one considers that the present Steyr, with 79 mm bore and compression ratio of 11 to 1, develops about 165 BHP at 5,500 RPM and the new barrels and heads incorporate a bore of 88 mm, compression ratio of 12.5 to 1, and larger valves with much improved breathing characteristics.

The transmission system has been especially designed to provide some control over the power transmitted to the front axle in relation to the rear. For many events (dependent on the venue), it is proposed to have two speeds only and accordingly the three speed and reverse auxiliary gearbox behind the engine can be removed. When the gearbox is used, in conjunction with the gears in the axles, four forward speeds and reverse are provided with two speeds to the front axle.

Both axles are the same, and the ratio of the rear axle only is changed when the gearbox is used. The driving mechanism in each axle consists of the usual crown wheel and pinion and two sets of electrically operated epicyclic gears which provide the two speeds previously mentioned. There is therefore, a total of 8 sets of epicyclic gears, two to each axle shafts. These units also incorporate separate clutches, there being no conventional clutch between engine and transmission. The differential action between each pair of wheels is obtained by varying the current supplied to the N/S or O/S epicyclic gears in each axle, this control being effected by an automatic switch actuated by cams on the steering column. The same principle of control is also used between front and rear axles, and although the normal maximum torque transmitted to the front is some 40% of the total, this can be reduced as required to suit prevailing conditions by a manual control fitted close to the driver's left hand. Gear ratios will be 3.5, 4.18, 5.47, and 7.65 to 1, with estimated speeds of 125 mph in top, 110/115 mph in third, 85/90 mph in second, and 60 mph in first gear. Tires will be 5.00 x 18 mounted on magnesium Z.5.Z alloy wheels.

Brakes are 10 inch hydraulically operated and mounted inboard on the axle cases. The axle shafts are all interchangeable and consist of a layrub coupling on the inside and an open Hardy Spicer joint at the wheel. In view of the light weight of the car it has not been considered necessary to use constant velocity joints with their unavoidable increase in weight. Layrub joints are also used on the propellor shafts.

Steering is by rack and pinion with the box mounted in the center of the frame in front of the engine. The steering column passes between the two banks of cylinders.

A single seater body will be fitted, probably with alternative sizes of petrol tank to suit the event, but these final detail items have not yet been settled.

The car has been designed expressly to be as light as possible. Accordingly, light alloys have been used everywhere possible. The frame, wishbones, suspension supports, hubs, drums, brake fittings, steering rods, and idler wheel, radius arms, etc., are of Duralumin or similar alloys, while the newly developed magnesum Z.5.Z (Zirconium) alloy is used for the wheels, gearbox, differential cases and steering box.

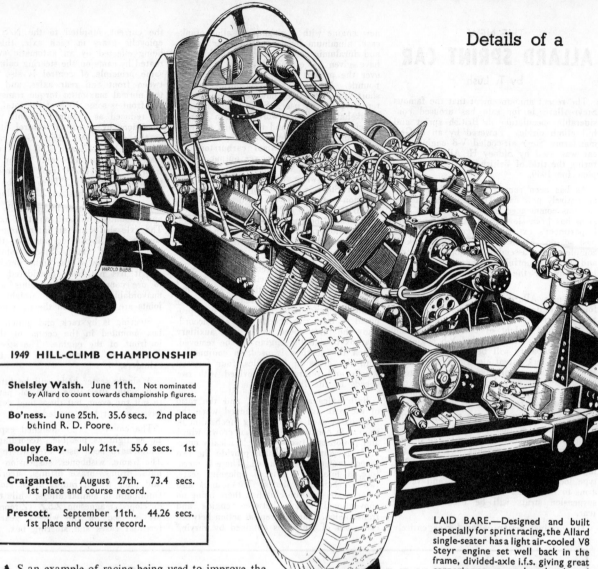

HAROLD BUBB

**LAID BARE.**—Designed and built especially for sprint racing, the Allard single-seater has a light air-cooled V8 Steyr engine set well back in the frame, divided-axle i.f.s. giving great cornering power on sharp bends, and a De Dion rear axle and cam-type differential for utmost acceleration from rest.

AS an example of racing being used to improve the breed it would be difficult to find anything better than the V8 single-seater which Sidney Allard, Director of the Allard Motor Co., Ltd., has raced during the 1947-8-9 seasons.  Built originally on a typically Allard layout, and largely from ordinary production parts, it has since been vastly improved by a steady development process and has pioneered new features for the catalogued cars.

In place of the Ford-built s.v. water-cooled V8 engine as used in sports models, the sprint car is powered by a larger o.h.v. air-cooled V8 evolved from a Steyr commercial vehicle design.  The individual cylinders have been slightly enlarged in bore and accommodate high-compression pistons, the light-alloy cylinder heads have enlarged inlet valves with inserted seatings, and each cylinder is fed by its own individual Amal carburetter. It is fair to say, however, that this unsupercharged engine is more notable for lightness and good torque at moderate speeds than for outstandingly high peak power output.

A perfectly normal Ford V8 clutch transmits the power of this engine to a Ford gearbox of the type which, designed for use with steering-column control, has its selector mechanism at the side.  The actual close-ratio gears inside the box are as fitted to the J2 competition two-seater Allard, and what would normally be the steering-column gear lever is in this case set on the driver's right with two rods linking it to the gearbox.

An enclosed propeller shaft couples the gearbox to the final-drive assembly, which is mounted on the chassis and comprises a Ford crown wheel and pinion in con-

junction with an Allard spin-limiting cam-type differential.  Except that a gear-type differential is more normally chosen for road use, this assembly was again the prototype for the J2 sports model.

One of the most valuable improvements made during the development of this car was the incorporation of a De Dion rear-axle arrangement, which very greatly improved the handling qualities.  The tubular axle beam which passes behind the final-drive assembly is located laterally by a peg sliding in a vertical slot, and the dual torque arms extend forwards and inwards to pivots on the chassis members—correct geometry is only attained with a common pivot for these torque arms, as has been arranged on subsequent two-seater cars, but with a narrow single-seater frame some theoretical imperfection has in fact proved acceptable.

Coil springs are used at the rear of the car, in conjunction with Girling hydraulic dampers—the actual decision to use coil springs having been largely a result of their fitting conveniently into the layout. At the front, in contrast, a transverse leaf spring has been retained throughout the car's career, in conjunction with friction shock absorbers. The divided axle layout of independent front-wheel suspension closely follows ordinary Allard practice, but at a time when (as was decided later) frame rigidity was somewhat inadequate the radius arm pivots were transferred from the frame side rails to a common point on the centre-line of the car.

# AMPION'S MOUNT

## The Allard V8 Single-seater With Which Sidney Allard Won the 1949 Hill-climb Championship

### ALLARD SINGLE-SEATER DATA

| Engine Dimensions : | | | Chassis Details : | | |
|---|---|---|---|---|---|
| Cylinders | .. .. | V-8 | Brakes | .. .. | Lockheed hydraulic |
| Bore | .. .. | 80 mm. | Brake drum diameter | | 12 in. |
| Stroke .. | .. | 92 mm. | Friction lining area | .. | 164 sq. in. |
| Cubic capacity | .. | 3,690 c.c. | Suspension : | | |
| Piston area | .. | 62.2 sq. in. | Front | .. .. | I.F.S., Transverse leaf |
| Valves .. | .. | Pushrod o.h.v. | | | spring and divided axle |
| | | Inlet 1⅜″ dia. | Rear .. | .. | De Dion type axle and |
| | | Exhaust 1⅜″ dia. | | | coil springs |
| Compression ratio | .. | 11/1 | Shock absorbers : | | |
| | | | Front | .. .. | Andre Hartford friction |
| **Engine Performance :** | | | Rear .. | .. .. | Girling Hydraulic |
| Max power | .. .. | Approx. 165 b.h.p. | | | |
| at | .. .. | 5,300 r.p.m. | Wheel type | .. .. | Pressed steel bolt-on |
| Max. b.m.e.p. | .. | Approx. 145 lb./sq. in. | | | (twin wheels at rear) |
| at | .. .. | 2,000 r.p.m. | Tyre size : | | |
| B.H.P. per sq. in. pis- | | | Front | .. .. | 5.75-16 |
| ton area | .. | Approx. 2.65 | Rear .. | .. | Double 5.00-18 |
| Piston speed at max. | | | Steering gear | .. | Marles |
| b.h.p. | .. .. | 3,200 ft. per min. | **Dimensions :** | | |
| | | | Wheelbase | .. .. | 8 ft. 4 in. |
| **Engine Details :** | | | Track : | | |
| Carburetter .. | .. | 8 Amal Type 289 | Front | .. .. | 4 ft 8 in. |
| Ignition | .. .. | Scintilla magneto | Rear (c/l of twin | | 4 ft. 4 in. |
| Plugs : make and type | | Lodge R49 | tyres) | .. .. | |
| Fuel pump | .. .. | Manual air pump | Dry weight | .. .. | Approx. 13 cwt. |
| Fuel capacity .. | .. | 2 gallons | Front rear weight | | |
| Oil capacity .. | .. | 2 gallons | distribution | .. | Approx. 42/58 |
| Cooling system | .. | Direct air cooling | | | |
| | | | **Performance Data :** | | (At assumed 15 cwt. |
| **Transmission :** | | | Piston area, sq. in. per | | running weight) |
| Clutch .. | .. .. | Ford V-8 semi-centri- | ton | .. .. | 83 |
| | | fugal single dry plate | Brake lining area, sq. | | |
| Gear ratios : Top | .. | 4.5 | in. per ton .. | .. | 218 |
| „ 2nd | .. | 5.89 | Top gear m.p.h. per | | |
| „ 1st | .. | 7.92 | 1,000 r.p.m | .. | 18.3 |
| Prop. shaft | .. | Enclosed | Top gear m.p.h. at | | |
| Final drive | .. | Ford V-8 Spiral bevel | 2,500 ft./min. piston | | |
| | | gears, and Allard (Z-F | speed | .. .. | 75.5 |
| | | type) differential, on | Litres per ton-mile .. | | 8,000 |
| | | frame | | | |

The actual frame, built from Allard-type pressings set close together to give single-seater width, is now boxed for torsional stiffness. The front cross-member is of inverted U shape, and encloses the transverse leaf spring, as well as supporting the high-mounted central steering gear. Similar to the unit mounted on one side of a normal Allard, the Marles steering gear actuates directly the two halves of a divided track rod, and is geared at 1¾ turns of the wheel from lock to lock: the side-by-side mounting of steering ball joints visible in the drawing is matched by correspondingly unequal-length steering arms on the stub axles.

The performance data for the complete car is interesting, and it may be mentioned that the same gear ratios have been used throughout the past sprint racing season. An engine speed of 5,300 r.p.m. gives speeds of 55, 74 and 97 m.p.h. respectively in the three gear ratios, and the *top-gear* specific displacement in litres per ton mile, allowing for the weight of the driver, closely approximates to the *bottom-gear* specific displacement of a modern 8 h.p. saloon carrying two people.

The overall effect? The R.A.C. Hill-climb Championship is based on performances in four out of five specified events, and Sidney Allard's score was three fastest times (including course records at Craigantlet and Prescott) and a second place.

Good enough? Apparently not, for already a good home is being sought for this car so that attention can be concentrated on the long job of constructing something quicker!          J.L.

GRAND FINALE.—On a day when he set a new sports-car course record and, with his wife, won the team award, Sidney Allard made f.t.d. and set a new course record at Prescott on September 11th, clinching his victory in the British Hill-climb Championship.

# ALLARD ACTIVITIES

❖

*NEW YORK ATTRACTION.—The new K-type Allard sports two-seater which will be exhibited at the New York Show with a Ford V8 30-h.p. engine "souped-up" with alloy heads and twin carburetters.*

THE Allard is a car which has earned a very warm place in the enthusiast's heart, for it evolved directly from the Ford Specials built by Sydney Allard when he was an amateur competitor in trials and rallies. Moreover, as Managing Director of the present Company, Allard drives as actively as ever in competition events, in direct contrast to the bowler-hatted, rolled-umbrella executives of many present-day manufacturers.

The present Allard range comprises tourer, coupé, saloon, K-type two-seater and the J2 Competition model. The ordinary models—if you can call any Allard ordinary !—normally have 30-h.p. Ford V8 engines, the new coil-spring, divided axle i.f.s., and steering-column gear-change. The use of coil springs in place of the former transverse leaf spring slightly lowers the chassis and provides a softer ride.

The K-type two-seater is a new model for those who require extremely high performance with more practical body-work than that of the J2. The frontal aspect is that of the J2, but the normal Allard front wings are used. There is a slab fuel tank behind the seat and behind that a luggage locker, while the spare wheel is enclosed. The K-type normally has a Ford V8 30 power unit, but with two Solex downdraught carburetters and alloy heads, the latter available to give a range of compression-ratios from 6.2 to 1 to 7.5 to 1. A rev.-counter is fitted, a remote-control central gear-lever is used and the frame is that of the J-type with the coil-spring i.f.s., but with the normal back axle in place of the de Dion axle used on the J-type. The new model will be at the New York Show and it is already proving extremely popular in the States.

The J2 Competition two-seater now has fairing over the front coil springs and detail improvements in appearance. It is normally supplied with a two-carburetter "stroked" V8 engine of 4,375 c.c., the alloy heads of which give a range of compression-ratios from 7.25 to 1 to 8.75 to 1.

We stated recently that Allards could be supplied with American engines other than Ford to clients' special requirements. These cars are, for instance, available from the American agents, and Tom Cole created a favourable impression at Palm Beach with his Cadillac-Allard. The Allard Motor Company is able to ship abroad cars ready to receive Cadillac V8, Ardun and other engines, the engine mountings, exhaust pipes, etc., being supplied to suit these installations. The Ford clutch is retained in such cases, adapted to the engine concerned.

It may not be generally known that Allard is concessionaire for the British-made Ardun engine. This engine is basically a Ford V8 engine with o.h.v. heads and valve operation *via* push-rods and rockers from the existing central Ford camshaft. The heads are of heat-treated Alcoa aluminium alloy, with bronze valve seat inserts and phosphor-bronze valve guides. A tulip inlet and exhaust valve with a stem diameter of 0.375 in. are inclined in each hemi-spherical combustion chamber, with a centrally located sparking plug. Double valve springs are used, tappets, push-rods and rockers are made of high-tensile nickel-chrome steel and the rockers are pressure lubricated. Ribbed cast-alloy valve covers are used and a downdraught carburetter feeds each bank of cylinders through a cast-alloy manifold. A four-branch exhaust manifold bolts on to the outside of each cylinder block. In 239-cu. in. form the Ardun V8 is claimed to develop 160 b.h.p. at 4,000 r.p.m., and 175 b.h.p. at 5,200 r.p.m. on 67 octane fuel, with a 7 to 1 compression-ratio. The rated torque is given as 225 ft./lb. at 2,500 r.p.m. The dimensions of the engine are 30 in. long, 30 in. wide and 27 in. high.

An Allard with an Ardun engine will be at the New York Show. The cost of converting existing Allards with 48-stud heads to this specification is in the region of £200.

Details of these intriguing Allard models are available from the Allard Motor Co., Ltd., 24/28, Clapham High Street, London, S.W.4, where overseas visitors are welcome, and from their many agents. In the States, E. Alan Moss, 3200, W. Olympic Boulevard, Los Angeles 6, John W. Forbes, Room 827, 60 State Street, Boston 9, Massachusetts, Fergus Motors, Inc., 290, Park Avenue, New York 17, Grancor Automotive Specialists, 5652, N. Broadway, Chicago 40, Illinois and Bell Auto Parts, 3633, E. Gage Avenue, Bell, California will be pleased to demonstrate Allard cars. If you are in Brazil, go to Cassio Muniz, S. A., Praca da Republica 309, Sao Paulo, if in Venezuela, to L. Bockh and Cia., San Isidro A San Julian II, Caracas. Enthusiasts in Uruguay should make for Emelas and Cia., Rincon 661, Montevideo, and those in Peru to Sociedad Mercantil International, Ayacucho 266, Lima. The Allard's suitability for rough roads and Ford service facilities, applicable to its major components, render it popular overseas.

Turning to Sydney Allard's competition plans, he intends to drive Allards in as many sports-car events as possible, for purposes of research and demonstration.

He is scheduled to run in the Targa-Florio on April 2nd, driving a standard J2 two-seater with an equally standard V8 Cadillac engine. He is very impressed with the possibilities of this push-rod o.h.v., 5,424-c.c. Cadillac power unit which, although designed for normal luxury-car duties, gives approximately 133 b.h.p. at 3,500 r.p.m., with a 7.5 to 1 compression-ratio. It has a five-bearing crankshaft, a bore and stroke of 90.4 by 92.1 mm., and weighs 699 lb. It will have to run on 80 octane fuel in the Targa, and a three-speed Ford gearbox will be used, in conjunction with the de Dion back axle with a ratio of 3.78 to 1 or perhaps 3.5 to 1. Allard will fly to Sicily and back, but the car is going by road, in his vast Ford van which was a familiar sight at sprint venues last year. If the planned hustle doesn't break down the car will be back just in time to run at Goodwood on Easter Monday.

For Le Mans the Allard Company has entered a Cadillac J2 Allard for Tom Cole, who will probably be partnered by Sydney Allard. This car runs under the prototype ruling, of course. There will be a strong Allard entry for this year's Alpine Trial, including three J2s to be driven by Allard, Clarkson, and that elusive and retiring person, A. N. Other. Allard teams will also run in the T.T. Allard will race on Dunlop tyres, Vigzol oil and will use Redex. He expects to employ the Ardun engine in certain races and may fit Alfin brake drums to the J2 later in the season.

This busy programme of sports-car racing will leave little time for sprints, and Allard has not entered for this year's R.A.C. Hill-Climb Championship. He may fit in a few hill-climbs with his new four-wheel-drive car but his famous Steyr-Allard single-seater is for sale.

W. B.

❖❖❖❖❖❖❖❖❖❖❖❖❖❖❖❖❖❖❖❖❖❖❖❖❖❖❖❖

# ALLARD MOTOR COMPANY LTD.

### 24 - 28 CLAPHAM HIGH STREET, LONDON, S.W.4. - - ENGLAND

*Telegraphic Address :* Inland - Almotco, Clapcom, London
Overseas - Almotco, London

*Telephone :* MACaulay 3201

# ANALYZING THE ALLARD

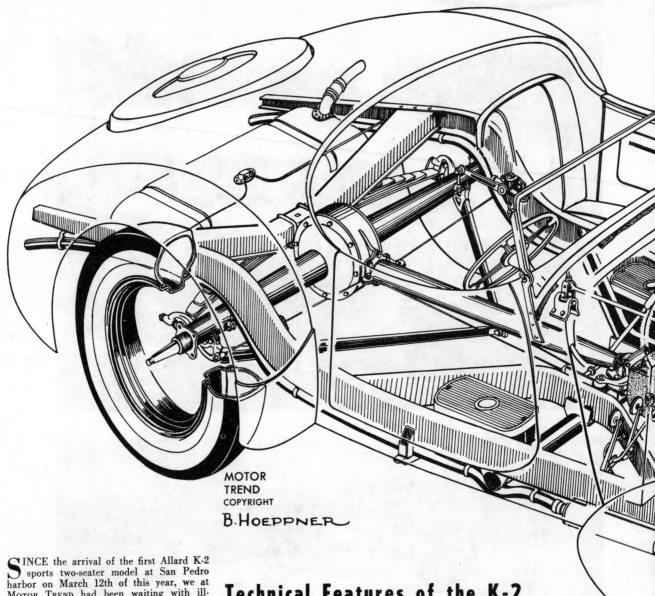

MOTOR
TREND
COPYRIGHT

B. HOEPPNER

SINCE the arrival of the first Allard K-2 sports two-seater model at San Pedro harbor on March 12th of this year, we at MOTOR TREND had been waiting with ill-concealed impatience for the opportunity to analyze the performance characteristics of the car. Our wishes were granted just recently when we were allowed the use of the car for a full day.

The Allard, which is notable for its use of Ford engine and chassis parts, was delivered to Moss Motors Ltd., 3200 W. Olympic Blvd., Los Angeles, equipped with a stock 85 hp Ford V-8 engine. To increase the performance of the car, this engine was replaced with an Edelbrock converted 1950 Mercury. The block is relieved and the ports polished. Compression ratio was increased to 8.5:1 and a dual intake manifold, with late Ford carburetors, was installed. Bore and stroke are standard. The engine is placed farther back in the chassis than is customary with standard passenger cars, which improves the handling characteristics. Engine torque is transmitted through a conventional Ford clutch and three-speed floor shift transmission to a torque tube type Ford rear axle, equipped with 3.54:1 gears.

Springs, front and rear, are transverse, semi-elliptical leaf type and provide a smooth, easy ride without body sway. The

## Technical Features of the K-2

### by Don Francisco, Technical Editor

front axle is novel in design, being essentially a Ford 'I' beam cut in two at the center and provided with suitable ends, which hinge in a bracket attached to the front crossmember. The frame is a conventional channel type complete with 'X' member. Lockheed hydraulic brakes of large diameter are fitted front and rear. Wheels are 16-inch, bolt-on type with 6.25 tires.

The passenger compartment has two leather upholstered bucket-type seats, which are quite comfortable. Seat cushions contain rubber bags, which may be inflated to suit the individual. Fore and aft position of the seats can be adjusted by removing and replacing the mounting bolts. All controls are easily reached from the driver's seat and the right hand drive steering wheel is mounted on a telescopic shaft which can be adjusted to suit. (Although this model had a right-hand drive, later models will be

left-hand drive.) The turtleback forms a small luggage and tool compartment which is concealed by a fabric curtain behind the seats. Gears are shifted by means of a simple, but very practical, remote lever mounted on the driveshaft tunnel in a convenient location. Clutch and brake controls are easily reached and it was not found necessary to raise the foot from the floor to transfer from the throttle to the brake. The combination parking and hand brake, located at the left of the gearshift, was found to be somewhat short for effective competition use.

Instruments consist of a large diameter speedometer, a tachometer and the usual ammeter, oil pressure gauge, heat indicator, and gasoline gauge. The instrument panel also has a small electric clock. A combination switch on the dash controls the lights and ignition while the dimmer switch, horn button, and turn indicator switch are mounted on the steering wheel hub. The 20-gallon fuel tank incorporates a reserve supply, which is controlled by a switch on the instrument panel.

From the mechanic's or service man's point of view the Allard is very well laid out. When the alligator-type hood is raised the engine and components are readily accessible. The hood is locked in position by means of two latches, one on each side at the front. A safety latch must be released before the hood can be lifted. Two jack pads, one on each side of the frame under the doors, are provided to facilitate wheel changing. The spare tire is carried in a recess on the turtleback.

Like most cars of its type, the Allard is a little harder to get in and out of than conventional American passenger cars, but, once seated, one gains a feeling of confidence in the machine. The four-spoke steering wheel is slightly smaller in diameter than average and has finger grips on the underside, which provide a non-slip grip on the wheel. With the top down, vision is unobstructed in all directions and both front fenders can be seen while sitting in a normal driving position. Shoulder room was found to be slightly inadequate for two average-size men, but caused no discomfort. Leg room on the passenger side is sufficient to allow a six footer to straighten his legs and place his feet on the firewall. The passenger compartment is well insulated as regards engine

noise, and ventilation is provided by two small ventilators on the sides of the body forward of the doors.

Once the various controls and switches were located, a flip of the ignition switch and a slight push on the starter button brought the engine to life with a low, deep-throated rumble that was very pleasing to the ear. The exhaust of this car is not noisy, as many dual systems are, but has a low, powerful sound of its own which is as audible while driving as it is from the outside of the car. The remote gearshift lever, which is approximately eight inches long, provides a short, fast, and easy change of gears. Shifting with the left hand might seem strange at first, but soon becomes quite natural.

The steering gear ratio is fairly high but does not require undue effort for fast turns at any speed. The long hood, combined with the seating location, which is just forward of the rear wheels, tends to give a peculiar sensation when rounding curves or turning corners. The car handles with ease in traffic,

*Continued on page 52*

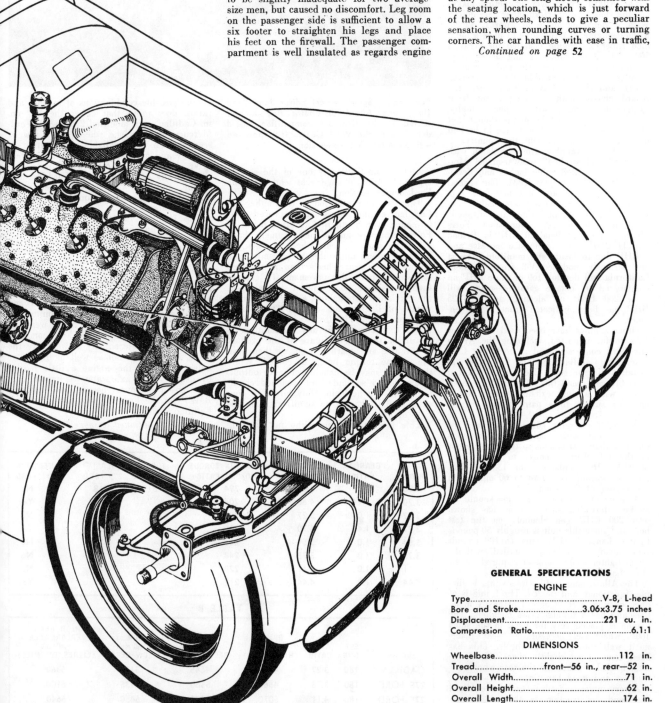

### GENERAL SPECIFICATIONS

#### ENGINE

| | |
|---|---|
| Type | V-8, L-head |
| Bore and Stroke | 3.06x3.75 inches |
| Displacement | 221 cu. in. |
| Compression Ratio | 6.1:1 |

#### DIMENSIONS

| | |
|---|---|
| Wheelbase | 112 in. |
| Tread | front—56 in., rear—52 in. |
| Overall Width | 71 in. |
| Overall Height | 62 in. |
| Overall Length | 174 in. |
| Weight | 2780 lbs. |

# ALLARD J-2

### An Analysis by our Technical Editor

### John R. Bond

To many sports car enthusiasts (including the writer) the new Allard J-2 Competition model is the outstanding sports car available today. While it is true that certain other makes offer more comfort, this feature is strictly secondary in importance with a car designed for competition activity, and it is axiomatic that in attaining comfort some measure of performance is lost by virtue of added weight.

The Allard scores over competing makes on the basis of performance per dollar. With a delivered price of approx. $2620, without engine, it is possible to have a modified American engine installed for between 500 and 1,000 dollars, giving acceleration second to none of currently available automobiles. For good road-holding, cornering power, and sheer safety at high speed, the Allard chassis with its independent front suspension system is without peer. Finally, the Allard is favored by many, though not all, because service and parts are to be had in any small town thruout the country.

The J-2 is available, from England, with a "bored and stroked" pre-war-model Mercury engine of 268 cubic inches and developing 120 BHP at 3800 RPM. The special aluminum alloy heads and manifold supplied with this engine are remarkably similar to Edelbrock, and since the displacement increase is 11% over stock Ford-Mercury, the additional 20 BHP is divided into 11 BHP gained from size increase and 9 BHP due to heads and manifold. Almost any seriously modified V-8 from Southern California will develop 160 or more BHP on commercial 91 octane gasoline—many will show 200 BHP on alcohol, and 220-225 BHP has been indicated from a few engines.

Other engines have been used in the few J-2's so far imported, including the Ardun ohv Ford conversion and a stock ohv Cadillac. The Cadillac develops 133 BHP "as installed" in the stock Cadillac chassis, but probably can reach the 160 BHP advertised figure with a dual exhaust system and a cool air supply to a pair of dual carburators.

A Cadillac engine coupled to the Ford gearbox, and with smaller radiator, adds no more than 100 pounds to the curb weight of the J-2. With a power to weight rate of 2100÷160 (unladen), or 13.- lbs./HP, the acceleration from zero to 60 mph is in the region of 7 seconds!

A Wayne-Chevrolet installation should also be interesting since Wayne has shown over 200 BHP (on alcohol) on the test bed, and since this unit is roughly 50 pounds lighter than a Ford-Mercury (a 100 pounds total saving, completely installed, with the much lighter cooling system required by the ohv Chevrolet).

The Allard chassis, like its styling, is simple, functional, and rugged. The frame is of open channel section devoid of any x members and has 4 tubular cross members. The engine is placed very far back in the short 100" wheelbase, necessitating seat placement well into the rear wheels. This has been done to get slightly over 50% of the total loaded weight onto the rear wheels for traction and good handling.

A very interesting advantage of the Allard rear end construction is the use of reworked Ford parts making it a very simple

Road and Track Technical Editor John Bond (left) and Allard distributor Roy Richter seated in the first J-2 competition Allard delivered to the West Coast. It is powered with an Allard V-8 conversion.

matter to substitute any one of the several types of quick change rear ends for the Ford center section.

There is some question as to whether the Cadillac engine offers an improved performance over Southern California modified Ford-Mercury engine. The argument boils down to one of rear wheel traction, it obviously being impossible to transmit more torque to the rear wheels than is required for wheelspin on dry pavement. To explain further, using a coefficient of .9 (taken as the maximum obtainable), a rear end loaded weight of 1220 pounds and 6.50 x 16 tires, a torque of 940 ft. lbs. on the axle shaft is all that can be usefully transmitted. If we divide this torque figure by the product of the axle and gearbox ratio, we then have the engine torque being developed. While the engine may be capable of more output, it cannot do so under the assumed conditions due to wheelspin. Only torque is considered, BHP having no significance in this type of analysis.

This brief tabulation, altho not showing all the possible combinations of engines and ratios, does prove that either the 331 cu. in. Cadillac, or a modified 275 cu. in. Ford-Mercury will produce wheelspin in low or second, with any available combination of gearbox and axle ratios. However, in direct drive, only the 4.44 ratio will give wheelspin on any surface with the Ford-Mercury engine, and then only in the speed range during which engine torque exceeds 212 foot pounds.

The Cadillac engined Allard owned by Briggs Cunningham has the heavier engine re-located slightly further aft than with the Ford-Mercury engine, necessitating a shortened torque tube and drive shaft. An axle ratio of 3.2 was obtained by fitting a quick change rear end. Acceleration from rest to 60 mph requires 7 seconds, and maximums of 80 mph in low and 100 mph in second engine speed of 6700 RPM assuming the Lincoln-Zephyr model 26H gears were installed. The proposed Mercury-Ford combination will accelerate equally as well thru the gears, but perhaps not as well in high gear unless we work the engine a little harder by using a 4.11 axle ratio. A hypothetical comparison follows, based on a higher BMEP for the Ford-Mercury than the stock Cadillac engine.

*(Continued on page 52)*

## TABLE A

| AXLE RATIO | GEARBOX RATIO | OVERALL RATIO | WHEELSPIN TORQUE = 940/O.A. RATIO | TORQUE AVAILABLE | | WHEELSPIN | |
|---|---|---|---|---|---|---|---|
| | | | | CADILLAC | 275 FORD | CAD | FORD |
| 3.20 | 1.0 | 3.20 | 294 | 312 | 218 | Yes | No |
| 3.20 | 1.44 | 4.60 | 204 | " | " | " | Yes |
| 3.27 | 1.0 | 3.27 | 288 | " | " | " | No |
| 3.27 | 1.44 | 4.70 | 200 | " | " | " | Yes |
| 3.54 | 1.0 | 3.54 | 256 | " | " | " | No |
| 3.78 | 1.0 | 3.78 | 248 | " | " | " | No |
| 4.11 | 1.0 | 4.11 | 228 | " | " | " | No |
| 4.44 | 1.0 | 4.44 | 212 | " | " | " | Yes |

## TABLE B

| ENGINE | EST. BHP | AXLE RATIO | RPM at 100 mph (HIGH GEAR) | RPM at 80 mph (SECOND GEAR) | RPM at 60 mph (LOW GEAR) | HIGH GEAR PERFORMANCE FACTOR (LITRES/TON-MILE) |
|---|---|---|---|---|---|---|
| CADILLAC | 180 | 3.27 | 4040 | 4645 | 5130 | 6360 |
| 275 FORD | 180 | 3.78 | 4660 | 5360 | 5935 | 6100 |
| 275 FORD | 180 | 4.11 | 5070 | 5825 | 6450 | 6640 |

## DATA FOR THE DRIVER

### 3.6-LITRE ALLARD

**PRICE**, with saloon body, £999, plus £278 5s British purchase tax. Total (in Great Britain), £1277 5s.

**ENGINE**: 30 h.p. (R.A.C. rating), eight cylinders, side valves, 77.8 × 95.2 mm, 3622 c.c. Brake Horse-power : 85 at 3,500 r.p.m. Compression Ratio : 6 to 1. Max Torque : 140 lb ft at 2,000 r.p.m. 21.5 m.p.h. per 1,000 r.p.m. on top gear.

**WEIGHT** : 28 cwt 2 qr 7 lb (3,199 lb). LB per C.C. : 0.88. B.H.P. per TON : 50.95.

**TYRE SIZE** : 6.25 × 16in on bolt-on steel disc wheels.

**TANK CAPACITY** : 17 English gallons (2 in reserve). Approximate fuel consumption range, 15-19 m.p.g. (18.8-14.9 litres per 100 km).

**TURNING CIRCLE** : 42ft 0in (L and R). Steering wheel movement from lock to lock : 2¾ turns. **LIGHTING SET** : 12-volt.

**MAIN DIMENSIONS** : Wheelbase, 9ft 4in. Track, 4ft 8in (front) 4ft 10½in (rear). Overall length, 15ft 9in ; width, 5ft 11in ; height, 5ft 0in. Minimum Ground Clearance : 9in.

### ACCELERATION

| Overall gear ratios | From steady m.p.h. of 10-30 sec | 20-40 sec | 30-50 sec |
|---|---|---|---|
| 3.78 to 1 | 10 0 | 10.7 | 12.1 |
| 6.68 to 1 | 5.8 | 6.5 | 8.8 |
| 11.75 to 1 | 4.5 | — | — |

From rest through gears to :—

| | sec | | sec |
|---|---|---|---|
| 30 m.p.h. .. | 6.0 | 60 m.p.h. | 23.4 |
| 50 m.p.h. .. | 15.0 | 70 m.p.h. | 35.0 |

### SPEEDS ON GEARS :

| (by Electric Speedometer) | M.p.h. (normal and max) | K.p.h. (normal and max) |
|---|---|---|
| 1st .. .. | 20—38 | 32—61 |
| 2nd .. .. | 40—60 | 64—96 |
| Top .. .. | 84/85 | 135/137 |

*Speedometer correction by Electric Speedometer:—*

| Car Speedometer | Electric Speedometer m.p.h. |
|---|---|
| 10 = | 8.75 |
| 20 = | 19.0 |
| 30 = | 27.0 |
| 40 = | 36.5 |
| 50 = | 45.0 |
| 60 = | 54.0 |
| 70 = | 63.5 |
| 80 = | 71.5 |

*WEATHER ; Dry, cool ; fresh wind.*
*Acceleration figures are the means of several runs in opposite directions.*
*Described in " The Autocar " of August 26, 1949.*

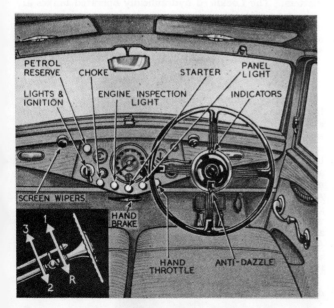

PETROL RESERVE — CHOKE — STARTER — PANEL LIGHT

LIGHTS & IGNITION — ENGINE INSPECTION LIGHT — INDICATORS

SCREEN WIPERS — HAND BRAKE — HAND THROTTLE — ANTI-DAZZLE

---

Except that it is "modern" in the approach, the Allard does not conform to any particular style of appearance. In other words, it is an individualist, as in road feel and general behaviour.

# No. 1414 : 3.6-LITRE ALLARD SALOON

A RECIPE for motoring which is in many ways unusual, even unique for these days, is contained in the Allard. This make in its more potent forms, although produced in relatively small numbers, has put itself very firmly on the map in the post-war years by notable and numerous successes in competitions of the kind in which keen private owners engage. A good deal in consequence of these successes it has attracted much attention abroad as well as at home among members of the motoring community who are appreciative of a highly individual car capable of high performance.

The Allard is chiefly known in its 3.6-litre V8 engined version, although this year the J2 sports model open two-seater has been introduced to be fitted at choice with other engines such as the V eight Cadillac for still greater performance potential. Hitherto the car had been seen, except for some examples of special bodywork, in open two-seater and drop-head coupé form, and only this year was a full-scale saloon put into production. It is an example of this that has now come under review.

It is not necessarily logical or necessary that performance comparisons should be made between the saloon and the open and coupé versions which have hitherto been tested in this way by *The Autocar*, although such a comparison will inevitably be made by some buyers. Unavoidably, the weight goes up appreciably with the saloon body in spite of aluminium panelling, but the closed car still retains a striking acceleration performance as well as the main features of appeal which have caused the Allard to become established as a serious make.

In the first place relative simplicity of design is an attractive feature and one of the unusual points in a car capable of high performance. The Ford V8 side valve engine that is used for the saloon has an excellent reputation for reliability. It gives sufficient power to be useful in a car which is still not of high weight, and as other Ford components are embodied in the chassis the Allard has the great advantage that world-wide servicing facilities as part of the Ford organization apply to it. Throughout, this car is simple and rugged, gaining its results through a useful power-to-weight ratio deriving from moderate total weight rather than from sheer power output. Because of this favourable ratio it can be successful with a three-speed gear box, the high second gear offering up to a genuine 60 m.p.h.

The most material factor governing the road behaviour is the use of high gearing, with the result that the Allard has that exceptional feeling of ease and lack of effort which come only from an engine of ample size operating at extremely moderate r.p.m. A top gear only slightly lower than 3¾ to 1 gives a cruising 70 m.p.h. at less than 3,500 r.p.m., an engine speed which can be maintained indefinitely, it would seem, without the car being in the

In the styling of the nosepiece this car is particularly bold. Although the bonnet is of modern one-piece type it has conveniently operated external catches, one of which incorporates a safety catch.

The rear part of the body is particularly clean, and there is no excessive overhang. Wheels are not enclosed.

## ROAD TESTS . . . . . . . . . . continued

least stressed. It is very noticeable on journeys of some length that the driver finishes with a particular sense of ease and well-being, for he has not been fussed by a busy engine, he has had a minimum of gear changing to perform, and always there have been the power and the speed to suit the traffic and road conditions.

Sheer maximum speed is, wisely—as a thought of general application—not claimed to be particularly high and the saloon would not readily see more than 85 m.p.h., readings over the genuine 80 mark needing, indeed, some appreciable stretch of clear road. The great point of the car is the ease with which it gets up to its 60-70 m.p.h. cruising rate and holds it. The getaway from rest can be snappy, though the high ratios are felt in conjunction with a centrifugally loaded clutch. In the range from about 30 to 50 m.p.h. there is real punch if second gear is used for maximum effect.

By contrast top gear can be used nearly all the time. As a demonstration the car can even be started on top, in spite of the high ratio, and it will trickle down to 4 or 5 m.p.h. smoothly on top gear and accelerate therefrom. It can weave through town traffic and round right-

The V8 engine is neat as regards wiring and pipes, and most of the auxiliaries, including the 18 mm. sparking plugs are accessible, there being plenty of room in the engine compartment. A lamp on the bulkhead can be switched on from the facia to provide useful illumination.

angle turns, or regain the cruising rate rapidly after a check, without a change down. Ordinary main-road gradients are swept at speed and a swift climb can be made of the 1 in 6-7 order of hills on second gear. No pinking or running-on tendency was experienced on the comparatively low-octane Pool petrol.

An integral part of the delightfully easy point-to-point performance of the car is its road holding and stability.

A rather striking compromise has been obtained in a suspension which takes up shock well, yet has really no lateral give at all, meaning that the car can be poked round bends and also quite acute turns with maximum enterprise, and yet no heel or sway occurs. It is not the softest kind of suspension for general riding that gives this effect, as might be expected, but there is no real harshness or any pronounced vertical motion on fair to moderately poor surfaces. Whilst the divided front axle design which has been previous practice on the Allard is still used, coil springs are now employed in place of a transverse half-elliptic spring formerly, and these give a softer effect than in earlier models without letting the car become at all spongy. At the rear a transverse half-elliptic spring is still used.

The steering is light for general driving and remains reasonably so down to manœuvring speeds, is definite in the way that is required for confidence at speeds of 70 m.p.h.-plus, has decisive castor action, and is not subject to reaction from the road wheels to any extent that matters. The Lockheed hydraulically operated brakes are in keeping with the performance. Moderate pedal pressure is sufficient for all ordinary braking and there is an excellent reserve of braking power for emergencies, still without excessive pedal pressure being required.

### Positive Gear Change

A steering-column gear lever is used and has one of the best, that is, tautest and most positive, movements experienced with this form of lever, such a result being easier to obtain when only three forward speeds are employed. The lever movements are not particularly light, but the travel is short and there is no uncertainty about obtaining the different gears. The first to reverse movement, and vice versa, is as good as could be wished. A driver has to accustom himself to the fact that the gear positions are different from those normally expected with a three-speed layout; that is, top gear position is away from the driver or upward, instead of towards him. At the furthest away setting of the telescopically adjustable steering wheel there is very little clearance between the gear lever and the wheel rim in reverse position.

The driving position bears evidence of the influence of drivers of sports-type cars. The driver sits low but well up to a large spring-spoked wheel, which is at just the right angle, and is supported amply in the back and shoulders by the nearly vertical back rest of a separately adjustable seat. Slight curvature of the back rest would be of value to "hold" the driver better when cornering fast. There is plenty of room for the left foot, but the right foot could do with more feeling of support in operating the pendant style of throttle pedal. A pull-and-push type of hand-brake control is within easy reach, whilst leaving the front compartment clear, and is powerful for holding the car stationary. The front seat cushions and back rest practically meet at the centre, and it would be possible to carry a third occupant on occasion. Although the bonnet is long it is not high or obstructive to driving vision, nor are the windscreen pillars noticed as an obstruction; the right-hand wing (in a right-hand drive car) is within view of an average-height driver and the other wing can be seen by leaning over slightly.

### Unusual Detail Equipment

Instrument layout again shows the good influence of the sports-car outlook. The gauges have "honest," circular dials, black with white markings and needles. They include an engine thermometer, reading in degrees F, as well as an ammeter. There is the now exceptional pro-

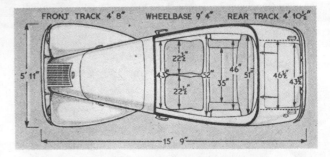

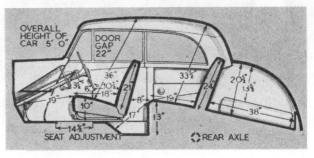

Measurements in these scale body diagrams are taken with the driving seat in the central position of fore and aft adjustment and with the seat cushions uncompressed.

There is useful capacity in the luggage compartment, although the spare wheel is prominent in it, as seen, and the floor of the locker slopes fairly sharply rearward. A useful light in the compartment is illuminated automatically by opening the lid, the struts of which are self-locking.

vision of a control on the facia for a reserve supply of petrol. A screw-type hand throttle is provided in addition to the choke control, and among the main group of minor controls is a switch for a light in the engine compartment. Other practical detail points have not been overlooked in the saloon body, which gives every impression of being well made, and which has the coachbuilt manner of the doors closing without being slammed. There is a shelf for packages under the facia, as well as pockets formed low down in the thickness of the doors.

This two-door body is somewhat "occasional," as distinct from "family," as regards the rear seats, although their upholstery in leather over a rubber underlay is comfortable. It would not be easy for the less agile and elderly to get in and out of the rear seats through the space given by tilting the back rests of the front seats, although the leg room is reasonable; there are elbow rests, set at an angle which robs them of maximum value, but a central arm rest is not fitted in the rear seat.

Again unusually nowadays, this unusual car has a windscreen which can be opened by means of a central toggle mechanism, but a sliding roof is not provided. Demisting vents for the windscreen are built in and the car can be

supplied with a heating installation of the type that takes in fresh air from a grille in the nose. This installation is standard for export and an extra for the home market. A degree of control over ventilation which is useful for some weather conditions is given by pivoting panels in the front of the doors, additional to the drop windows.

The excellent detail feature of a rear window blind is included. The view provided by the driving mirror is all but comprehensive. Twin horns give a quite powerful but still pleasing note. The head-lamp beam is satisfactory up to about 70 m.p.h. Always the engine started immediately and required very little use of the mixture control from cold.

Access to the rear seats through the single wide door on each side is by tilting the back rests of the front seats and leg room for back passengers is given by shallow wells. The upholstery is in good leather over foam rubber. The roof light is switched on by opening the doors.

# The 4·4-Litre J.2 Allard

*Ready for action; the very rapid J.2 Allard poses for a picture. The tubular luggage-rack is not fitted.*

DESIGNED primarily for competitions, the J.2 Allard two-seater is a straightforward, no frills no non-sense sports car of great charm. Bodywork, although undeniably attractive, is distinctly functional; the manufacturers have obviously made certain that the J.2 carries the minimum possible weight around with it. As a result, the car has a remarkable power-weight ratio for a large-engined vehicle.

The car tested was fitted with a "stroked" Mercury V-8 power-unit of 4,375 c.c. (84.13 × 98.42 mm.), developing 120 b.h.p. at 3,800 r.p.m. The longer stroke is obtained by reducing the crankpin diameter slightly and fitting special con. rods. The engine is further modified to the extent of aluminium-alloy cylinder heads and twin, downdraught, large-bore carburetters. A further refinement is the fitting of an oil cooler.

Road-holding is exceptionally good; the J.2 appears to be one of the few modern cars that can be cornered at high speeds without displaying the slightest tendency to roll. Despite all that has been said in the past concerning split-axle i.f.s., the helically sprung arrangement on the Allard is beyond criticism. Combined with the De Dion pattern rear axle (also helically-sprung) which was developed on Sidney Allard's famous Steyr-engined sprint car, the J.2 can be said to possess a suspension system which would do credit to the designer of a Grand Prix racing car.

Fast drivers will also appreciate the slight degree of understeer, so necessary when "feeling" a really high-speed bend. The steering itself is light and commendably self-centring. In fact, one of the outstanding features of the J.2 is that it can be driven over very long distances without in the least fatiguing the driver.

It is quite true to say that cruising speeds are limited only by road conditions. The big, side-valve Mercury power-plant burbles along with a healthy note from the twin exhaust pipes on fast stretches with the rev. counter at "three-five", and plenty more to come. With the usual

*FUNCTIONAL : The row of switches on the nearside of the Allard's facia panel are (L. to R.), dash, side and head lamps, fuel reserve, pump, ignition, magneto cut-off and mixture control.*

# AN 100 m.p.h. TWO-SEATER WITH REMARKABLE ACCELERATION

accuracy of Ford-type instruments, this shows a top-gear speed on the speedometer of 81 m.p.h. Working it out properly (3.5 to 1 axle, 600 × 16 tyres), 3,500 r.p.m. is equal to a top gear speed of 79.8 m.p.h.

For normal road use, the J.2 Allard is a top-gear car, with astonishing flexibility in the lower speed ranges. It is possible to accelerate from walking pace on an uphill gradient. Bottom gear can be ignored except for starting off on very steep hills, although we must admit that the temptation to use maximum acceleration in that gear, from traffic lights, is overwhelming. Particularly when standstill to 50 m.p.h. can be achieved in just 6.7 secs.

The clutch is delightfully smooth, with a complete absence of judder Gear-changing is effected as rapidly as the stubby, remote-control lever can be moved. The usually tricky 1st to 2nd "straight-through" change with the Ford box can be quickly mastered on the Allard. This is evident in the matter of improving acceleration figures with constant practice. A preliminary "standing-quarter" of 18.5 secs., was eventually reduced to 16.9 secs.

The car was tested under the most favourable conditions possible, on AUTOSPORT's airfield circuit, which has a main runway of more than average length. Despite the need for a spot of Benzol to counteract a certain amount of pinking, only normal pump fuel was used. The

(two up) at exactly 103.6 m.p.h.

On the debit side, we did not care for the door-catches and the lack of rigidity of the doors themselves. The latter are easily distorted, making it difficult to close them securely. We would suggest that ultra-lightness might be sacrificed a trifle, by providing some form of bracing, whereby this distortion could not occur. The catches are simple, spring-loaded affairs of the meat-safe type, which do provide positive locking when everything is in order. However, their efficiency is entirely dependent on the doors closing properly, and on more than one occasion the catch failed to operate, and the driver's door flew open.

The headlamps are scarcely powerful enough for fast night driving, and the makers might consider fitting longer-range units, even if it means

## SPECIFICATION AND PERFORMANCE DATA

**Car Tested.** Allard, J.2. Competition two-seater: chassis No. J.888; engine No. 1721162. Mileage at conclusion of test, 9,000. List Price, £999 (plus £278 5s. P.T.).

**Engine.** V-8, 84.13 × 98.42 mm. (4,375 c.c. side valves) 120 b.h.p. at 3,800 r.p.m. 8 to 1 compression ratio. Twin downdraught carburetters; mechanical and electrical fuel pumps with dual feed lines; water pump coolant circulation; aluminium-alloy cylinder heads; Lucas 12-volt coil ignition. (Car tested had vertical magneto fitted). External oil cooler; full-flow oil filter.

**Engine Performance Factors.** Piston area, 68.9 sq. in.; b.h.p. per sq. in. of piston area, 1.74; piston speed at 3,800 r.p.m. (86.9 m.p.h. in top gear), 2,453 ft. per min. 1,000 r.p.m. (top gear) = 22.8 m.p.h.

**Transmission.** Ford heavy-duty single plate dry clutch. Gear ratios, 3.5, 5.6 and 9.87 to 1. Final drive by enclosed propeller shaft to spiral bevel axle = Hardy-Spicer universally-jointed driving shafts.

**Chassis.** Independent front suspension (swing-axle and helical springs). De Dion type rear with helical springs; Woodhead-Monroe telescopic hydraulic dampers. Lockheed hydraulic brakes with 12-in. "Alfin" ribbed drums (2LS at front). Inboard rear

drums Cable-operated handbrake (fly-off pattern). Bolt-on steel wheels with 600 × 16 Dunlop tyres.

**Equipment.** 12-volt lighting and starting (twin 6-volt batteries). Speedometer, revolution counter, oil pressure, water temperature and fuel gauges, ammeter; twin tail lights (stop light combined), spring-spoked stearing wheel.

**Dimensions, etc.** Wheelbase, 8 ft. 4 in. Track (front), 4 ft. 8 in. (rear), 4 ft. 4 in. Overall length, 12 ft. 4 in. Ground clearance 6¼ in. Turning circle, 39 ft. Weight (dry), 17 cwt. (as tested, c.w. fuel, oil, spare wheel, hood, etc.), 19 cwt.

**Performance.** Maximum speed (mean of four runs), 102.10 m.p.h. Fastest in one direction, 103.60 m.p.h. **Speeds in gears,** 1st, 72 m.p.h. 2nd., 90 m.p.h. **Acceleration,** Standing quarter-mile, 16.9 secs. 0–50 m.p.h., 6.70 secs. 0–60 m.p.h., 8.30 secs. 0–70 m.p.h., 10.65 secs. 0–80 m.p.h., 13.75 secs. 0–90 m.p.h., 17.50 secs. 0–100 m.p.h., 23.50 secs. **Top gear acceleration,** 20–40 m.p.h., 3.90 secs. 30–50 m.p.h. 4.25 secs. 40–60 m.p.h. 4.30 secs. 50–70 m.p.h., 5.00 secs.

**Fuel Consumption.** 23 m.p.g. at steady 30 m.p.h., 21.5 m.p.g. at 40 m.p.h. 19.6 m.p.g. at 50 m.p.h., 17.8 m.p.g. at 60 m.p.h.

engine had a tendency to "run on" after a series of acceleration and maximum speed tests, probably due to fairly low quality petrol.

The brakes are extremely powerful, and there is never the slightest suggestion of tail-wag, even when they are applied hard on a downhill straight with "four-eight" showing on the tachometer, which is equal to a speed of 109.4 m.p.h., the highest non-timed rate achieved with the car. Against the watch, the J.2 covered a flying quarter-mile

*CENTURY-MAKER: The J.2 is rock-steady as it flashes over the measured quarter-mile at something over the "ton". Passenger Roy Clarkson owns a similar car.*

extra cost, now that double-purchase tax no longer applies. We also suggest that the deep well between the accelerator pedal and the body side might well be eliminated, as it was found that the driver's heel was apt to be trapped. It is also difficult to enter the car with the handbrake "on", as it completely obstructs the doorway.

On the car tested, the turning circle had been decreased by altering the drag link, and providing recesses on the body sides to give the front wheels maximum lock. As originally delivered, the turning circle was about 44 ft., which was too great a

*(continued overleaf)*

## ALLARD ROAD TEST—*continued*

radius for a vehicle with a wheelbase of just 8 ft. 4 ins. After modification, the figure was reduced to 39 ft.

This particular car was also fitted with a windscreen, as well as aeroscreens, full all-weather equipment and a neat tubular luggage-rack on the tail. There is no enclosed luggage space, the entire area being taken up with a 25-gallon fuel tank (including two in reserve) and a compartment for tools and spare wheel. The hood is a well-designed fitment, which, when not in use, can be stowed behind the seat squab.

In view of the performance of this likeable Allard with the side-valve motor, it would be interesting to compare it with the smaller capacity, o.h.v. engine now being specially made for the J.2. This is, as on all production Allards, basically a Ford unit of 3,622 c.c., but with "Ardun" heads, dual Solex carburettors, a compression ratio of eight to one, and a power-output of 140 b.h.p. at 3,800 r.p.m. The other version of the J.2, the "export-only" Cadillac-engined job, is also down on our list for road-testing.

*POWER-PLANT: Close-up of the modified Mercury engine, showing the ribbed, light-alloy cylinder heads. This particular car was fitted with a Scintilla magneto, and the fan was removed.*

The car tested went well in the recent Ulster Trophy race, until it was eliminated with a blown gasket. In to-morrow's One Hour Production Car Race at Silverstone, all three types of engine will be represented, the Cadillac version being, of course, available on the American market.

Without a doubt, the excellent road-holding and all-round performance of this very sporting Allard, are the results of Sidney Allard's unshaken belief that vehicles intended for competition use, should be developed in competitions, before being placed on the market.

## Analyzing the Allard

*Continued from page 45*

DASH and cab compartment of the Allard K-2 shows the neat arrangement of instruments and convenient gearshift lever on floor

having good acceleration in any gear and ample braking capacity for quick, safe stopping. The engine in this car was new, so high speed driving and acceleration tests were postponed to a later date. Cornering on winding mountain roads was very good and was accomplished without any tendency toward skidding or wheel fight.

It was noticed when driving over sharp bumps, such as chuck holes or railroad tracks, that the impact was transmitted to

WITH the alligator type hood opened wide, easy access is permitted to all parts of the 1950 Mercury engine converted by Vic Edelbrock

the steering wheel and caused a definite reaction. Although severe in some instances, this reaction did not occur so often as to become objectionable, nor did it cause the car to deviate from its path.

The Allard K-2 should be received with enthusiasm by the sports car fraternity as its design permits it to be adapted, through minor modifications and adjustments, to suit ones driving habits and desires.

## ALLARD J-2

*(Continued from page 46)*

From this it can be said that a much modified Ford-Merc can only be made to equal a slightly modified Cadillac installation by using gear ratios to take advantage of the higher revving capabilities of the Ford-Mercury—with consequent sacrifice in durability due to much higher piston speed. The cost of the two engines is nearly equal, but the Cadillac installation requires either specially cut non-Ford gears giving 3.27 to 1, (about $65.00) or the still more expensive quick change center section.

The writer's choice is the Ford-Mercury, with 3.78 axle ratio, because road surface coefficients are often much less than .9 (as low as .6 dry). Even in this higher gear the acceleration will be virtually equal to the big engine and the handling qualities will definitely be better. Finally, it's too easy to drop in a big klunker, or add a super-charger—I like to do things the hard way!

# ALLARD WINS at SANTA ANA

PHOTOGRAPHS BY E. RICKMAN

MOST hazardous 'S' turn of Santa Ana course

### by G. Thatcher Darwin

AFTER showing his Allard's stubby tail to the cream of Southern California's sports car pilots, red-headed Roy Richter took the checkered flag and cheers of 14,000 spectators at Santa Ana on June 25th. The genial Bell, Calif., business man sped over the finish line 39:16.10 seconds after starting the 20-lap premier road race. Second man home was Phil Hill, and third was Jack Mc-Afee (both drove Jaguar XK-120's). Laid out to simulate as closely as possible actual road conditions, the tricky, two-mile asphalt circuit included every type of curve and corner, and required the highest order of driver skill and car stamina.

Richter's win underlined recent Allard successes elsewhere, and has made the name an important factor in west coast competition. Other cars of the same make were handled by Basil Panzer and Tom Frisbey, and these finished fourth and fifth, respectively. Panzer drove his black J-2 with much restraint, since the car was delivered just prior to the race, and he had not become accustomed to it. His speed increased noticeably as the race went on, and in the eleventh lap, he passed Frisbey, who was driving a steady race with the heavier K-2 model.

The winning J-2 has remained practically unaltered since original delivery to its owner. Other than a careful tune-up, no special preparation was made for this race. Although the Allards are usually ordered "less engine," and fitted with Mercury power-plants after delivery, Richter's machine is powered with a British-built, 21-stud Ford V-8, modified to Allard factory specifications. These changes include ⅛-over standard bore and stroke, Allard heads and manifold and a Harman & Collins ¾ cam. For this version, the makers claim a modest 120 hp. The Santa Ana course placed a high premium on cornering ability, and the Allard's unique L.M.B. independent front suspension and DeDion rear axle appeared to be ideally suited to the conditions.

The two Jaguar XK-120's, driven by Hill and McAfee, were very consistent in the hands of these experienced drivers. Hill, with the faster of the pair, had the misfortune to spin while trying to match Richter's pace into the first curve, and was passed by the entire field. Evidently inspired by this adversity, Hill resumed the battle with such verve that by the end of lap three, he had motored through all the traffic to regain second place behind Richter—a spirited exhibition. Although Hill remained within striking distance until the end, 17 laps later, the Allard held its lead with apparent ease.

An interesting feature of Phil Hill's campaign was his use of "asphalt slicks" on the Jaguar. These smooth tread, track-type tires proved very effective, and mark a significant innovation in western sports car racing.

The feature event was, in a sense, two races in one. The larger-engined cars naturally filled the first positions, but farther back a no-less-exciting struggle was going on among the MG's for leadership of the smaller-engined contingent. After the first lap, Bill Kerrigan's light green TC freed itself from the pack and set sail for Arnold Stubb's yellow machine which led the MG's. For the next seven laps Kerrigan hounded the other car, never more than a few feet away, but not quite able to pass. Finally in the ninth lap he succeeded in passing but soon thereafter he charged a hay bale, bending the MG's tie rod and forcing its retirement on the next circuit. Stubbs roared on without slackening pace, and became the first MG driver to cross the line—a fine showing.

Small car fans found delight in the performance of several Crosley Hotshots. These sturdy little machines ran very smoothly, and put up an excellent race considering that their 720 cc engines were pitted against MG's of 1250 cc's. In the first event William Palmer's Crosley actually passed a brace of MG's, and held second place for a time before being overtaken. He eventually finished in third spot. It was unfortunate that the Hotshots' performance appeared eclipsed by

that of the larger-engined cars against which they were ranged. If enough Crosley's had been entered to form a 750 cc class, the resulting competition would have been very keen indeed.

In evaluating the performance of all the entrants, it must be kept in mind that these are true sports cars, driven by their owners for normal usage as well as for competition. With the exception of two "specials," all carried full road equipment, and most of them were driven to the circuit and home again, unlike race cars which are towed or transported on trailers. Generally speaking, all the cars ran well, and retirements from the races were rare. This was, no doubt, partly due to the perfect weather which prevailed, a welcome change from the blistering heat which attended the earlier Palm Springs road race.

Sterling Edwards, winner of the Palm Springs race, was again on hand with his splendid Edwards car, which was rated a pre-race favorite. The car won its heat race, and then starting from the last row in the main event, Edwards came through the field to fourth place by the end of lap three, only

CROSSING the finish line as winner of the main event is Roy Richter, driving an Allard J-2

to retire on the back stretch in the next circuit due to a bent clutch pedal link. The car was running beautifully, and no doubt would have been among the leaders at the finish. The way this machine handled on the twisty course leaves no question as to the merit of its four-wheel independent suspension.

In marked contrast was the Baldwin Special exemplifying the solid axle school of design. This car possesses a simply fantastic power-to-weight ratio, and the bellow of its open exhaust headers is certainly impressive. As was anticipated, the Baldwin repeated its Palm Springs success by qualifying fastest, several seconds ahead of its nearest rival. This machine snakes badly under full acceleration, and although this gives the spectators thrills, the car is obviously quite a handful to manage.

Fortunately no accidents occurred to mar the day's pleasure, and spectator control, usually a tough problem on a road course, was satisfactory. Some grumbling was heard in the bleachers because it was difficult to see cars clearly on the back stretches, and at one point on each lap, the drivers passed completely out of sight. It should be made clear to all that amateur road racing is fundamentally a competitor sport, and spectators cannot expect to have the whole show go on under their noses. Airport circuits, such as the Santa Ana layout, actually provide the best spectator visibility because of their flat terrain. A race run over real roads including hills and valleys would be much more difficult to follow.

Incidentally, "amateur" in this sense means only that the drivers and car owners participate purely for the love of the sport, and do not race for any monetary gain or awards of tangible value. The word carries no connotation of inexperience or indifferent ability. Generally the standard of driving was quite competent, and the degree of skill which some of these "amateurs" are acquiring is a good indication of what may be expected at Pebble Beach this fall.

LINEUP for the main event, with Richter (J-2) on pole, Hill (XK-120) on outside, Edwards fifth

# The Motor Continental Road Test No. 3C/51—

**Make:** Allard. **Type:** J2 (Cadillac engine) 2-seater.

**Makers:** Allard Motor Co., Ltd., 26, High Street, Clapham, London, S.W.4.

## Dimensions and Seating

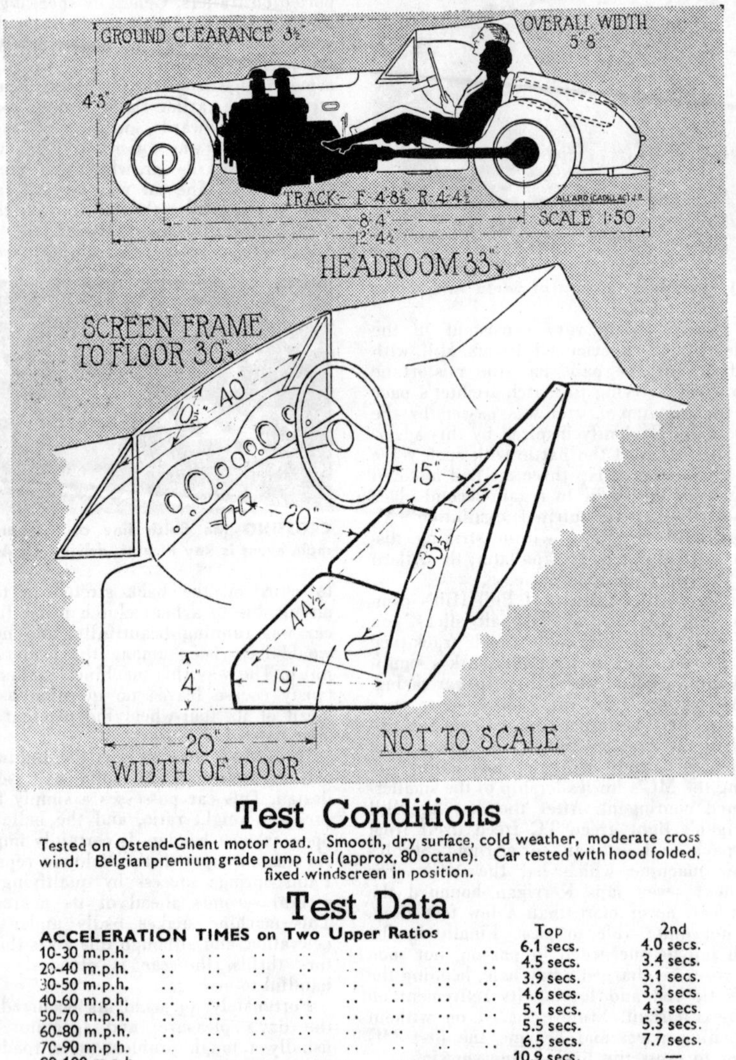

GROUND CLEARANCE 3½"
OVERALL WIDTH 5' 8"
4' 3"
TRACK– F 4' 8¾" R 4' 4½"
8' 4"
12' 4½"
SCALE 1:50
HEADROOM 33"
SCREEN FRAME TO FLOOR 30"
40"
10½"
15"
20"
33½"
44½"
4"
19"
20"
WIDTH OF DOOR
NOT TO SCALE


## Test Conditions

Tested on Ostend-Ghent motor road. Smooth, dry surface, cold weather, moderate cross wind. Belgian premium grade pump fuel (approx. 80 octane). Car tested with hood folded, fixed windscreen in position.

## Test Data

**ACCELERATION TIMES on Two Upper Ratios**

| | Top | 2nd |
|---|---|---|
| 10-30 m.p.h. | 6.1 secs. | 4.0 secs. |
| 20-40 m.p.h. | 4.5 secs. | 3.4 secs. |
| 30-50 m.p.h. | 3.9 secs. | 3.1 secs. |
| 40-60 m.p.h. | 4.6 secs. | 3.3 secs. |
| 50-70 m.p.h. | 5.1 secs. | 4.3 secs. |
| 60-80 m.p.h. | 5.5 secs. | 5.3 secs. |
| 70-90 m.p.h. | 6.5 secs. | 7.7 secs. |
| 80-100 m.p.h. | 10.9 secs. | |

**ACCELERATION TIMES Through Gears**

| | |
|---|---|
| 0-30 m.p.h. | 3.4 secs. |
| 0-40 m.p.h. | 4.6 secs. |
| 0-50 m.p.h. | 5.9 secs. |
| 0-60 m.p.h. | 7.4 secs. |
| 0-70 m.p.h. | 10.2 secs. |
| 0-80 m.p.h. | 13.1 secs. |
| 0-90 m.p.h. | 16.8 secs. |
| 0-100 m.p.h. | 23.6 secs. |
| Standing quarter-mile | 16.25 secs. |

**MAXIMUM SPEEDS**

**Flying Quarter-mile**

| | |
|---|---|
| Mean of four opposite runs | 110.8 m.p.h. |
| Best time equals | 111.8 m.p.h. |

**Speed in Gears**

| | |
|---|---|
| Max. speed in 2nd gear | 94 m.p.h. |
| Max. speed in 1st gear | 64 m.p.h. |

**WEIGHT**

| | |
|---|---|
| Unladen kerb weight | 21 cwt. |
| Front/rear weight distribution | 47/53 |
| Weight laden as tested | 24 cwt. |

**INSTRUMENTS**

| | |
|---|---|
| Speedometer at 30 m.p.h. | 7% slow |
| Speedometer at 60 m.p.h. | 7% slow |
| Speedometer at 90 m.p.h. | 5% slow |
| Distance recorder | 8% slow |

**FUEL CONSUMPTION**

19.0 m.p.g. at constant 30 m.p.h.
18.0 m.p.g. at constant 40 m.p.h.
18.0 m.p.g. at constant 50 m.p.h.
16.0 m.p.g. at constant 60 m.p.h.
15.0 m.p.g. at constant 70 m.p.h.
12.5 m.p.g. at constant 80 m.p.h.
10.5 m.p.g. at constant 90 m.p.h.

**HILL CLIMBING** (at steady speeds)

| | |
|---|---|
| Max. top-gear speed on 1 in 20 | 107 m.p.h. |
| Max. top-gear speed on 1 in 15 | 105 m.p.h. |
| Max. top-gear speed on 1 in 10 | 95 m.p.h. |
| Max. gradient on top gear | 1 in 4.4 (Tapley 500 lb./ton) |
| Max. gradient on 2nd gear | 1 in 3.2 (Tapley 660 lb./ton) |

**BRAKES at 30 m.p.h.**

0.90 g. retardation (=33½ ft. stopping distance) with 150 lb. pedal pressure.
0.70 g. retardation (=43 ft. stopping distance) with 100 lb. pedal pressure.
0.44 g. retardation (=68½ ft. stopping distance) with 50 lb. pedal pressure.
0.24 g. retardation (=125 ft. stopping distance) with 25 lb. pedal pressure.

## In Brief

| | |
|---|---|
| Price £1,200 (Model not available in England, no purchase tax quoted). | |
| Capacity | 5,440 c.c. |
| Unladen kerb weight | 21 cwt. |
| Fuel consumption | approx. 11 m.p.g. |
| Maximum speed | 110.8 m.p.h. |
| Maximum speed on 1 in 20 gradient | 107 m.p.h. |
| Maximum top-gear gradient | 1 in 4.4 |
| Acceleration | |
| 10-30 m.p.h. in top | 6.1 secs. |
| 0-50 m.p.h. through gears | 5.9 secs. |
| Gearing 25.1 m.p.h. in top at 1,000 r.p.m., 104 m.p.h. at 2,500 ft. per min. piston speed. | |

## Specification

| | |
|---|---|
| **Engine** | |
| Cylinders | V-8 |
| Bore | 96.8 mm. |
| Stroke | 92 mm. |
| Cubic capacity | 5,440 c.c |
| Piston area | 91.3 sq. ins. |
| Valves | Push-rod o.h.v. |
| Compression ratio | 7.5/1 |
| Max. power | Approx. 160 b.h.p |
| at | 4,000 r.p.m. |
| Piston speed at max. b.h.p. | 2,420 ft. per min. |
| Carburetter | 2 Carter downdraught |
| Ignition | Lucas-Delco Remy, 12-volt coil |
| Sparking plugs | 14 mm. Lodge R47 |
| Fuel pump | A.C. mechanical and S.U. electrical, in parallel |
| Oil filter | Floating oil-pump intake |
| **Transmission** | |
| Clutch | Single dry plate |
| Top gear (s/m) | 3.2 |
| 2nd gear (s/m) | 4.35 |
| 1st gear | 5.75 |
| Propeller shaft | Tubular, enclosed |
| Final drive | Spiral bevel |
| **Chassis** | |
| Brakes | Lockheed hydrauli |
| Brake-drum diameter | 12 ins. |
| Friction lining area | 156 sq. ins. |
| Suspension: | |
| front | Divided axle I.F.S. (coil springs) |
| rear | de Dion axle (coil springs) |
| Shock absorbers | Woodhead telescopic |
| Tyres | Dunlop, 6.00 mult. 16 |
| **Steering** | |
| Steering gear | Adamant (worm and roller) |
| Turning circle | 38 feet |
| Turns of steering wheel, lock to lock | 2½ |
| **Performance factors** (at laden weight as tested) | |
| Piston area, sq. ins. per ton | 76.0 |
| Brake lining area, sq. ins. per ton | 130 |
| Specific displacement, litres per ton-mile | 5,400 |

*Described in "The Motor," August 24, 1949 (Home market model with 4.4-litre engine).*

## Maintenance

**Fuel tank:** 20 gallons (Warning light operate at 3 gallons). **Sump:** 16 pints, S.A.E. 20 **Gearbox:** 2 pints, S.A.E. 90 E.P. gear oil. **Rear Axle:** 2 pints S.A.E. 90 E.P. gear oil **Steering Gear:** ⅔-pint semi-fluid grease. **Radiator:** 32 pints. **Chassis lubrication:** by grease gun to 19 points. **Ignition timing:** fully advanced, 32° b.t.d.c. **Spark plug gap:** 0.030 in. **Contact breaker gap:** 0.012 in. **Valve Timing:** I.O., 19° b.t.d.c., I.C., 83° a.b.d.c. E.O., 53° b.b.d.c., E.C., 49° a.t.d.c. **Tappets:** self-adjusting. **Front wheel toe-in:** ⅛ in.—$\frac{3}{16}$ in. **Camber angle:** 3°. **Castor angle:** 3°—4°. **Tyre pressures:** Front 22 lb., Rear 25 lb. **Brake fluid:** Lockheed. **Battery:** Two Lucas 6-volt 60 amp. hour, in series. **Lamp bulbs:** 12 volt. Headlamps 36/36 watt. Side lamps 3 watt. Tail/stop lamp 6/36 watt. Number plate 6 watt. M.C.C.

Ref. B-U.S./55/51.

# —The ALLARD J2 (Cadillac engine)

## Remarkable Acceleration and Responsive Handling Qualities Combined in a Car Suitable for Many Types of Speed Event

The purpose of the Allard is to provide a fast car shorn of non-essentials. The lines of the J2 model are straightforward and attractive

ON rare occasions cars which are road tested by "The Motor" produce figures and comment which make history. Not all such vehicles become memorable on account of their high performance—some reveal outstanding advancement in suspension or general ease of handling, others impress by an exceptional degree of silence or comfort.

It must be admitted, however, that there is a very great fascination about the ultimate in high performance machines of all sorts, and the number of types of car built in the past 20 years which come within this category can be counted on two hands.

### Le Mans Performance

The figures which we obtained in Belgium from the Cadillac-engined Allard are, in several instances, unique but not entirely unexpected. It will be recalled that at Le Mans last year the J2 put up an outstanding performance and finished third in the race. Clearly a car able to maintain an average of 87.8 m.p.h. for 24 hours must be an outstanding performer in many ways, and at the end of a week's driving in three different countries "The Motor" test team suffered no disappointments.

It is only fair to record that although the 5.4-litre eight-cylinder engine propels the Allard in any of its three remarkably high and close ratios in a manner more docile than that offered by most family saloons, the car as tested by us could hardly be considered a suitable touring machine. Rather should it be regarded as a vehicle eminently suitable for road racing, or as a provider of a superb method of high-speed travel in warm countries on dry days.

On the model tested there was virtually no luggage room whatever. With the hood raised it became possible to lash a kitbag behind the occupants' heads, but due to the absence of side screens and the modest dimensions of the front wings, a great deal of mud and water penetrated to the passengers' compartment and on many occasions smeared the inside of the windscreen and, in fact, most of the rest of the interior of the car.

Clearly, the man who purchases this model of the Allard should not expect luxury travel. What he gets might be described as the finest sports motor bicycle on four wheels ever conceived. No lack of creature comforts can, however, disguise the splendid handling qualities or the outstanding performance offered by the J2. The figures attained for acceleration through the gears are in most instances the best ever recorded in the history of our road tests. The maximum speed was slightly disappointing, particularly as it is known that the car has travelled considerably faster in races, but the absolute regularity with which we drove the car up and down our measured section of the Jabbeke Highway, recording between 110 and 112 m.p.h., made it fairly obvious that this was, in fact, the true figure for this particular car, running in touring trim under entirely normal conditions.

Such tremendous powers of acceleration

would be useless without the compensating ability to stop from high speeds, together with an outstanding degree of merit in the matter of road holding and steering. The brakes on the Allard are first class and seem remarkably free from fade. They are, of course, so far as the front drums are concerned, set well out in the air stream and provided with a generous wind scoop. A series of stops from maximum revealed no weakness, and it is important to record that the clutch stood up to heavy punishment during our test without any signs of deterioration.

To get the best out of the Allard takes a little practice. Steering is delightfully sensitive and direct, and on dry roads it is possible to corner with an abandon associated only with a select few in the world of fast motoring. On ice and roads made slippery by rain we never entirely mastered the motor-car, because there appeared to be a slight tendency to

The front suspension and brakes fitted with air scoops can be seen in this illustration.

The Cadillac engine on the car tested was an almost standard power unit with the addition of two Carter down-draught carburetters.

(Left) Although not provided with side screens, the Allard has a useful hood which folds away in the tail of the car when not in use. (Below) In the best traditions of the past is the layout of essential instruments designed to a size which can be read at speed. The very large rear mirror is a great asset. The gear lever position can also be seen.

## The Allard J2 - - - Contd.

wander which had nothing to do with the formidable power available to the back wheels. In fact, it is noteworthy that even on ice only the most ham-footed tactics could produce serious wheelspin except during cornering, and on dry roads such tendencies are virtually unknown even when using full throttle in low gear, circumstances for which the De Dion rear axle is largely responsible.

Extraordinary performance figures do not always present to the reader a true idea of what really occurs. For example, the car tested could be stationary at the side of a road when overtaken by another vehicle doing a steady 55 m.p.h. If the Allard was taken off the line at the precise moment of passing, the 55 m.p.h. car would be caught in considerably less than 500 yards! In practice the Allard can be cruised comfortably and quietly at anything between 40 and 80 m.p.h., and there still remains such an astonishing reserve of power in top gear as to make the overhauling of other fast vehicles the whim of an instant. Controlled by a central remote lever, the extremely close-ratio gearbox is a sheer joy to use.

We have said that the body styling of the Allard is spartan. This does not mean that anything essential to the purpose for which the car is designed is lacking Everything, in fact, is functional. The lights are adequate for speeds up to 100 m.p.h. and, though the horn is not, the Allard Company can hardly be blamed, because we have yet to experience any post-war British electric horn that is. The body panels are naturally extremely light,

but the doors fit well and are quite unaffected by distortion. The instruments covered most requirements, and it must always be remembered that the fortunate overseas buyer, for whom this model is designed exclusively, can order his car with a very wide variation of equipment and finish. Consequently, anything reasonably desired can be supplied.

### Essential Equipment

The windscreen is robust and sensible, and the hood is well thought out and folds completely away behind the seats. The large fuel tank is clearly desirable for such a thirsty engine, and the seats are reasonably comfortable even when occupied for long periods. The car is completely without temperament and can be started up and driven away in the manner of any of the better family saloons, engine flexibility and good steering lock combining to make turning

around in a wide road in top gear a smooth operation. The exhaust note is reasonably pronounced, but at speeds in excess of one mile a minute the Allard settles down to a pleasant blend of air rush and other sounds which enables loud-voiced conversation to be carried on with the passenger right up to maximum m.p.h.

The cockpit is commendably free from draughts and likewise devoid of those desultory air eddies which whisk maps out of some open cars without warning. Similarly, owing to the small side panels which reinforce the windscreen, there is not enough air disturbance even at maximum speed to make goggles for either driver or passenger a necessity. The tools are housed under the bonnet and there is ample space for additional emergency gear such as snow chains, spare sparking plugs and any other equipment of this type. When the bonnet is raised the V-8 engine becomes extremely accessible. The unusual bulge in the bonnet top covers the special dual carburetters fitted to this model Allard, and on each side of this projection are located spring-loaded straps which provide security in addition to the aircraft-type fastenings also standardized. Incidentally, this metal hump in the centre of the bonnet does not interfere with forward visibility, which is excellent.

The steering wheel is not adjustable, the cars being, as previously mentioned, tailored to fit their prospective owner. The body is wide enough to carry two broad passengers wearing full winter kit without any inconvenience.

The car is not seriously affected by cross-winds—a matter of some importance when sustained high speed is contemplated. The ground clearance, however, is limited by the special deeply finned sump which measures only three and a half inches from the surface of the road. Consequently, this model is not suitable for rough country and care must be taken when traversing village streets abroad.

These things, however, are of little significance when compared with the tremendous performance offered by the car, and to take the J2 Allard with Cadillac engine on a 100-mile journey away from towns on a fine day is one of the most memorable experiences which a motoring enthusiast can achieve.

Perhaps the best-known view of this particular car! The locker contains the spare wheel.

# HIGH PERFORMANCE MODELS FOR ALL OCCASIONS

The ALLARD Saloon, with aluminium-panelled coachbuilt body, incorporates all the good features of the previous models, including sports-car manners on the road, plus such refinements as independently-adjustable close-fitting front seats allowing ample room for 3 abreast, luxurious hide upholstery with Latex cushion rubber, controlled air conditioning, interior lighting with door-operated switch, and, for overseas models only at present, heating equipment.

Other good points are an opening windscreen for safe driving in fog and comfort in heat, and a very spacious lockable luggage boot with interior lighting.

**P.1 2-DOOR SALOON**

**J.2 COMPETITION 2-SEATER**

Built mainly for participation in sporting events, the J.2 Competition 2-Seater is undoubtedly destined to create many sensations in that field and to add to the long list of successes achieved by previous ALLARD models.

For the benefit of sporting enthusiasts overseas, the chassis is specially designed to accommodate many of the larger capacity American engines, and the car can be supplied less engine if preferred.

With its aluminium body the dry weight of the complete car is only 2006 lb.

The K.2. Sports 2-Seater has been designed for the motorist who prefers a touring car which is capable of putting up a good sports performance.

It has high-compression cylinder heads, dual induction with twin Solex carburetters, remote centre gear change and racing-type fly-off handbrake. Like the J.2, the chassis has been designed to accommodate alternative engines if required.

The body is aluminium-panelled and has a large lockable luggage boot and all-weather equipment.

**K.2 SPORTS 2-SEATER**

DISTINCTION

IN

APPEARANCE

AND

PERFORMANCE

## 50 POST-WAR INTERNATIONAL COMPETITION SUCCESSES

## Saloon

ENGINE rated at 30 h.p. 77.79 mm. bore by 95.25 mm. stroke—3622 ccs. capacity. V.8 L head side valve—2 banks of 4 cylinders at 90 degrees off-set. Cast alloy crankshaft carried in 3 large diameter main bearings—detachable cylinder heads—valves of silicon chromium alloy steel—pistons of aluminium alloy—full force oil lubrication system—floating power 3 point suspension—dual down-draught carburetter with single control—special coil and distributor for high revs. with automatic control—large area single plate cushioned clutch centrifugally assisted.

TRANSMISSION gear box providing 3 forward speeds and reverse—synchromesh 2nd and top—all gears helically cut and silent—steering column gear change.

Ratios :—3.78 top ; 6.7 second ; 11.8 first ; 15.1 reverse. Drive between gear box and rear axle is by tubular propeller shaft with single universal joint enclosed in torque tube.

REAR AXLE. Three-quarter floating axle shafts carried on roller bearings—robust spiral bevel crown and pinion carried on double bearings, with outrigger bearing supporting pinion. Ratio 3.78 to 1.

FRONT AXLE. Independently sprung—adjustable hub bearings—axle pivots and steering arm fitted with oilless silent bloc bushes—self-adjusting type steering knuckle joints.

## J.2 Competition 2-Seater

ENGINE. 81 mm. bore by 95.25 mm. stroke—3917 ccs. capacity—V.8 overhead valves—detachable aluminium heads—compression ratio 7 to 1 (optional 8 to 1)—develops 140 b.h.p. at 4000 r.p.m.—valves 1.875 in. inlet, 1.500 in. exhaust—hemispherical combustion space with centrally placed plugs—dual Solex carburetters—aluminium alloy pistons—full-force oil lubrication—3-point floating power suspension—large area single-plate clutch.

TRANSMISSION. Gear box providing 3 forward speeds and reverse—synchromesh 2nd and top—all gears helically cut and silent—remote control gear change lever.

Ratios :—3.5 top ; 6.19 second ; 10.9 first ; Close ratio :—(3.5 ; 4.69 ; 6.2) at extra cost.

REAR AXLE. de Dion type, located by radius arms to centre of frame, brakes located on axle—robust spiral bevel crown and pinion carried on double bearings, with outrigger bearing supporting pinion. Ratio :—3.5 to 1 ; Optional ratios :—3.78 or 4.11 to 1.

FRONT AXLE. Independent swing arm axles—adjustable hub bearings—axle pivots and steering arm fitted with oilless silent bloc bushes—self adjusting type steering knuckle joints.

STEERING. Marles cam gear, high ratio, provided with spring type steering wheel. Column is adjustable for position. Left or right hand drive optional to order.

BRAKES. Four wheel two shoe assemblies—2 leading shoe type on front wheels—hydraulically operated—Alfin drums—handbrake quick release racing type operating on rear wheels only—forged dural pedals.

SUSPENSION—Coil springs front and rear—tubular hydraulic shock-absorbers all round.

## K.2 Sports 2-Seater

ENGINE rated at 30 h.p. 77.79 mm. bore by 95.25 mm. stroke—3622 ccs. capacity. V.8 L head side valve—2 banks of 4 cylinders at 90 degrees off-set—Special high-compression aluminium cylinder heads. Ratio :—⅛ to 1. Optional : 8 to 1. Cast alloy crankshaft carried in 3 large diameter main bearings—detachable cylinder heads—valves of silicon chromium alloy steel—pistons of aluminium alloy—full force oil lubrication system—floating power 3 point suspension—dual induction with twin Solex carburetters—special coil and distributor for high revs. with automatic control—large area single plate cushioned clutch centrifugally assisted.

TRANSMISSION gear box providing 3 forward speeds and reverse—synchromesh 2nd and top—all gears helically cut and silent—remote control centre gear change.

Ratios :—3.78 top ; 6.7 second ; 11.8 first ; 15.1 reverse. Drive between gear box and rear axle is by tubular propeller shaft with single universal joint enclosed in torque tube.

REAR AXLE. Three-quarter floating axle shafts carried on roller bearings—robust spiral bevel crown and pinion carried on double bearings, with outrigger bearing supporting pinion. Ratio, 3.78 to 1.

FRONT AXLE. Independently sprung—adjustable hub bearings—axle pivots and steering arm fitted with oilless silent bloc bushes—self-adjusting type steering knuckle joints.

STEERING. Marles cam gear, high ratio, provided with full adjustment spring type telescopic steering wheel. Column is adjustable for position. Left or right hand drive optional to order.

BRAKES. 12 in. Lockheed hydraulic, 2 leading shoes at front.

SUSPENSION. Coil springs on front transverse cantilever spring at rear—oilless shackles—hydraulic shock absorbers all round.

FRAME. Heavy box section well braced with cross members. Track:—front 4 ft. 8 in.; rear 4 ft. 10 in. Wheel-base—9 ft. 4 in. Ground clearance 9 in.

WHEELS. Easy clean type. TYRES. 5—6.25 by 16.

FUEL SYSTEM.—Rear petrol tank capacity of 20 gallons—petrol feed incorporating an electrically operated reserve.

EXHAUST SYSTEM. Dual manifolds and large diameter pipes with straight through silencers.

LIGHTING. 12 volt compensated voltage control with large capacity battery. Head lamps with hand-operated dipper switch—dual stop and tail lamps—automatic reversing light.

EQUIPMENT. Fitted facia board with speedometer, oil pressure, petrol and water gauges, ammeter, clock, dash lights, etc. Dual arm electric wiper and interior mirror. Self-cancelling trafficators.

WEIGHT. Approx. 29 cwts.

FRAME. Heavy section well braced with tubular cross members. Track :—front, 4 ft. 8 in. ; rear, 4 ft. 4 in. Wheel-base :—8 ft. 4 in.

WHEELS. Easy clean type. TYRES. 6.00 by 16.

FUEL SYSTEM. Rear petrol tank capacity 20 gallons—petrol feed incorporating a reserve. Dual feed through SU electric pump and AC mechanical pump, with dual piping to tank.

EXHAUST SYSTEM. 3-branch manifolds and large diameter pipes with straight through silencers.

LIGHTING. 12 volt compensated voltage control with large capacity battery. Head lamps with hand operated dipper switch.

EQUIPMENT. Fitted facia board with speedometer, rev. counter, oil pressure, petrol and water gauges, ammeter, etc.

BODYWORK. Competition 2-Seater, 2-door, aluminium lightweight shell body conforms with International Sportscar Regulations—body constructed in two pieces to facilitate removal from the chassis, leaving all instruments wiring and flooring intact and attached to the chassis—3 steel tubes have been expressly designed to carry the body shell and ensure extreme rigidity—body is fitted with small cycle-type front wings and 2 aero screens.

WEIGHT. Approx. 18 cwts.

EXTRAS. Orders can be accepted, at extra cost, for the following items :—

Full size wings.
Full size windscreen with dual electric wipers and hood.
Non-standard gears.
Luggage grid.

STEERING. Marles cam gear, high ratio, provided with full adjustment spring type telescopic steering wheel. Column is adjustable for position. Left or right hand drive optional to order.

BRAKES. 12 in. Lockheed hydraulic, 2 leading shoes at front.

SUSPENSION. Coil springs on front, transverse cantilever spring at rear—oilless shackles—hydraulic shock absorbers all round.

FRAME. Heavy box section well braced with cross members. Track :—front 4 ft. 8 in. ; rear 4 ft. 4 in. Wheel-base—8 ft. 10 in. Ground clearance 9 in.

WHEELS. Easy clean type. TYRES. 5—6.25 by 16.

FUEL SYSTEM. Rear petrol tank capacity of 17½ gallons—petrol feed incorporating an electrically operated reserve.

EXHAUST SYSTEM. Dual manifolds and large diameter pipes with straight through silencers.

LIGHTING. 12 volt compensated voltage control with large capacity battery. Head lamps with hand-operated dipper switch—dual stop and tail lamps.

EQUIPMENT. Fitted facia board with rev. counter, speedometer, oil pressure, petrol and water gauges, ammeter, clock, dash lights, etc. Dual arm electric wiper and interior mirror.

WEIGHT. Approx. 22 cwts.

**ALLARD MOTOR COMPANY LTD., 24-28 CLAPHAM HIGH STREET, LONDON, S.W.4**

*Cables :* Almotco, London          *Telegrams :* Almotco, Clapcom, London.          *'Phone :* Macaulay 3201-2-3

# Emphasis On Sports Cars—

# On the Road with the T.T. Chrysler-Allard

IT never rains but it pours. And pour it did most of the time we had the Chrysler-Allard out on test. Whatever else this car has, so far as protection from the elements is concerned you might just as well jump into a river. The fact that in spite of repeated drenchings driver and passenger developed a warm respect for this motor car is mainly attributable to the splendid cornering, roadholding and suspension factors of the latest Allard chassis.

This is not to suggest that these cars do not GO in a very notable manner; but wet roads strewn with a carpet of autumn leaves do not permit of satisfactory experimentation with 180 b.h.p. in a 24 cwt. car so far as logging good acceleration times are concerned. That driving the T.T. Chrysler-Allard, with its power/weight ratio of 215 b.h.p./ton was pleasurable even under these conditions is a fine tribute to the excellence of its roadholding. But before we go on to discuss details of this exciting car's make-up, we had better explain the Allard which had unexpectedly come into our hands during the wettest part of November.

It was the car driven by Sydney Allard in this year's T.T. race, when it proved less potent than he had hoped and finally retired with back axle trouble. Since the race the four-carburetter Chrysler "Fire Power" V8 engine has been replaced by a standard single-carburetter unit of this kind, so that what we had for test was virtually a normal J2X Allard, with the important proviso that most customers would want to put back the four "gas works" and probably do other "souping" besides.

The engine apart, the car was in T.T. guise, even to white racing number discs on the green body, and all the more exciting for that. It has the divided-axle coil spring i.f.s. with the long radius arms running forward, a three-speed Ford gearbox with remote control and the Allard de Dion back end with inboard brake drums and coil spring suspension. Weather protection was confined to twin aero screens, or rather, mica wind-breaks, but you sit well above these! The tail is full of fuel tank, accessible through a hole at the back covered with a panel held by quick-action fasteners. The capacity of this fuel tank constitutes a minor mystery, for although Mr. Bullen, Allard's publicity man, quoted 36 gallons in his Motor Show literature, he later brought this up to 42 gallons in a MOTOR SPORT advertisement, whereas technical-chap Tom Lush says no, it's 38 gallons, plus two in reserve. Not that it really matters; the point is that the J2 Allard had a capacity of about 20 gallons, whereas the new J2X carries something in the region of twice as much fuel, to obviate refuelling pauses in races and to give a touring range of some 400 miles.

Continuing with detail, the car came with Dunlop racing tyres on its smart centre-lock wire wheels, 7.00 by 16 at the back, 6.00 by 16 at the front and for a spare. The double-hump scuttle is backed by an instrument panel that carries only necessities—a 5-in. 6,000-r.p.m. Smiths rev.-counter before the driver, matched by a Smiths speedometer calibrated to 140 m.p.h., and notable for a highly commendable steadiness of recording, a combined oil gauge and water

thermometer dial, a happy fuel gauge that registered "full" continually whatever the content of the tank (a pleasant contrast to that of the Editorial vehicle, which habitually registers all but "empty"!), an ammeter and the usual switches and controls, of which those for wipers, panel light and mixture (automatic choke) were inoperative.

The gear-lever is a rather wobbly affair set a thought far forward, the hand-brake lies horizontally neatly below the driver's door-sill, but its fly-off action was rather difficult to appreciate after the release mechanism had come out by the roots. The driving position was clearly meant for a *big* man like Sydney Allard and as the Editor is a *medium* man and his colleague on this occasion was a *small* man, both had to take cushions with them, like a 'bus driver. They reflected a bit about expensive cars with non-adjustable seats, decided that on a competition job like this Allard the car would be tailored to its owner, but were left wondering what would happen if said owner ever wanted to lend the car to wife or friends. A further embarrassment, but only because we were respectively *medium* and *small*, was the fact that the treadle accelerator was further forward than the other pedals, and possessed of *very* strong springs—even the clutch pedal required to be pushed right down to obtain grate-free gear engagement and this also was awkward. However, we found *more* cushions.

Once properly settled in the driving seat the panorama ahead could be admired; and admire is the right word, for in spite of the long lift-up bonnet with its air-intake goitre (replacing the rather naughty twin affairs which Sydney affected for the T.T.) visibility is first-class, even the front wheels being visible beneath their helmet wings. Elbow room, too, is entirely unrestricted. Entry and egress does not call for slacks-for-women and the light, simple doors shut and open easily.

To digress for a moment, the air-intake goitre is the new one which lets plenty of the surrounding atmosphere into the engine, so that it can be used with one, two or four carburetters without modification. We unstrapped, undid and raised the featherweight bonnet-panel to see what one Carter carburetter looks like and there it was sitting on a scientific maze of aluminium-painted inlet and water piping too complex to describe. Room has been found for an F.4 Fram filter, ignition is by Lucas coil and Auto-Lite Splashproof distributor, and the dipstick is very accessible providing you have room to walk away from the car as you withdraw it, sabre-fashion, from its scabbard. A belt over a huge pulley drives a big water impeller and from this another belt drives the little dynamo, from which a flexible drive *via* a reduction gearbox goes to the rev.-counter. The plugs

*EXCITING MOTOR-CAR.—The 5.4-litre 180 b.h.p. Chrysler-engined T.T. Allard tested by* MOTOR SPORT, *seen in action at Dundrod. The twin air-intakes, here covering four carburetters, have been replaced by a new style of air-inlet.*

[MOTOR SPORT *copyright.*]

live under metal strips along each o.h.v. cover and we wouldn't like to have to change one during a hard-fought race. Hot air leaves the bonnet through three little peep-holes on each side, so these are *not* purely for show. Fuel feed is by a mechanical pump, abetted by an electric pump which also feeds the reserve fuel.

That, then, is the T.T. Allard as presented to us. Someone said that not only has it i.f.s., but b.f. and i., but we professed not to understand.

There is, however, great charm in the way the 5.4-litre V8 Chrysler engine delivers the urge. It will " pobble " you along in top gear at 10 m.p.h. with scarcely a sound or you can open up, still in top, to the " typically Sydney " beat of those dual twin-exhausts and, after 40 m.p.h. be wafted straight up to 90 m.p.h. almost before you have got your eyes off the speedometer and onto the terrain ahead. On the other hand you can rev.-up quite briskly, change down, and enjoy acceleration that journalists like myself describe as electrifying. As you lift your foot, the exhausts bellow an inspiring war song on the over-run.

Two things occur about this short-stroke V8 engine. One is that, although it looks a fearful mass of metal, which only an Allard's broad bonnet amongst sports cars could accommodate, the total weight of the J2X is only 24 cwt. 14 lb., ready to run, with about seven gallons of fuel but without occupants—a reasonable figure for a 5.4-litre car. The other point is that, like other many-litred cars in the past, the J2X's big engine provides effortless cruising—this T.T. version was geared 26.5 m.p.h. per 1,000 r.p.m. in top gear, so that, cruising at 70, the crankshaft was turning at less than 2,650 r.p.m.

The remote gear-lever, which has no stop for reverse, is not up to the best sports car standards, but as the two lower ratios are either not required at all in a downward direction, or would not be needed quickly except during a race, it is easy to overlook the difficulty Allard has had in coupling three Ford speeds to a sports car change. The clutch tended to drag, so that some gear crunching resulted, but take-up is very smooth, although a tendency to slip was noticed when trying a standing start quarter-mile.

We have said that rain defeated accurate logging of speed and acceleration. We got as far as checking the speedometer, finding that at 53 m.p.h. it indicated 60 and we did a few very wet s.s. quarter miles and a few 0-50s, after which notebook was converted to porridge and pneumonia seemed imminent.—N.B, the seat cushions are firmly attached to the body, annoying when you wish to wring them out ! We discovered two things while thus wetly engaged—the de Dion back axle is thoroughly worth while, reducing to a minimum wheelspin under fierce acceleration where many cars would have spun sideways, while the Chrysler develops its power at modest speeds, so that early changes out of bottom and middle cogs caught us up quickest with the stop-watch. Conditions were wholly unfavourable ; the best s.s. quarter mile time was 18.1 sec., the best 0-50 m.p.h. time 8.8 sec.

As it happened, there was little point in logging the performance of this particular Allard, for these reasons : It is confessedly slower than the Cadillac-

powered cars because it has only one carburetter. In the States they would soon throw away the one-carburetter manifolding and pour the soup, when the performance characteristics would presumably be transformed. Finally, we were warned that the hydraulic tappets get a thought confused above 4,200 r.p.m. One shot at a timed quarter-mile approached through an 80-m.p.h. bend in pouring rain to be confronted by an onward-coming van, gave us 90 m.p.h. when, in spite of the speedometer saying 100, both driver and passenger would have settled for 75/80. In brief, 90 m.p.h. is chicken-feed to the T.T. Allard " anywhere, anytime," with lots more to come under that stiff throttle, so that a comfortable maximum of over 100 m.p.h. is definitely to be expected.

Leaving performance logging for finer days we concentrated on the brilliant

---

### THE J2X ALLARD TWO-SEATER

(Standard Competition Version)

*Engine :* V8, 96.8 by 92 mm (5,420 c.c.) ; 180 b.h.p. at 3,800 r.p.m. (180 b.h.p. with four carburetters).

*Gear Ratios:* first, 10.0 to 1 ; second, 5.75 to 1 ; top, 3.27 to 1.

*Tyres :* 6.00 by 16 Dunlop on centre-lock wire wheels.

*Weight :* (T.T. car) 24 cwt 14 lb., less occupants, with approximately seven gallons of fuel.

*Steering Ratio :* 3¼ turns, lock to lock.

*Fuel Capacity :* 40 gallons (two in reserve). Range approximately 400 miles.

*Wheelbase :* 8 ft. 4 in.

*Track :* Front, 4 ft. 8 in. ; rear, 4 ft. 4 in.

*Price :* £1,100 (£1,712 12s. 4d. with p.t.).

*Makers :* Allard Motor Co., Ltd., 24–28, High Street, Clapham. London, S.W.4.

---

handling qualities of this he-man motor car. Here the slippery roads enhanced, rather than diminished, the Allard's behaviour and our esteem of it. The steering is extremely light and smooth and at first seems low-geared, asking 3¼ turns, lock to lock. But the lock is generous, so that in normal motoring the low-geared effect is not pronounced, especially as there is powerful castor-action, although the thought persists that if a high-speed slide were to develop, winding the Allard out might prove next to impossible. Return motion is not transmitted except when the front wheels strike a particularly severe bump. There is, however, some movement of the scuttle which moves the column with it on bad roads, suggesting that the body frame is not so stiff as the excellent chassis.

Round bends and corners the Allard holds a predetermined course impeccably ; over or under-steer not pronounced but with emphasis on the latter. Somewhat more than wrist flexion is needed to change direction, but the steering is entirely effortless. What is so very im-

pressive is the way the car sits down and the manner in which the de Dion back axle kills both wheelspin and sideslip on slippery surfaces. Round a corner you can kick the power on and the car remains stable, when in other cars correction would be necessary. In the same way the J2X Allard rushes round corners at speed so that the driver feels that the back wheels *must* slip an inch or two, yet they follow strictly the correct path. It is this safety factor that makes so pleasant to drive a car which, contemplated beforehand, looks as if it could be a " handful." Roll is a word outside the vocabulary of the Allard driver when discussing his own car.

Over bad roads the Allard is very comfortable, too, even when the front wheels are being encouraged to use the full travel of the Armstrong-damped front suspension. Add to this Lockheed brakes with 2LS at the front, inboard Alfin drums at the back, which can be stamped on hard from 90 m.p.h. in the wet and still pull up the car " all-square " and which, given fairly determined pressure, are amply powerful, and the Allard emerges as one of those desirable motor cars it is a rare pleasure to drive for driving's sake. Sydney Allard is a past master at adapting low-stressed American-style engines to fast chassis and his Chrysler JX2 is an intriguing proposition, although no doubt the Cadillac or Ardun versions are nearly as entertaining. We believe, however, that the considerable mass of the Chrysler engine, moved 7½ in. further forward in the chassis to provide a more roomy cockpit, humours weight distribution and eliminates a tendency to pitch noticeable in the earlier J2 Allard.

Purposely, this " Competition " model is spartan, body frame tubes unconcealed in places, upholstery sparse but comfortable where provided, the body not devoid of rattles. But, a slight imperfection in the gear-change apart, any criticisms we have are of a minor nature—such as a tendency for a bonnet stud to chafe the top water hose, the hand-brake defect, and an annoying tendency for the throttle to stick partly open in spite of three throttle springs. Incidentally, the engine started impeccably and pulled away from stone cold ; it normally ran at less than 170 degrees F. and the pressure of the S.A.E. 20 oil rose with engine speed to a maximum of 50 lb./sq. in.

Details of the standard J2X model are appended in the table and we wi l sum up by saying that, like a Comper Swift to aviation enthusiasts, the Chrysler-Allard is a fine car for the purpose for which it is intended—competition work, or for taking out in good weather for the sheer fun to be had from so doing.

Alack, that it is for export only.—W. B.

◆◆◆◆◆◆◆◆◆◆◆◆◆◆◆◆◆◆◆◆◆◆◆◆◆◆◆◆◆◆◆◆◆◆

### ALLARD SUCCESS

Bill Pollack, driving Tom Carstens' Allard J2, won the Reno Road Race, while the owner took the car over to win the Virginia Lake Handicap Race at the same meeting, making fastest qualifying time. The car was the only Allard in either event, out of an entry list of 38 in the first and 24 in the latter event.

# The Allard Drophead Coupe

## A High-performance Convertible with a Strong Appeal to Drivers Who Want Motoring Rather than Mere Transport

comparisons, it is worth relating the figures to those of other contemporary cars. That can well be done by considering the 27 varied cars tested by "The Motor" in the "car year," October, 1950, to October, 1951. If, for the purpose in hand, one takes the aggregate time to accelerate from 0-60 m.p.h. through the gears and from 20-60 m.p.h. in top gear, then this 3·6-litre V8-engined Allard model has been beaten by only three other cars—very handsomely by another Allard (the 5½-litre Cadillac-engined J2), by a margin of 3·2 secs by a 4½-litre saloon costing two and a half times the price, and by 0·8 sec. by a two-seater, two-litre sports

COMING to the Allard M2X drophead coupé with a mind conditioned by the standards of normal post-war cars, one very rapidly decides that the engine is rough and mechanically noisy, that the suspension is harsh and that the steering is sensitive to a rather disconcerting degree. All this is undeniably true, and yet one feels oddly good-humoured about it all. More oddly still, one's good humour is not entirely accounted for by the inevitable afterthought, ". . . but it *does* go!" Sheer performance is certainly the outstanding merit of this, the most staid model in the Allard range, but there is much more to it than that, an indefinable feeling of affection that mounts with the miles.

How much this is due to the now rare combination of a big engine, light weight, and a preponderance of load on the rear wheels, and how much to other qualities, readers will have to decide for themselves on the more detailed analysis of performance characteristics which follow.

Before coming to that, however, we must talk about the weather. During our tenure as an M2X driver, the following conditions were encountered: Dry roads and a howling gale; wet roads with the same howling gale plus teeming rain; wet cobbles and tramlines with Christmas shoppers acting as Christmas shoppers

**TOURING TRIM**—The canvas top of the Allard convertible disappears completely from view to leave a good-looking four seater touring car.

**POTTED POWER**—The test car was equipped with the British-built 30 h.p. type of Ford V8 engine, light alloy cylinder heads giving some extra power. For export markets, the chassis can also accommodate V8 engines of greater size.

will on a wet evening; dry, clear roads and crisp winter sunshine with the thermometer dropping rapidly below freezing as the sun went down; and finally, hard frosty roads, showing white with rime in the headlamp beams and just a trace of mist to make unexpected corners more unexpected. No one can say that the car did not have opportunities to reveal its vices and its virtues.

Performance being one of the outstanding qualities of this car, more should be said on this point at the outset; as mere figures do not convey so much to some as

car which, however, was fractionally slower on maximum speed.

The fact that another Allard easily headed the list on this basis, places the car under review in its correct perspective—as the model intended by its makers for the driver whose sporting leanings are strong but who, for reasons of Anno Domini, family, business, or just simple preference, requires four seats and coupé comfort.

To revert to acceleration, the M2X is one of those accommodating motor cars with an extremely wide overlap on its gear capabilities. In top, it reveals almost constant acceleration from 10 to 60 m.p.h., and remains very lively right up to its maximum of over 85 m.p.h.; in second, its range is from a walking pace to 67 m.p.h., if taken to the limit; and first gear will take one from rest to the legal limit in built-up areas in a single exhilarating bound, with still more in hand.

In practice, the Allard can also be used as a top-gear car, since it will climb a gradient of approximately 1-in-8 without a change and is pleasantly flexible, although a momentary hesitation is noticeable if the throttle is opened suddenly below 20 m.p.h. As already hinted,

**CLASSIC STYLE**—Adjustable spring-spoke steering wheel, central remote gear control, well-placed hand brake, neat facia panel carrying easy-to-read instruments, opening windscreen: such details as these can endear a car to the keen motorist.

there is a distinct degree of roughness when the engine is working hard, and the unit is mechanically noisy under the same conditions (although, oddly enough, very quiet on tick-over), but the pronounced growl it emits when called upon to scamper rapidly past a car ahead is somehow reassuring rather than displeasing. This ability to overtake and revert rapidly to its own side of the road as though nothing had happened is, in fact, one of the great charms of the car.

Another is the capacity of the engine for high revs, this, no doubt, being due to the use of a special high-compression finned alloy cylinder head fitted to the Ford V8 engine by Allard. Pinking is, however, rather obtrusive on Pool petrol. Starting proved remarkably rapid and sure, even with the temperature well below freezing.

### Wide Cruising Range

With most cars, one feels that a particular speed represents a desirable cruising limit; in this case, cruising speed is what one likes to make it within the very wide top-gear range and it is interesting to note, in this connection, that maximum speed and a piston speed of 2,500 ft. per min. almost exactly synchronize.

In handling qualities, the car is unusual in that the combination of suspension (divided axle and coil springs at the front and transverse leaf at the rear) and weight distribution (with 55 per cent. of the load on the back axle) produce characteristics which are distinctly individual. On the straight, there is a degree of oversteer which makes the car unusually sensitive to cross winds or changing camber, the effect being particularly noticeable if the tyre pressures are allowed to drop even a pound or two below recommendations; against that, the steering is light and moderately high-geared, so that correction becomes almost second nature after a few miles.

On corners, the oversteer characteristic is less pronounced and never involves the driver in any disconcerting paying-out of lock. Hard acceleration, of course, emphasizes the oversteer tendency and can in fact usefully be employed at the right moment to assist cornering.

With the weight distribution employed,

**ADEQUATE ACCESS** —Two doors of large size, in conjunction with tipping seat backs (prone as usual to contact the horn button!) provide reasonably easy access to back seats which are comfortable for use on long journeys.

break-away, if a slide does occur, is always at the rear and can be checked instantly and with no trouble before it has time to develop. In practice, the car shows an unusual reluctance to slide at all, unless deliberately provoked; wheel adhesion is, in fact, of a very high order, the car revealing a very distinct reluctance to spin its wheels even on slippery roads, despite the power available. All these characteristics, difficult to put adequately into words, add up to handling qualities which not only inspire confidence, but give a driver familiar with the car both an unusual sense of mastery and a pleasure in driving, *per se*, which is not so usual as it used to be.

To these points, one can add that the brakes respond excellently and have no vices bar the merest suggestion of squeak occasionally, and that the suspension, although harsh by modern standards (and thereby apt to emphasize one or two body rattles on the car tried), offers a very satisfactory standard of all-round journey comfort.

Fuel consumption checks were made under a variety of conditions (none calculated to be flattering) and varied from 16·3 m.p.g. for 326 miles which included the performance tests to 17·4 m.p.g. for 174 miles of fast main road running. Both figures could obviously be bettered under touring conditions. Oil consumption was less satisfactory, however, the engine showing a distinct thirst in this direction.

In the matter of amenities, the M2X has obviously been designed with a practical appreciation of the needs of people who *like* motoring. The controls are well placed and reveal no awkward oversights, the instruments and switches are equally well planned, the seats give good support

in an alert position, and a Bluemel spring-spoke wheel and adjustable column help to accommodate drivers of varying height and reach. Separately-adjustable close-up seats have the advantage that, at a pinch, three can be accommodated in the front (there being room for the extra passenger's legs to the left of the gear lever) and the squabs tip forward to give access (without too much agility) to the rear seats; the latter, whilst not offering luxury or providing an excess of knee-room, do provide comfortable seating for two full-sized people who, incidentally, enjoy better side vision than in most cars of this type.

Visibility, in fact, is generally very good (apart from a mirror so placed as to give an indiscreetly short range of view for so lively a car) and many will appreciate the opening windscreen.

### Conversion is Easy

Bar the fact that the fabric material used is of a type which shrinks when wet and stretches when dry, the head is well planned and proved water- and draughtproof in high wind and rain; erection and furling call for no irritating struggles and the job can be tackled by one person, although frankly easier with two. With the head down, motoring is really pleasant and the inevitable back draught is not obtrusive except at high speeds.

Luggage accommodation is adequate (it would be generous if the spare wheel did not occupy part of the boot floor) and neat tool lockers are built into the boot sides; inside the body, there is a parcel shelf below the facia, really large door pockets and two handy ledges (excellent for cups or glasses) just forward of the hood trough which, in itself, offers commodious stowage space when the car is closed.

As for equipment, all the usual fittings are provided, including a really efficient Clayton heater and demister of the fresh-air type, twin visors, boot and under-bonnet lights, a reserve tap for the 20-gallon tank, courtesy lights under the facia and double-dipping headlamps which are adequate but could be very much better for high speeds.

Altogether, the Allard M2X drophead coupé is a most likeable car, the faults in which one is ready to forgive because (quite apart from the advantages of Ford service in respect of the main components) it has so much else to offer the driver who does not want transport so much as motoring—and there is a world of difference between the two.

CLOSED UP—In wet weather trim, the car has neat roof contours and ample window areas, the rear window panel being removable to provide ventilation for the opposite extreme conditions of hot sunshine. Much greater luggage space is provided in this body than in earlier types of Allard convertible.

**Make:** Allard  **Type:** M2X Drophead Coupé

**Makers:** The Allard Motor Co., Ltd., 24-28, Clapham High St., London, S.W.4

## Dimensions and Seating

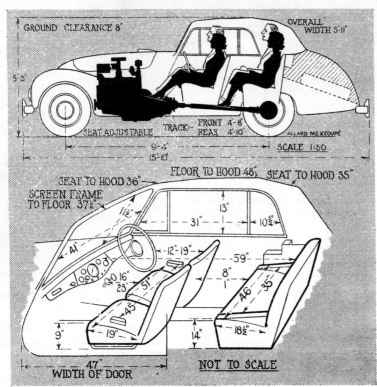

GROUND CLEARANCE 8"
OVERALL WIDTH 5'-11"
5'-3"
SEAT ADJUSTABLE  TRACK:- FRONT 4'-8"  REAR 4'-10"
ALLARD M2X COUPÉ
9'-4"
15'-10"
SCALE 1:50

SEAT TO HOOD 36"  FLOOR TO HOOD 48½"  SEAT TO HOOD 35"
SCREEN FRAME TO FLOOR 37½"
11½"  13"  10¾"
41"  31"
12"-19"  59"
16"  8"
23"  46"  35"
9"  5'1"  19"  14"  18½"
WIDTH OF DOOR 47"  NOT TO SCALE

## In Brief

Price £1,150, plus purchase tax £640 7s. 11d., equals £1,790 7s. 11d.
Capacity .. .. .. 3,622 c.c.
Unladen kerb weight .. 28 cwt.
Fuel consumption .. ..17.4 m.p.g.
Maximum speed .. ..85.5 m.p.h.
Maximum speed on 1 in 20 gradient .. .. 77 m.p.h.
Maximum top gear gradient  1 in 8.2
Acceleration
10-30 m.p.h. in top .. 8.4 secs.
0-50 m.p.h. through gears 10.3 secs.
Gearing 21.5 m.p.h. in top at 1,000 r.p.m. 86 m.p.h. at 2,500 ft. per min. piston speed.

## Specification

**Engine**

| | | |
|---|---|---|
| Cylinders .. .. .. .. .. | V8 |
| Bore .. .. .. .. .. | 78 mm. |
| Stroke .. .. .. .. | 95.2 mm. |
| Cubic capacity .. .. .. | 3,622 c.c. |
| Piston area .. .. .. | 59.2 sq. in. |
| Valves .. .. .. .. .. | Side |
| Compression ratio .. .. .. | 7/1 |
| Max. power .. .. .. | 90 b.h.p. |
| at .. .. .. .. | 3,600 r.p.m. |
| Piston speed at max. b.h.p. | 2,250 ft. per. min. |
| Carburetter  Ford downdraught (double choke) |
| Ignition .. .. .. .. | Lucas coil |
| Sparking plugs .. Champion j10 com. (14 mm.) |
| Fuel pump .. .. .. | AC. mechanical |
| Oil filter .. .. .. | Gauze at oil pump |

**Transmission**

| | | |
|---|---|---|
| Clutch .. Ford S.D.P. (centrifugally assisted) |
| Top gear (s/m) .. .. .. .. | 3.78 |
| 2nd gear (s/m) .. .. .. | 6.7 |
| 1st gear .. .. .. .. | 11.8 |
| Propeller shaft .. Enclosed (torque tube) |
| Final drive .. .. .. | Spiral bevel |

**Chassis**

| | | |
|---|---|---|
| Brakes .. Lockheed Hydraulic (2 LS on front) |
| Brake drum diameter .. .. | 12 ins. |
| Friction lining area .. | 165 sq. ins. |
| Suspension | |
| front .. Independent (coil and divided axle) |
| rear .. .. .. | Transverse leaf |
| Shock absorbers.. .. Armstrong telescopic |
| Tyres .. .. .. .. | 6.25 × 16 |

**Steering**

| | | |
|---|---|---|
| Steering gear .. .. .. | Marles |
| Turning circle .. 45 ft. (right), 49 ft. (left) |
| Turns of steering wheel, lock to lock .. | 3 |

**Performance factors** (at laden weight as tested)

| | |
|---|---|
| Piston area, sq. in. per ton .. | 37.0 |
| Brake lining area, sq. in. per ton .. | 103 |
| Specific displacement, litres per ton mile | 3,180 |

## Maintenance

**Fuel tank:** 20 gallons (including 2 reserve). **Sump:** 8 pints, S.A.E. 30 (summer), S.A.E. 20 (winter). **Gearbox:** 2 pints S.A.E. 90 (E.P.). **Rear axle:** 2½ pints S.A.E. 90 (E.P.). **Steering gear:** S.A.E. 90 (E.P.). **Radiator:** 36 pints (2 drain taps). **Chassis lubrication:** By grease gun every 1,000 miles to 16 points. **Ignition timing:** 4 degrees before T.D.C. **Spark plug gap:** 0.022 in. **Contact breaker gap:** 0.014 in.—0.016 in. **Valve timing:** Inlet opens at T.D.C. and closes 44 degrees after B.D.C. Exhaust opens 48 degrees before B.D.C. and closes 6½ degrees after T.D.C. **Tappet clearances (cold):** Inlet 0.0125 in. Exhaust 0.016 in. **Front wheel toe-in:** ⅛ in. **Camber angle:** 2-4 degrees at normal loading. **Caster angle:** 2 degrees. **Tyre pressures:** Front 22 lb., rear 28 lb. **Brake Fluid:** Lockheed. **Battery:** Lucas (two 6-volt, 60 amp/hr. units). **Lamp bulbs:** 12-volt: Head lamps, 42/36 watt (Lucas No. 354); side lamps, 3 watt; stop and tail light, 36/6 watt; number plate, 6 watt.

Ref. B/37/52

## Test Conditions

Very cold dry weather with little wind, smooth tarmac surface. Pool petrol. Performance tests carried out with head and windows in closed position.

## Test Data

**ACCELERATION TIMES on two Upper Ratios**

| | Top | 2nd |
|---|---|---|
| 10-30 m.p.h. .. .. .. .. .. .. | 8.4 secs. | 4.4 secs. |
| 20-40 m.p.h. .. .. .. .. .. .. | 7.8 secs. | 4.2 secs. |
| 30-50 m.p.h. .. .. .. .. .. .. | 8.3 secs. | 5.5 secs. |
| 40-60 m.p.h. .. .. .. .. .. .. | 9.9 secs. | — |
| 50-70 m.p.h. .. .. .. .. .. .. | 12.1 secs. | — |

**ACCELERATION TIMES Through Gears**

| | |
|---|---|
| 0-30 m.p.h. .. .. .. .. | 4.1 secs. |
| 0-40 m.p.h. .. .. .. .. | 7.1 secs. |
| 0-50 m.p.h. .. .. .. .. | 10.3 secs. |
| 0-60 m.p.h. .. .. .. .. | 15.7 secs. |
| 0-70 m.p.h. .. .. .. .. | 22.9 secs. |
| Standing Quarter Mile .. .. | 20.3 secs. |

**FUEL CONSUMPTION**

25.5 m.p.g. at constant 30 m.p.h.
24.0 m.p.g. at constant 40 m.p.h.
21.5 m.p.g. at constant 50 m.p.h.
18.0 m.p.g. at constant 60 m.p.h.
15.5 m.p.g. at constant 70 m.p.h.
Overall consumption for 174 miles, 10 gallons, equals 17.4 m.p.g. (see text).

**HILL CLIMBING** (at steady speeds)

| | |
|---|---|
| Max. top gear speed on 1 in 20 .. .. .. | 77 m.p.h. |
| Max. top gear speed on 1 in 15 .. .. .. | 72 m.p.h. |
| Max. top gear speed on 1 in 10 .. .. .. | 56 m.p.h. |
| Max. gradient on top gear .. .. 1 in 8.2 (Tapley 270 lb./ton) |
| Max. gradient on 2nd gear .. .. 1 in 4.7 (Tapley 470 lb./ton) |

**BRAKES at 30 m.p.h.**

| | | | |
|---|---|---|---|
| 0.96g retardation | (= 31¼ ft. stopping distance) with | 120 lb. | pedal pressure |
| 0.87g retardation | (= 34½ ft. stopping distance) with | 100 lb. | pedal pressure |
| 0.68g retardation | (= 44½ ft. stopping distance) with | 75 lb. | pedal pressure |
| 0.38g retardation | (= 79½ ft. stopping distance) with | 50 lb. | pedal pressure |

**MAXIMUM SPEEDS**

**Flying Quarter Mile**

| | |
|---|---|
| Mean of four opposite runs .. | 85.5 m.p.h. |
| Best time equals .. .. | 87.4 m.p.h. |

**Speed in Gears**

| | |
|---|---|
| Max. speed in 2nd gear .. | 67 m.p.h. |
| Max. speed in 1st gear.. .. | 36 m.p.h. |

**WEIGHT**

| | |
|---|---|
| Unladen kerb weight .. .. | 28 cwt. |
| Front/rear weight distribution | 45/55 |
| Weight laden as tested .. | 32 cwt. |

**INSTRUMENTS**

| | |
|---|---|
| Speedometer at 30 m.p.h. .. | Accurate |
| Speedometer at 60 m.p.h. .. | 5% fast |
| Speedometer at 80 m.p.h. .. | 4% fast |
| Distance recorder .. .. | Accurate |

*(Above) The J2X flat-out on an airfield circuit.*

*(Right) Low, wicked - looking lines characterize the latest Allard. The side-mounting of the spare wheel is unusual on modern sports-cars.*

AT this year's Motor Show, the competition model two-seater Allard was exhibited in a modified form. Not only was the big Chrysler engine a new departure, but it was mounted 7 ins. farther forward than the power unit of the previous J2 type. This entailed the radius arms of the well-known split axle i.f.s. being carried forward instead of back, which is actually an advantageous arrangement. Naturally, especially having regard to the high reputation of its predecessor, I was all agog to try this latest version.

The car that I took over was of the J2X series, which is an export model. Instead of the four carburetters that are used for racing, a single Carter instrument was fitted, and a wide ratio gearbox replaced the "high first" job.

On taking my seat, I was amazed that a 5½-litre car could feel almost as small as an Austin Seven. The engine fired instantly, the automatic mixture control working perfectly at all times, and the tickover seemed impossibly slow, though there was never any tendency to stall. On moving off, it was at once apparent that the big motor developed a phenomenal torque at low speeds, and I soon realized that for normal road work the gear lever was all but superfluous. A touch of the accelerator was sufficient to send the machine surging forward, with the curiously typical "V8 beat" rumbling from the four exhaust pipes. The Chrysler engine was

entirely silent mechanically, and at a high cruising speed one heard nothing but the hum of the tyres and the wind. It was all most exhilarating, and quite unlike any other car on the market.

The three-speed gearbox is no disadvantage on the road, but for racing one would prefer four speeds, or at least the close ratio version of the present arrangement. The excellent acceleration figures could certainly be improved with a higher intermediate gear, but on top the performance, from 35 m.p.h. onwards, is better than that of most sports-cars using their four speeds to the full.

Such a car deserves good brakes, and that is a department in which the Allard excels. The big Lockheeds are well cooled, and never fade. The front ones, in particular, are really out in the airstream, for the separate mudguards do not obstruct the flow, nor do the proper racing wire wheels screen the drums. The cooling arrangements for the inboard mounted rear brakes seem to work well, too. There is a "fly off" type of hand brake lever mounted horizontally to the right of the driver's seat, and this gets full marks for efficiency and convenient location. How one appreciates it after a surfeit of pistol-grip devices!

The Allard suspension system is unconventional, and I shall therefore go fairly fully into its characteristics. In front, the swing axle system is employed, with helical springs and very large telescopic

dampers. It allows considerable deflection to take place, and an extra severe bump may cause a momentary bottoming. Let me say, straight away, that the results are excellent. It is difficult to combine very soft front springing with good wheel adhesion and adequate roll resistance, but the Allard system does all these things.

### Exemplary Front-end Behaviour

It is obvious that the divided axle must cause appreciable tilting of the wheels, and that gyroscopic forces are thereby engendered. In practice, one can see the typical flick of gyroscopic precession if one watches the front wheels on a bumpy road. There is normally no reaction to be felt through the steering, however, and the control is light, precise, and has good caster action. Such exemplary front-end behaviour is conditional on a rigid chassis frame being provided, and that has certainly been done in this case.

At the rear, a de Dion axle is employed. This consists of a tubular axle beam, offset to the back of the hubs so that they can

# CHRYSLER-ENGINED ALLARD

## J2X "Export" Model Reveals a Remarkable Flexibility — Inboard Rear Brakes and De Dion Axle Features of Popular British Sports-Car

be driven through articulated half shafts. These shafts also take the braking torque, for the back plates of the brakes are secured to the chassis-mounted final drive unit. All this results in commendably low unsprung weight, and the absence of wheelspin on rough surfaces is most noticeable. As the axle beam is freed of propeller shaft torque, violent acceleration on a low gear produces two identical black marks on the road surface.

The suspension medium is again hydraulically damped helical springs. As is customary today, the back springs are appreciably harder than those in front, and a very level ride is consequently secured. The comfort of the suspension is outstanding, and the new weight distribution entirely eliminates pitching. The car can be cornered fast without a trace of roll, in fact, a premonitory whistle from the tyres is the only sign that rapid negotiation of a curve is taking place.

My only criticism of the suspen-

*Frontal aspect of the J2X Allard. As on the latest unsupercharged racing-cars, an air-scoop is fitted on top of the bonnet.*

sion concerns its behaviour when a corner is taken at racing speed. Under those conditions, the rear end breaks away rather suddenly, particularly on wet roads. This makes it difficult to slide a corner in one smooth sweep, without a certain amount of "dicing" at the wheel. I may be hypercritical, or airing an individual preference, but

in any case a very slight alteration of the rear suspension would lower the roll centre and eliminate the effect. I don't say that this would get one through the swerves any faster, but I think that one could then make a tidier job of it.

The body is entirely functional, and achieves exactly the right degree of sleek raciness, allied with almost animal ferocity. An admiring crowd forms wherever the car is parked, and the traditional green, with white number discs, certainly suits it very well. There is not an ounce of superfluous weight, yet there is nothing flimsy about the construction. It would be impossible to better the view from the driving seat, and all the controls are well placed, though the accelerator seems a thought far away. Naturally, one does not expect much luggage space in this sort of body.

### Space for Four Carburetters

On the top of the alligator bonnet, there is a large air intake, so schemed that there is ample room to fit four down-draught carburetters if these are required. It is interesting that, as one gets above the 90 mark, this grille emits a shrill whistle that sounds exactly like a supercharger.

Particularly in the States, the Chrysler engines of race-winning Allards are made to produce far more power than the standard article. They are of very rugged construction, and stand up to this

*OFFICE: Dominated by a large 160 m.p.h. speedometer, and a "six-thou" revolution counter, the facia panel of the J2X Allard is that of a true sports-car.*

**Transmission.** Chrysler single plate clutch. Ford three-speed gearbox with remote control, ratios 3.27, 5.75, and 10 to 1. Spiral bevel final drive with Hardy Spicer articulated half shafts, 26 m.p.h. per 1,000 r.p.m.

**Equipment.** 12 volt lighting and starting. Speedometer, revolution counter, ammeter, water temperature, oil pressure and fuel gauges.

**Dimensions, etc.** Wheelbase 8 ft. 4 ins. Track (front) 4 ft. 8 ins. (rear) 4 ft. 4 ins. Overall length 12 ft. 4 ins. Turning circle 39 ft. Weight 24 cwt.

**Performance.** Maximum speed 100 m.p.h. Speeds in gears, 2nd 65 m.p.h., 1st 37 m.p.h. Acceleration (wet road) standing quarter-mile 18.5 secs. 0-50 m.p.h., 7.2 secs. 0-60 m.p.h., 10 secs. 0-70 m.p.h., 14 secs. 0-80 m.p.h., 21 secs. 0-90 m.p.h., 29.2 secs.

**Fuel Consumption.** Driven hard, 12 m.p.g. 40 gallon tank, two in reserve.

\*     \*     \*

## The Chrysler-Engined Allard—*contd*

treatment quite well. For road work, however, few people would ask for more performance than the model I drove provides, and the unusual combination of steam engine flexibility and a super sporting-car is most attractive. I am quite sure that one could not over-drive this motor, and the cruising speed could be anything up to the maximum. Actually, the unit rushes straight up to 4,000 r.p.m., where it peaks, after which the hydraulic tappets get out of breath, and prevent over-revving. The Smith rev-counter was commendably accurate at all relevant readings, but the speedometer had a considerable degree of optimism.

The J2X Allard is a very unusual car. It combines stark sporting coachwork with flexibility of a rare order and remarkably comfortable suspension. A really big engine, which simply plays with its very high top gear, gives probably a greater ease of travel than can be secured by any other means. I am sure that many Americans will get a great deal of excitement out of this new model, particularly those who live in the warmer states, and at \$4,500 delivered in New York, it should find a ready sale.

*POWER-HOUSE: The car tested was fitted with a standard production, single-carburetter 5½-litre, V8 Chrysler "Fire Power" motor. Sports-racing version of this engine normally has four Carter carburetters.*

## SPECIFICATION AND PERFORMANCE DATA

**Car Tested.** Allard J2X Sports two-seater, price \$4,500, delivered in New York.

**Engine.** Eight cylinders, 96.8 x 92 mm. (5,420 c.c.). Inclined overhead valves, operated by pushrods and rockers. 172 b.h.p. at 4,000 r.p.m. 7½ to 1 compression ratio. One Carter down-draught carburetter. Lucas coil and Autolite distributor.

**Chassis.** Swing axle i.f.s., and de Dion rear. Helical springs and hydraulic dampers all round. Lockheed hydraulic brakes, 2LS front, inboard rear, 12 in. Alfin drums, 156 sq. in. lining area. Racing type wire wheels with knock-off caps, fitted 7.00-16 in. rear tyres and 6.00-16 in. front tyres.

# The WINNER'S MOUNT

*Details of the Allard Saloon with which S. H. Allard and his crew won the 1952 Monte-Carlo Rally*

TO win the Monte-Carlo Rally is, first and foremost, a supreme personal achievement, by drivers Sydney Allard and Guy Warburton and by navigator Tom Lush. Nevertheless, the best of crews could not attain such success without a car of unusual merit, and the Allard saloon in which Britain's long-awaited success was won is a car which will undoubtedly go down in British motoring history.

The whole character of the car which is illustrated on these pages, the car with which three (very large) men were able to win the world's greatest winter motoring event, can be clearly understood only in terms of the fact that its driver is also managing director of the company which built it. The Allard V8 saloon is, up to a point, a perfectly ordinary touring motor car; but only up to a point, because the men who build them know that now as for many years past "the guvnor" expects to be able to take one of the cars and thrash it mercilessly in some major motoring contest, be it an Alpine Trial or a Tourist Trophy Race or a Monte-Carlo Rally. With that background, one can expect to find that an Allard is built with rather less regard than usual to current fashions, and with rather more regard than usual to ability to withstand hard work or ill treatment.

One of the special characteristics of the Allard range of cars is the fact that, out of a relatively straightforward series of components, a surprisingly wide variety of different cars can be built to special order. The maximum range of choice is open only to customers in dollar markets, but there are for example five different sizes of engine in current use, some of them in both side-valve and overhead valve forms: there are conventional and de Dion pattern rear axles: there are four main types of bodywork to suit three

## " MONTE-CARLO " ALLARD SALOON SPECIFICATION

| | | |
|---|---|---|
| **Engine Dimensions** | | |
| Cylinders | ... ... | V-8 |
| Bore | ... ... | 84.13 mm. |
| Stroke | ... ... | 98.42 mm. |
| Cubic capacity | ... | 4,375 c.c. |
| Piston area | ... | 68.9 sq. in. |
| Valves | ... ... | Side |
| Compression ratio | | 7.0/1 |
| **Engine Performance** | | |
| Max. b.h.p. | ... | Approx. 100 |
| B.H.P. per sq. in. piston area | ... | 1.45 |
| **Engine Details** | | |
| Carburetter | ... | 1 dual-choke down-draught. |
| Ignition | ... ... | Lucas coil |
| Plugs | ... ... | Lodge |
| Fuel pump | ... ... | Mechanical |
| Fuel capacity | ... | 20 gallons |
| Oil capacity | ... | 8 pints |
| Cooling system | ... | Pumps and fan |
| Water capacity | ... | 36 pints |
| Electrical system | ... | Lucas, 12-volt |
| **Transmission** | | |
| Clutch | ... ... | Ford s.d.p. |
| Gear ratios: Top | ... | 3.78 |
| 2nd | ... | 6.7 |
| 1st | ... | 11.8 |
| Rev. | ... | 15.1 |
| Prop. shaft | ... | Enclosed in torque tube. |
| Final drive | ... ... | Spiral bevel |
| **Chassis Details** | | |
| Brakes | ... ... | Lockheed hydraulic (2 l.s. front) |
| Brake drum diameter | | 12 ins. |
| Friction lining area | | .165 sq. ins. |
| Suspension: Front | ... | Coil springs and divided axle I.F.S. |
| Rear | | Transverse leaf spring and rigid axle. |
| Shock absorbers | ... | Armstrong telescopic. |
| Wheel type | ... | Steel disc |
| Tyres | ... ... | Dunlop Trak-grip, 6.00-16 |
| Steering gear | ... | Marles |
| **Dimensions** | | |
| Wheelbase | ... ... | 9 ft. 4 ins. |
| Track: Front | ... | 4 ft. 8 ins. |
| Rear | ... | 4 ft. 10 ins. |
| Overal, length | ... | 15 ft. 6 ins. |
| Overall width | ... | 5 ft. 8 ins. |
| Overall height | ... | 5 ft. 2 ins. |
| Ground clearance | ... | 8 ins. |
| Turning circle | ... | 41 ft. |
| Dry weight (without extra equipment) | | 27 cwt. |
| **Performance Data** | | |
| Piston area, sq. in. per ton | ... ... | 51 sq. ins. |
| Brake lining area, sq. in. per ton | | 122 |
| Top gear m.p.h. per 1,000 r.p.m. | | 21.5 |
| Top gear m.p.h. at 2,500 ft./min. piston speed | | 83.5 |
| Litres per ton-mile, dry | ... ... | 4,520 |

FACIA DETAILS do not differ from normal Allard specification, except for the fitting of a speedometer calibrated in kilometres per hour. Note that the two spanners which serve for most minor jobs on a Ford power unit are held to the gear lever by rubber bands, ready for instant use if needed.

### The Winner's Mount - - - Contd.

different lengths of chassis: and so the possibilities go on.

The car which won the Rally to Monte-Carlo, however, is the most "ordinary" model in the range, the comfortable saloon which is sold in very considerable numbers for a price of £1,100. It was of course equipped with various extras to suit the job in hand, but mechanically it departed in only two respects from "basic" specification. The V8 side valve engine was enlarged to the optional "oversize" of 4,375 c.c., by an increase in cylinder dimensions of $\frac{1}{4}$ inch on the bore and $\frac{1}{8}$ inch on the stroke: and Allard light-alloy cylinder heads were fitted, giving the moderate compression ratio of 7.0/1. A single carburetter was retained (the catalogued alternative twin-carburetter induction system was not thought necessary for this event), as were the usual side valves of the Ford-built engine.

One of the vital requirements of the car which wins the Monte-Carlo Rally in a "difficult" year such as this, is the ability to keep going on snow and ice, and to keep going fast. There must be good wheel adhesion, for getting up and down hills: there must be good controllability on treacherous

corners: and last but not least there must be sheer strength of construction, so that the occasional inadvertent departure from the fairway into the rough will not cause serious harm.

In "The Motor" Road Test Report on the Allard convertible coupé, published on January 2, 1952, it was recorded that 55 per cent. of the unladen weight was carried on the driving wheels, the corresponding average figure for the ten preceding test cars having been just under 47 per cent. That alone means that in slippery conditions an Allard convertible should be able to surmount a hill 17 per cent. steeper than could an average car: and as the saloon Allard has heavier bodywork than the coupe, and a slightly different layout of the I.F.S. linkage which also sets the weight further back, the Allard saloon which won the rally obviously has a much more-than-average amount of traction available on slippery surfaces. Interestingly, tyre chains were not carried, but "sliced" Dunlop Trakgrip tyres of 6.00-16 size were fitted to all wheels—this type of tyre is not claimed to have any special merit for use on hard ice surfaces, but its bold tread is very helpful on soft snow: the "Vee" treads were fitted facing in opposite directions on the front and rear wheels, to give best braking adhesion and best traction respectively.

The chassis of these cars, it may be recalled, uses two box-section longerons with a central X-bracing. At the front, the I.F.S. system incorporates swinging half-axles and coil springs, whilst at the rear there is a conventional axle with torque tube, transverse panhard rod, and transverse leaf spring. The V8 engine, of Ford manufacture, is set much further back in the frame than is nowadays customary, and whilst a steering column gear lever is available if preferred the gear lever on the rally car was a conventional floor-mounted central remote control.

MOVING HOUSE is the description which might applied to a good Rally car, provision being made by su details as a fold-flat passenger's seat for rest during hours of almost continuous motoring.

...der the bonnet are such items as a lead lamp for nocturnal wheel changing, a spare set of sparking plugs, a duplicate ignition coil and other minor replacement parts. Personal impedimenta fills the luggage locker, and an additional spare wheel is recessed into one front wing.

To suit extreme climatic conditions, the highly effective Allard heating system was backed up by the installation of a Berkshire de-mister on the inside of the windscreen: outside the screen, a windscreen washing spray was provided, its container filled with a Bluecol-water mixture which would not freeze in frosty conditions: finally, in case of dense fog, provision was made for securing the usual opening windscreen in the wide open position.

Inside the car, the nearside front seat was fitted with a hinged backrest, so that the driver off duty could lie down and sleep. To make sure that a very tall navigator could

survive 3 days of imprisonment in what remained of the rear compartment, incidentally, the cushions of what was in fact a new car were "settled" in advance as much as possible.

The conventional lighting system was supplemented by two more Lucas lamps, mounted on a bar in front of the radiator cowling, a flat-beam unit on the left side and a pencil-beam "flame thrower" on the right. To prevent soft snow being thrown up in front of the lights, a horizontal baffle was mounted below and ahead of them: also, interestingly, special provision was made for easy removal of packed snow from inside the radiator cowling, just in case a bank of soft snow beside the icy road had to be used as an emergency substitute for brakes ! A leadlight was arranged under the bonnet, with a long lead so that it could be used if any wheel needed to be changed after dark.

### For Mechanical First-aid

A certain number of spare parts were carried, of course, not major components but merely those which could be used quickly by the roadside if needed. For example, spare sparking plugs and a duplicate ignition coil were accessibly mounted under the bonnet; a duplicate horn with its own horn button and fuse was fitted; a 6-volt battery was carried which could replace either of the two units in series normally fitted to Allard cars. Such spares as fan belts and a dynamo had been "tried on for size" before the start, using the tools in the standard kit. The radiator hoses had duplicated clamps, and spare hoses were threaded onto the pipes in case of need. A duplicate ignition key was hidden outside the car in case the other was mislaid in the rush at some control.

Such are the details of preparation which, in an event settled by minutes, seconds and fractions of a second, cut down to a minimum the element of chance. If floods were encountered, then the distributor was already waterproofed but could breathe through a pipe leading into the body of the car. If on the other hand hard driving on dry roads took the fine edge of adjustment off the brakes, external adjusters outside the drums would allow for a rapid re-adjustment whenever moments could be spared. If by any misfortune the car got into a ditch, then unditching gear was available with which it could be hauled back onto the road.

That is the recipe for winning the Monte-Carlo Rally, then. A car which is fast, sturdy, and has a useful measure of go-anywhere character; a car prepared carefully so that those misfortunes which are called "bad luck" are to a surprisingly large extent foreseen and prevented from occurring; a car, in fact, with which a first class crew will have a sporting chance of success.

# MONTE CARLO RALLY
## Won by

## Powered by the Famous FORD V.8 Engine

The first British car to win
outright for twenty-one years

*Photo by " The Motor "*

*The Overseas Prestige of the British Motor Industry
will be increased by this Magnificent Success*

# ALLARD MOTOR COMPANY LTD.
### 24-28, CLAPHAM HIGH STREET, LONDON, S.W.4

PHONE : MACAULAY 3201                    CABLES : ALMOTCO, LONDON

The distinctive sporting line can be appreciated in this view. The one-piece bonnet is held in place by the racing car and reliable method of a leather strap. Below each built-in Trafficator is a cockpit ventilator.

## No. 1457 : K2 ALLARD TWO-SEATER

IN the sporting world the name Allard is well known, not only as that of a driver in trials and rallies, including the Monte Carlo Rally of 1952, when S. H. Allard won the event in a car bearing his name—the first British driver to do so for twenty-one years—but also as a manufacturer of a range of sporting mounts from stark two-seaters to four-seater saloons. Like some other specialist car producers manufacturing cars on a small scale, the Allard company uses a number of proprietary chassis and engine components; as is well known, the early cars were based on Ford V8 parts. This policy is a sound one as it relieves the specialist producer of a certain amount of costly basic development work. From the owner's point of view, too, such a policy has the advantage that spares will be much more readily available than if every component was peculiar to the particular car.

However, with a continual quest for improved performance and road holding, modifications to this general principle must, of course, be made; and this has resulted in several variations on the original theme. To improve road-holding a form of swing axle independent front suspension was adopted in the early history of the Allard, while on some models a De Dion rear end is available. A range of V-eight engines is available to suit the requirements of the owner, and units ranging from the Ford V8 to the o.h.v. Cadillac can be fitted.

The car recently tested by *The Autocar* in Belgium, as regards maximum performance figures, was powered by the Ardun engine, which is a massive light-alloy overhead valve conversion unit built on to a modified Ford Mercury bottom end. This engine with a capacity of almost four litres develops 140 b.h.p. at 4,000 r.p.m. compared with 85 b.h.p. for the 3.6-litre side-valve Ford engine, and in the slim two-seater chassis it produces a real performance mount, as reference

### DATA

**PRICE** (basic), with open two-seater body, £1,200.
British purchase tax, £668 3s 4d.
Total (in Great Britain), £1,868 3s 4d.

**ENGINE** : Capacity : 3,917 c.c. (239 cu. in.)
Number of cylinders : 8.
Bore and stroke : 81 × 98.43 mm. (3.189 × 3.875in).
Valve gear : o.h.v., by push-rods.
Compression ratio : 7.5 to 1.
B.H.P.: 140 at 4,000 r.p.m. (101.5 B.H.P. per ton laden).
Torque : 225 lb ft at 2,500 r.p.m.
M.P.H. per 1,000 r.p.m. on top gear, 21.43.

**WEIGHT** (with 5 galls fuel), 24 cwt. (2,689lb).
Weight distribution (per cent) : 48 F ; 52 R.
Laden as tested : 27½ cwt. (3,081 lb).
Lb per c.c. (laden) : 0.79.

**TYRES** : 6.25-16 in.
Pressures (lb per sq in) : 22 F ; 24 R.

**TANK CAPACITY** : 17 Imperial gallons.
Oil sump, 8 pints.
Cooling system, 36 pints.

**TURNING CIRCLE** : 42ft 0in. (L and R).
Steering wheel turns (lock to lock) : 2¾.

**DIMENSIONS** : Wheelbase : 8ft 10in.
Track : 4ft 8½in (F) ; 4ft 4½in (R).
Length (overall) : 14ft 0in.
Height : 4ft 8in.
Width : 5ft 11in.
Ground clearance : 9in.
Frontal area : 19 sq ft (approx.).

**ELECTRICAL SYSTEM** : 12-volt. Two 6-volt 60 ampère-hour batteries.
Head lights : Double dip, 36/36 watt.

**SUSPENSION** : Front, coil springs; swing axles.
Rear, transverse leaf spring.

### PERFORMANCE

**K2 ALLARD**

**ACCELERATION** : from constant speeds.
Speed, Gear Ratios and time in sec.

| M.P.H. | 3.78 to 1 | 6.7 to 1 | 11.77 to 1 |
|---|---|---|---|
| 10—30 | .. | — | 4.4 | 3.0 |
| 20—40 | .. | 7.4 | 4.2 | — |
| 30—50 | .. | 7.5 | 4.5 | — |
| 40—60 | .. | 7.8 | 5.5 | — |

From rest through gears to :

| M.P.H. | | | sec. |
|---|---|---|---|
| 30 | .. | .. | 3.4 |
| 50 | .. | .. | 8.5 |
| 60 | .. | .. | 11.6 |
| 70 | .. | .. | 14.7 |
| 80 | .. | .. | 19.8 |
| 90 | .. | .. | 27.5 |

Standing quarter mile, 18.1 sec.

**SPEEDS ON GEARS :**

| Gear | | M.P.H. (normal and max.) | K.P.H. (normal and max.) |
|---|---|---|---|
| Top | (mean) | 101.25 | 163 |
| | (best) | 102 | 164 |
| 2nd | .. .. | 50—60 | 80—97 |
| 1st | .. .. | 22—34 | 35—55 |

**TRACTIVE RESISTANCE** : 32.5 lb per ton at 10 M.P.H.

**TRACTIVE EFFORT :**

| | Pull (lb per ton) | Equivalent Gradient |
|---|---|---|
| Top | .. .. | 319 | 1 in 7 |
| Second | .. .. | 520 | 1 in 4.25 |

**BRAKES :**

| Efficiency | Pedal Pressure (lb) |
|---|---|
| 87 per cent | 119 |
| 80 per cent | 100 |
| 63 per cent | 50 |

**FUEL CONSUMPTION :**
12.3 m.p.g. overall for 111 miles. 23 litres per 100 km.
Approximate normal range 12-15 m.p.g. 23.5-18.8 litres per 100 km.
Fuel : Belgian Premium-grade (approximately 80 octane).

**WEATHER :** Dry surface ; fresh cross-wind. Air temperature 35 degrees F.
Acceleration figures are the means of several runs in opposite directions.
Tractive effort and resistance obtained by Tapley meter.

**SPEEDOMETER CORRECTION : M.P.H.**

| Car speedometer | .. | 10 | 20 | 30 | 40 | 50 | 60 | 70 | 80 | 90 | 100 | 107 |
|---|---|---|---|---|---|---|---|---|---|---|---|---|
| True speed | .. | 14 | 22 | 30 | 38 | 46.5 | 55.5 | 64.5 | 74 | 84 | 94 | 102 |

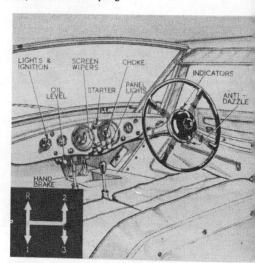

The slim tail and crab track are unduly emphasized in this view of the Allard. A neat grille of simple design is in keeping with the character of the car. Double bumpers give good protection.

The K2 has a well-shaped hood which blends into the general contours of the car. Double quarter bumpers protect the vulnerable "corners."

## ROAD TEST . . . . . . . continued

to the test figures will show. The Allard does not have the degree of silence and smoothness of some cars; however, this is perhaps of little importance to the enthusiast interested chiefly in performance. It is well to remember that this car is one of the very few that will do a genuine mean maximum speed of over one hundred miles an hour, without very favourable conditions such as a down grade and a following wind. It also has flashing acceleration (0 to 90 m.p.h. in well under half a minute), a quality often lacking on some cars geared to attain a high maximum. In spite of its large capacity the engine does not possess the degree of flexibility associated with its type, as it is designed to give extra urge at the top end; gear boxes on sports cars are, after all, there to be used.

One very experienced driver remarked after a brief run in the car that it was the fastest thing up to 90 that he could remember for a very long time. The quality of good acceleration cannot be too highly stressed, as it applies to the whole speed range and can be used whenever the car is driven. On one run, for example, a 48 m.p.h. average was recorded for a distance of well over 100 miles without

ever showing more than 75 on the speedometer, and including several built-up areas.

The name Allard and hill-climbing go together in the sporting world, and it is not surprising to find that the hill-climbing powers of this car are very much above average. It is an understatement to say that all main-road hills can be taken on top gear; in fact, some of the steeper variety such as Sunrising, a Cotswolds area trials hill in earlier times (1 in 6½ gradient), was climbed without changing down. Gear changing by means of the remote control lever is not quite as positive as some of its kind, and the lever could with advantage be placed farther rearward to avoid the driver having to reach so far forward, especially if he has to use the full range of seat adjustment to accommodate himself. The clutch, designed to deal with lots of willing horses, is heavier than most and neat footwork is necessary for a smooth take-off.

The leather upholstery and polished metal facia finish the car in true sports car fashion. When the hood is down all hood irons are neatly stowed out of sight. With the all-weather equipment in place (right) the car has a snug interior. The rear "quarter light" gives extra visibility for manoeuvring.

The fly-off hand brake is very effective, although the lever is quite short; positioned as it is to the front and a little to the left of the gear lever, it can be operated more easily by the passenger than the driver. Although this would perhaps be of little importance on an average touring car where such a brake is chiefly used for parking, the fact that a fly-off type is fitted may be taken to indicate that the component is intended as a service brake.

The K2 is a car that takes some little time to get to know thoroughly, and this is perhaps in part because of its near-vintage characteristics, not frequently found today but longed for by some enthusiasts. The suspension is firm but not to the point of being harsh, although even the more mild forms of Belgian pavé could be felt. A weight distribution such as this car has considerably assists getting off the mark quickly with the minimum of wheelspin, yet this is perhaps offset in part by loss of directional stability at high speeds brought about by the tendency for the car to over-steer.

With two and three-quarter turns from lock to lock the steering is light, yet sufficiently positive to enable the car to be accurately placed. There is a good self-centring action, and a light and lively feel to the car as a whole. For practical purposes there is no roll on corners. Not only does the Allard go, it also stops. The hydraulically operated brakes are very powerful yet smooth in operation. At no time during the performance testing or on the road was any fade or judder experienced. Nor for that matter, was any brake adjustment found necessary during the whole of the time that the car was in the hands of *The Autocar* over the usual substantial distance, hard driving included.

A high ground clearance necessary for some types of competition work, plus a low overall height and modest frontal area to help to cheat the wind, result in a rather limited amount of space in the cockpit. There is plenty of leg room

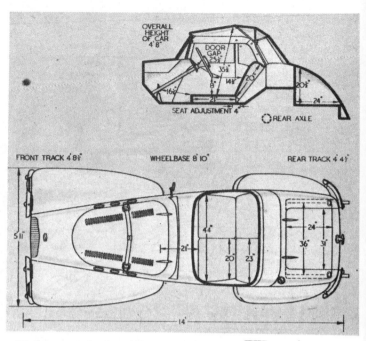

Measurements in these ⅛in to 1ft scale body diagrams are taken with the driving seat in the central position of fore and aft adjustment and with the seat cushions uncompressed.

The top-hinged luggage locker lid also encloses the spare-wheel compartment, and is held in the open position by pivoting arms. A canvas bag in the locker protects the side screens when they are not in use.

for the passenger, and for the driver's left leg, strangely enough, but his right one is rather cramped. To help matters the floor in front of the pedals is shaped to form a well. Because of the pedal arrangement it is very difficult to "heel and toe." Seat adjustment is provided by moving the whole of the squab backward or forward, while a further adjustment for height is possible by regulating the amount of air in the seat cushion pneumatic bags. The steering column, too, can be adjusted for length. The seats insulate the driver from general road shocks and are quite comfortable. For long journeys comfort could be further increased by lengthening the seat cushion to give more support to the driver's leg muscles. Some form of positive division between the two seats would be a distinct advantage, as, although the driver is firmly held in place if there is a passenger, when the car is driven solo the effects of "g" can shift him to the passenger seat during quick cornering.

From the driving seat the forward view is very good; the sloping bonnet and both wings are in full view, and this fact gives the driver every facility to line up and to position the car accurately. By contrast, with the hood up the view to the rear is somewhat limited; an interior mirror would be a useful addition, as the single outside mirror does not show the vehicle that is tucked in right behind.

As is, of course, expected with a car of this type, the equipment is limited to the bare essentials, in the interests of weight saving, yet the interior is well appointed with most if not all of the driver's requirements, including Trafficators, which are often omitted on cars of this type. The windscreen wipers sweep a very wide arc, but the blades could with advantage be set to wipe more of the top of the screen. The electrical equipment is well up to its job; the horns in particular are very powerful and have a pleasing sound. The head lights, too, are well placed and give a good spread

of light, yet for fast night driving a longer range would be an advantage. Starting from cold was a first-press matter every time, even at temperatures below freezing point. With the engine hot, starting was sometimes not immediate. Although it is not apparently essential for this engine, the car tested was running on Castrol R. This contributed a great deal to the "atmosphere" of the test and the individual nature of this interesting car, the exhaust aroma of vegetable oil bringing back a great deal of sports car motoring in the past.

The K2 is a car for the driver who likes his motoring "in the raw," and who wants a car that must really be driven, and one that in return gives results.

The space under the bonnet is completely filled by the engine. Two Solex downdraught carburettors are used. Both mechanical and electrical fuel pumps are fitted.

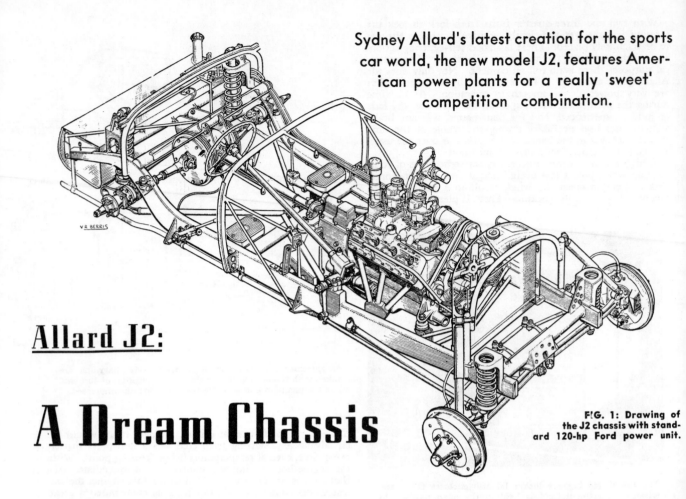

Sydney Allard's latest creation for the sports car world, the new model J2, features American power plants for a really 'sweet' competition combination.

# Allard J2:
# A Dream Chassis

**FIG. 1: Drawing of the J2 chassis with standard 120-hp Ford power unit.**

## By ROGER HUNTINGTON

SAE, TECHNICAL EDITOR, SPEED AGE

TO THE man who looks at everything through a slide rule, or to the guy who just wants to get from A to B in the shortest possible time, the Allard J2 is not a car —it's a chassis!

And this fabulous reputation is not built solely on a drawing board theory. A lot of fancy sports chassis have looked good in the blueprint; but rack 'em through a 90° corner at 40 MPH, or run 'em up to 120 on a rough dirt road, and some looked too much like Detroit cars!

The Allard J2, on the other hand, has proved itself on the road, until today it stands head and shoulders above the rest of the field as the most successful competition sports car in history. And the secret is all in the chassis.

Britisher Sidney Allard was always a great one for hot competition cars with highly-advanced chassis and scientific weight distribution. He began in the mid-1930s with modest home-built specials based on Ford parts, and by the start of the war, his cars were the most successful 'trials' jobs in England.

Shortly after the war, Allard went into production on the Model K sports touring type, based on Ford chassis parts and the V8-85 engine. In 1949 he saw a market for a more elaborate model, designed especially for road competition, and thus the J2 was born. Let's look it over:

In the first place, Mr. Allard considered several factors to be especially important in the basic layout of this car, and these were followed closely throughout the design:

Low cost, using as many standard Ford parts as possible;

Low weight;

Moderate wheelbase of 100 inches;

Four-wheel independent suspension designed for best road-holding; and

A weight distribution putting about 55% of the total weight on the rear driving wheels.

Allard felt that, if these requirements could be met, and providing he could get 200 HP from a semi-stock engine weighing under 700 pounds, he'd have a relatively

**FIG. 2: Cockpit of the J2; everything functional and convenient for competition motorists—but no deal for getting Milady from A to B in the plush comfort she likes!**

inexpensive bundle of powerful dynamite.

How right he was! Fig. 1 shows the resulting chassis layout of the J2, using the original modified Ford V8 power plant.

### FRAME

Frame stiffness is very essential in any high-speed car in order to form a perfectly rigid base for the wheel suspension. Allard has achieved this stiffness, without going into the expensive all-tubular construction, by using box-section side rails at the front, welded tubular cross-members, and building up the body bracing as part of the frame. The resulting structure is rigid, fairly light and inexpensive.

### FRONT SUSPENSION

Allard uses a very unorthodox front end layout to achieve fast cornering at the lowest possible cost. It's nothing more than an old-style Ford beam axle cut in two and pivoted at the inner ends (see Fig. 1); coil springs are used for the suspension medium and the swinging arms are located by radius rods running back to pivots on the frame rails. This layout saves costs and gives a high roll center at the front, which greatly increases the roll resistance and stability in cornering.

But it's also, necessarily, a great compromise for high speeds on rough surfaces. As the wheels rise and fall, the tread varies (the tires scrub in and out on the road surface) and the camber changes (wheels tip in and out). Theoretically this would cause considerable front-end instability on rough surfaces and set up some vicious

FIG. 3: Side view of the Allard J2; it weighs only 2,300 pounds at the curb. The driving seat is set back to put weight on the rear driving wheels.

gyroscopic forces at high speeds. In practice, however, the resistance of the tires to sidewise scrubbing, in conjunction with 'sea legs' mounting of the shock absorbers, seems to give fairly good front end stability at the higher speeds.

So once again Mr. Allard has gotten out of a complicated muddle at a low dollar—but it's not the kind of front end I'd put on my dream car!

### STEERING

Close attention has been paid to getting correct steering geometry. One steering fault of many high-speed cars with wishbone front suspension is that, for reasons of cost and convenience, a simple divided track or tie rod is used, with each rod considerably longer than its wishbone. When the wheels move up and down, they strike arcs of different radius and the wheels toe in and out, which upsets the steering geometry and makes a bad deal all around. Allard has solved this by using a three-piece track linkage (see Fig. 1) with the outside rods the same length as the suspension arms, giving perfect geometry at all wheel positions. Steering is through a high-geared Marles worm-and-roller box giving 2.3 turns of the wheel over full lock.

### REAR SUSPENSION

Right here is the big secret of the J2's amazing road performance. When it comes to getting around a road circuit in the shortest possible time, the conventional solid rear axle is strictly for the birds.

Maserati has tried to prove it isn't, and all they've gotten out of their experiment is dust in their grilles!

There are three basic reasons why the solid axle is no good:

When one wheel goes over a bump, it causes the opposite wheel to deflect a little, which breaks traction and causes instability at high speed;

The high unsprung weight of a solid rear axle in a very light car causes it to bounce at high speed; and

Crosswise or transverse engine torque on a solid axle tends to lift the right rear wheel when accelerating hard, which, of course, breaks the traction. The solid axle is a bad deal all around.

Now there are a number of ways you can lay out the rear end to give independent

suspension. Allard didn't try to use the less effective swing-axle system, but faced right up to the difficult job of building an inexpensive deDion layout. This is the best design of all, since it maintains the wheels vertical at all times and there is no sidewise tire scrub or gyroscopic forces from the wheels pivoting up and down.

Fig. 4 shows the rear layout on the J2. There is a separate dead axle tube fixed to each hub, linked together at the center so they can pivot independently; they are located in a sidewise direction by a bronze peg sliding up and down in a slot mounted on the differential case, which in turn is bolted to the frame. The drive to the road wheels is taken through splined universally-jointed shafts; the shafts can move in and out as well as up and down to accommodate the vertical wheel movement. Radius rods from each hub to the center of the frame locate the wheels (see Fig. 1). Coil springs carry the load. It's really a very beautiful and simple thing, costs are cut by using standard Ford torque tube, differential housing and hubs—and road-holding is much better than with the swing-axles.

### BRAKES

Powerful braking without fade is also an important factor on a competition road car. Allard uses Lockheed four-wheel hydraulics for the J2. The front brakes are of the two-leading-shoe type—that is, there are two piston units on each brake and both shoes utilize the friction of the lining against the drum to pivot them harder against the drum surface than the pedal pressure alone would do. Most stock cars have one piston and only one shoe is self-energizing. Front brakes are cooled by air scoops on the back plate. Additional cooling is obtained by using Alfin drums; aluminum fins are bonded to a cast iron drum surface to help conduct the heat to the outside air.

The rear brakes are unorthodox, mounted inboard next to the differential case and exerting their braking torque through the drive shafts to the wheels. Hard braking in this case is pretty rough on the universal joints and it's not a recommended layout. Allard has used it mainly to reduce unsprung weight to a minimum and to cut costs. In practice, these J2 brakes work very well and are said to be unusually free from fade.

### ENGINES

Several power plant options are available from the factory. The standard fitment is a regular Ford V8 100-HP engine

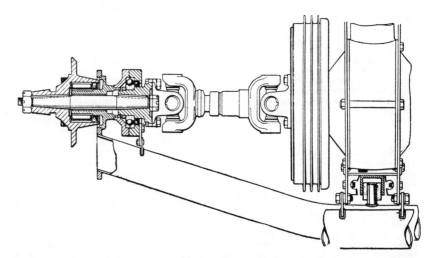

FIG. 4: The deDion rear end layout of the J2 gives vertical wheel movement and maximum road-holding, but has slightly higher unsprung weight than the swing-axle system.

(239 cubic inches). Or this same engine can be had with special Allard dual Solex manifold and 7½:1 aluminum heads, developing 120 HP at 3800 RPM. Optionally, this engine is available bored and stroked ⅛ of an inch to give 140 HP on 8½:1 compression.

For the last year they've also had a Cadillac engine conversion in the catalog; this is the regular overhead-valve V8 (331 cubic inches), but with a special Allard dual manifold and eight-quart shallow oil sump for ground clearance. The output here is stated to be 160 HP at 4000 RPM, as installed in the car. In all cases, a dry-plate clutch and modified Ford three-speed transmission are used, with several gear box and rear axle gear sets optional.

Incidentally, though not available at the factory, the J2 has been very successful this year with converted Chrysler V8 power units. This combinaton has proved to be the fastest yet.

### ROAD PERFORMANCE

With the J2's low weight, small frontal area, and high HP, we'd expect the performance on the road to be something pretty special. And it is! As sold from the factory, the Allard J2 carries a light two-seat aluminum competition body with the seats well back, just ahead of the rear axle (see Fig. 3); this puts about 53% of the loaded weight on the rear wheels for best traction and road-holding, and total curb weight runs 2,300 pounds.

Reliable performance figures with all engine combinations are scarce, but London *Motor* magazine recently ran full road tests on the J2 with the standard Cadillac 160-HP plant and 3.27:1 axle ratio. We can quote a few figures from this. To tell the truth, top speed was à bit of a disappointment to all concerned. Running on 80-octane pump fuel, the absolute true top was 110.8 MPH at 4400 RPM!

Since it was known that the car would exceed 100 MPH with the 100-HP Ford engine, top speed here should theoretically have been 115-120 MPH. It is now known that the standard Cadillac hydraulic tappets had begun to float and pump up at this high RPM, which caused the HP to drop off. Dynamometer tests show that the Caddie will cut right out above 4500 RPM from this tappet pump-up! No solid tappets are yet available for this engine in England.

To offset the disappointing maximum speed, however, some truly astonishing acceleration times were clocked. From a standing start to 60 MPH, using first and second gears, took a mere 7.4 seconds, and the standing quarter-mile was covered in 16.3 seconds. The J2 will reach 100 MPH from a dead stop in no more than 23.6 seconds. It should be remembered that much of this terrific acceleration is due to the increased traction of the right rear wheel with the deDion rear suspension. It'll burn rubber to 80 MPH, but it keeps digging all the way!

In road racing, they generally run up to 60 MPH in low gear and maybe 90 in second (using solid tappets). Maximum top gear speeds reached on the road circuits like Bridgehampton and Watkins Glen, with moderately-souped Cadillac and Chrysler engines of 200-250 HP, range around 130 MPH, at which speeds the J2 is said to be very stable and controllable.

When you combine this top speed with the blinding acceleration getting away from slow corners, it's no wonder that the J2 is having little trouble staying in front of the Ferraris and Jaguars! In fact, it's generally agreed that acceleration—and not top speed—is the Allard's big trump card.

So that's the story. Sidney Allard has succeeded very nicely in his original purpose—he's producing an extremely successful competition sports model for a price of only $3,350 (with the Cadillac engine).

But I'm compelled to conclude on a sour note. There is another impressive sports car on the British horizon that's stealing the Allard's thunder—that is the new Jaguar XK-120-C competition model. This short-chassis, lightened version of the famous '120' won this year's LeMans race and easily out-lapped the Cadillac-Allards.

With an entirely new rear end layout that eliminates transverse axle torque, and a fully-streamlined body, the 120-C got good acceleration and hit better than 150 MPH on the straights with its 195 HP. The J2 can still out-accelerate the 120-C, and could doubtless stay in front on a slow road course where extremely high speeds are not a factor, but on the faster courses it hasn't a chance.

Now if Allard would toss out those cycle-type mudguards and go to a fully-enveloping body. . . . What do they say? "The wheel of progress spins, and where it stops—well, it just never does!"  ☆ ☆

---

# MONTE CARLO RALLY IMPRESSIONS

### —by Sydney Allard

MY crew consisted of Guy Warburton and Tom Lush, and the crew arrangements were that Guy and I should share the driving and Tom be responsible for navigating and time-keeping. The same crew had done the Rally previously and this arrangement had proved satisfactory.

We selected Glasgow as our starting point, as the alternative starting places in Europe meant too long a time away from the office desk. We found we were the last but one to leave, there being 72 cars in front of us. Mrs. Allard and her sisters, in an Allard, were 15 numbers ahead of us, and this order was kept until their unfortunate retirement some 300 miles from Monte Carlo.

The weather conditions between Glasgow and Carlisle were fairly bad, the roads being covered in snow with patches of ice, and these conditions were again met some 50 miles from Llandrindod.

From Wales we headed for Folkestone. The channel crossing was accomplished without trouble and we were soon on our way to the first foreign control at Lille. From Lille we turned northwards towards Liége and from there northwards again into the flat lands of Holland. We crossed the new Arnhem Bridge in the early hours of the morning and were in Amsterdam in time for a very early breakfast. Here we joined up with competitors from some of the other starting controls and began to see foreign makes of cars bearing the registration plates of most of the European countries. An amusing incident occurred at this control. When we came to get back in our car, we were horrified to see that somebody had painted an enormous greyhound on the side. We were rather annoyed and it was not until we attempted to unlock the car and found our key would not fit that we discovered it was not our car but another Allard of identical colour ; it had started from Norway ! We had a lot of fun over this coincidence during the rest of the Rally when we watched other people making the same mistake. The weather so far had been dry and cold but nothing had yet occurred which could affect our timekeeping.

From Amsterdam we turned southward through Antwerp, Brussels and Rheims to Paris. We were escorted through Paris by motor-cycle police who led the cars in convoy to the outskirts of the city. The police entered thoroughly into the spirit of the thing and our average speed for the short distance through the Paris traffic was very high indeed ! Just south of Paris we turned off the main road, which until now had been used for the entire route, and for the first time made our way over secondary roads towards the mountains which lay ahead.

At Bourges, which lay in the valley, we were told that the roads ahead were deeply snow-bound and that heavy snow was falling in the mountains. We pressed on, travelling as fast as possible, because we knew that the critical part of the Rally now lay ahead. The snow was being blown horizontally against the windscreen and thick patches of fog made visibility extremely poor. The width of the road was considerably reduced by the high snow banks on either side and this made passing a matter of waiting one's chance at a wider section, or perhaps a bend, and then and there pressing on without hesitation. This was a very interesting procedure as one never quite knew what lay ahead !

We covered all sections without loss of time, although the last one from Le Puy down through the Rhone Valley to Valance, a distance of some 80 miles, was completed with only a minute in hand. This was where most of the other competitors lost marks and we were the only Glasgow starter to get through on time. The rest of the run was uneventful although the roads were snowbound.

We spent the whole of Saturday, in company with many others, going round the course of the Regularity Test, and at the end of the day thought we had memorised all the most difficult parts.

We were horrified to find on Sunday morning that it had been snowing hard all night, which meant that most of our landmarks were obliterated ; however, we started the test, together with 50 other competitors, and by lunchtime we had all finished. I spent the afternoon waiting for the results. We were having tea when the news came through that we had won the Rally.

# EVOLUTION OF THE ALLARD

*THE FIRST ALLARD, subsequent to S. H. Allard's prototype CLK5—*

SYDNEY ALLARD'S first Allard, the famous CLK5, was built in 1936. It was evolved from a crashed Ford V8 saloon. The chassis was cut down, normal Ford suspension, rod-operated brakes and welded Ford wheels retained, while the body had a G.P. Bugatti tail, and the steering box was also Bugatti. The engine was a standard 30-h.p. V8. Incidentally, Warburton later acquired it and today it still exists.

CLK5 was so successful that two more similar Allards were built, using longer, "imitation-Bugatti" tails and sloping vee radiator grilles coming to a point at the base. These cars incorporated new side- and cross-members purchased from the Ford Co., Ford steel disc wheels, and divided axle i.f.s. FGP 750 had a drilled chassis, was very light, and Allard used it to collect many awards. The sister car was bought by K. Hutchison and driven by him in a pre-war Experts' Trial, amongst many other events.

The next three Allards had 2/4-seater bodies and flat instead of vee radiator grilles, with inbuilt stoneguards. The first, AUX 59, was supplied to Sydney's father and often chauffeur driven; it is now in Scotland. The next, EXX 455, was owned by Mr. Gilson, went to Ireland, but is now back in this country and has been converted by its present owner to coil-spring i.f.s. These cars had Ford wheels but the third, EXP 469, had wire wheels and Rudge hubs. It was sold to someone in Berkhamsted and last year was driven in trials by Hancock.

A more exciting car came next, for whereas those mentioned so far used V8 30 engines with iron heads, FXP 470, built for Ken Hutchison, had a Lincoln Zephyr V12 engine. A Ford gearbox was retained and the engine accommodated by shortening the torque-tube. A 30-gallon slab-tank was fitted, and the flat radiator grille retained. Hutchison drove this car in the 6-Hour Sports Car Race at Brooklands but the fan belt fell off. Pulling a 4.11 to 1 axle ratio it would do 60 in second, 90 m.p.h. in top and the s.s. ¼-mile in 17.8 sec. Later Len Parker made this Allard the basis of his fearsome rear-engined Parker Special trials car.

We come now to three more-civilised Allards built just prior to the war. They had full four-seater bodies, streamlined wings, spatted at the back, and the sloping vee radiator grille coming to a point at the base. EXP 470 was a Zephyr V12-engined car built for Silcock and driven in the Alpine Rally after the war by Len Potter. ELL 300 was a similar Allard, but with V8 engine, delivered to V. S. A. Biggs. One of these cars was later driven in trials by K. McAlpine, who increased its ground clearance and fitted strip wings, etc.

The last of this series, LMG 192, was another V12, intended for the 1939 Show but unfinished when war intervened. It was later completed and driven by Allard in the first speed trial after the war at Bristol, and also in trials, including an "Experts'." Experimental work leading up to the production cars was performed on it, then Wick acquired it and now it resides at Banstead.

By 1945 Allard was supplying cars to order, to comply with the clamour of connoisseurs. In 1946 he formed the Allard Motor Co., Ltd., and a white two-seater and red four-seater, having new curved grilles and low alligator bonnets, appeared in the London Cavalcade that year, driven by Imhof and Hutchison. Canham completed the trio in Silcock's pre-war V12.

Production commenced with rather stark two-seaters, which had V8 engines and the same 8 ft. 4 in. wheelbase of the pre-war cars. They were known as the J-type. The more refined K-type two-seater, of 8 ft. 10 in. wheelbase, followed. A four-seater L-type was also produced at this time, and in June, 1947, these were joined by a drophead coupé—the M-type—on the four-seater chassis. This coupé proved so popular that the J and L-type Allards were gradually discontinued and the K made only in small numbers.

In August, 1949, coil springs replaced a transverse leaf spring for the divided-axle i.f.s., 2LS Lockheed brakes were adopted and the P-type saloon, Monte Carlo Rally winner this year, was introduced at the Show on the coupé chassis. This was a winner also in the commercial sense and to meet the demand for saloons the coupé was gradually dropped. It was, however, re-introduced at the 1951 Show in revised form, known as the M2. The K-type two-seater, after slight modification, re-emerged in 1950 as the K2, with larger body, new-type front grille and bumpers and a big luggage locker. Before this, in August, 1949, a new sports Allard, very stark, with oversize Mercury engine, made its debut at Prescott and this went into production as the famous J2 with coil springs all round and de Dion back-end, a Cadillac engine being available as an alternative for U.S.A. customers. This in turn has given way to the J2X, with Ardun-Ford, or 5.4-litre Cadillac or Chrysler o.h.v. V8 engine, as tested by MOTOR SPORT in Chrysler form last December, when the differences between J2X and the J2 were described. In its various guises the Allard has won 92 important awards, and has set seal to its world-wide fame by its victory in the recent Monte Carlo Rally.—W. B.

*—AND the present-day Type P saloon, on its way to its great victory in the Monte Carlo Rally.*

NEW LINES.—The all-enveloping coachwork, in the continental style, gives the car a completely different appearance from any of the standard Allard models.

CONTROLS.—A good deal of thought has gone into the facia arrangement. Apart from the lamps, each electrical component has its individual switch and the instruments are all plain and grouped in front of the driver. The horn button, on the right, and trafficator switch, just visible below the left-hand wheel spoke, can both be operated without removing the hand from the wheel.

# MADE T

carry cold air directly to the engine compartment.

Interior accommodation extends the full width of the all-enveloping body so that, apart from the obtrusion of the centrally placed gear lever, three people can sit abreast on the single-piece, pneumatic upholstered seat. The luggage space between the back of the seat and the rear window is of such capacity that two or three sizeable suitcases plus other items of baggage can be stowed without coming above the bottom line of the deep rear window.

Visibility in all directions has obviously received a fair measure of study with the result that, despite a long bonnet and an overall height of only 4½ feet, one has a remarkably

TAKE a car which, when road tested by "The Motor" in February last year, was described as "the finest sports motor bicycle on four wheels ever conceived"; reclothe it with wind-cheating, coupé coachwork, add a few chassis modifications to suit and you have . . . not everybody's choice of a motor car, perhaps, but one possessing all the necessities for competition work, plus the protection, passenger accommodation and luggage space required for practical, long-distance touring.

Such a car has just taken shape. The basis is a J2 Allard chassis and the coachwork is of all-enveloping, continental style, designed and developed by the car's owner, Mr. A. G. Imhof, the well-known trials and rally driver.

To allow for the increased accommodation which the body design provides, certain chassis modifications have been found necessary, the major change being an increase in length of 1 foot; as an illustration shows, this increase occurs between the back of the seat and the rear axle. To deal with the increased body width, special outriggers have been provided for front and rear mounting and the tubular chassis hoop which supports the dash and bulkhead has been widened by 14 ins. The steering column is moved 7 ins. to the right, to bring it into line with the new driving position and the pedal position altered accordingly. Other chassis changes consist of shorter coil springs at the rear and re-positioning of the telescopic dampers which are now of the heavy-duty type.

For the present, the power unit is a Ford V-8 bored out to 4½-litres capacity and equipped with aluminium cylinder heads and twin carburetters. Running on pump fuel, with a 7 to 1 compression ratio, an output of 120 b.h.p., at 3,800 r.p.m. is available which, it is stated, has propelled the car over an electrically-timed quarter mile at 102 m.p.h. Later on, it is intended to install a Cadillac engine which should considerably step up the performance.

The main air flow from the low-set front aperture is ducted direct to the radiator, while two smaller ducts

RELATIVE PROPORTIONS.—The increase in size of the coupé mo the standard J2 is clearly seen in this illustration where the outlin seater, to the same scale, has been superimposed

good all-round view helped by very careful choice and placing of the rear-view mirror. The doors, being hollowed-out inside, make no provision for winding glass windows; the material used is Perspex, arranged, in the case of the door windows, to slide manually up and down. The rear quarter windows have a limited degree of outward opening.

The windscreen is of the divided type with the driver's side made to open, another practical feature in this department being a special linkage in the screen-wiper arms, altering the angle of the blade as the arm moves upwards, so that, in the topmost extremity of the sweep, each blade fits right up against the screen centre pillar. A further item which gives emphasis to the practical planning which has gone into this car, is the arrangement whereby the headlights, which are of the dip-and-switch variety, can be changed over to meet continental or British requirements, simply by moving a switch beneath the facia.

The rear end of the car, beneath the luggage compartment, is devoted to carrying the spare wheel, access being obtained through a movable panel which also carries the rear number plate. Fuel is accommodated in two separate

# MEASURE

## A Special Coupé Version of a Popular Competition Machine

10-gallon tanks, situated in the rear wings, each with its own filler, individual fuel line and pump.

We were fortunate in being able to test this Allard coupé throughout a 700-mile weekend during which time the weather conditions ranged between sleet and brilliant sunshine, while road surfaces alternated from billiard table by-pass to mud-packed track.

### Further Developments Planned

It would be wrong to imagine that the introduction of a streamlined all-enveloping form of coachwork must automatically turn a rip-snorting road racing car into a docile town carriage. The qualities of the Allard, which may be summed up as rough, rugged and reliable, are not necessarily concealed beneath an elegant coupé. On the car now under review virtually no attention has yet been paid to sound damping or luxurious equipment. Such improvements are, however, in the course of preparation and undoubtedly this J2 will emerge, when powered by the Cadillac engine, as an infinitely quieter and more docile machine than is at present the case.

Nevertheless, the experience of driving the Imhof Allard is one which no car enthusiast would gladly forgo.

As in the case of the open two-seater version, it is necessary to "play oneself in." Unlike many lesser motor-cars, the Allard simply cannot safely be driven fast within a few miles of takeover. The combination of all-round independent suspension, extremely high-geared and accurate steering and a weight distribution which centres well aft, means that the machine must be "learned" much in the same way as a successful racing yacht, which seldom responds to inexperienced hands.

It takes about 100 miles of hard driving to weigh up the Imhof Allard and then the reward is perceived because there are only a few production models which are faster or safer on four wheels, provided that the driver knows the form.

Obviously a car which can overtake slower traffic with such all-conquering ease must be less prone to hazard than the slower brethren. Equally a car equipped with such outstanding brakes can be relied upon to look after itself when the inevitable emergency does arise. The Imhof Allard, painted a rather pleasant shade of cherry red, with its combination of an immensely long bonnet (by modern standards) and low overall height, caused us some speculation as to the reception the car might have in industrial and agricultural districts. We need not have worried. Clearly the British are now motor-minded to an extent not known before the war. Whenever the car arrived at a garage

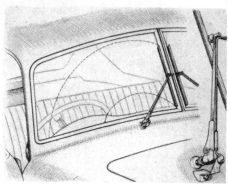

**FULL SWEEP.**—A special linkage has been devised to change the angle of the wiper arms as they traverse their arc, so that they abut completely with the screen centre pillar and the bottom screen edge at each extremity of travel.

**LUGGAGE ROOM.**—A surprising quantity of luggage can be carried without interrupting rearward vision.

or paused outside a shop, crowds began to gather. An interesting point emerged throughout that, as a result of the tremendous publicity arising from the Monte-Carlo Rally, the name of Allard has become a household word.

Reviewing the Imhof version of an Allard, it is clear that this particular car has been built to suit both the physique and general requirements of one man. The intention has been to create an immensely fast and practicable road car combining the exceptionally fine qualities of the competition machine with a measure of weather protection and comfort which cannot be expected from an open body. To a large extent we believe that this courageous experiment has succeeded and it will be interesting to see if the final outcome inspires a production model following the same general specification.

### ALLARD J.2 SPECIAL COUPÉ

| Engine Dimensions | | Chassis Details | | |
|---|---|---|---|---|
| Cylinders ... ... | 8 | Brakes ... ... | Lockheed hydraulic, 2 L.S. front |  |
| Bore ... ... | 84.13 mm. | Brake drum diameter | 12 ins. |  |
| Stroke ... ... | 98.42 mm. | Friction lining area... | 156 sq. ins. |  |
| Cubic capacity ... | 4,375 c.c. | Suspension: Front ... | Swing axle with coil spring |  |
| Piston area ... | 67.6 sq. ins. | Rear ... | Coil spring with de Dion axle |  |
| Valve ... ... | Side | Shock absorbers ... | Woodhead Munroe telescopic |  |
| Compression ratio ... | 7/1 | Wheel type ... | Pressed steel |  |
| Engine Performance | | Tyre size ... | 6.00-16 |  |
| Max. b.h.p. ... | 120 | Steering gear ... | Marles |  |
| at ... | 3,800 r.p.m. | Steering wheel ... | Bluemel 4 spring spoke |  |
| B.H.P. per sq. in. | | | | |
| Piston area ... | 1.77 | Dimensions | | |
| Peak piston speed ft. | | Wheelbase ... ... | 9 ft. 4 ins. |  |
| per min. ... | 2,400 | Track: Front ... | 4 ft. 8 ins. |  |
| | | Rear ... | 4 ft. 4 ins. |  |
| Engine Details | | Overall length ... | 15 ft. 8 ins. |  |
| Carburetter ... | Two Ford downdraught | Overall width ... | 5 ft. 7 ins. |  |
| Ignition ... | Coil | Overall height ... | 4 ft. 6 ins. |  |
| Plug make and type | 14 mm. Champion | Ground clearance ... | 4½ ins. |  |
| Fuel pump ... | Two S.U. | Turning circle ... | 36 ft. |  |
| Fuel capacity ... | 20 gallons | Dry weight ... | 25½ cwt. |  |
| Cooling system ... | 2 gallons | Performance Data | | |
| Sump capacity ... | Twin pump | Piston area, sq. in. | | |
| Gearbox capacity ... | 4½ gallons | per ton ... | 53.0 |  |
| Electrical system ... | 12 volt | Brake lining area, sq. | | |
| | | in. per ton ... | 122 |  |
| Transmission | | Top gear m.p.h. per | | |
| Clutch ... | Ford single dry plate, heavy duty | 1,000 r.p.m. ... | 23.0 |  |
| Gear ratios: Top ... | 3.5 | Top gear m.p.h. at | | |
| 2nd ... | 6.2 | 2,500 ft./min. piston | | |
| 1st ... | 10.8 | speed ... | 89 |  |
| Rev. ... | 14.0 | Litres per ton-mile, | | |
| Prop. shaft ... | Torque tube | dry... ... | 4,480 |  |
| Final drive ... | Spiral bevel | | | |

# FOR ALL TYPES OF MOTORING

ALLARD

## PALM BEACH OPEN THREE SEATER

The ideal small touring car, with two doors, detachable sliding windows and a bench type front seat. Powered with the Ford Consul or Zodiac O.H.V. engine.

4 cyl. Consul 1,508 c.c. 47 B.H.P. 6 cyl. Zodiac 2,262 c.c. 71 B.H.P. Gear ratios: 4.11 top, 6.96 second, 13.45 first, 16.87 reverse. Hypoid final drive. Centre gear change. Coil suspension front and rear. Girling hydraulic brakes with 2 leading shoes on front. 12-volt electrical system. 6.40 x 13 tyres. Fuel tank capacity 8½ gallons. Wheelbase 8'. Overall length 13' 1½" Width 4' 11". Ground clearance 5". Turning circle 28'. Additional equipment available includes wire wheels, overdrive, multiple carburetters, etc.

PRICE : CONSUL £720 plus P.T. £301 2s. 6d.

ZODIAC £750 plus P.T. £313 12s. 6d.

## 2¼ litre COACHBUILT SALOON

Built on the same chassis as the Palm Beach, the 2 seater Saloon body constructed by Messrs. Abbott Limited, has a low drag form, and has aluminium panelling on a frame of Ash mounted in one with the tubes of the chassis to form a very rigid structure. Visibility is exceedingly good with the low front, and large windscreen. A large carpet-lined luggage locker is fitted and supplemented by considerable space behind the Dunlopillo trimmed bucket seats.

PRICE : £1,250 plus P.T. £521 19s. 2d.

## THE "MONTE CARLO" SALOON

Five-six seater with full equipment including heating and air conditioning with de-mister. Radio set at extra cost.

8 cyl. Ford V.8 engine, 3,622 c.c. 85 B.H.P. Gear ratios: 3.78 top, 6.7 second, 11.8 first, and 15.1 reverse. Spiral bevel final drive. Side gear change. Coil suspension front and rear. De-Dion type rear axle. Lockheed hydraulic brakes with 2 leading shoes on front. 12-volt electrical system. 6.25 x 16 tyres. Fuel tank capacity 18 gallons. Wheelbase 9' 4". Overall length 16'. Width 5' 11". Height 5'. Ground clearance 8". Turning circle 41'.

PRICE : £1,375 plus P.T. £574 0s. 10d.

## THE "SAFARI" ESTATE CAR

Built on the same chassis as the Saloon, this is a full six seater with two extra occasional seats at rear. All, except front seat with room for three, fold away leaving flat floor luggage space 72" x 50".

PRICE : £1,375 plus P.T. £574 0s. 10d.

## THE K.3 TOURING THREE SEATER

A grand touring car with two doors, a bench type front seat, wind-up windows and a large luggage boot.

8 cyl. Ford V.8 engine with aluminium cylinder heads, 3,622 c.c. 95 B.H.P. Gear ratios: 3.5 top, 6.2 second, 10.8 first, 14.0 reverse. Spiral bevel final drive. Side gear change. Coil suspension front and rear. De-Dion type rear axle. Lockheed hydraulic brakes with 2 leading shoes on front. 12-volt electrical system. 6.25 x 16 tyres. Fuel tank capacity 13 gallons. Wheelbase 8' 4". Overall length 14' 9". Width 5' 6½". Height 4' 6". Ground clearance 8". Turning circle 38'.

PRICE : £1,100 plus P.T. £459 9s. 2d.

# ALLARD MOTOR COMPANY LTD. 24 - 28 CLAPHAM HIGH STREET, LONDON, S.W.4 - - ENGLAND

*Telegraphic Address:* Inland - Almotco, Clapcom, London
Overseas - Almotco, London

*Telephone :* MACaulay 3201

The  P2 Tubular Chassis

The 3·6 litre **ALLARD** chassis offers a real opportunity to individual stylists and enthusiasts. It provides a first class basis for a first class car. The ability of the V.8 engine to pull strongly and smoothly at any speed, the powerful and progressive hydraulic brakes, the light but positive handling at high speeds plus tractability at low speeds conferred by the divided axle front suspension and the De-Dion axle rear suspension, the rigidity of the new tubular chassis frame with room for six comfortable seats and luggage room unimpaired by the spare wheel

Incorporating a Ford V.8 engine has the additional advantage-*and an all important one from the owners viewpoint* -**the servicing facilities of a world wide organisation are available at all times in all districts**

This servicing feature also applies to: Wheel Bearings, Oil Seals, King Pins and Bushes, Track Rod Ball ends and Rear Axle Unit including Crown Wheel and Pinion

> **HEATING AND VENTILATING ARE BUILT IN FEATURES OF THE NEW P.2 CHASSIS**

**THE NEW TUBULAR CHASSIS is designed also to accommodate the LINCOLN CHRYSLER and CADILLAC V.8 Engines for Dollar Areas**

FULL CONVERSION SETS SUPPLIED AT AN EXTRA COST

# *Specifications*

### ENGINE DETAILS

Cylinders: V.8
Valves: Side
Bore: 77·8 mm.
Stroke: 95·2 mm.
Capacity: 3622 cc.
Compression Ratio: 6·15 : 1
Max. BHP: 85 at 3500 r.p.m.
Carburettor: Ford-Chandr. Groves
Ignition: Battery and Coil
Spark Plugs: Champion 7
Fuel Pump: Ford A.C.
Fuel Capacity: 18 Imp. Gall.
Oil Capacity: 1 Gall.
12 Volt. Lighting Equipment

### TRANSMISSON

3 Speed Gearbox.  Overall Gear ratios:
    Top: 3·78:1  2nd: 6·68:1  1st:11·75:1
Clutch: Single Dry Plate

### CHASSIS DETAILS

Brakes: Lockheed Hydraulic
Suspension: Front, Divided Axle, Coil Springs
              Rear, De-Dion Axle,  ,,     ,,
Tyres: 625 x 16
Shock Absorbers: Hydraulic
Steering Gear: Marles patent

### DIMENSIONS

Wheelbase: 9ft. 4ins.
Width: 5ft. 11ins.
Weight: 19½ cwts. as shown
Ground Clearance: 8ins.
Turning Circle: 40ft.
Floor Height: 15ins.

The P.2 Chassis is available complete as shown
with full instruments including rev-counter, speedometer, warning lights, head and side lights, bulkhead, front and rear bumpers

★ Tubular Chassis Frame

★ De-Dion Rear Type Axle

★ 30 h.p. V.8 Engine

★ Air-Conditioning and Heating

★ Lockheed Hydraulic Brakes

★ 8in. Ground Clearance

★ Trickle charger or lead light plug provided under bonnet

**ALLARD MOTOR COMPANY LTD**    24-28 CLAPHAM HIGH STREET
LONDON S.W.4  -  ENGLAND

LE MANS

## EXHILARATING MOTORING WITH COMPLETE SAFETY

*The* **ALLARD** *J.2.X. Competition*

*2 Seater - Custom Built Body*

The **ALLARD J.2.X.** standard competition 2 seater, has a 2-door aluminium light-weight body with cycle type front wings and aero screens. The Le Mans Body a 2-door aerodynamic body - both body styles conform with International Sports car regulations.

The J.2.X. Chassis is fitted with a 3.9 litre overhead valve V8 engine, and offers a real opportunity to the competition driver and enthusiast, and with the ability of the V8 engine to pull strongly and smoothly at any speed - the powerful and progressive hydraulic brakes - the light but positive handling at high speeds, conferred by the divided axle front suspension, and the De-Dion type rear suspension, makes either model a most delightful car to drive, with power and speed when required - strikingly modern in design and unequalled servicing facilities of a world wide organisation.

The Le Mans body when fitted is an additional cost. Both body styles can be fitted with Wire wheels, Hood and full width Windscreen as an extra.

★ **De-Dion Type Rear Axle**

★ **Divided Front Axle**

★ **3·9 Litre V8 Engine**

★ **Coil Spring Suspension**

★ **Lockheed Hydraulic Brakes**

★ **Al-Fin Drums**

★ **Marles Steering**

★ **6½″ Ground Clearance**

**Performance Extraordinary !**

At the 1952 Monte Carlo Rally the Allard P.1. Saloon had an outright win against 328 competitors . . . scoring the first British Victory in 21 years.

# The  ALLARD J.2.X. Competition
## 2 Seater

# Specifications

### ENGINE DETAILS

Cylinders : V8
Valves : Overhead
Bore : 81 m.m.
Stroke : 95·25 m.m.
Cubic Capacity : 3917 c.c.
Compression Ratio : 7·0 : 1
Max. BHP 140 at 4000 RPM.
Carburettor : Twin
Ignition : Battery and Coil
Fuel Pump : Mech. and Electric
Fuel Capacity : 22 Imp. Gall.
Oil Capacity : 2 gall.
12 Volt Lighting Equipment

### TRANSMISSION

3 Speed Gearbox (Centre Change)
Overall Gear Ratios :
    Top : 3·27 : 1 — 2nd : 5·8 : 1
        1st : 10·02 : 1
Clutch : Single Dry Plate

### CHASSIS DETAILS

Brakes : Lockheed Hydraulic 2 L. S.
Suspension :
    Front : Divided Axle, Coil Springs
    Rear : De-Dion Type Coil Springs
Tyres : 6·00 × 16
Shock Absorbers : Hydraulic

### DIMENSIONS

Wheelbase : 8′ 4″
Width : 5′ 8″
Height : 3′ 8½″
Weight Approx. 18 cwts.
Ground Clearance : 6½″
Turning Circle : 38′
Front Track : 4′ 8″
Rear    ,,    4′ 4½″
Overall Length : 12′ 11″

> **Both models are designed to accommodate the Lincoln, Cadillac and Chrysler V8 engines for dollar areas only at extra cost.**

Tests of a stock model **ALLARD J.2.X.** made under average conditions showed the following acceleration times — stationary to 30 m.p.h. in 3·5 secs., to 40 m.p.h. in 5·7 secs., to 50 m.p.h. in 6·8 secs., to 80 m.p.h. in 15·3 secs., maximum speed 120 m.p.h.

**ALLARD MOTOR COMPANY LTD** 24-28 CLAPHAM HIGH STREET
LONDON S.W.4 - ENGLAND

*Telegraphic Address : Inland - Almotco, Clapcom, London*    Telephone : MACaulay 3201

# EXHILARATING MOTORING WITH COMPLETE SAFETY

The  "Safari" Estate Car

The 3·6 litre **ALLARD SAFARI** estate car is the outstanding result of long research into the possibilities of combining a superior European type chassis with an American type power unit. The advantages immediately became apparent - performance and reliability of the robust V8 engine is combined with the roadability of a high-class sports car. Capable of maintaining high speeds the **ALLARD** will maintain a perfectly straight course without effort, and will swing through a tortuous series of corners with equal facility.

Incorporating a Ford V8 engine has an additional advantage — *and an all-important one from the owners viewpoint*—**the servicing facilities of a world wide organisation are available at all times in all districts.**

**This servicing feature also applies to Wheel Bearings, Oil Seals, King Pins and Bushes, Track Rod Ball Ends and Rear Axle Unit including Crown Wheel and Pinion.**

Full SIX SEATER with occasional seat for two or Luggage space

★ Tubular Chassis Frame
★ De-Dion Rear Type Axle
★ 30 h.p. V8 Engine
★ Coil Spring Suspension
★ Air-Conditioning and Heating
★ High power to weight ratio

★ Lockheed Hydraulic Brakes
★ 8ins. Ground Clearance
★ Luxury Hide Upholstery
★ Interior Light with door operated switch
★ Automatic Reverse Light
★ Hydraulically Operated Bonnet
★ Built-in Wireless Aerial
★ Trickle Charger or Lead Light Plug provided under Bonnet
★ Laminated Wind Screen

**CARS**

PERFORMANCE EXTRAORDINARY!
At the 1952 Monte Carlo Rally the Allard Saloon had an outright win against 328 competitors . . . scoring the first British victory in 21 years

# THE NEW [ ALLARD ] "SAFARI" ESTATE CAR

## *Specifications*

### ENGINE DETAILS

Cylinders : V8
Valves : Side
Bore : 77·8 mm.
Stroke : 95·2 mm.
Cubic Capacity : 3622 cc.
Compression Ratio : 6·15 : 1
Max. BHP : 85 at 3500 r.p.m.
Carburettor : Ford-Chandler-Groves
Ignition : Battery and Coil
Sparking Plugs : Champion 7
Fuel Pump : Ford A.C.
Fuel Capacity : 18 Imp. Gall.
Oil Capacity : 1 Gall.
12 Volt Lighting Equipment

### TRANSMISSION

3 Speed Gearbox. Overall Gear ratios :
Top : 3·78 : 1 — 2nd. 6·68 : 1
1st. 11·75 : 1
Clutch : Single Dry Plate

### CHASSIS DETAILS

Brakes : Lockheed
Suspension :
   Front : Divided Axle, Coil Springs
   Rear : De Dion  ,.  ,,  ,,
Tyres : 625 x 16
Shock Absorbers : Hydraulic

### DIMENSIONS

Wheelbase : 9ft. 4ins.
Width : 5ft. 11ins.
Height : 5ft.
Weight : 30 cwt.
Ground Clearance : 8ins.
Turning Circle . 40ft.
Floor Height : 15ins.

Tests of a stock model **ALLARD** made under average conditions showed the following acceleration times — stationary to 30 mph. in 5·6 secs., to 40 mph. in 8·8 secs., to 50 mph. in 12·8 secs. Shock stopping distance of the brakes from 30 mph. was 27ft. 10in.

Strikingly modern in design, the **ALLARD "SAFARI"** is the perfect combination of a comfortable saloon car with the sleek lines and general roadworthiness of the sports car.

The **ALLARD** has all the features to make the ideal car for any conditions — comfortable driving, plenty of power, speed when you want it, and unequalled servicing facilities throughout the world by FORD MAIN DEALERS.

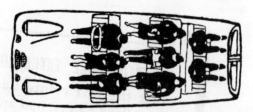

The New Tubular Chassis Frame is design
also to accommodate the
   LINCOLN
     CHRYSLER
      and CADILLAC V.8 Engines
        for Dollar Are

Full Conversion Sets supplied at an extra cost

---

**ALLARD MOTOR COMPANY LTD** 24-28 CLAPHAM HIGH STREE
LONDON S.W.4 - ENGLAN

A Spacious New Model on a
Tubular Chassis, Designed
to Go Far and Fast

CAPACITY.—The Safari transports six people in comfort at speed, with 45 cubic feet of luggage space behind them. Alternatively, eight people with less luggage space, or three people with 95 cubic feet of space can be accommodated.

# Allard Introduce "The SAFARI"

ORIGINALLY, the V-8 Allard was a trials car, and although the make is no longer regularly represented in such events, the outright victory of Sydney Allard in this year's Monte-Carlo Rally is still fresh in memory. These things are recalled to emphasize how truly in the Allard tradition is the new model announced this week, the "Safari" estate car, which combines great roominess and rugged go-anywhere characteristics with the promise of sports-car speed and controllability.

The new body may be described as an eight-seater, the individual front seats being arranged to form a single

three-seater bench when required, and the gear lever being set on the floor to the right of the driver. Behind the front seats there is a bench-type seat, comfortable, but readily folded away beneath a flat floor, and behind this again is a rearward-facing bench seat with ample foot-room, which can also be folded out of sight. Luggage accommodation varies with the number of seats in use, amounting to 45 cubic ft. if the rearmost seat is folded, or 95 cubic ft. on a single flat floor if the car is only in use as a three-seater.

Beneath the new body there is a totally new chassis based upon Allard racing experience. There is the latest layout of divided-axle I.F.S. as evolved for the J2X model, and a de Dion-pattern rear axle with sprung differential to give low unsprung weight and exceptionally good traction on slippery surfaces. These features are now built

into a multi-tubular chassis frame, two large diameter tubes which form each chassis longeron being linked by welded-in connecting members and boxed together at the points of maximum stress. This new chassis has been on test since last summer, on pavé and other bad surfaces, and should be of very great strength.

The new model, which is intended for export and is priced at $3,500 (£1,250), has all the usual saloon-car amenities such as a built-in fresh-air heater, long-range headlamps, instrumentation which includes a rev. counter, and provision for the mounting of car radio. As shown in the photographs, unusually full access to the mechanism is provided by a hydraulically-raised body front section, either electrical or hand pump operation of this lifting section being available.

## ═══ Allard Safari Data ═══

### ENGINE
Cylinders, V-8; bore, 77.8 mm.; stroke, 95.2 mm.; cubic capacity, 3,622 c.c.; piston area, 58.9 sq. ins.; valves, side; compression ratio, 6.1/1; alternative engines, Lincoln, Cadillac, Chrysler.

Max. power, 85 b.h.p. at 3,500 r.p.m.; Max. b.m.e.p., 102 lb./sq. in. at 2,000 r.p.m.; b.h.p. per sq. in. piston area, 1.44; peak piston speed ft. per min., 2,190.

Carburetter, twin-choke downdraught; ignition, 12-volt coil; plugs: make and type, 18 mm. Champion C7; fuel pump, AC mechanical; fuel capacity, 20 gallons; oil capacity, 8 pints; cooling system, pumps and fan; water capacity, 4½ gallons; electrical system. 12-volt.

### TRANSMISSION
Clutch, Ford s.d.p.; gear ratios: top. 3.78 (options, 3.50 and 3.27); 2nd, 6.7; 1st, 11.8; rev., 15.1; prop. shaft, enclosed; final drive, spiral bevel gears, in casing rubber-mounted on chassis.

### CHASSIS DETAILS
Brakes, Lockheed hydraulic, 2 l.s. front; brake drum diameter, 12 ins.; friction lining area, 165 sq. ins.; suspension: front, coil spring and swinging half axles; rear, coil springs and de Dion type axle; shock absorbers, Armstrong telescopic; wheel type, steel disc, 4½-inch rims; tyre size, 6.25 x 16 (up to 7.50 x 16 available at rear); steering gear, Marles worm-and-roller; steering wheel, telescopic adjustable.

### DIMENSIONS
Wheelbase, 9 ft. 4 in.; track: front, 4 ft. 8½ in.; rear, 4 ft. 10½ in.; overall length, 16 ft. 0 in.; overall width, 5 ft. 10in.; overall height, 5 ft. 3 in.; ground clearance, 7½ in.; turning circle, 41 ft.; kerb weight, 29 cwt.

ACCESS.—The whole front assembly is hinged to lift at its rear allowing access to the engine and the spare wheel which is mounted on the left-hand side. In common with other Allard models, the wearing parts of this car are mainly of Ford design, replacements therefore being internationally available.

The Allard Safari is a big, fast, roadworthy estate car which can seat six in comfort and carry eight or nine people if required. The Ford V8 is the standard power unit, but other American V-eight engines can be accommodated.

# *Allard Safari*

## A FAST AND ROADWORTHY UTILITY MODEL FOR EXPORT

VICTORY in the Monte Carlo Rally must have made the name of Allard familiar in many markets where sports cars are not of great interest, and the appeal of the Allard range to owners who require fast and roadworthy cars for daily use has been broadened by the introduction of the Allard Safari estate car to supplement the existing saloon and convertible models.

The Safari should have the excellent roadholding and rugged reliability for which this make is well known, coupled with a very large amount of practical carrying space. It will seat six people comfortably and has in addition 45 cubic feet of luggage space. If this luggage space is not required, a further two occasional seats are available. With the centre and rear seats folded away, three people can be accommodated on the front seat, leaving a total of 95 cubic feet behind them for the carriage of luggage or for

sleeping accommodation. The car has already been tested for twelve months in prototype form on road and track and over the Belgian *pavé* road surface at the M.I.R.A. proving ground.

It incorporates the same suspension system as on the famous J2X sports model, the fastest car in the Allard range, but has an entirely new and very rigid chassis frame. Whereas the J2X has a short channel section frame, the Safari has a frame in which the side members are built up from twin steel tubes joined by steel plates, a variant of the method employed on the B.R.M. Tubes are also used for the cross-members.

The J2X-type front suspension and steering layout has proved itself in sporting events throughout the world and differs from former Allard practice in that the radius arms which brace the divided front axle are taken forward instead of to the rear. Moreover, the pivots of the

──────── SPECIFICATION ────────

**Engine.**—V8, 77.9 × 95.25 mm, 3,622 c.c. 85 b.h.p. at 3,500 r.p.m.

**Transmission.** — Single-plate dry clutch. Three-speed synchromesh gear box. Remote control lever. Overall ratios 3.78, 6.7, 11.73. Alternative axle ratios 3.5 or 3.27 to 1.

**Suspension and Steering.**—Divided axle independent, with coil springs and forward projecting radius arms at front. De Dion with coil springs and Panhard rod at rear. Marles hour-glass worm and roller steering.

**Wheels and Tyres.**—6.25-16in tyres on steel disc wheels. Tyres up to 7.50in section can be fitted.

**Dimensions.**—Wheelbase 9ft 4in. Track (front) 4ft 8½in; (rear) 4ft 10½in. Overall length 16ft, width 5ft 10in, height 5ft 3in. Kerb weight 3,250 lb.

**Price.**—£1,250. Export only.

radius arms and divided half axle are on lines parallel with the chassis centre line. Coil springs are used at the front and also at the rear, where a De Dion axle is located by a Panhard rod. The brakes are by Lockheed with 12in drums and two leading shoes at the front, the system again being the same as that used on the J2X. A comprehensive heating, ventilating and demisting system is standard on the Safari, a Clayton unit being employed.

The normal engine is a side-valve Ford V.8 giving 85 b.h.p., but the car can be delivered to the United States complete with the necessary fittings to allow the installation of the new 5.4-litre Lincoln V8, the Cadillac or the Chrysler. A stan-

With the centre and rear seats folded away, 95 cubic feet of carrying capacity is available on a completely flat floor.

The third row of seats faces rearwards and the passengers' feet are accommodated in a well which houses the seat when it is not in use.

The spare wheel is neatly accommodated under the bonnet, where it does not restrict the space available for passengers and luggage.

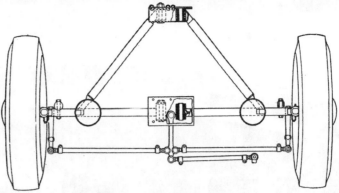

A plan view of the front suspension used on the Safari and J2X, showing the swinging half axles and forward projecting radius arms pivoted parallel with the car centre line. Suspension is by coil springs with telescopic dampers. With this layout the caster angle does not change as the wheels rise and fall.

Looking down from above the engine on one of the two hydraulic rams which lift the complete bonnet, front wing, lamp and grille assembly.

Seen here are the Ford V8 engine, the chassis frame built up from twin tubes joined by steel plates, and the electrically driven hydraulic pump which lifts the bonnet.

dard Ford three-speed gear box is employed on the normal version, but a new remote control gear change is used to bring the lever alongside the driving seat, the right-hand-drive car having a right-hand lever placed alongside the seat cushion, where it is easy to reach but causes no obstruction.

The layout of the Safari body and chassis includes several ingenious features. The spare wheel, always a problem, has been accommodated under the bonnet alongside the engine. The whole of the bonnet and front wing assembly, together with the grille and head lamps, lifts forward to allow access to the engine, front suspension and steering. It is lifted by two hydraulic rams supplied with oil under pressure by a hydraulic pump driven by an electric motor situated under the bonnet.

### Third Row

The third row of seats at the extreme rear of the vehicle faces rearwards and the passengers sit with their feet in a deep well which lies behind the fuel tank. When the seat is not required it folds away completely into the foot well, leaving a flat, unobstructed floor for luggage.

All Safaris are at present reserved for export and service is, as usual, simplified by the fact that all wearing parts in the chassis, such as bearings, pivots and oil seals are standard Ford parts or directly interchangeable with Ford parts. All screws, nuts and bolts have American standard S.A.E. threads. A wide selection of colours is available for body and trim and numerous extras are provided for, including radio and seat covers.

There is a neat engine-turned instrument panel in the centre of the facia with equipment comprising speedometer, rev counter, water temperature gauge, fuel gauge with reserve warning light, oil pressure gauge, cigar lighter, indicator warning light and main head lamp beam warning light. An adjustable telescopic steering column contributes to driving comfort.

The J2X sports model, which was first revealed at the London Show last autumn, is now in steady production. The great majority go overseas, but a few have been released on the home market. Overseas buyers can have the car fitted with the American type of quick-change rear axle in which the drive passes under the differential to a pair of spur gears at the back of the housing and then forward to the final drive. Removal of the cover plate, which is held by six nuts, gives access to the pair of gears, which can be changed in a few minutes to vary the final drive ratio. A large selection of different ratios is available to suit all types of sporting event.

The engine of the J2X is carried $7\frac{1}{2}$in farther forward in the chassis than it was in the former J2. This allows more room in the cockpit and produces a desirable increase in the weight carried on the front wheels.

The remote control lever for the three-speed gear box is conveniently located alongside the driving seat. Other items visible are the horn ring, the engine-turned instrument panel and the radio loudspeaker alongside the door pillar.

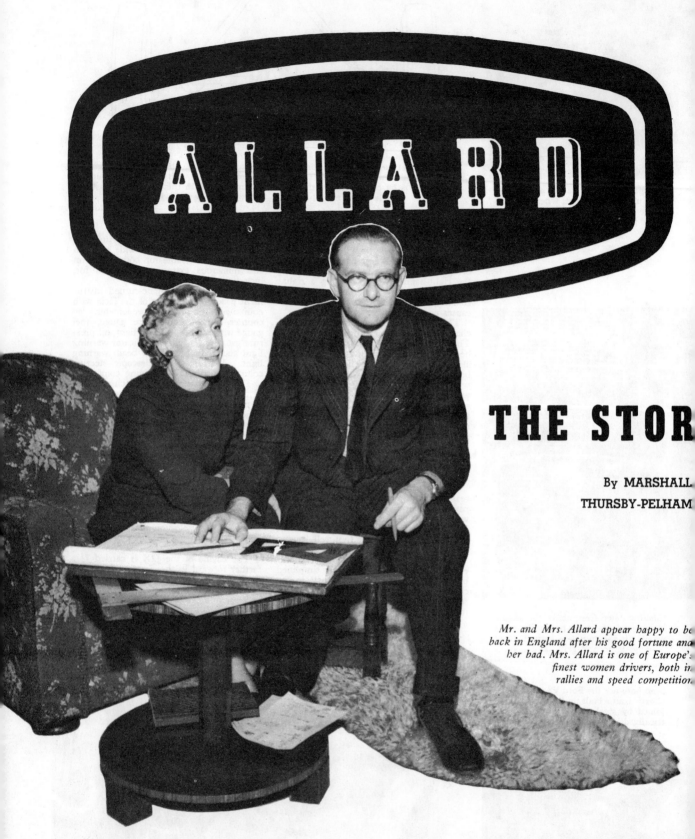

# ALLARD

## THE STOR

By MARSHALL
THURSBY-PELHAM

*Mr. and Mrs. Allard appear happy to be
back in England after his good fortune and
her bad. Mrs. Allard is one of Europe's
finest women drivers, both in
rallies and speed competition.*

*The V-8 Steyr-engined hillclimb car with which Allard
won the 1949 British Hillclimb Championship.
The 3½-liter (213.6 cu. in.) engine used eight carburetor*

WHEN SIDNEY ALLARD drove his Allard Sedan to an overall first place in the Monte Carlo Rally this year, he gained the first win in this event for a British car and driver in 21 years . . . a historic moment for Great Britain. However, to Allard this success represents just one more in an almost monotonous series of wins for himself and his automobiles since 1936 when the first "Allard Special" was slammed together in 20 successive days and nights from T.T. Ford components wedded to a G.P. Bugatti's steering gear and body.

Today, we have become accustomed to Allards. We watch the almost savagely functional brutes hurtling past the checkered flag, or see them in photographs among the leaders in race after race. So it is rather amazing to learn that the Allard Motor Co. Ltd. was formed in 1946—just six years ago, and that the total pre-war yield was represented by only *a score or so of "Allard Specials,"* no two quite alike.

Since these specials were constructed by Allard, and most of them driven by himself and his associates, it becomes apparent that the story of the Allard is the story of the man.

From childhood on, Allard's thoughts centered around automobiles and motors. He successfully avoided being led into his father's firm as a building contractor and persuaded this parent to get him a job with F. W. Lucas Ltd.—a garage and motor dealership—where he worked first as a helper and later as a mechanic. During this time he went to night school at the Battersea Polytechnic Institute, and took a correspondence course in auto engineering. Later he passed the examination for Associate Members of the Institute of Automobile Engineering.

His first motoring interests seemed to focus around the powerful motorcycles of that time, the Francis-Barnett and his broth-

er Denis' Brough Superior. In 1929 he won his first race, a three-lap novices' handicap on the Brooklands outer circuit, driving his super-sports Morgan three-wheeler.

The Morgan of that time weighed under 900 pounds and mounted a powerful 1000 cc (61 cu. in.) Vee-twin engine. In it he was able to "beat up" his motorcyclist friends on a 10-mile stretch from Reigate the first time he took the new Morgan out with them. This early experience with the small, powerful Morgan and the Brough-Superior may be the reason his designs have always favored a large capacity, comparatively slow revving engine of moderate compression and output per cu. in., mounted in a body and chassis of functional design with little or no excessive weight.

This formula was applied to the first Allard Special, the 20-day wonder compounded of Ford components and a Bugatti body, which first hurled Sidney into the foreground of British motorsportsmen. The machine was so well adapted to "mud-plugging" and hill climbing trials that Allard drove it to nine wins in a row including a win at Brighton for the fastest unsupercharged sports-car time in the standing half mile at 61.64 mph.

Two more specials were then constructed from the existing Fords of Chappell and Hutchison. Ken Hutchison, the famous Bugatti and ERA racing driver, was a power-weight ratio fanatic and insisted on having a V-12 Lincoln Zephyr engine installed. This car developed 110 bhp at under 4000 rpm, and with it Allard broke the Prescott sports car record. With these specials, "The Tailwagger" team was formed in 1937 consisting of Hutchison, Warburton, and Allard, and British racing history between 1937 and the outbreak of the war in 1939 became a methodical recording of their trial wins.

# F A MAN AND HIS CAR

**ALLARD** continued

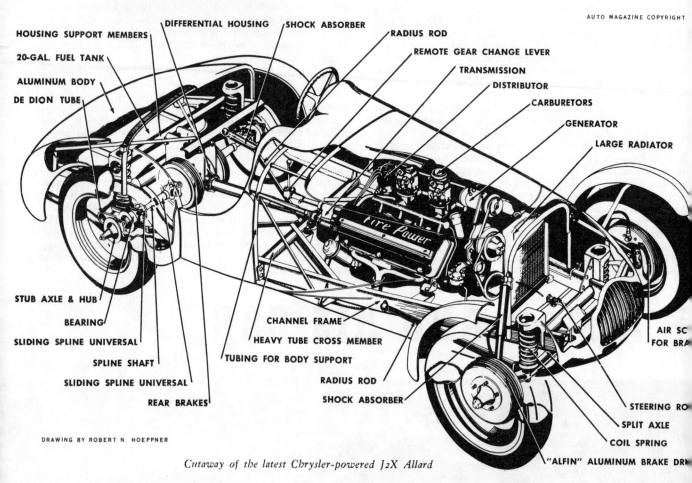

HOUSING SUPPORT MEMBERS
DIFFERENTIAL HOUSING
SHOCK ABSORBER
RADIUS ROD
20-GAL. FUEL TANK
REMOTE GEAR CHANGE LEVER
ALUMINUM BODY
TRANSMISSION
DE DION TUBE
DISTRIBUTOR
CARBURETORS
GENERATOR
LARGE RADIATOR

Fire Power

STUB AXLE & HUB
BEARING
SLIDING SPLINE UNIVERSAL
SPLINE SHAFT
SLIDING SPLINE UNIVERSAL
REAR BRAKES
CHANNEL FRAME
HEAVY TUBE CROSS MEMBER
TUBING FOR BODY SUPPORT
RADIUS ROD
SHOCK ABSORBER

AIR SC
FOR BRA

STEERING RO
SPLIT AXLE
COIL SPRING
"ALFIN" ALUMINUM BRAKE DR

DRAWING BY ROBERT N. HOEPPNER

*Cutaway of the latest Chrysler-powered J2X Allard*

As near as Sidney can remember, the name "Tailwaggers" was first coined by Guy Warburton to describe the motion of the Allard Specials. Sidney always built his cars with a greater proportion of weight to the rear, and Allard drivers approached rough or muddy sections in high confidence – rear wheels spinning madly, the tail end slewing from side to side under power. In addition, the rear ends of the Allards, even the late models, seem to have a tendency to break loose suddenly at high cornering speeds. Many drivers appreciated this courteous, easily correctible wag of the tail as a warning of excessive cornering speeds, and preferred it to a sudden all-out-for-the-hay-bales, four-wheel slide that might come on without warning. From all reports on this characteristic of the Allard Specials and the lead-footed character of the drivers, it is apparent that "The Tailwaggers" team came by its name honestly.

At this time Sidney Allard was known chiefly as a *racing driver* who built his own cars, and not as an auto manufacturer. A chronicle of his successes would fill pages.

The war put a stop to racing, so Sidney and his two brothers ran the firm of Adlard, at that time engaged in the repair of military vehicles. The similarity of the name "Allard" and "Adlard" is purely coincidental, although Sidney retains a controlling interest in the Adlard Company.

Although the war forced retirement from actual racing, the sport was never out of Sidney's mind; and when the Royal Navy intercepted a consignment of 3½-liter (214.3 cu. in.) V-8 air-cooled, German Steyr engines en route to North Africa for use in Steyr-Puch staff cars, he approached the British Admiralty and acquired three of them. The engines are just like two banks of four motorcycle engines in vee formation, with cooling fins and detachable cylinder heads.

Allard tuned one of the Steyr engines so effectively that the initial bhp delivery of 85 at 3500 rpm was stepped up to 140 at 4000. It was fitted with eight carburetors and mounted in a sprint machine for the 1946 season. Two years later he modified it to take de Dion-type rear suspension and fitted close ratio gears of 6.5,

5.5, and 4.1:1 in place of the standard Ford gearing. With this happy combination, he won at Prescott and Craigantlet in 1947 and broke the unblown record at Shelseley Walsh Hillclimb by over three seconds with a meteoric ascent in 19.56 seconds. In 1949 he finally won the British Hillclimb championship, having finished among the first three since the event's inception in 1947.

Throughout this entire period the Allard formula for racing success remained constant. The machines characteristically have a high power to weight ratio with the greater percentage of the weight to the rear. The engines are large and develop high torque at reasonably low revs (about 100 bhp at 2500 rpm), whereas a competitor with a much higher specific output – say 150 bhp – is not obtaining full urge until he is doing something like 5000 rpm. In other words, the Allard's

*An early (1939) Allard powered by a V-12 Lincoln-Zephyr engine. This car was an outgrowth of famous "Tailwaggers" specials, Britain's top trials' team*

power comes in at *usable* speeds, giving a steam engine power and flexibility without the need for constant shifting. Too potent an engine in slippery conditions is a hindrance rather than a help, owing to the difficulty of controlling wheelspin. As Sidney Allard mentioned in a personal interview with the writer, with a supercharged car the throttle is either fully closed or fully open—there are no half measures about it.

Although many conservatives among racing circles remain cool toward the Allard design, it is hardly necessary to defend it. The Allard Motor Co. was formed in 1946, just ten years after the first specials made their boisterous appearance. It was formed, as has been pointed out, merely on the basis of the success of a handful of specials. His comparatively unknown product had to sell against formidable and well-established competition; and the fact that he did succeed speaks eloquently for the quality of his product and, of course, for his personal enterprise and business acumen.

He changed over from the "one off" production of the Trials Specials to sports and road-racing cars because there is a vast potential market for these types, whereas there are comparatively few trials

fans, and in any case, those enthusiasts usually build their own cars. The decision to depend largely on Ford components was based on several factors: economy, availability, performance, and the advantages of utilizing a world-wide service organization. Parts for the standard Allards can be purchased as readily in Calcutta as in London or Chicago.

The first more or less standard cars produced at the Allard works were the two-seater "K" and the four-seater "L" models powered by 85 hp Ford engines. In addition to these, a few two-seaters of similar appearance to the "K," but with a six-inch shorter wheelbase and fitted with tuned 95 hp Mercury engines, were made to special order. These cars were termed "J." In 1948 a convertible was added to the range. In 1949 a sedan was introduced to fill a public demand, and also the world famous "J2" competition two-seater made its bow. The dry weight of this aluminum-bodied projectile is a mere 2006 pounds, and it can be supplied with a variety of engines to the customer's requirements.

The "K2" sports two-seater roadster first appeared in 1950 and was an immediate success with its high compression cylinder heads, twin carburetors, racing-type fly-off handbrake, full size fenders,

windshield, and all-weather equipment. This auto demonstrates a dual personality, giving comfortable transportation as well as sports performance.

The Allard plant is of considerable interest. It is an unpretentious double-fronted showroom and shop in Clapham, S.W. London. It is purely a family business, since the shares belong to Sidney, his wife, and his brother. The total staff is a mere 250 employees who manage to turn out about 400 vehicles per year.

Roughly speaking, the structural components of the Allard are constructed especially for the vehicle, while the moving parts which might need replacement through wear are either Ford parts or are interchangeable with Ford components. Hilton Brothers of Fulham, London, a subsidiary firm, manufacture the bodywork. The frames and bodies of the car are built on jigs so that many assemblies are interchangeable throughout the different models. As far as possible, the most modern assembly techniques are employed: the vehicles are moved in orderly fashion around the shop with no wasted effort or time as components are added to build up the finished product. The result of this miniature mass production is a hand-made vehicle capable (*turn to next page*)

LEN THORPE. FINCHLEY

*Sidney Allard in the 1950 Le Mans race placed third overall. Two cars were
entered in the 1951 event, but both had mechanical difficulties
and were forced to withdraw after putting up some very fast laps*

of sports performance, that is marketed at a competitive price.

When I called at the head office, I was immediately struck by the friendly and informal atmosphere prevailing. A blonde receptionist smilingly offered me a cup of tea upon my arrival and showed me into Sidney's private office, a small room on the first floor. The only hint that this was the personal sanctum of an established motor manufacturer was in the few action photos on the wall, his two engineering certificates, and several ashtrays which he had won in past competitive events. There was one small desk with one inside and one outside phone, but nothing flamboyant or even mildly luxurious about the place.

Sidney Allard, in his early forties, is a tall man who dresses quietly, wears spectacles, and has slightly thinning light-brown hair. I got the impression that, as with many large men, he has a slight stoop. Upon meeting him as a stranger, his appearance would suggest a university professor or a doctor. He has a most kindly, one might say benevolent, expression, and an infectious schoolboy grin. I was a bit diffident about meeting the man, particularly since he had just won the Monte Carlo Rally and was then being lionized at every conceivable function in honor of his performance. However, he was quick to put me at ease and we were

soon chatting together quite informally.

Sidney manages to combine his abilities and activity with devotion to the duties of a family man, and takes great pleasure in his home in Esher, Surrey and his three children, ages four to nine. He met his wife, Eleanor, who is blonde and petite, through motoring. She comes from a large family of rabid motoring enthusiasts, and some of Sidney's most cherished memories involve driving one of his latest creations over a *motorcycle* trials course with his wife leaning over the side of the car picking up route cards on the fly.

When I first broached the subject of the Monte Carlo Rally, he said, "We felt that if others could maintain a 31-mph average, so could we." The extraordinary modesty of the man made it difficult to get much relevant information. I did elicit the fact that they only stopped once in 14 hours' driving. He quite casually mentioned driving through a blizzard on an unfenced and very slippery mountain road at night . . . this is typical of the man.

Although the experience gained on "loose stuff" purely for fun during his days as a "Tailwagger" was of inestimable value on the treacherous, icy surfaces encountered on the continent, a great share of credit for his success must be given to preparation and ingenuity. One month prior to the rally he went to France and cov-

ered the course. As a result of this preliminary survey, he returned and had a special speedometer constructed and calibrated so that one complete revolution of the needle equaled one kilometer: similarly, a clock was also made to show time taken for the same distance at the requisite average speed, so that it could be seen at a glance by the navigator, Tom Lush. If the hands were at the same relative positions (*i.e.*, parallel), they were on time. The plan was that Lush would watch the instruments during the all-important regularity test and call out, "15 seconds to the next kilometer post, 14-13-12, etc.," and Sidney had to be there when he said "Now." However, the posts were obscured by snow, and they had to rely entirely on instruments, with enough success to make history.

Sidney's wife also competed in the Monte Carlo Rally, but had the misfortune to slide off the road into a ditch. Sidney, running to schedule with only five minutes in hand, drove past the accident and, after assuring himself that the crew had sustained no injuries and that help was on the way from a nearby village, was forced to press on.

After this major triumph for both the automobile and the man, it is interesting to hear him say that he does not particularly want to expand the (*turn to page 96*)

Adlards Motors Ltd., a subsidiary of the Allard firm, was operated during the war as a repair depot for military vehicles

The main Allard "plant" has an unassuming store front that occupies small space. This shot was taken just as Allard arrived in London after his Monte Carlo victory

This was the 1938 version of an Allard four-seater sports tourer. Even in those days, the full utilization of Ford components was obvious. Note the early-type Ford wheels and the front radius rods

# A New Export ALLARD

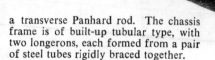

OFF to America by air yesterday was Sydney Allard, of the Allard Motor Co., Ltd., to finalize marketing arrangements for the new Allard model illustrated on this page. Following successful tests on the M.I.R.A. proving ground, a prototype of the Allard "Palm Beach" model was shipped to the United States secretly some weeks ago.

With a wheelbase of 8 ft. and a track of 4 ft. 4 ins., this new car, at 15 cwt., is very much lighter than any preceding Allard sports model. Alternative overhead-valve power units for it are the 2¼-litre Ford Zephyr-Six, with which it is known as the type 21Z, and the 1½-litre Ford Consul 4-cylinder, in which form it is known as the type 21C. Whichever power unit is fitted, the suspension is by coil springs all round; drawings on this page show the well-tried Allard layout of divided axle I.F.S., and the hypoid rear axle located by parallelogram linkages and a transverse Panhard rod. The chassis frame is of built-up tubular type, with two longerons, each formed from a pair of steel tubes rigidly braced together.

TUBULAR - FRAMED and coil-sprung, the "Palm Beach" 4- and 6-cylinder Allard models incorporate divided-axle independent front - wheel suspension, a correspondingly divided steering track rod, a hypoid rear axle located by radius arms, and Girling hydraulic brakes.

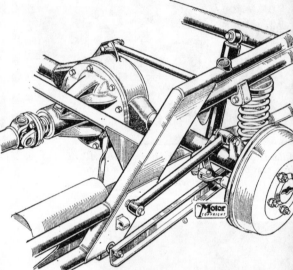

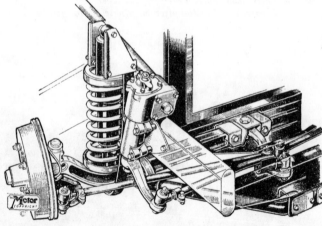

It is emphasized that this new model is an addition to the Allard range, and does not replace the well-proven V-8 powered cars. It is reported that the "Safari" tubular-framed utility car, described in "The Motor" of April 2, 1952, is proving popular in export markets, in which the "best seller" has hitherto been the J2X competition model.

## allard

(from page 95) business and would certainly refuse to "sell out" to a larger company. He is most concerned with the welfare of his staff of hand-picked enthusiasts "to whom a successful business is necessary for their happiness."

Sidney went on to say, "The aims of the Allard Motor Company are, as they have always been, to produce high-performance cars and sell them at the lowest possible price consistent with limited and specialized production. As a private company and a 'family concern,' we have no necessity to constantly aim at increased turnover and profits in order to satisfy shareholders whose natural interest is in dividends rather than motorcars. We shall continue to offer cars for which we claim a high all-round performance with complete safety, distinctive appearance, and world-wide service, and a model to suit every taste from the out-and-out competition motorist to the businessman who wishes to travel far, fast and safely."

Permits, forms, and low steel allocations bedevil the company, which is forced to export much of its output in order to get a small quantity of material to continue manufacture for the English market. However, Sidney's future plans are to build prototype small Allards utilizing the Ford Consul or Zephyr four- and six-cylinder engines. These, if brought to the production stage, would be for export only, and would entitle him to a little more steel for home use.

## Imhof Allard

Sidney Allard supplied Geoffrey Imhof with a lengthened (12″) chassis and the latter came up with this combination of a stout (4375 cc Ford) American engine, traditionally roadworthy British chassis, and a Continental body design. This passenger and luggage accommodating, high speed (102 mph) touring coupe, is capable of 0-50 in 7.9 sec. With the new Cadillac or Chrysler engine, Imhof calculates a possible 130 mph. Vertically sectioned foto above left shows the reader same design on regular wheelbase.

The newly announced J2X streamlined Allard will be a strong contender at the 1952 Le Mans 24 Hour Race. It will be put into production and be available to the general public. Driving the two entries will be Sidney Allard and Frank Curtiss, with Jack Fairman and Zora Duntov acting as co-pilots. The car should (because of smoother body contours) come up with some exceptionally high speeds on the three-mile-long Le Mans straights.

## Le Mans Allard

Well known throughout the sports car world, Allard has now invaded the station wagon set. Called the Safari Estate Car, it is designed to carry six passengers comfortably and in dire emergency, a total of eight passengers can be accommodated.

# ALLARD

# SAFARI

The Ford, Cadillac and Chrysler engines can be used and all around access to the engine is possible due to the unusual hydraulically-opened hood which pivots at the front bumper bar.

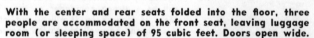

With the center and rear seats folded into the floor, three people are accommodated on the front seat, leaving luggage room (or sleeping space) of 95 cubic feet. Doors open wide.

BACKED by an enviable reputation in the sports car field, Allard has introduced a six passenger station wagon—the Safari Estate Car. Built on a tubular chassis designed to insure lightness and freedom from twisting often induced from driving over rough roads, the Safari also provides in comfort, road holding, ground clearance and performance.

The J2X-type front suspension and steering, proven in road races and hill climbs, are linked with the deDion type rear axle to provide for stability. Lockheed brakes, the same as those used on the Allard competition car, are fitted to the Safari.

Powerplant is either the Ford, Cadillac or Chrysler engines installed beneath a hydraulically operated hood. This hood also conceals the spare tire and wheel, a novel arrangement which leaves considerable body space free.

In addition to seating six persons comfortably, the Safari provides 45 cubic feet of luggage space; this space can also be used for two additional emergency seats which are folded into the floor.

An engine turned instrument panel includes speedometer, tachometer, temperature, fuel and oil gauges, reserve warning light, cigar lighter, indicator warning light and main beam warning light.

The remote control gear shift lever is mounted to the right of the driver and below the seat cushion while the hand brake is at waist level on the same side leaving the center of the car unobstructed for the seating of three persons.

The overall length of the Safari is 16 feet. Width is 70 inches. Shades and colors of body and trim are varied to suit all tastes as well as extras in the form of seat covers and radios. The Safari sells for $5200 with a Chrysler engine in this country.

# ALLARD SAFARI
## SPECIFICATIONS

DIMENSIONS:
Overall length ....................................... 16 feet
Overall width ....................................... 70 inches
Curb weight ....................................... 2900 pounds
Maximum height ....................................... 63 inches
Ground clearance ....................................... 7½ inches
Track front ....................................... 56½ inches
Track rear ....................................... 58½ inches
Wheelbase ....................................... 112 inches
Brakes ....................................... Lockheed two leading shoe, front
Wheels and tires—6.25 x 16. Up to 7.50 tires may be fitted on rear to increase ground clearance by 1¼ inches and to suit soft or sandy tracks. 16 x 4.50 wheels.

ENGINE:
Stock Engines:—3622 cc (220.98 cubic inches) side valve Ford V8. (30 HP) 85 BHP at 3500 RPM.
Complete parts can be supplied to allow fitting for export to U. S. of:
5.4 liter (329.50 CI) Lincoln V8. 160 BHP engine.
5.4 liter (329.50 CI) Cadillac engine 160 BHP at 3800 RPM.
or 5420 cc (330.68 CI) Chrysler 'Firepower' OHV V8. 180 BHP at 3800 RPM.

REAR AXLE:
deDion type suspension, inboard brakes, coil springs, ratio of drive, 3.78; one standard, also 3.5; I, and 3.27; I, alternative.

GEARBOX: Standard Ford, straight drive on top gear.

BOX RATIOS:
Top ................ 1 ; 1
Inter ............... 1.773 ; 1
Low ................ 3.114 ; 1
Reverse ............. 4.005 ; 1

GEAR CHANGE: Remote control.
FRONT AXLE: Independent swinging half axle, with forward facing radius rods, axle pivots and radius rod pivots are rubber bushed. Suspension by coil springs, telescopic type shock absorbers.
STEERING: Marles patent hour-glass worm and roller type, transverse drag-link, telescopic steering wheel—3 inches adjustment.
TOP: Hydraulic actuation by either electric pump or hand pump, bonnet assembly pivots at front end and rises sufficiently to allow all-round access to engine. ☆ ☆

The remote control gear change lever is mounted to the right of the driver while the hand brake is at waist level on the same side, leaving the center of the car free from obstruction.

The J2X-type front suspension and steering have already been proven in road races and hill climbs throughout the world. With the tubular chassis frame, formidable strength is obtained, yet there still remains the lightness typical of European cars.

Bumpers and overriders are standard equipment, very necessary on a car destined for export to the United States. The production models will have a more graceful windscreen, tapering towards the top. There are separate side lamps below the head lamps. Although the car is of low build, there is a good ground clearance.

# A Small Allard

## THREE-SEATER SPORTS CAR TO TAKE A FORD CONSUL OR ZEPHYR ENGINE

ALLARD, who have gained fame by building exclusively large sports cars with V-eight engines, are breaking into an entirely new market with the introduction of a small three-seater sports car which is fitted with either the four-cylinder Ford Consul or the six-cylinder Ford Zephyr engine. The new model is named the Palm Beach Allard, which is a sufficient indication of the market for which it is intended, and practically the whole output is reserved for United States buyers for some time to come. The considerable gap between the popular M.G. and the more powerful and expensive European sports cars has for some time represented one of the major sales opportunities for foreign cars in the United States market, and the new Allard should receive an enthusiastic welcome. Mr. Sydney Allard has been in America for some weeks demonstrating the prototype and completing distribution arrangements.

In general layout the Palm Beach is similar to the larger Allards, and it follows the tradition of using the maximum number of standard Ford parts, thus ensuring a ready supply of spares at low prices in all overseas markets. The power units are the standard Consul or Zephyr engines with normal clutches and gear boxes. The rear axle is the standard spiral bevel unit employed in the Ford Zephyr saloon, but it is used in conjunction with a special Allard rear suspension which achieves very precise location of the axle with the minimum of weight. The suspension is by coil springs and telescopic dampers, and the axle is located in a fore-and-aft direction by twin radius arms at each side. The lower radius arms are robust members built up from twin channel pressings in steel, joined by flat plates; the upper arms are steel tubes. Lateral location is by a Panhard rod pivoting on the frame side member and on a small bracket welded to the top of the differential housing.

The independent front suspension follows standard Allard practice by employing the divided axle layout in conjunction with coil springs and telescopic dampers mounted inside the springs. Long experience with this layout has produced numerous detail refinements, and a short road test demonstrated that it is now possible to drive over quite rough ground without any movement being transmitted to the rim of the steering wheel. The radius arms run forward of the main half axles, and all the pivots lie parallel with the longitudinal central line of the chassis, following the layout introduced on the J2X sports racing model. The Marles steering box is the same as employed on the larger cars and is mounted on the outside of the frame, with its drop arm connected to a transverse rod which moves a centrally placed slave-arm, from which two half track rods of equal length run to the front wheels. Front hubs, bearings and oil seals are standard Ford parts, and the standard Ford Girling hydraulic braking system is retained.

The chassis frame has been evolved after successful experience with the tubular frame on the Allard Safari station wagon, which is torsionally five times as stiff as the previous channel and box section frame, for approximately the same weight. On the Palm Beach chassis the side members are formed of twin steel tubes, one above the other, joined by steel plates. The tubes are of 1⅜in diameter and 16 gauge, and the thickness of the plates is 14 gauge. Maximum depth of the side member thus produced is 6⅛in. To complete the frame, there are six tubular cross members, plus a strong steel plate cross member of inverted top-hat section in the region of the front suspension. The scuttle is supported on a substantial steel tube arch carried on outriggers, and there are additional box section outriggers fore and aft to carry the weight of the bodywork.

At present there is one standard body, a low-built three-seater of simple modern lines, panelled entirely in 14 gauge aluminium. It has a single bench-type seat 52in wide, providing space for three people abreast. The upholstery for both seat cushion and back rest is in leather, over normal spring cases with overlays of rubberized hair. Located by pegs in the floor, the seat cushion has a simple fore-and-aft adjustment, and there is a quick method for varying the slope of the back rest.

The Ford steering column gear change

The metal facia panel is coloured to match the exterior; also visible are the short central gear lever and the pull-out hand brake.

The light but very rigid chassis frame is made from steel tube electrically welded. The side members are twin tubes joined by steel plates. Engine and transmission, rear axle, radiator, brakes, wheels and wheel bearings are standard Ford parts.

has been replaced by a specially designed remote control connected to a small central lever on the floor; and there is a pull-out hand brake under the instrument panel. Standard equipment includes a rev counter, and a speedometer with trip and total mileage recorders and a dial calibrated in both m.p.h. and k.p.h. There are also an oil pressure gauge, water thermometer, ammeter and fuel gauge.

The windscreen, which has a sloping single main panel and triangular side panels, has a light frame made from aluminium extrusions. There is a quickly erected hood, which stows away behind the seat; and side screens are provided. In the tail is a useful luggage locker with a total capacity of 9 cu ft. The spare wheel is carried flat on the floor of the locker,

and the tools are accommodated in a box alongside the battery on the scuttle.

Electrical equipment includes a two-brush dynamo with compensated voltage control, double-dipping sealed beam head lamps of 7in diameter, separate side lamps, twin Windtone horns, and a separate lamp (protected by the bumper) to illuminate the rear number plate. The steering wheel is the same as that on the Ford Zephyr and carries a plated horn ring. There is also a central switch controlling the self-cancelling direction indicators.

Normally the power units will be in completely standard forms: the four-cylinder Consul engine of 1,508 c.c. gives 47 b.h.p. at 4,400 r.p.m., and the six-cylinder Zephyr unit of 2,667 c.c. gives 68 b.h.p. at 4,000 r.p.m. In view of the car's low weight, clean shape and small

frontal area, this output should yield a performance that will meet the needs of a large number of owners; and with the Zephyr unit speeds approaching 100 m.p.h. are expected. It is, however, inevitable that owners interested in competitions will ultimately seek ways and means of obtaining still more power, and there are plans for specially tuned engines at a higher price.

The Consul is being offered with the cylinder head milled to raise the compression ratio from 6.8 to 7.5 to 1. Two additional single Zenith downdraught carburettors can be fitted, and a four-branch exhaust manifold will be available. These modifications raise the power output to 68 b.h.p. at 5,000 r.p.m., thus equalling the output of the untuned Zephyr. The torque of the tuned Consul

The Ford Zephyr rear axle is used on the Palm Beach Allard with coil springs and twin radius arms. Lateral location is by a Panhard rod attached to the differential housing. All pivots have Silentbloc rubber bushes, needing no lubrication.

The divided axle independent front suspension resembles the layout used on the J2X. Half axles and forward-projecting torque arms are pivoted parallel to the car centre line. The steering linkage is designed to prevent reactions through the steering wheel.

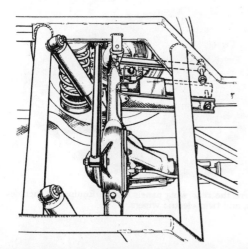

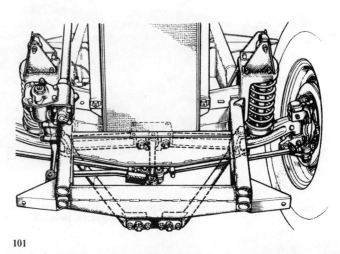

is also improved, reaching 105 lb ft at 2,500 r.p.m. At present all cars will have the standard Ford gear box ratios, and the Zephyr hypoid rear axle with a ratio of 4.375 to 1. The wheels are the steel disc type used for the Zephyr, with tyres of 6.40in section on 13in rims.

Owners who wish to change engines can do so very easily, since the only new part required (apart from a larger radiator for the Zephyr engine) is a propeller shaft, which is shorter for the Zephyr engine than for the Consul.

At present only one body style is offered, but plans have been discussed in the United States for the production of alternative bodies in resin-bonded fibre glass, and a few chassis are being supplied to British coachbuilders. Right- or left-hand drive can be provided, and, in order to accommodate four-seater coachwork, a shorter steering column is available, together with a more forward mounting of the pedals. Incidentally, the Ford hydraulic control for the clutch is retained.

For owners interested in competitions, the surplus 8 c.c. that brings the standard Consul engine into the 2-litre category is a severe handicap, and there are plans to make available a special linered-down engine to enable Consul-engined cars to compete in the 1½-litre category.

Weight of the standard Consul-engined car is only 1,850lb, with oil, water and five gallons of petrol; with the Zephyr engine the car is 100lb heavier. With the Consul engine, slightly less than 55 per cent of the unladen weight is carried on the front wheels, and with the Zephyr

The big J2X Allard continues in the maker's range. Here is one of these cars during a pit stop in the recent Nine-hour Race meeting at Goodwood. The flush-sided model introduced at Le Mans has now been added to the range.

unit the figure is slightly over 55 per cent. Both front and rear suspensions allow a total wheel movement of about 6in, the spring periodicity being 68 at the front and 85 at the rear. The turning circle is only 28ft, left and right, and only 2¾ turns of the wheel are required from lock to lock.

Among the larger Allard cars the V-eight Safari station wagon has had an excellent reception overseas, and a very few have recently been released on the home market. The J2X sports racing model

is continued in standard form as exhibited at the last London Show, and in addition there is a new Le Mans version with flush-sided streamlined coachwork based on that of the car that ran in the 24-hour race in June this year. Normally, the power units for the larger cars are the standard Ford V8 engines, with single carburettors. Aluminium cylinder heads can be supplied to order. For export, conversion kits are available which allow the Chrysler or Cadillac V-eight engine to be fitted.

---

## SPECIFICATION

**Engine.**—Palm Beach C. 4 cyl, 79.37 × 76.2 mm, 1,508 c.c. O.h.v. in line, push rod operated. Single downdraught Zenith carburettor. Compression ratio 6.8 to 1, 47 b.h.p. at 4,400 r.p.m. Maximum torque 74 lb ft at 2,400 r.p.m.
**Palm Beach Z.**—6 cyl, 79.37 × 76.2 mm 2,267 c.c. 68 b.h.p. at 4,000 r.p.m. Maximum torque 112 lb ft at 2,000 r.p.m.
**Transmission.**—Dry single-plate clutch with hydraulic pedal operation. Three-speed gear box with synchromesh second and top. Central lever. Open propeller shaft, hypoid final drive. Overall gear ratios: 4.375, 7.187 and 12.434 to 1.
**Suspension and Steering.**—Independent front suspension by swinging half-axles and radius arms with parallel pivot layout and coil springs. Coil springs and twin parallel

radius arms at rear, with Panhard rod. Telescopic dampers all round. Marles steering with central slave arm and equal-length track rods.

**Wheels, Brakes and Tyres.**—Bolt on steel disc wheels with 6.40—13in tyres. Girling hydraulic brakes; 2LS at front. Drums 9 × 1½in. Brake lining area 121 sq in. Mechanical hand brake on rear wheels.

**Dimensions.**—Wheelbase, 8ft. Track (front) 4ft 3in; (rear) 4ft 2in. Overall length 13ft. Width 4ft 10in. Height (hood up) 4ft 3in. Weight, C, 1,850 lb; Z, 1,950 lb.

**Prices.**—Palm Beach C two-three-seater £800, plus £445 18s 11d British purchase tax, total £1,245 18s 11d. Palm Beach Z £865, plus £482 1s 2d British purchase tax, total £1,347 1s 2d.

The spare wheel is housed in the floor of the luggage locker, which has a total capacity of 9 cu ft and can be locked.

The sides of the Palm Beach Allard taper slightly inwards to the point where the rear wing panels begin. Equipment includes self-cancelling indicators, twin tail and stop lamps, and twin electric wipers.

*A New Saloon and an Improved Tourer Added to a Range of Sporting Cars*

**GREATER ROOMINESS** within the body is offered by the new Monte Carlo saloon, coil sprung, tubular framed, and with a more forward engine position.

## 1953 CARS

# Two additional ALLARD models

CENTRE of interest on the Allard stand at Earls Court this week will be a new saloon model, which should offer better roominess and riding comfort than the existing P1 saloon (this, costing less than the new model, continues to be listed) as well as having appearances which many will adjudge to be more pleasing.

The basis of this new model, which carries the type name "Monte Carlo," is the tubular chassis announced earlier this year for the "Safari" estate car. A pair of steel tubes are linked together to form each frame side member, just as on the smaller Palm Beach chassis, and in this chassis frame the V-8 engine is mounted appreciably further forwards than have been the power units of other recent Allard cars. This more forward location of the power unit has left more space for passengers within the wheelbase, and incidentally allows the complete car to be of rather better balanced appearance.

### Roll Resistance

Divided-axle independent front wheel suspension is a unique Allard feature which is retained on the new model. Coil springs controlled by Armstrong telescopic dampers are the shock cushioning medium, and there is considerably greater suspension flexibility than on previous models, but the unique combination of high roll axis and wide effective springbase which this suspension layout provides should ensure roll-free high-speed cornering. One of the departures from earlier Allard practice is the use of forward torque arms which take braking drag loads in tension.

Straightforwardness characterizes the steering linkage; a short transverse drag link extends from the drop arm of a Marles steering gear to an idler arm on the chassis centre line, and from this idler arm there are two half track-rods which swing about identical arcs to the axle halves. Thus, correct geometry is obtained without the complexity of numerous joints at which wear can develop.

Race-bred is the phrase which must inevitably be used concerning the rear suspension of this car, which follows along lines proved on the J2 and later J2X competition two-seaters. A tubular axle beam links the rear wheels, but the final drive gears and the rear

brakes are mounted on the chassis, universally jointed shafts linking this assembly to the rear hubs. On racing models, the absence of any tendency for engine torque to lift one rear wheel has been a great advantage of this layout, but touring car buyers will equally appreciate the rear-seat riding comfort resulting from low unsprung weight. As at the front of the car, coil springs are used to absorb road shocks, in conjunction with telescopic dampers, and it is interesting to note that this chassis and suspension system was first seen on test on the M.I.R.A. proving ground pavé tracks considerably more than a year ago.

Of two-door four-light type, the five-six-seater saloon body is styled in the modern full-width manner, and incorporates as standard equipment a Clayton fresh-air heating and de-misting system. The complete bonnet and front wing assembly is pivoted on the front cross member, and a hand pump inside the body lifts this whole assembly to

give ideal accessibility around the power unit—as an extra, electrical operation of this bonnet opening may be provided.

Alongside the Monte Carlo saloon at Earls Court will be a new version of the K-type three-four-seater tourer Allard. This incorporates the modern Allard features such as coil springing and de Dion-type rear axle. As with other Allard models, a majority of the wearing parts of the chassis (as distinct from the structure) are British-made Ford parts backed by the Ford service organization, and cars delivered in this country are equipped with Ford Dagenham-built engines. All chassis are, however, designed to accommodate larger sizes of V8 engine, and export cars for dollar areas can be supplied with the appropriate mountings for Lincoln, Cadillac or Chrysler engines; also, many specification items such as top-gear ratio or gear lever position (side, central or steering column) can be modified to individual order.

=====ALLARD DATA=====

### "Monte Carlo" Saloon

**ENGINE.—Dimensions:** Cylinders, V8; bore, 78 mm.; stroke, 95.2 mm.; cubic capacity, 3,622 c.c.; piston area, 58.9 sq. ins.; valves, side; compression ratio, 6.12 : 1. **Performance:** Max. b.h.p., 85 at 3,500 r.p.m.; b.h.p. per sq. in. piston area, 1.45; max. b.m.e.p., 102 lb./sq. in. at 2,000 r.p.m.; b.h.p. per sq. in. piston area, 1.45; piston speed at max. b.h.p., 2,190 ft./min. **Details:** Carburetter, double choke downdraught; ignition, coil; plugs (make and type) Champion Type 7 standard; fuel pump, AC mechanical; fuel capacity, 18 gallons; oil filter, Ford; oil capacity, 1 gallon; cooling system, twin pumps and fan; electrical system, 12-volt; battery capacity, 63 amp. hr. (Chassis will also accommodate Lincoln, Cadillac and Chrysler V8 engines.)

**TRANSMISSION.—Clutch,** single dry plate; overall gear ratios: top, 3.78; 2nd, 6.7; 1st, 11.8; rev., 15.1; prop shaft, torque tube; final drive, spiral bevel; De Dion type rear axle.

**CHASSIS DETAILS.—Brakes,** Lockheed, hydraulic (2 LS at front); brake drum diameter, 12 ins.; friction lining area, 165 sq. in.; front suspension, coil springs and divided axle I.F.S.; rear suspension, coil springs and De Dion rear axle; shock absorbers, Armstrong telescopic; tyre size, 6.25-16; steering gear, Marles cam and double roller.

**DIMENSIONS.—Wheelbase,** 9' 4"; track, front, 4' 8½"; rear, 4' 10½"; overall length, 16' 0"; overall width, 5' 11"; overall height, 5' 0"; ground clearance, 8"; turning circle, 40'; dry weight, 29 cwt.

**PERFORMANCE DATA.—Piston area, sq. in. per ton, 40.5; brake lining area, sq. in. per ton, 114; top gear m.p.h. per 1,000 r.p.m., 21.8; top gear m.p.h. at 2,500 ft./min. piston speed 87.2 litres per ton-mile, dry 3,440.**

### K.3 Three-four-seater Tourer

**ENGINE.—Dimensions:** Cylinders, V8; bore, 78 mm.; stroke, 95.2 mm.; cubic capacity, 3,622 c.c.; piston area, 58.9 sq. ins.; valves, side; compression ratio, 7 : 1. **Performance:** Max. b.h.p., 95 at 3,800 r.p.m.; b.h.p. per sq. in. piston area, 1.61; piston speed at max. b.h.p., 2,380 ft./min. **Details:** Carburetter, double choke downdraught; ignition, coil; plugs (make and type), Champion Type 7; fuel pump, AC mechanical; fuel capacity, 18 galls.; oil filter, Ford; oil capacity, 1 gall.; cooling system, twin pumps and fan; electrical system, 12 volt; battery capacity, 63 amp. hr. (Chassis will also accommodate Lincoln, Cadillac and Chrysler V8 engines.)

**TRANSMISSION.—Clutch,** single dry plate; overall gear ratios: top, 3.5; 2nd, 6.2; 1st, 10.08; rev., 14.0; prop. shaft, torque tube; final drive, spiral bevel; De Dion type rear axle.

**CHASSIS DETAILS.—Brakes,** Lockheed hydraulic (2LS at front); brake drum diameter, 12 ins.; friction lining area, 165 sq. in.; front suspension, coil springs and divided axle I.F.S.; rear suspension, coil springs and de Dion rear axle; shock absorber, Armstrong telescopic; tyre size, 6.25-16; steering gear, Marles cam and double roller.

**DIMENSIONS.—Wheelbase,** 8' 4"; track, front, 4' 8½"; rear, 4' 10½"; overall length, 14' 9"; overall width, 5' 6½"; overall height, 4' 6"; ground clearance, 8"; turning circle, 38'; dry weight, 23¼ cwt.

**PERFORMANCE DATA.—Piston area, sq. in. per ton, 50.5; brake lining area, sq. in. per ton, 142; top gear m.p.h. per 1,000 r.p.m., 23.5; top gear m.p.h. at 2,500 ft./min. piston speed, 94; litres per ton-mile, dry, 3,980.**

# ALLARD
## "Palm Beach"

### New "baby" Allard does 100 mph

Specifically designed to fill the gap (both as to size and price) between the MG and the Jaguar XK, the newly announced Allard "Palm Beach" is expected to enjoy substantial sales in the United States. The prototype, which attained over 100 mph in timed tests, has already been shipped to this country.

This new "baby" Allard is offered with a choice of powerplants . . . the new ohv six-cylinder Ford Zephyr or the ohv four-cylinder Ford Consul. Both engines are "oversquare," have interchangeable parts, and are capable of sustained high speeds.

Based on a tubular frame which utilizes parallel steel tubes joined by welded strips to form an oval box section, the chassis is both light and strong. Aluminum body panels are on steel formers attached directly to steel tube hoops. These hoops are, in turn, welded directly to the frame. The 52 inch wide bench type seat will accommodate three people. A large (for this type car) 9 cubic foot luggage compartment also houses the spare tire. The top folds out of sight and is easy to erect.

Front suspension is independent . . . of the familiar Allard split axle type with parallel axis geometry as on the P-2. Low periodicity coil springs are used with Armstrong telescopic shock absorbers. Stock Ford wheel bearings, oil seals, and hubs are employed. The rear suspension uses near-parallel trailing links with lateral location by Panhard rod. All bearings are of the silent bloc type, requiring no lubrication. The rear end is stock Ford Zephyr with three-quarter hypoid final drive and 4.375:1 ratio.

Brakes are Girling hydraulic, two leading shoe front, with stock Ford Zephyr-Consul at the rear. The electrical system is 12 volt, the battery is very accessible, the generator has compensated voltage control, and the 7″ sealed-beam headlights have foot dipping, with separate side lights.

At a later date, a five passenger tourer will be available . . . with the Consul engine only because of need for space.

### SPECIFICATIONS

| | |
|---|---|
| Wheelbase (either engine) | 96 inches |
| Track, front | 51 inches |
| rear | 50 inches |
| Overall length | 13 feet |
| Overall height | 52 inches |
| Curb weight, with Zephyr engine | 1950 pounds |
| Curb weight, with Consul engine | 1850 pounds |
| Fuel tank capacity | 10 gallons |

### ENGINE OPTIONS

**Stock Ford Zephyr . . .**

6-cylinder, 2267 cc displacement, bore 3.125″, stroke 3.0″, push rod ohv, 6.8:1 compression ratio, 68 bhp @ 4000 rpm. Torque 112 lbs/ft @ 2000 rpm. Single downdraft carburetor.

**Stock Ford Consul . . .**

4-cylinder, 1508 cc displacement, bore 3.125″, stroke 3.0″, push rod ohv, 6.8:1 compression ratio, 47 bhp @ 4400 rpm. Single Zenith downdraft.

**Modified Ford Consul . . .**

7.5:1 compression ratio, 2 Zenith downdraft carburetors, exhaust headers, 68 bhp @ 5000 rpm. Torque 105 lbs/ft @ 2500 rpm.

### FOTO CAPTIONS . . .

1—British Ford components used include pedals (inverted), steering, brakes, and accessory units. Clever conversion uses floor-mounted shift lever on column-shift gearbox.

2—Typical Allard split axle independent front suspension uses telescopic shock absorbers mounted inside the coil springs.

3—Track arm is mounted on differential housing while near-parallel trailing links take the driving and braking loads.

# ALLARD
## custom tailored transportation

### By Major Peter D. Sheridan-Young

Louis Klementaski and I spent a most interesting day at the London factory of the Allard Motor Company. There we learned the real meaning of custom tailoring; how in these days of mass production, there still exists a manufacturer who sets out to produce a high performance car that is fixed just the way the customer likes it . . . be it special ratios, particular seating arrangements, oversize gas tank, or his pet shade of blue.

The Allard offers serviceability hitherto unknown (in a European car sold in the States). The components are extensively Ford or made up in special metals to Ford dimensions. Whilst the powerplant (Ford, Cadillac, Lincoln, or Chrysler) can be fitted by the dealer in the States, according to the customer's specifications, all the necessary "plumbing" for the customer's engine is done in England . . . and an engine of the required type is actually fitted for the final inspection, then removed prior to shipping.

Sydney Allard was a "hop up" enthusiast par excellence, starting out in trials before the war with his own brand of very successful special. The Allard Motor Company was formed shortly after the war and in 1946 production was started. The works have now built up from that simple beginning to a firm employing close to 400 people, spread out over the chassis plant and three body shops. On the night before our visit, Sydney had been working with the experts in his racing shop until three a.m.!

Let us follow for a moment *your* order . . . placed with your local Allard dealer in the States. Along with the order, you are asked to complete a specification form which is then air mailed to the London export office. Here it is checked, then sent on to the chassis plant where a chassis is laid down and a chassis number allocated to you. With great care, that chassis is built up with components made exclusively by Allard to exacting specifications, or with proprietary components which have been time-tested—such as the electrical system or the Lockheed brake operating mechanism. This takes under three weeks. After that, the chassis is taken to the body shop where the body is made and fitted—on to the trim shop, and finally the paint shop. Putting the body on and finishing takes a further 5 to 6 weeks, making a total time of 8 to 9 weeks. Did you order a

*Continued on page* 123

1 Welding in the lamp mounting on a J-2.
2 All Allard bodies are carefully hand-fitted.
3 Sydney Allard . . . his development of the Ford-based trials special into a high performance sports car has been an international success.
4 Sam Whittingham, foreman of the body shop.
5 Chassis assembly shop . . . note hood-fender assembly for 'Palm Beach' model in background.

# 1953 CARS
# The Allard

## A STURDY MEDIUM-SIZED NEW

TOTALLY ENCLOSED accommodation for luggage is available in a roomy rear locker which also houses the spare wheel.

LARGER UNIT of the alternatives which the "Palm Beach" chassis can accommodate is the Ford Zephyr Six engine seen in this under-bonnet view.

TYPICALLY Allard qualities of vivid acceleration and sensitive steering, but lower costs for purchase and operation, are the salient points of the "Palm Beach" model which is to be exhibited on the Allard stand at Earls Court. Familiar design characteristics have been incorporated in a new chassis which is smaller and lighter than those of previous Allards, and although wide use continues to be made of Ford components which may readily be serviced or replaced in any part of the world, Ford Consul and Zephyr Six components replace the heavier V-8 parts previously favoured.

As the drawing on these pages shows, the new chassis follows closely along the lines of the V-8 "Safari" model which was announced earlier this year. It is conventional in so far as it uses two frame longerons linked by cross members, but unconventional in respect of the type of longeron used. At each side of the car there are two steel tubes of 1¾ ins. diameter, set vertically above one another and linked together at frequent intervals by steel plates welded into position. Each individual side member of this frame is immensely strong in bending and of very considerable torsional rigidity: tubular cross members welded into position complete a structure of great torsional rigidity.

For suspension, well-tried Allard principles are adopted, coil springs controlled by Armstrong telescopic shock absorbers being used at both front and rear. The rear axle is a hypoid-geared Ford Zephyr Six unit, positively located laterally and fore-and-aft by radius arms, and the front wheels are independently located by pivoted half-axles. In more detail, at each side of the car there are a pair of radius arms to take the reactions of drive or braking torque and thrust from the rear axle to the chassis frame, and a Panhard rod resists cornering loads. At the front of the car, the swinging half axles are braced against braking loads by radius arms extending forwards and inwards to pivots near to the chassis centre line.

As on other Allard models, a Marles steering gear is used, and may be installed on either side of the car as required. The drag link extends transversely to an idler arm at the centre of the chassis, from which two track-rod halves (swinging about the same arc as the axle halves) extend to the steering arms on the front hubs. Parts such as the hub bearings and the Girling hydraulic brakes are of Ford pattern, very conservatively stressed on these lightweight sporting cars.

Two sizes of power unit may be accommodated in this chassis, without alterations being required to parts other than the propeller shaft and radiator. These are the four-cylinder Consul engine of fractionally over 1½ litres displacement, and the 2.3-litre Zephyr Six. Both engines are of modern short-stroke design, with overhead valves operated by pushrods and rockers, and they are built in unit with single dry-plate clutches and three-speed synchromesh gearboxes.

For ordinary road use, either the Consul engine in a 16½-cwt. car or the Zephyr Six unit in a car weighing 17½ cwt. are expected to give very usefully lively and economical performance without requiring high-octane fuel. Competitions are inevitably envisaged when a sports car is marketed, however, and already bench tests have resulted in the Consul engine being made available to order in specially tuned form. An increased compression ratio, the fitting of twin downdraught carburetters, and installation of a four-branch exhaust manifold, together allow the power output to go up from 47 b.h.p. at 4,000 r.p.m. to 68 b.h.p. at 5,000 r.p.m.

Full-width bodywork has been standardized for the "Palm Beach," the light and sturdy structure incorporating a framework of **steel tubes** covered by

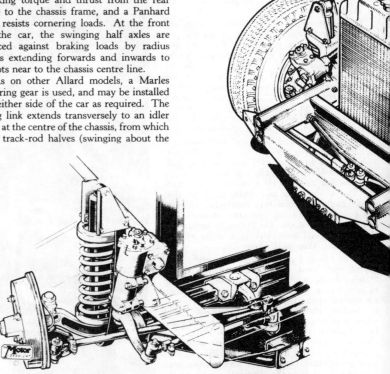

CORRECT GEOMETRY of the steering connections to the independently sprung front wheels is provided by the divided track rod, set ahead of the swinging half-axles.

O THE SPORTS-CAR FIELD

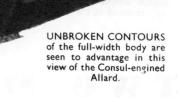

**UNBROKEN CONTOURS** of the full-width body are seen to advantage in this view of the Consul-engined Allard.

DOUBLE TUBES are linked together to form each side member of the chassis. Coil springs controlled by telescopic dampers are used for the suspension of all four wheels.

aluminium panels. Essentially of two-seater type, the body can in fact accommodate three people when required, as the bench-type seat is 52 ins. wide, and the floor-mounted gear lever is offset slightly from the centre-line of the car towards the driver. In order to leave the floor completely free from obstructions, a handbrake of pistol grip type has been chosen, and this is mounted beneath the instrument panel. There is a completely disappearing hood, and the non-folding raked windscreen is a full-width unit with draught-deflecting side extensions. Useful luggage accommodation is provided, in a tail locker of 9 cubic feet capacity which also accommodates the spare wheel.

Additionally to the "Palm Beach," examples of the larger Allard models with V-8 engines will be exhibited at Earls Court. These will comprise the J2X competition model with full-width bodywork, the K3 3/4 seat sports tourer, the tubular-chassis Safari estate car, and the "Monte Carlo" saloon of which the name recalls Sydney Allard's outright victory in the 1952 Monte-Carlo Rally.

## ALLARD "PALM BEACH" SPECIFICATIONS

| | Type 21C | Type 21Z | | Type 21C | Type 21Z |
|---|---|---|---|---|---|
| **Engine Dimensions:** | (Tuned Engine data in brackets) | | **Transmission—Contd.** | | |
| | | | Prop. shaft ... | Open | Open |
| Cylinders ... | 4 | 6 | Final drive ... | Hypoid bevel | Hypoid bevel |
| Bore ... | 79.4 mm. | 79.4 mm. | **Chassis Details:** | | |
| Stroke ... | 76.2 mm. | 76.2 mm. | Brakes ... | Girling hydraulic | Girling hydraulic |
| Cubic capacity ... | 1,508 c.c. | 2,262 c.c. | | (2 l.s. front) | (2 l.s. front) |
| Piston area ... | 30.7 sq. in. | 46.0 sq. in. | Brake drum diameter | 9 in. | 9 in. |
| Valves ... | Pushrod o.h.v. | Pushrod o.h.v. | Friction lining area | 121 sq. in. | 121 sq. in. |
| Compression ratio ... | 6.8/1 (7.5/1) | 6.8/1 | Suspension: Front ... | Coil springs and divided axle i.f.s. | Coil springs and divided axle i.f.s. |
| **Engine performance:** | | | Rear . | Coil springs and rigid axle | Coil springs and rigid axle |
| Max. power ... | 47 b.h.p. (68) | 68 b.h.p. | Shock absorbers ... | Armstrong telescopic | Armstrong telescopic |
| at ... | 4,400 r.p.m. (5,000) | 4,000 r.p.m. | Wheel type ... | Steel disc | Steel disc |
| Max. b.m.e.p. ... | 121 lb./sq. in. (172) | 122 lb./sq. in. | Tyre size ... | 6.40-13 | 6.40-13 |
| at ... | 2,400 r.p.m. (2,500) | 2,000 r.p.m. | Steering gear ... | Marles | Marles |
| B.H.P. per sq. in. pis- | | | Steering wheel ... | 17 in., spring spoke | 17 in., spring spoke |
| ton area ... | 1.53 (2.22) | 1.48 | **Dimensions:** | | |
| Peak piston speed ft. | | | Wheelbase ... | 8 ft. | 8 ft. |
| per min. ... | 2,200 (2,500) | 2,000 | Track: Front ... | 4 ft. 3 in. | 4 ft 3 in. |
| **Engine Details:** | | | Rear ... | 4 ft. 2 in. | 4 ft. 2 in. |
| Carburetter ... | 30 mm. downdraught | 30 mm. downdraught | Overall length ... | 13 ft. | 13 ft. |
| | (2 Zenith downdraught) | | Overall width ... | 4 ft. 10 in. | 4 ft. 10 in. |
| Ignition ... | 12-volt coil | 12-volt coil | Overall height (over | | |
| Plugs: make and type | Champion NA8 | Champion NA8 | hood) ... | 4 ft. 3 in. | 4 ft. 3 in. |
| Fuel pump ... | AC mechanical | AC mechanical | Ground clearance ... | 5½ in. | 5½ in. |
| Fuel capacity ... | 10 gallons | 10 gallons | Turning circle ... | 30 ft. | 30 ft. |
| Oil filter (make, by- | | | Dry weight ... | 16½ cwt. | 17½ cwt. |
| pass or full flow).. | AC full-flow | AC full-flow | **Performance Data:** | | |
| Oil capacity ... | 6½ pints | 8 pints | Piston area, sq. in. | | |
| Cooling system ... | Pump and fan | Pump and fan | per ton ... | 37.2 | 52.6 |
| Water capacity ... | | | Brake lining area, sq. | | |
| Electrical system ... | 12-volt Lucas | 12-volt Lucas | in. per ton ... | 147 | 138 |
| Battery capacity ... | 45 amp. hr. | 45 amp. hr. | Top gear m.p.h. per | | |
| | | | 1,000 r.p.m. ... | 16.0 | 16.0 |
| **Transmission:** | | | Top gear m.p.h. at | | |
| Clutch ... | 8 in. single dry plate | 8 in. single dry plate. | 2,500 ft./min. pis- | | |
| Gear ratios: Top ... | 4.444 | 4.444 | ton speed ... | 80 | 80 |
| 2nd ... | 7.297 | 7.297 | Litres per ton-mile, | | |
| 1st ... | 12.62 | 12.62 | dry ... | 3,420 | 4,850 |
| Rev. ... | 17.15 | 17.15 | | | |

The new Allard P2 Monte Carlo saloon has a bold frontal grille based on the letter "A." The intake for the ventilation system is visible on the scuttle and direction indicators are recessed in the front wings.

# TWO MORE ALLARDS

## MONTE CARLO SALOON AND K3 TOURING THREE - FOUR - SEATER

THE Allard stand at the London Show enjoyed a unique distinction, all the more remarkable for a small company, as there were on display four new models, not one of which had previously been exhibited in this country.

The Palm Beach sports two-seater, which can be had with either the Ford Consul or the Zephyr engine, was described in *The Autocar* of August 29, 1952, and the big Safari station wagon was fully illustrated in the issue of April 11, but the other two cars, the Monte Carlo saloon and the K3 sports touring model, were being revealed for the first time and are worth closer examination than was possible in the Show numbers.

Despite its name, the Monte Carlo

saloon is not directly developed from the P1 saloon in which Sydney Allard achieved a victory for Britain in the classic winter rally earlier this year. It has a different chassis, different front suspension and a de Dion rear axle, while the bodywork is entirely new and roomier than that of the P1. Basically, the chassis is very much the same as the one recently introduced for the Safari station wagon, having very strong side members made of twin steel tubes joined by webs of steel plate; it has the latest type front suspension with the torque arms projecting forward of the divided axle beam. The front suspension is by coil springs, and the rear suspension is also by coil springs in conjunction with the de Dion axle, transverse location of the axle beam being assisted by a Panhard rod.

The standard power unit for this car is the Ford V8 side-valve engine of 3,622 c.c., but the chassis is also designed to accommodate the Lincoln, Cadillac or Chrysler V-eight engines for the benefit of purchasers in America, who are thus able to buy the car without an engine and have their own power unit fitted in the United States. Like the station wagon, the P2 Monte Carlo saloon, to give it its full name, has the front wings, bonnet, radiator grille, and head lamps all built as one structure which pivots on the front end of the chassis. To facilitate lifting the whole assembly, it is fitted with two hydraulic rams, and by working a small hand pump similar to the type employed for hydraulic jacking systems the whole front panel unit can be lifted without any great effort, giving

Right : On the Monte Carlo saloon and the Safari station wagon the bonnet and wing assembly is raised hydraulically. Shown in the sketch are the hand-operated pump and double rams at the front.

Below : The chassis of the Monte Carlo saloon is the same as that used for the Safari station wagon. When the bonnet and front wing assembly is lifted the spare wheel is revealed mounted on the scuttle. The right-hand gear lever is visible below the steering wheel and also in place is the handle for the hydraulic pump which lifts the bonnet.

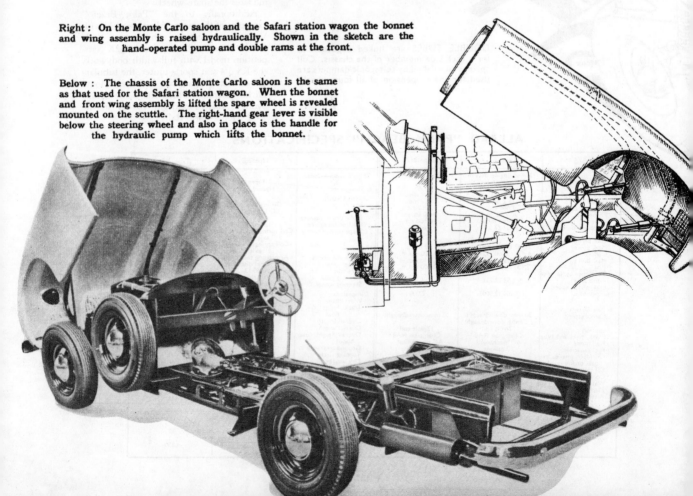

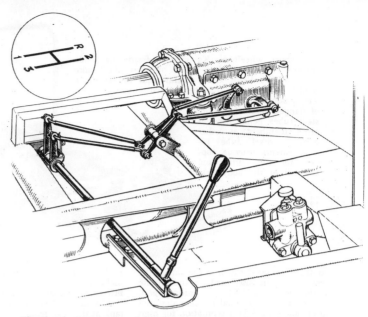

The simple linkage by which the remote control gear lever on the right- or left-hand side of the chassis is connected to the striker and selector controls on the side of the gear box. It is arranged to accommodate movement of the power unit on its flexible mounting.

Left : The interior of the Monte Carlo saloon, showing the facia with engine-turned instrument panel, the three-spoke steering wheel with horn ring and the right-hand gear change lever. Demister slots are provided at the base of the windscreen and there are two ashtrays on the facia.

unrestricted access to the engine, steering, suspension and front brakes. The pump is located under the floor carpet in front of the driving seat and is worked by a detachable handle which is normally carried in the door pocket. A cut-off control allows the bonnet to be lifted by hand in the event of any trouble arising in the hydraulic system.

The spare wheel is mounted under the bonnet, leaving valuable extra space free in the luggage locker. Auxiliaries such as the electric control units and screenwiper motor are also revealed when the bonnet is lifted. The 12-volt battery is carried under one of the front seats and is accessible from inside the car.

Construction of the saloon body is on orthodox coachbuilt lines, with a wooden frame covered by aluminium panels. It is easily the roomiest Allard saloon to date, and the large window areas all round ensure excellent vision for driver and passengers. Included in the equipment

are an interior light with door-operated switches, automatic reversing lights, a built-in radio aerial and a trickle charger plug by which the battery can be charged overnight from the electric mains. The front seat is a split bench with two halves separately adjustable and the upholstery is in real hide throughout. The heating and ventilation system is standard equipment and employs a Clayton-Dewandre heater unit with fan, drawing fresh air from an external intake on the scuttle.

### A Fast Tourer

The K3 touring car represents a new departure in styling of the larger Allard models, as it has a simple oval radiator grille giving it a family resemblance to the small Palm Beach sports model. The chassis is a shorter version of the chassis used for the new saloon, with coil spring suspension all round and a de Dion axle at the rear. This car has a

single bench seat, but this is 56in wide and the internal body width at this point is a generous 58 inches. The model is therefore described as a three-four-seater, and one of the first cars to be delivered has gone to an American family comprising husband, wife and two children. There is a fixed V windscreen, and wind-up safety glass windows are fitted in the doors. The head folds away completely behind the seat and, when erected, transforms the car into a snug coupé.

On the K3 the bonnet opening is by a single rear-hinged panel giving access to the engine, similar to that used on the Palm Beach model. The front wings are not movable and the spare wheel is therefore housed in the luggage locker. A considerable increase in luggage space has, however, been achieved by carrying the fuel in two seven-gallon tanks concealed in the rear wings. To allow the maximum unrestricted floor space in the driving compartment, the gear change is by a remote

The Allard K3 is a fast touring model with space for three or even four people on a wide single seat. Substantial bumpers and over-riders are fitted, as this model is destined primarily for America. Centre lock wire wheels, as shown, are an optional extra.

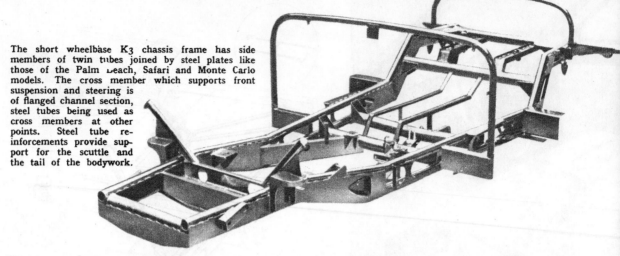

The short wheelbase K3 chassis frame has side members of twin tubes joined by steel plates like those of the Palm Beach, Safari and Monte Carlo models. The cross member which supports front suspension and steering is of flanged channel section, steel tubes being used as cross members at other points. Steel tube reinforcements provide support for the scuttle and the tail of the bodywork.

control lever on the floor at the side of the seat, a system also used in the Monte Carlo saloon and the Safari station wagon.

Both these new models seem destined to enhance the Allard reputation for high performance and controllability, but they are also thoroughly practical vehicles for operation over indifferent roads, as is shown by their ground clearance of a full eight inches. Brakes are Lockheed hydraulic with 12-inch drums and two-leading shoes at the front, and telescopic spring dampers are used at front and rear.

As with all Allards, the main items which may require replacement in the life of the car, such as wheel bearings, oil seals, king pins and bushes, track rod ends and final drive pinions are standard Ford parts which are readily obtainable throughout the world. The Ford-engined cars have in addition the advantage of Ford service for the power unit. At the same time, steady progress is being made in lightening the chassis parts where possible. The differential housing is already supplied with aluminium alloy side pieces, and arrangements are in hand to replace the central iron casting with one of light alloy. The standard Ford crown wheel and pinion are employed for the Monte Carlo saloon, giving a final drive ratio of 3.78

to 1, but three other ratios are available, including one of 3.5 to 1 which is normally fitted as standard on the K3 open car.

The saloon has an eighteen-gallon fuel tank at the rear from which fuel is drawn by the mechanical pump on the engine, supplemented by an electric pump under the bonnet, and a warning light glows on the facia when the last three gallons have been reached.

## World-Wide Service

The introduction of these two models marks steady progress in the rationalization of Allard design. The chassis frames of the Palm Beach range and of these new cars are very similar, although naturally the smaller car uses lighter gauge tubes. The front suspension and steering layouts are also similar. A further step has been the provision of a common design of facia panel for the Safari, Monte Carlo saloon and the K3. A neat engine-turned metal panel in the centre accommodates the tachometer, speedometer, ammeter, fuel gauge, oil gauge and water thermometer. There are also a cigarette lighter, control for the heater, a rheostat for instrument illumination, main beam head lamp light and petrol reserve warning lamp.

## SPECIFICATIONS
### P2 Monte Carlo Saloon

**Engine.**—Ford V8, 77.9 × 95.2 mm (3,622 c.c.). Side valves, compression ratio 6.12 to 1. 85 b.h.p. at 3,500 r.p.m.

**Transmission.**—Single-plate dry clutch. Three-speed synchromesh gear box. Remote control lever. Overall ratios 3.78, 6.68, 11.75 to 1.

**Suspension and Steering.**—Front, divided axle independent with coil springs and forward projecting radius arms. Rear, de Dion with coil springs and Panhard rod. Marles worm and roller steering.

**Wheels and Tyres.**—6.25-16in tyres on steel disc wheels.

**Dimensions.**—Wheelbase 9ft 4in. Track (front) 4ft 8½in; (rear) 4ft 10½in. Overall length 16ft. Width 5ft 11in. Height 5ft. Ground clearance 8in. Kerb weight 3,190 lb.

**Price.**—£1,650 plus £918 3s 4d British purchase tax. Total in Great Britain, £2,568 3s 4d.

### K3 Touring Three-four-seater

**Transmission.**—Overall ratios 3.5, 6.2, and 10.08 to 1. Reverse, 14 to 1. Alternative axle ratios available include 3.78 to 1.

**Dimensions.**—Wheelbase 8ft 4in. Overall length 14ft 9in. Width 5ft 6in. Weight with Ford V8 engine, 2,580 lb. Otherwise as Monte Carlo saloon.

**Price.**—£1,100 plus £612 12s 4d British purchase tax. Total in Great Britain, £1,712 12s 4d.

Right : The left-hand drive version of the K3 touring model has a left-hand gear lever and an adjustable steering wheel. Instruments are mounted on an engine-turned panel in the centre of a metal facia coloured to match the exterior of the car.

Rear end of the K3 chassis, showing the de Dion rear axle with coil springs and tubular axle beam. Axle location is by two arms running diagonally to a central pivot pin which carries a steel ball encased in rubber. At the rear of the axle there is a Panhard rod. Also shown is the method of mounting the twin fuel tanks, which are enclosed within the rear wings.

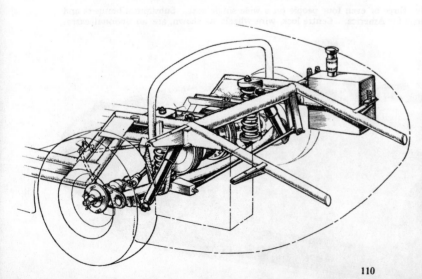

# Allard "Palm Beach"

photographs by
Louis Klemantaski

Twin carburetor Ford Consul engine.

full instrument complement . . .

llard Palm Beach, featured in October Road and Track,
ses 4 or 6 cylinder British Ford ovh engines . . .

enter gear shift and room for three.

Full weather protection . . . .

inch wheelbase .

Low frontal area . . .

Neat, sleek over all.

Slimmer, shorter and lighter than the previous Allards in this category, the JR is also one of the best looking Allards yet built. With the Cadillac engine giving between 200 and 300 h.p. according to tune, it should also be the fastest yet. The slim tail houses the spare wheel and main fuel tank. The exhaust from the V-eight engine is conducted away through triple pipes at each side of the car.

# The JR ALLARD

## NEW CADILLAC-ENGINED SPORTS CAR WILL RUN AT LE MANS

THE success of the Allard J2X sports car when fitted with American V-eight engines has led to the evolution of a new, lighter and more compact model known as the JR, designed specifically for sports car races. It complies with the international sports car regulations, but passenger comfort has been subordinated to performance. There are two comfortable seats in the big cockpit, but interior trim has been kept to the minimum and there is a single small wind-deflecting screen in front of the driver.

The JR has a wheelbase 4in shorter and the maximum track is 5in narrower than on the J2X. To achieve these reductions in size it has been designed round one specific engine, the Cadillac V-eight, which is not only more compact, but is also nearly 130lb lighter than the Chrysler. With the aid of various special parts provided by Detroit Racing Equipment, the output of the Cadillac engine can be raised from the standard 210 b.h.p. to approximately 300 b.h.p., and, as the weight of the complete car is only 2,200lb, the performance will obviously be very fine indeed. The engine is fitted with two four-choke Rochester downdraught carburettors. Only two chokes on each carburettor are in use during the first part of the throttle range, the remaining two being brought into use progressively as the throttle pedal is depressed.

Transmission is through a single-plate clutch and a Cadillac three-speed gear box with synchromesh for second and top. A right-hand change is used. The drive is taken through a short open propeller-shaft to a new De Dion axle incorporating the quick-change final drive produced by Allard in collaboration with H.W.M. The drive passes under the crown wheel and pinion to a pair of spur gears retained by circlips, then forward again to the crown wheel and pinion. Final drive ratios can thus be changed in a few moments by removing the cover plate and putting on a different pair of transfer gears. A selection of four crown wheel and pinion ratios is also available, so that the car can be geared to suit any type of circuit. The power-to-weight ratio is such that, once geared correctly, the car can be driven for most of the time in top gear.

The axle tube is deeply curved to pass behind the transmission casing, and it is located by twin parallel radius arms at each side. Additional location is provided in the centre by a new arrangement of twin A-brackets, one pivoted to the frame, one pivoted on the axle, meeting in a universal joint at the apex of the two brackets. Silentbloc bushes are used for the pivots, with bronze packing pieces to limit end float without impeding radial flexibility.

Regulations for Indianapolis racing cars.

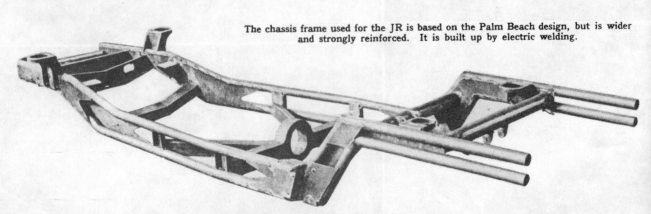

The chassis frame used for the JR is based on the Palm Beach design, but is wider and strongly reinforced. It is built up by electric welding.

# The JR ALLARD

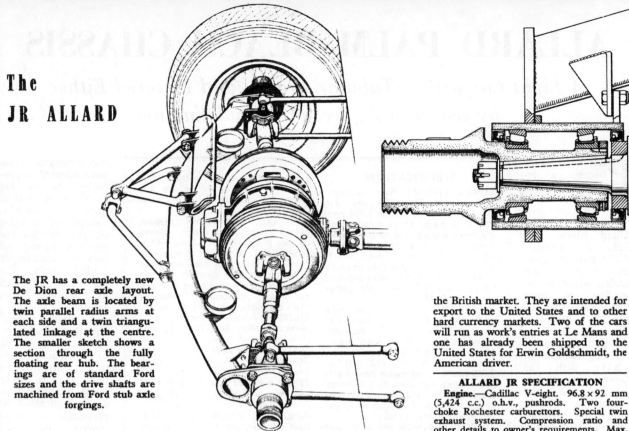

The JR has a completely new De Dion rear axle layout. The axle beam is located by twin parallel radius arms at each side and a twin triangulated linkage at the centre. The smaller sketch shows a section through the fully floating rear hub. The bearings are of standard Ford sizes and the drive shafts are machined from Ford stub axle forgings.

insist on what are known as "safety hubs," and this has helped to produce an interest in sports car racing circles in the United States in types of hub where wheel location is not affected by breakage of a drive shaft. This requirement has been met on the new Allard by fully floating hubs carried in twin taper roller bearings. The drive shaft simply transmits the drive and the braking effort from the rear brakes, which are mounted on each side of the differential housing. The bearings are of standard Ford sizes and the short drive shafts are machined from Ford stub axle forgings. Coil springs form the suspension medium, at front and rear.

The JR frame is developed from that used on the Palm Beach model, but is wider. To this basic frame are welded strong tubular hoops which support the body panelling in front of the cockpit and immediately behind it, thus affording a substantial measure of protection to the occupants if the car rolls over. The weight of the complete frame is only 180lb. The body panelling, in aluminium, can quickly

be removed, while the complete front wing and bonnet assembly is hinged at the forward edge, giving access to engine, radiator, front suspension, steering and brakes.

The engine is carried farther forward in the frame than has been Allard practice in the past, and the weight distribution, unladen, is approximately 57 per cent on the front axle and 43 per cent on the rear. With a load of fuel and the driver on board the weight distribution is roughly equal on front and rear axles. The main tank holds 25 gallons and the auxiliary a further 25. Fuel is fed by two Bendix electric pumps, each of which gives an output of twenty gallons per hour for a weight of about 1½lb.

To cope with the very high performance of which this car is capable, the brakes are bigger than before. They are of Lockheed manufacture with Al-fin drums, 12in in diameter and 2¼in wide, the front brakes having two-leading shoes.

These cars cannot be sold in Britain, as the Cadillac engines are not available on

the British market. They are intended for export to the United States and to other hard currency markets. Two of the cars will run as work's entries at Le Mans and one has already been shipped to the United States for Erwin Goldschmidt, the American driver.

## ALLARD JR SPECIFICATION

**Engine.**—Cadillac V-eight. 96.8 × 92 mm (5,424 c.c.) o.h.v., pushrods. Two four-choke Rochester carburettors. Special twin exhaust system. Compression ratio and other details to owner's requirements. Max. power 200-300 b.h.p. according to tune.

**Transmission.**—Single-plate dry clutch. 3-speed synchromesh gear box; open propeller-shaft; spiral bevel final drive with quick change transfer gears. Gear box ratios: top 1.0, second 1.5, first 2.4 to 1. Crown wheel and pinion ratios: 3.29, 3.5, 3.78 or 4.1 to 1. Further changes of overall ratio possible by a selection of transfer gears.

**Suspension.**—Divided axle independent front, with parallel axis forward projecting radius arms, and coil springs. De Dion rear, with twin parallel radius arms, and twin triangulated A brackets; coil springs. Telescopic dampers all round.

**Frame.**—Twin tubular side members joined by steel plates; tubular and box section cross members.

**Wheels and Tyres.**—Centre lock wire wheels with 6.00-16in tyres.

**Brakes.**—Lockheed hydraulic, 2LS at front. 12in × 2¼in drums. Mechanical hand brake on rear wheels.

**Dimensions.** — Wheelbase 8ft. Track 4ft 3in. Overall length 12ft 6in. Width 4ft 11in. Height to scuttle 2ft 10½in. Kerb weight 2,200 lb approx. Weight distribution, front 57 per cent, rear 43 per cent.

**Price.**—Export only. With fully modified engine, approximately $8,500 in U.S.A.

Alongside the passenger seat are the twin electric fuel pumps, and the removable auxiliary fuel tank which is filled via the main tank. The seats are carried within the chassis frame members, but the driver's feet straddle the frame. Instruments include speedometer, rev counter, ammeter, fuel gauge, oil gauge and two thermometers. The duct on the bonnet covers the two four-choke carburettors.

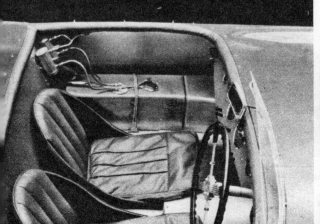

# ALLARD PALM BEACH CHASSIS

## A Light Car with a Tubular Frame, and Powered Either by the Ford Zephyr or Consul Engines

**P**RICE has now become a decisive factor in selling cars both at home and overseas. Because of this, the Allard Motor Co., Ltd., of Clapham, S.W.4, have designed the Palm Beach model, which is the smallest of their post war vehicles. The 21C model is powered by the Consul engine, and its dry weight is 1700 lb, while with the Zephyr installation, the 21Z model, the weight is 1780 lb. With the smaller power unit, the front/rear weight distribution is 55:45, and with the larger one, $57\frac{1}{2}:42\frac{1}{2}$. This should tend to give a slight understeering tendency and help to give good handling characteristics.

The wheelbase is 8 ft, and the front and rear track are respectively 4 ft 3 in and 4 ft 1 in. With the hood up, the overall height is 4 ft 3 in. The other principal dimensions are: width 4 ft 10 in, length 13 ft, ground clearance 5 in to the exhaust silencer and 7 in to the frame. It is stated by the manufacturers that frontal area is about 10 ft².

In order to accommodate the divided front axle, the engine has been positioned to the rear of the wheel axes. This has made it necessary to carry the steering box and divided track rod steering system in front of the suspension units. At the rear, the Ford Zephyr axle is employed in conjunction with coil springs, trailing links and a Panhard rod. It is for cost reasons that

this arrangement has been adopted in preference to the De Dion layout used in previous models. Except for welding on one bracket for the Panhard rod and lugs for the upper trailing links, the axle unit is used as received from Fords.

A tubular frame has been adopted because it is simple to repair, and modifications to the design may be more easily made if required at a later date. No pressings are employed, and even circular dished components, such as suspension spring pans, are fabricated by welding. Two petrol tanks are employed, one over each rear wheelarch, and a filler tube projects through each rear quarter. The advantage of this arrangement is that it has made possible the provision of an exceptionally large boot. The spare wheel is carried on the boot floor.

One of the greatest difficulties that the small motor car manufacturer has to face is that of providing an adequate spare parts service. This is particularly

---

### SPECIFICATION

**CONSUL ENGINE:** Four cylinders. Bore and stroke $3\frac{1}{8}$ in (79·4 mm) × 3 in (76·2 mm). Swept volume 1,508 cm³. Maximum b.h.p. 47 at 4,400 r.p.m. Maximum b.m.e.p. and torque respectively 121 lb/in² and 74 lb-ft at 2,400 r.p.m. Compression ratio 6·8:1. Three-bearing, cast steel, fully balanced crankshaft. Push rod operated overhead valves. Zenith downdraught carburettor, with a 26 mm choke.

**ZEPHYR ENGINE:** Six cylinders. Bore and stroke $3\frac{1}{8}$ in (79·4 mm) × 3 in (76·2 mm). Swept volume 2,662 cm³. Maximum b.h.p. 68 at 4,000 r.p.m. Maximum b.m.e.p. and torque respectively 122 lb/in² and 112 lb-ft at 2,000 r.p.m. Compression ratio 6·8:1. Four-bearing, cast steel, fully balanced crankshaft. Push rod operated overhead valves. Zenith downdraught carburettor, with a 30 mm choke.

**CLUTCH:** Ford single dry plate, 8 in diameter, with hydraulic withdrawal unit.

**GEARBOX:** Three forward speeds and one reverse, baulked synchromesh on top and second. Ratios: top 1:1, second

1·642:1, first 2·48:1, reverse 3·86:1. In later models they will be: top 1:1, second 1·692:1, first 3·273:1, reverse 3·975:1.

**REAR AXLE:** Ford Zephyr. Hypoid, $\frac{3}{4}$-floating with banjo casing. Driven by open propeller shaft. Ratio 4·44:1.

**SUSPENSION:** Rear, coil springs with almost parallel trailing links. Armstrong AT7 telescopic shock absorbers, $\frac{7}{8}$ in bore × 7 in stroke. Front, divided axle and coil springs. Armstrong AT7 telescopic shock absorbers, $\frac{7}{8}$ in bore × 4 in stroke.

**STEERING:** Adamant Marles Hourglass worm and roller. Ratio 14:1. $2\frac{1}{4}$ turns from lock to lock. Turning circle 28 ft.

**BRAKES:** Girling hydraulic, 2LS front. Drum diameter 9 in. Shoe width $1\frac{3}{4}$ in. Friction lining area 121 in².

**TYRES:** 6·40 × 13·0 at 18 lb/in² front and rear, or 5·50 × 15·0 at 20 lb/in² front and rear.

**DIMENSIONS:** Wheelbase 8 ft. Track, front 4 ft 3 in, rear 4 ft 1 in. Ground clearance minimum 5 in. Overall length 13 ft. Overall width 4 ft 10 in. Overall height 4 ft 3 in with hood up. Frontal area 10 ft². Dry weight: Consul 1,700 lb, Zephyr 1,780 lb.

---

In the Allard Palm Beach, the petrol tanks behind the rear wheel-arches do not restrict luggage space

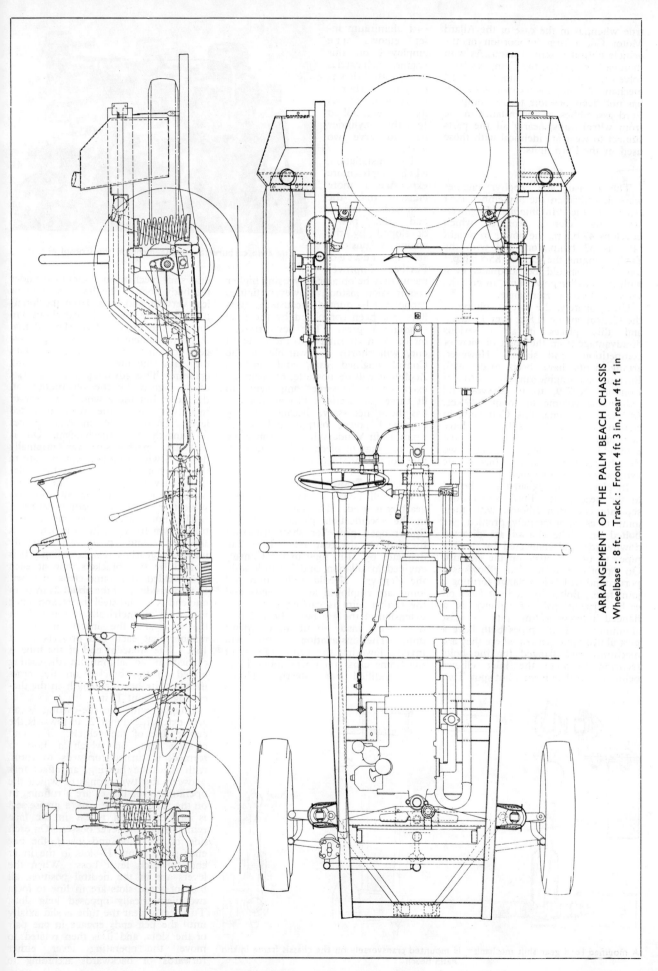

ARRANGEMENT OF THE PALM BEACH CHASSIS

Wheelbase : 8 ft.   Track : Front 4 ft 3 in, rear 4 ft 1 in

true when, as in the case of the Allard Motor Co, a large proportion of the vehicle output is sent overseas. As with their earlier models, the Company have solved the problem by employing Ford mechanical components, and where it has not been possible to use complete Ford assemblies, as for instance in the front wheel hubs, nearly all the parts subject to wear are identical with those used in the Ford units.

### Engines

The Consul and Zephyr engines were described in the September 1951 issue of the *Automobile Engineer*. With the Consul engine, which develops 47 b.h.p., the power to weight ratio is 62 b.h.p./ton, and with the Zephyr engine the ratio is 85·5 b.h.p./ton. This should be adequate, even with the smaller power unit, to give the vehicle a lively performance.

Unfortunately, the swept volume of the Consul engine is 8 cc over 1½ litres, and this places it at a serious disadvantage from the point of view of competition enthusiasts. However, arrangements have been made with Burtonwood Engineering Co., Ltd., of London, N.W.9, to fit sleeves and reduce the volume to about 1,495 cc. At the same time, this Company, in conjunction with Allards, have developed a different inlet and exhaust manifold arrangement to take two Zenith carburettors and to incorporate exhaust heated hot spots.

In place of the exhaust pipe bolted to the head in the Ford layout, four separate cast iron elbows, with their joint faces appropriately profiled, are bolted on. The elbows are directed downwards and connected by flexible pipes to branch pipes on the exhaust. On top of each of the four elbows is a port round which is a flange forming a joint face. Bolted to the joint faces on each adjacent pair of elbows is a flanged interconnecting pipe of cast aluminium. These pipes both have a port above their centres where they are machined and flanged for the bolts securing them to the inlet elbows below which they form a hot spot. Two

cast aluminium inlet elbows are employed on this engine. Each carries a Zenith downdraught carburettor on top, and has its lower end bolted to the cylinder head to serve two ports.

This installation, although more expensive, is more efficient than the standard layout, and the power developed by the engine is considerably increased. Further improvements may be obtained by using higher compression pistons. However, figures cannot yet be quoted because the tests have not been completed by the time of going to press. The new arrangement, as an alternative to the standard one, will shortly be available on the Consul engined cars, and on the Zephyr it will be possible, by using an extra set of the same components, to fit three carburettors. In all cases it has been necessary, because of the improved power output and higher r.p.m. to fit Vandervell lead bronze big end bearings in place of those used in the normal production engines.

### Transmission

With all power units, the Zephyr gearbox is used. The ratios are given in the specification panel. A Hardy Spicer open propeller shaft transmits the drive to the rear axle. It is 2 in diameter by 31 in long in the Consul-engined installation, and 22¾ in long in the Zephyr. Needle roller universal joints are employed at both ends and the sliding joint is carried in the rear extension of the gearbox. Provision is now being made to fit an overdrive unit. The installation of this will involve lowering the centre of one of the frame cross members about 1½ in.

A modified Ford steering column

The twin carburettor arrangement on the Consul engine

gear shift mechanism is mounted under the body floor. The lever is more or less vertical, and offset from the longitudinal centre line of the car about 3 in towards the driver. It is claimed that this arrangement gives a more positive gear shift motion than is possible with the unit mounted on the steering column. This advantage is, of course, offset slightly by the obstruction on the floor, but those who buy a car of this type prefer the floor mounted lever. There are two more advantages in using the Ford mechanism. One is that the mechanism was originally designed with a motion appropriate to this gearbox, and it is therefore relatively easy to adapt it. The second advantage is that replacements for parts subject to wear are readily available.

The Ford steering column control tube, which is ¾ in diameter, is shortened and positioned laterally under the gearbox rear extension. It is carried by two brackets, one at each end, welded to a frame cross member. Brazed inside the tube about 2⅜ in from one end is a solid steel insert, and a peg is passed diametrically through both the tube and the insert in such a manner that each end projects about ¼ in. The adjacent end of the tube is carried in an aluminium die-casting bolted to the bracket on the cross member; its bearing length in the die-casting is about 1⅛ in.

Integral with the die-casting is an arm extending about 2¼ in towards the centre line of the vehicle. The end of the arm, on which a boss is formed, is turned forwards to form, with the tube bearing, an offset fork between the two prongs of which the operating lever bosses are a running fit on the tube. In the arm, a grease seal is pressed into a recess in the face remote from the lever bosses. On each side of the tube and insert, the peg ends project into D-slots in the inner ends of each lever boss. When the levers are in the neutral position, all four of these slots are in line to form two diametrically opposed long slots. To select a gear the tube is slid axially until the peg ends engage in one pair of the slots, and it is then rotated to move the operating lever either forwards or backwards according to

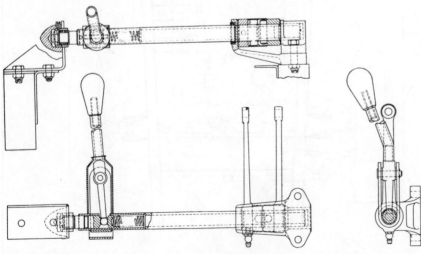

A modified Ford gear shift mechanism is mounted transversely on the chassis frame in the Palm Beach

In the Palm Beach, twin trailing links are employed in conjunction with coil springs and the Ford Zephyr rear axle

in the support bracket. Axial location is effected by a horseshoe washer engaging in two diametrically opposite grooves on the insert. This washer is retained in position by a domed cap passed over the end of the insert and carried on the tubular housing for the bearing ring. A grub screw in a hole in the side of the cap engages in the housing to lock the assembly.

The gear shift lever is pinned between two lugs welded to the control tube. Its lower, or striker end projects through a hole in the tube into a large notch in the steel insert. A rubber gaiter protects this part of the assembly from dust. The pivot pin is positioned with its axis fore and aft so that when the lever is moved from left to right the lower end is held stationary in the notch while the lugs and tube slide from left to right with the lever. If a fore and aft motion is given to the lever, the whole assembly comprising the tube, insert, and an operating lever at the other end rotates about the axis of the tube.

The Zephyr-Six rear axle is fitted on both the 21C and 21Z models. It is a hypoid bevel, three-quarter floating unit with a banjo type casing. The final drive ratio is 4·444:1. Hypoid gear oil is recommended and the capacity is 2½ pints.

Black heart malleable cast iron, B.S. 310:1947 grade 2 is employed for the nose piece which carries all the gears, and which is secured to the casing by eight $\frac{3}{8}$ in diameter bolts. The axis of the En 35A hypoid pinion is offset 0·88 in to the right of the plane of the differential spindle axis, and 1·375 in below the crown wheel axis. Two taper roller bearings spaced approximately 3 in apart, between centres, support the En 35A crown wheel pinion spindle which is overhung in the usual manner. The 9-toothed pinion is upset forged on the end of the spindle. At the front bearing, the spindle diameter is 1 in and at the rear one it is 1½ in. Splines on the front end of the spindle transmit the drive from the companion flange of the universal joint. This flange is held on by a nut on the $\frac{3}{4}$ in diameter threaded end of the spindle. The nut is tightened until the pre-load on the roller bearings is such that the torque required to turn the spindle is 12 to 15 lb-in. The outer races of both bearings are pulled up against shoulders in the nose piece, and the inner ones are separated by a tubular distance piece.

Adjustment of the axial position of the pinion is effected by means of washers of suitable thickness interposed between the gear and the inner race of the rear bearing. An oil seal is housed in the front end of the nose piece, and bears round the boss of the companion flange for the universal joint. This seal, which is supplied by the Super Oil Seals and Gaskets Ltd., is protected by a shroud ring pressed on to the boss of the companion flange.

An En 35A forged crown wheel with 40 teeth is employed. The outside diameter is 7·23 in and the inside diameter 4·06 in. It is drilled and tapped for eight $\frac{5}{16}$ in diameter set bolts which secure it to the inner face of the flange around the one-piece, black heart malleable cast iron differential cage.

which gear is to be selected.

The link between the end of each lever and the gearbox is a simple tube with rod inserts in its ends. These inserts are bent at right angles to engage in the holes in the ends of the levers where they are retained by split pins and plain washers. At the control end the insert is welded in, but at the gearbox it is screwed into the tube, and secured with a lock nut.

A fabricated steel bracket, bolted to the bracket on the frame cross member, carries a steel insert in the other end of the control tube where the gear shift lever is mounted. This insert is a running fit in the tube, and its outer end is shouldered and bears in a bush. The bush is of an absorbent material to retain the lubricant, and is in a steel channel section ring which is pressed into a tubular housing welded in a hole

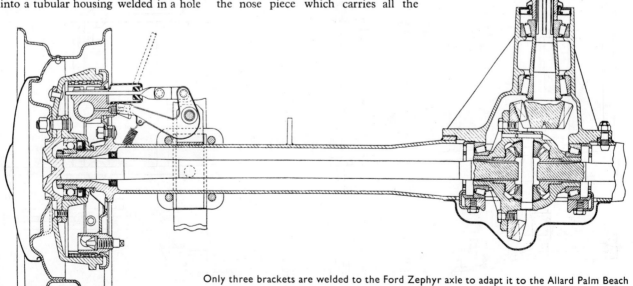

Only three brackets are welded to the Ford Zephyr axle to adapt it to the Allard Palm Beach

The two differential pinions are of En 362. They are carried on a $\frac{5}{8}$ in diameter En 18B pinion spindle which is secured by a peg in a hole through the differential cage and one end of the spindle. Phosphor bronze, spherical thrust washers, $1\frac{1}{2}$ in outside diameter, are interposed between the outer ends of the pinions and the cage.

The En 35A forged differential gears are slightly more than $2\frac{5}{8}$ in diameter, and the length of the tooth engagement is approximately $\frac{5}{8}$ in. Flat, phosphor bronze thrust washers of $2\frac{1}{8}$ in outside diameter are employed, and the bearing length of the 1·32 in diameter gear boss in the differential cage is 0·56 in. The back lash between the differential gears and pinions is 0·005-0·007 in.

Two taper roller bearings carry the differential cage. They are spaced approximately 5 in apart between centres. Their inner races bear against shoulders on the cage, and their outer races are held by ring nuts screwed into the housings in the nose piece. These ring nuts control the mesh of the crown wheel and pinion, as well as the bearing pre-load which is gauged by measuring the spring of the bearing caps. The amount of spring should be 0·01-0·012 in.

The En 18A shafts are 1·06 in diameter at the ends, but they are reduced to 0·94 in diameter over most of the centre portion. Splines on the inner ends transmit the drive from the differential gears. The spline root diameter is 0·865-0·875 in, and the depth is 0·0548-0·0610 in. On the outer end of each shaft, a flange is upset to carry the cast iron brake drum, wheel and En 5B or En 8B forged bearing housing. A single row ball bearing is employed. Its outer face is clamped between the housing and the upset flange on the half shaft, and the inner race is pulled against a shoulder on the hub by a ring nut tightened against its outer face. This nut is locked by a tab washer.

Two oil seals are employed, one in the bearing housing to prevent grease or oil passing from the bearing into the brake drum; the other is carried in the hub, and bears on the periphery of the half shaft to prevent the escape of oil from the axle. The hub and brake back plate carrier are an integral En 8B forging welded on to the axle tube which is $2\frac{1}{2}$ in outside diameter by 0·152-0·168 in. thick. The inner ends of the axle tubes are welded to the banjo casing. Knock-on wheel hubs may be fitted if required by the customer. They are used in conjunction with the larger wheels which are wire braced. Although these hub assemblies are not Ford components, all parts such as bearings, seals, etc., subject to wear are common to both types of hub.

### Rear suspension

Coil springs are used on the rear suspension. With this arrangement it is necessary, of course, to provide positive longitudinal and lateral location. For this reason, almost parallel trailing links are employed in conjunction with a Panhard rod. The unsprung weight is 190 lb. At the wheel, the rate is 105 lb-in. It is obtained with a spring that has a rate of 56 lb-in. This arrangement gives a periodicity of 92 cycles/min. The height of the roll, which is assumed to be the height of the lower bearing of the Panhard rod, is 16·5 in above the ground. The wheel deflection to fully laden position is 4·1 in, and to full bump 3 in.

On each side, the En 45A spring is mounted between two fabricated steel pans, one under the frame side member and the other on an extension of the lower trailing link. The free length of the spring is 16·19 in, and in the static fully laden position it is 10·5 in long. Its overall diameter is $4\frac{7}{16}$—the wire is $\frac{13}{32}$ in diameter and there are 10·7

A Panhard rod, attached at one end to the frame and at the other to the differential casing, provides the necessary lateral location for the rear axle

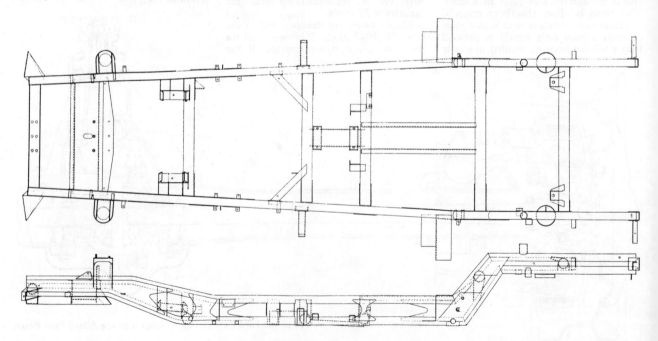

No pressings are employed in the chassis frame, the main members of which are constructed from steel tube

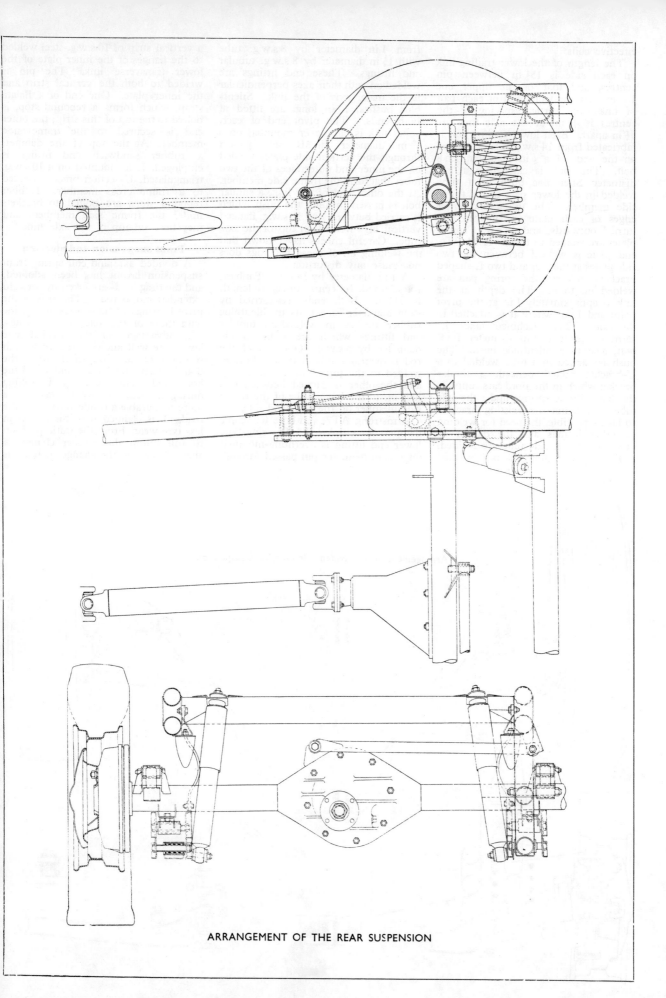

ARRANGEMENT OF THE REAR SUSPENSION

effective coils.

The length of the lower trailing link on each side is $15\frac{1}{2}$ in between pin centres, and that of the upper one $13\frac{1}{8}$ in. At the front end of each pair of links, the vertical spacing of the centres is $4\frac{3}{4}$ in; at the axle they are $5\frac{1}{4}$ in apart. Each lower trailing link is fabricated from 14 s.w.g. plates pivoted on the ends of a $\frac{1}{2}$ in diameter, En 8 bolt. This bolt is carried in a 1 in diameter Silentbloc bush in a tube welded in the lower part of the frame side member. The upper and lower edges of each plate are flanged and turned outwards, and 14 s.w.g. spacer plates are welded to them. A 14 s.w.g. end plate is welded between the two side plates at the rear and two L-shaped brackets to carry the spring pan are welded on to it. The depth of the link is approximately 1 in at the pivot point and $1\frac{1}{8}$ in where it is attached to the axle. This attachment takes the form of another $\frac{1}{2}$ in diameter En 8 bolt, also in a Silentbloc bush. The bush is carried in a tube welded to a U-bracket bolted beneath a similar bracket which in the Ford cars supports the semi-elliptic springs under the axle tube. By using the existing brackets so far as possible, the need for welding on other fittings and the danger of distortion of the axle tube are avoided.

The upper trailing link is fabricated from 1 in diameter by 8 s.w.g. tube with $1\frac{1}{4}$ in diameter by 8 s.w.g. tubular end fittings. These end fittings are welded on with their axes perpendicular to the major axis of the link. Silent-bloc bushes, $1\frac{1}{4}$ in long, are fitted at both ends. The pivot end of each upper link is cantilever mounted on a $\frac{7}{16}$ in diameter En 8B bolt passed through the vertical side-plates welded on the inner and outer faces of the two tubes that form the frame side member. At the other end of the link, a similar bolt is passed through the bush which is carried between two 10 s.w.g. flanged vertical lugs welded on top of the axle tube. Careful checks have shown that the welding on of these two lugs does not cause any distortion.

A 1 in diameter by 14 s.w.g. Panhard rod is fitted. Its centre-to-centre length is $21\frac{1}{4}$ in. Both ends are carried by $\frac{7}{16}$ in diameter En 8 bolts in Silentbloc rubber bushes in welded-on tubular end fittings which are $1\frac{1}{4}$ in outside diameter by 8 s.w.g. One end of the rod is overhung mounted on a bracket welded to the top of the banjo casing and the other is carried between two lugs on to the lower tube of the frame side member on the left-hand side.

Armstrong AT7, $\frac{7}{8}$ in bore telescopic dampers are employed. The ring-type lower end fitting is overhung-mounted on a $\frac{7}{16}$ in diameter pin passed through

a vertical strip of 10 s.w.g. steel welded to the flanges of the inner plate of the lower transverse link. The pin is welded to both the vertical strip and the inner plate. One end of a Balata strap, which forms a rebound stop, is bolted to the top of this strip; the other end is secured to the frame side member. At the top of the damper, a rubber sandwich end fitting is employed. It is mounted on a 10 s.w.g. triangulated, U-section bracket welded to a frame cross member. Rubber rebound stops are bolted to brackets under the frame side members and they bear on top of the axle tube.

### Front suspension and steering

A divided axle and coil spring front suspension layout has been adopted, and the drag loads are taken by forward extended radius rods. The axes of the pivot bearings of these rods are in line with those of the axle pivot bearings. The advantages of the divided axle layout are well known. It gives a high roll centre as compared with the double wishbone layout, and when the body and frame structure is rolling during a turn, the wheels take up a more favourable attitude relative to the road. It is claimed that this results in less tyre wear. From the static position to full bump the camber change is about 7 deg and the change in track is

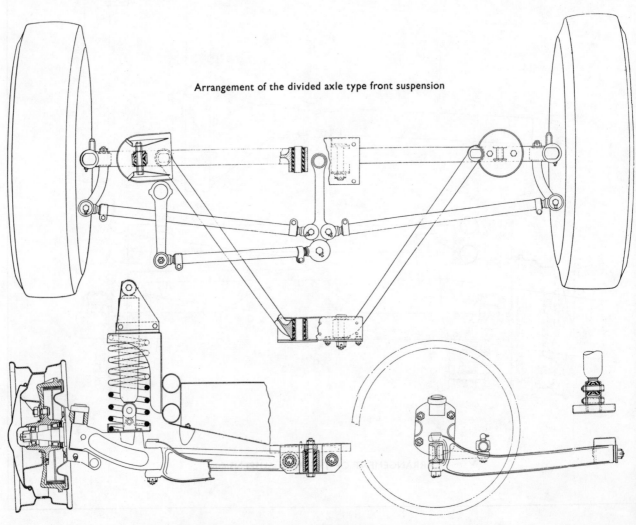

Arrangement of the divided axle type front suspension

In this illustration, the front end pivot of the radius rod is shown in a partly assembled condition

approximately $\frac{7}{8}$ in. The normal camber and castor angles are respectively $2\frac{1}{2}$ deg and 2 deg while the swivel pin angle is 7 deg. A toe in of $0-\frac{1}{8}$ in is incorporated.

The wheel deflection to the static laden position is 8·25 in, and to full bump 11·25 in. With the vehicle in the normal laden state, the height of the roll centre above the ground is ·10·75 in. The rate at the wheel is 52 lb/in and at the spring 140 lb/in. This gives a periodicity of 65 cycles/min with the Zephyr engine installed, and 68 cycles/min with the Consul. The unsprung weight is $66\frac{1}{2}$ lb on each side.

A co-axial coil spring and telescopic damper arrangement has been adopted. The spring is made from $\frac{7}{16}$ in diameter, En 45A ground bar. It has a free length of 13·4 in, and its installed length in the fully laden position is 8·5 in with the Consul, and 8·0 in with the Zephyr engined chassis. The overall diameter of the spring is 4 in and there are 8·34 effective coils. At the upper end, the spring bears on a fabricated steel pan welded to the frame side member. The Armstrong AT7 damper passes through a clearance hole in the centre of the pan. The

ring type end fitting at the top of the damper is rubber bushed and carried about $4\frac{1}{4}$ in above the spring pan by a $\frac{3}{8}$ in diameter bolt between two 14 s.w.g. lugs. Each of these lugs is bolted to a 14 s.w.g. right angle bracket welded on top of the pan. This arrangement is necessary in order that the appropriate axial compression may be applied to the bush. The lower end of the spring rests on a 14 s.w.g. pan bolted to a boss on top of the divided axle. Another rubber bushed ring type end fitting at the bottom of the shock absorber is carried in a similar manner to the upper one between two 10 s.w.g. lugs bolted to a 10 s.w.g. U-bracket welded to the lower spring pan. The effective radius of the line of action of the spring and shock absorber is $15\frac{1}{4}$ in from the pivot point of the swing axle.

An En 18A I-section forging forms the divided axle. Its effective radius measured to the wheel centre is 25 in. The inner bearing is a Silentbloc bush, and is carried on a $\frac{5}{8}$ in diameter mild steel pin 2 in from the centre line of the chassis, in a 10 s.w.g. inverted U-bracket. About 15 in outboard of the pivot point, the forged fork-end fitting of the tubular radius rod is secured to the axle by a $\frac{1}{2}$ in diameter

pin. In a tubular fitting at the other end of this rod, there is a Silentbloc flanged bush with its axis in line with, and its centre about 16 in in front of, that of the swing axle pivot bush. A $\frac{5}{8}$ in diameter mild steel bolt carries the radius rod bush in a 14 s.w.g. inverted U-bracket bolted to the underside of the frame cross member. An inverted U-shaped cut-out in the front face of this bracket clears the bush when it is assembled and a separate bolted on plate is fitted in front of it to apply the compressive pre-load. The rubber bump stop is mounted just inboard of the side member under the cross member supporting the axle pivot bearings. At full bump it bears directly on the axle. The rebound stop is formed by a Balata strap passed under the axle just outboard of the point of attachment of the drag link. The ends of the strap are bolted to the lower ends of the side plates which form gussets between the upper spring pan and the outer face of the frame side member.

A $1\frac{3}{16}$ in diameter, En 207 swivel pin is carried in a boss on the outer end of the axle, and is secured by a cotter pin. This pin is passed through the axle boss and engages in a groove in the swivel pin. Phosphor bronze bushes, spaced $2\frac{1}{2}$ in apart in bosses on the stub axle forging, form the upper and lower swivel pin bearings. These bushes are $1\frac{1}{16}$ in long. They are lubricated through a grease nipple in the lower bearing boss and drillings in the pin. The thrust is taken by a ball thrust bearing between a head on the swivel pin and the top face of the upper bearing boss. A felt seal is interposed between the upper face of the bottom bearing and the axle.

The stub axle forging is of En 18A. Two taper roller bearings carry the wheel, the inner bearing being mounted on the $1\frac{1}{8}$ in diameter portion of the stub axle and the outer one on the $\frac{3}{4}$ in diameter portion. The two bearings are spaced approximately $1\frac{1}{2}$ in apart. They are assembled from each end into the wheel hub. A Superfelt "G" type grease seal is carried in the inner end of the hub and bears on a $1\frac{1}{2}$ in diameter portion of the stub axle. The whole wheel hub assembly is

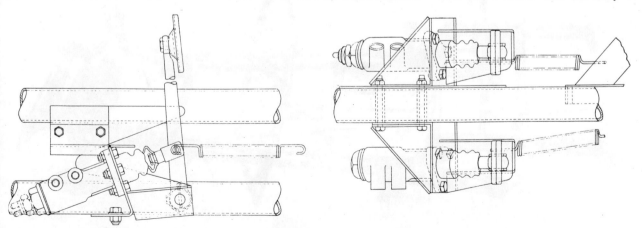

The brake and clutch master cylinders are mounted on brackets on each side of a frame side member

pulled on to the stub axle by a $\frac{5}{8}$ in nut and washer. The inner race of the rear bearing is against a shoulder on the stub axle and the two outer races bear against shoulders on the hub. A pressed steel cap over the outer end of the hub serves to retain the grease. If any grease should escape past the seal on the inner end, it is caught in a trap formed by a shroud ring surrounding the inner end of the hub and bolted to the brake back plate. The brake drum is secured in the conventional manner to a flange around the hub.

Marles Hourglass worm and roller steering gear, manufactured by Adamant Engineering Co., Ltd., of Luton, is fitted. The steering box is mounted on the side frame approximately 6 in in front of the swing axle. The ratio is 14:1, giving $2\frac{1}{4}$ turns from lock to lock. On front lock, the wheel angle is 34 deg, and it is 36 deg on the other lock. This gives a turning circle of 28 ft. A 17 in diameter steering wheel is employed.

A divided track rod system has been adopted. Thompson or Ford adjustable ball joints are fitted throughout. They are lubricated by grease nipples. The ball joints are screwed into the split ends of the $\frac{7}{8}$ in diameter by 9 s.w.g. tubes. The setting is fixed by tightening a bolt passed through a clamping ring round the tube. At their outer ends the track rods are each connected to an En 18A steering arm, which is a push fit in a lug on the lower swivel pin bearing boss. The arm is retained in the lug by a split pinned slotted nut on its end. The effective length of the arm is 5 in.

The track rods are $21\frac{7}{8}$ in long. At their inner ends they are attached to an idler lever, at a point $6\frac{1}{2}$ in from its pivot. The pivot pin in this lever is $\frac{7}{16}$ in diameter and is carried in a Silentbloc bush, $1\frac{7}{8}$ in long. At the outer end of the idler lever is attached the connecting link to the steering drop arm. The effective radius from the line of action of this link about the

idler pivot centre is $8\frac{1}{4}$ in, and that of the drop arm is $6\frac{1}{2}$ in.

### Brakes

Girling two leading shoe hydraulic brakes are fitted at the front, and two trailing shoe units are employed at the rear. The cast iron brake drums are 9 in diameter, the shoe width is $1\frac{3}{4}$ in and the friction lining area is 121 sq in. A pistol grip type hand brake is mounted under the dash. It operates a lever pivoted on a bolt in a bracket on a frame cross member under the engine. A lever ratio of 12:1 has been adopted. The brake control cable is pinned to the lower end of the lever and passed back and attached to the centre of a cross link compensator. Each end of the cross link is pinned to a Bowden cable control. These controls are connected to the bell crank brake operating levers mounted one on each end of the axle tube.

A mild steel pivot pin with a phosphor bronze bush, $\frac{7}{8}$ in inside diameter by $1\frac{1}{2}$ in long, carries the lower end of the brake pedal. This pin is in a bracket on the inner face of the frame side member. The master cylinder is bolted to the same bracket, and the fork end of its plunger is attached to the pedal stem at a point about $2\frac{7}{16}$ in above the pivot to give a lever ratio of 4.25:1. A similar bracket on the other face of the frame side member carries the clutch pedal and master cylinder. The principal dimensions and the lever ratio of the clutch control are approximately the same as those of the brake unit.

### Frame

A notable feature of the frame is that in order to avoid the use of pressed steel components it is built up almost entirely of tubular members. As a result, it is possible to manufacture and assemble all parts of the frame at the Clapham factory. Moreover, should modifications be required in the future, to adapt the frame to different vehicles. there are no undue restric-

Brake and clutch master cylinders

tions imposed by the necessity of recovering the high cost of press tools. In order to localize distortion, almost all the welded joints are arranged parallel to the axis of the tube.

Seven cross members are incorporated. All except the main cross member that supports the suspension are $2\frac{1}{2}$ in diameter by 16 s.w.g. mild steel tube. The first carries the bearings for the radius rods of the front suspension. The second is the cross member supporting the axle and suspension components. It is fabricated as follows: Two plates vertically positioned and flanged outwards at their top and bottom edges form the front and rear walls which are about $5\frac{1}{2}$ in apart. A flat plate is welded up to the bottom two flanges, and another is welded horizontally about $1\frac{1}{4}$ in above it between the two vertical plates. Thus, a box section is formed beneath the second horizontal plate and a channel section above it. The swing axles are pivoted in an inverted U-bracket at the centre of the member

The frame is of sturdy construction

under the lower plate beneath the rear wall.

The next cross member to the rear helps to support the brackets for the front engine mountings. These brackets are welded to the cross member and the frame side members. Then there are two cross members underneath the seats. Additional support for the foremost of these two members is afforded by box section gussets to the side frames. Welded beneath these two members at the centre line of the chassis is a longitudinal inverted channel section. It carries two brackets for the engine mounting points under the gearbox rear extension. Two more brackets, one on each side of the longitudinal channel, are welded on the rearmost of the two cross members to carry the gear shift mechanism. Two longitudinal pieces of angle section extend back from the rearmost cross member to a bracket suspended under another cross member where the frame is cranked upwards to clear the rear axle. These two angle pieces support the propeller shaft tunnel. Another cross member is positioned approximately 4 in behind the axle and two 10 s.w.g. brackets are welded to it to carry the telescopic shock absorbers.

The frame side members are each fabricated from two 1¾ in diameter by 16 s.w.g. mild steel tubes positioned one above the other and spaced apart by 14 s.w.g. or alternatively 16 s.w.g. plates. These plates are positioned on each side member as follows. Two are welded, one on each side, at the front, where the members are bent to form an upward crank so that the front end is approximately 4 in above the centre. The outer plate extends back to the cross member supporting the front engine mountings, and the inner one to a point about 15½ in further to the rear. Immediately to the rear of this cross member a similar plate, but of I-shape, is welded on the outer face of each side member.

Five more interconnecting plates are welded between the tubes in the centre portion of the frame where the axes of the tubes are 5 in apart. Three of them are on the inner face, two being U-sections into which are welded the ends of the two tubular cross members, while the third is flanged outwards, and supports the gusset which is welded to its flat inner face to support a cross member. One of the two plates on the outer face of each side member is flanged inwards and carries a body mounting outrigger bracket, while the other is an I-section plate positioned in line with the rearmost of the two centre cross members.

Near the back, the frame is cut, mitred and welded together again to form an upward crank to clear the rear axle. A 14 or 16 s.w.g. plate is welded on the inner face of each side member from the rear cross member forwards to about 12 in in front of the lower part of the crank. Two more plates are welded on, one at the lower crank and the other at the upper one. The rear ends of each pair of tubes are welded inside short vertical channel sections. Carried on the outer face of each channel is a body mounting bracket.

The 14 s.w.g. spring pans are welded under the side members at the rear and gusseted to the inner plate. At the front they are welded and gusseted to the outer plate. Three 14 s.w.g. Z-section outrigger brackets for the body mountings are carried on each side frame. These are the two already mentioned, one in line with the foremost of the two centre cross members, the other at the extreme back, and the third is at the lower portion of the rear crank. Two more brackets, one on each side at the extreme front end, carry the bumper irons. Two hoops, 1½ in diameter by 16 s.w.g., are mounted on the frame, one under the scuttle and the other under the rear decking.

---

### ALLARD . . . custom tailored
*(Continued from page 105)*

Chrysler engine for your J-2X, sir? Then it is fitted at the works, is works-tested, the test engine removed, and your order is on its way. You can keep the 6 volt starter which comes with the engine . . . it works well on 12 volts!

As to the selection you have to choose from, the most popular of the Allard stable is the sports-racing model . . . the J-2X with Ford, Cadillac, Lincoln, or Chrysler engine—according to your taste and pocket. You can have the J-2X either in racing trim or with the new envelope-type body, as used at Le Mans. The spare wheel of the Le Mans is tucked away so that it does not interfere with the improved luggage accommodation which this super-sports car provides; this results in a much improved aerodynamic form for high speed work. The new K-3—successor to the K-2—is going to be a most desirable piece of high speed transportation. It will employ all the best features of the other models. It will have the new tubular chassis, as used in the P-2 Safari* (but only 100″ wheelbase). The chassis will be much lighter and stiffer than the former K-2, a de Dion axle will be fitted, and wire wheels are optional. The forward half of the Le Mans style envelope body will be hinged at the front to allow easy access to the engine and to the spare wheel, which is also enveloped by the body! Naturally, the car will be equipped with all-weather equipment. The P-2 will be continued with the Safari type body, providing immense room for man and baggage, for which the tubular chassis is excellent.

The latest addition is the new "baby" Allard, described on page 26. It will be fitted with a sleek 2/3 seater sports car body (later on in plastic perhaps). On this chassis, Allard will eventually offer a 4-seater. The family sports enthusiast who, in the past, has been neglected will then be nicely (and inexpensively) accommodated.

It is the policy of the company to make the Allard chassis available for the specialist body builders . . . who are increasing in number in the States. Thus, the Allard buyer may have the choice of a complete ready-to-go car in a wide variety of types, body styles, and engines . . . or he may use his own modified engine in any of the Allard cars . . . or he may utilize his own ability and facilities by building a completely individualized car around any one of the Allard chassis. •

*Allard's "station wagon."—Ed.

3 port Cadillac head is exhausted by individual pipes on each side.

Unusual painting around the grille for easy pit identification

# NEW FROM ENGLAND

# The Allard "JR"

**Photographs by Klemantaski**

Standard Ford column shift mechanism provides convenient right hand shifting for R.H.D. car. Brake is racing type.

In order to save weight, the tail structure is extremely light and carries the spare wheel only. Hood and front fenders lift as a unit

**The Allard "JR" for Le Mans . . .**

The latest product of Sidney Allard's genius points up the fierce competition now being waged for sports car supremacy at Le-Mans. The J in "JR" obviously comes from the company's line of competition models, with the R denoting "racing". However, the "JR" could also be interpreted "junior", since the goal was to produce a car 20% smaller, lighter and faster than the 1952 LeMans model, a J2X chassis with full width body.

Consequently the wheelbase of the JR is only 96 inches, the tread only 51 inches. Designed by Mr. D. Hume, the body has been carefully engineered to reduce weight, improve the "coefficient of penetration" and to lower the frontal area. With an overall width of 59 inches and a height of 34.5 inches, the frontal area must be under 13 sq. ft. The "all up" weight is given as 2200 lbs.—probably without fuel, and weight distribution is 57/43 (without driver or fuel).

The engine is a 5.4 litre Cadillac (stock bore and stroke) with two four barrel carburetors and coil ignition. Since the Cadillac "LeMans" (sports car?) is stated to develop 250 bhp, this output can reasonably be expected, and barring the "fortunes of battle", the new JR Allard must be reckoned with as a potential LeMans winner.

The JR chassis shows no important departures from the later Allard designs, with its double tube frame, parallel axis swinging axle type I.F.S., deDion rear suspension, and coil springs all around. The clutch and 3-speed transmission are standard Cadillac units, coupled to an open drive shaft and Allard's own quick change differential. A gear ratio between 2.6 and 2.9 is contemplated for LeMans. Assuming a ratio midway between these limits, the overall ratios would be 2.75, 4.15, and 6.68, with corresponding road speeds at 5000 rpm of 150, 99 and 62 mph respectively.

In order to cope with these road speeds, Dunlop knock off wire wheels, 6.00 x 16 tires and 12 x 2¼ Alfin brake drums with Lockheed two leading shoes on the front wheels are employed. Special attention has been paid to the shape of the body to facilitate brake cooling, particularly for the front drums which do most of the work. With a body requiring compromises to secure low weight, compromises to reduce wind resistance and yet give good air flow to the brakes, it is not surprising to find a car whose general appearance is rather ugly.

**THE ALLARD "BRIDGEHAMPTON" . . .**

Another new competition model from Allard (not illustrated) will be announced shortly. This is a 1500 cc car, with an estimated weight of 1450 lbs. without driver. The engine will be a Ford Consul, reduced to 1495 cc by sleeving instead of the more usual de-stroking method. The engine is expected to develop 70 bhp with a pair of Zenith carburetors and other modifications not yet fully decided upon.

Wheelbase of the 1500 cc Bridgehampton is 91 inches, tread is 48 inches front and rear, overall width is 56 inches, and height 33.5 inches.

Knock-off wire wheels carrying 5:50-15 tires are specified despite the severe weight penalty. Like the JR model, coil springs are used all-around, and the brake drums are the Alfin type. However, the smaller car uses Girling hydraulic shoes in 9 x 1.75 inch drums.

No information has been released on the transmission or rear axle, but it appears that the Bridgehampton model is to the 'Palm Beach', what the JR is to the K-3—similar, but smaller and lighter for all-out road racing competition. J.B.  •

# MAY 24th, 1952

# BRIDGEHAMPTON SPORTS CAR ROAD RACES

**Bridgehampton, L.I., New York**

Sponsored by

# Sports Car Club of America

By Invitation

*AUSPICES OF THE LIONS CLUB*

*OF BRIDGEHAMPTON FOR THESE CHARITIES*

A fast 3-seater, the K3 tourer has the tubular frame now common to all Allards, with a de Dion rear axle and alternative V8 engines available to "dollar" customers.

**1954 CARS**

# The ALLARD Programme

## Five Basic Models Continue Unchanged

FIVE cars, most of them with one or more alternative engines available, form the 1954 range of the Allard Motor Co., of Clapham. They include the big Monte Carlo saloon and Safari estate car, the K3 and Palm Beach three-seater tourers and, a newcomer, the JR sports-racing car with the 5½-litre Cadillac engine.

Exhibits at Earls Court will be the two tourers and the saloon, which made its first appearance on that occasion in 1952. Based on the Safari chassis, this car has a wheelbase of 9 ft. 4 in. with a tubular steel frame of great stiffness, each side member being built up of two tubes, one above the other. The familiar Allard divided-axle front suspension is used with forward radius arms which take the braking loads, and the rear suspension has the rare distinction among production cars of a de Dion layout, both differential casing and brake drums being mounted on the chassis, so that the unsprung weight is extremely light. Coil springs are used front and rear, with telescopic dampers. Steering is by Marles, the drag link being connected to a central idler arm on the frame. Two half track rods are hinged to this idler, and are so arranged that they move in the same arcs as the swing axles, so that accurate steering is obtained without either kick-back or a complexity of joints.

As an alternative to the standard 3,622 c.c. Ford V8 engine which, with side valves and a compression ratio of 6.12:1 develops 85 b.h.p., the Monte Carlo saloon can be supplied to "dollar" customers with either the Cadillac, Lincoln or Chrysler V8 end. The Ford engine, however, has special aluminium cylinder heads and a compression ratio of 7:1, giving an output of 95 b.h.p. at 3,800 r.p.m. The normal three-speed gearbox and transmission has overall ratios of 3.78, 6.7 and 11.8:1, and alternative final drive ratios are available of 3.27, 3.5 and

engines with normal three-speed transmission, or the Cadillac unit with Hydra-Matic transmission. When a conventional clutch and gearbox are fitted the floor-mounted remote-control change is placed on the driver's off side so that there is no obstruction to the use of the wide bench seat.

Most of the chassis features of the saloon are common in principle to the smaller K3 touring three-seater, including a tubular frame and coil springing with divided axles and a de Dion rear

The Monte Carlo saloon has a very large interior and excellent performance. The basic price is now reduced to £1,375.

4.1:1. Again, the car may be fitted with Cadillac, Chrysler or Lincoln engines if required. The attractive open body has a wide bench seat with off-side gear change, and accommodation for luggage is increased by mounting the fuel tanks, with a total capacity of 13 gallons, in the rear wings. Standard equipment includes hood and side-screens and pressed-steel wheels, but wire wheels may be had as an extra.

Similar in shape to the K3, the two Palm Beach models also have tubular frames, but to reduce costs a 4.11/1 Salisbury back axle is used, with suspension by coil springs and a pair of almost parallel trailing links at each side to take driving and braking torques, while the axle is located laterally by a Panhard rod. The result is simple and light with very accurate geometry.

The greatest difference between these cars and previous Allards is the use of the Ford Consul and Zephyr-Six engines of 1,508 c.c. and 2,267 c.c. respectively in place of the V8. With one eye, as always, on competition possibilities, Allard offer a number of modifications to increase the power of the Consul

engine to that of the Zephyr, 68 b.h.p., and by another arrangement it can be linered down to the 1½-litre category.

The normal Ford Zephyr-Consul gearbox is used, with a modified control by a short lever on the floor. As the car is wide enough to accommodate three people on occasion, the gear lever is offset to just beside the transmission line, either right or left, according to the driving position.

Of the two remaining Allard models, the Safari estate car appeared on the stand at Earls Court last year and differs from the saloon only in the vast wooden-framed body. The JR racing two-seater was introduced earlier this year and is designed specifically for the Cadillac 5½-litre V-8 engine, being an export-only car for the American racing enthusiast. As installed, the engine develops 250 b.h.p. and can be tuned to give considerably more. A special final drive has been produced for the de Dion rear axle of this car, enabling any of a number of alternative ratios to be fitted very quickly.

The style of the modern sports car is exemplified in the small Allard with its flat sides and exposed rear wheels. Larger tyres than standard are fitted to the centre lock wire wheels, which are available as an optional extra. A large windscreen gives full protection for the crew, and the doors, which have handles only on the inside, are of very reasonable dimensions.

# The Autocar ROAD TESTS

## No. 1520:

## ALLARD PALM BEACH TWO-THREE-SEATER

THE design of the original Allard, which first saw the light of day in the middle nineteen thirties, was based on a very favourable power-weight ratio. This car, which made hay of Kent and Surrey trials hills, was followed by others when people began to realize that to reap success in the pre-war trials world it was almost essential to possess

The Palm Beach has a smooth frontal appearance broken only by the plated ribs of the radiator air intake. Louvres cut in the bonnet top help the passage of air through the engine compartment.

a Ford V8-engined special bearing the name Allard on the radiator cowling. Since those days production has increased and the trials specials have been replaced by saloons, sports models and the Safari station wagon. The highlight of recent years was the winning of the Monte Carlo Rally of 1952 by an Allard saloon driven by S. H. Allard himself.

The design of the Palm Beach roadster, which is the subject of this Road Test, incorporates a similar layout to that of the larger Allards, and it follows the principle of using the maximum number of standard Ford parts, with the result that repairs and so on can be carried out speedily and inexpensively. The chassis frame is similar to that of the Safari station wagon, and consists of tubular steel side-members one above the other joined by steel plates; tubular cross-members are used and the suspension is by coil springs front and rear. The standard six-cylinder Zephyr engine is mounted behind the front " axle " line and the drive passes through a normal Ford three-speed gear box to a Salisbury rear axle.

The very name of this model conjures up visions of blue skies, hot sunshine and long straight ribbons of tarmac or concrete, but nearly all the test motoring was done under conditions exactly the reverse, as rain, fog and the usual English traffic conditions prevailed. However, the competition background of the Palm Beach showed up right away and because of the character and roadworthiness of the car it was possible to beat the adverse conditions. On getting into the car one feels at home straight away; a long

There is a good-sized cubby-hole on either side of the facia panel, which is positioned beneath the facia rail so as not to throw reflections in the windscreen at night. Twin electric windscreen wipers park out of the driver's view when not in use ; they clean a good area of glass. It is possible to cast a reassuring eye on the instruments through the top half of the steering wheel.

bonnet stretches out in front and the natural inclination is to drive in an enthusiastic manner. The single-carburettor Zephyr engine warms up quickly and will pull away without using the choke after the initial start, and in the short space of time required to reach the operating temperature the car and driver have settled down and can co-operate as a team.

This car likes to be hurried and covers the ground in a quiet, deceptive fashion. The first hour of a 360-mile journey accounted for 48 miles, which included six miles of narrow country lanes, and incidentally gave a reading of 52 on the mileometer. This was followed by another similar reading until fog put paid to that light-hearted progress. The willing six-cylinder engine laughs at main road gradients with little drop in engine revs and does its work without any fuss or feeling of being overworked. The only apparent noise is the rather healthy exhaust note when revving up to engage a lower gear and some flapping from the hood, which unfortunately had to be erected.

### Acceleration

If full use is made of the acceleration the engine responds at once to abrupt throttle openings; the front of the car lifts slightly and there is a definite hit in the back feeling. When cornering on wet surfaces it does not pay to take liberties with the throttle pedal, as the tail will swing round, but this playfulness can be quickly corrected, and it was found that the Allard was very nearly as fast on wet roads as under more pleasant conditions. With the use of full power whenever possible the fuel consumption will drop to approximately 20 m.p.g., but while still keeping up a very respectable average speed this can be improved by some two or three miles to the gallon. At its maximum one-way speed of 87 m.p.h., which was achieved with the hood and side curtains raised, the car is quite steady, only a light hold on the steering wheel being necessary. Also, in this speed range, the general noise level is such that it is possible for the occupants to converse in more or less normal tones.

The manner of the cornering leaves no room for complaints, and even when an unfamiliar bend is taken rather fast there is no protest from the tyres. Abrupt, snappy bends or fast curves give the same result; the car keeps to the line chosen at the start of the radius and follows it through with the minimum of guidance from the driver.

With such cornering abilities one would prefer separate bucket-type seats, and a grab handle for the passenger would be an advantage, as with two people only on the quite wide bench-type seat there is a tendency to slide about the cockpit. There is no doubt that the ability to corner well, as this Allard does, enables a high average to be maintained and the easy manner in which it swallows up the miles is aided by the independent suspension. Whenever possible, the car was cruised at a reading of 70-75 on the somewhat optimistic speedometer, and at this speed the engine had a comparatively easy time, developing, as it does, its maximum b.h.p. at 4,000 r.p.m. The 5.50-15in tyres fitted on the car tested have a bigger diameter than the standard size of 6.40-13in on the steel disc wheels that are normal equipment, and this, by giving slightly higher gearing, helps the cruising speed.

At speeds of this order, and higher, the car seemed to settle itself down and gave the impression of being able to keep up the pace endlessly. There is no hopping about at the front end and the car holds its course well on most kinds of surface. Some gradients in the nature of 1 in 10 called for the use of second gear, but it was more often by choice and not necessity that the lower gear was used. The untuned Zephyr engine gives plenty of performance for road conditions in Great Britain and the ratios in the three-speed gear box are well chosen. Minimum top gear speed from which the car will accelerate smoothly without a change down is about 12 to 15 m.p.h.

### Steering

The directional stability is good and in spite of a certain amount of lost movement at the wheel rim, the steering has a positive feeling with a definite but slight amount of understeer. The steering lock is good and is a great aid in congested traffic conditions. This lock and the acceleration of the Palm Beach enable most traffic problems to be dealt with in a favourable manner. A short central gear lever is used and although there is some "float" in the mechanism, it is a pleasant, quick change. Support given by the bench-type seat is firm but not uncomfortably so and the steering wheel comes low down, towards the vertical, and almost into the driver's lap.

The Ford hydraulic method of clutch operation is employed and the drive is taken up smoothly, the clutch also standing up well to snap gear changes. There is ample room for the foot away from the clutch pedal, while the right foot rests in what might be described as a separate compartment, as the floor is divided by projections of the frame members. The brakes did all that was asked of them, although towards the end of the test, during which 1,000 miles were covered in little less than a week, all the pedal travel was being used. The retarding effect is smooth and a comparatively light pressure is required when slowing the car from high speeds. Under maximum pressure the brakes pulled up the car in a straight line and no trace of fade was apparent during the taking of the somewhat exacting performance figures. One always hopes for a fly-off type of hand brake lever on a sports car, but here again is the umbrella handle, placed centrally under the facia. However, it does its job well and is comparatively easy to reach.

The coil spring suspension is firm enough to allow corner-ing without any trace of heeling over, yet is sufficiently supple to absorb shocks. Under maximum acceleration from rest there was no juddering of the rear axle, the spring dampers keeping the wheels on the ground in a most satis-factory manner. This car's general behaviour, indeed, gives the driver confidence and the driving position helps towards this feeling in spite of one or two criticisms of measurements.

A tall driver finds that his eye level is on a line with the top rail of the windscreen and, with the seat right back, he has to reach for the gear lever when second or reverse is engaged. A short driver, having adjusted the seat to reach the pedals, finds difficulty in engaging top gear as the lever then fouls the seat, whilst the pedals are still inclined to involve an over-long reach for him. A compromise can be found, however, to suit most people and it is understood that future production cars will be modified to obviate these points. Three adults *can* be accommodated on the seat, but two

## ALLARD PALM BEACH TWO-THREE-SEATER

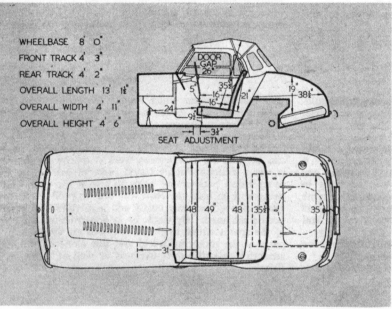

WHEELBASE 8' 0"
FRONT TRACK 4' 3"
REAR TRACK 4' 2"
OVERALL LENGTH 13' 1¼"
OVERALL WIDTH 4' 11"
OVERALL HEIGHT 4' 6"

DOOR GAP 26"
SEAT ADJUSTMENT

Measurements in these ¼in to 1ft scale body diagrams are taken with the driving seat in the central position of fore and aft adjustment and with the seat cushions uncompressed.

─────────── DATA ───────────

PRICE (basic), with open two-three-seater body, £750.
British purchase tax, £313 12s 6d.
Total (in Great Britain), £1,063 12s 6d.
Extras :
Centre lock wire wheels, £80.

ENGINE : Capacity : 2,262 c.c. (138 cu in) Number of cylinders : 6.
Bore and stroke : 79.37 × 76.20 mm (3.125 × 3.0in).
Valve gear : overhead, push rods.
Compression ratio : 6.8 to 1.
B.H.P. : 68 at 4,000 r.p.m. (B.H.P. per ton laden 56.6).
Torque : 112 lb ft at 2,000 r.p.m.
M.P.H. per 1,000 r.p.m. on top gear, 18.1.

WEIGHT : (with 5 gals fuel), 19¼ cwt (2,156 lb).
Weight distribution (per cent): F, 51 ; R, 49.
Laden as tested : 22¾ cwt (2,566 lb).
Lb per c.c. (laden) : 1.13.

BRAKES : Type : F, Two-leading shoe ; R, Leading and trailing.
Method of operation : F, Hydraulic ; R, Hydraulic.
Drum dimensions : F 9in diameter ; 1¾in wide. R, 9in diameter ; 1¾in wide.
Lining area : F, 60.5 sq in. R, 60.5 sq in (105 sq in per ton laden).

TYRES : 5.50 – 15in.
Pressures (lb per sq in): F, 22 ; R, 22 (normal). F, 24 ; R, 25 (for fast driving).

TANK CAPACITY : 8½ Imperial gallons.
Oil sump, 8 pints.
Cooling system, 22 pints.

TURNING CIRCLE : 28ft 0in (L and R).
Steering wheel turns (lock to lock) : 2¾.

DIMENSIONS : Wheelbase : 8ft 0in.
Track : F, 4ft 3in ; R, 4ft 2in.
Length (overall) : 13ft 1¼in.
Height : 4ft 6in.
Width : 4ft 11in.
Ground clearance : 5in.
Frontal area : 17 sq ft (approximately).

ELECTRICAL SYSTEM : 12-volt ; 45 ampère-hour battery.
Head lights : Double dip ; 36–36 watt bulbs.

SUSPENSION : Front, Independent ; coil springs, divided axle. Rear, Coil springs ; parallel trailing links.

## PERFORMANCE

ACCELERATION : from constant speeds. Speed Range, Gear Ratios and Time in sec.

| M.P.H. | 4.11 to 1 | 6.96 to 1 | 13.45 to 1 |
|---|---|---|---|
| 10—30 .. .. | — | 5.0 | 3.9 |
| 20—40 .. .. | 8.0 | 5.0 | — |
| 30—50 .. .. | 8.4 | 6.2 | — |
| 40—60 .. .. | 9.4 | — | — |
| 50—70 .. .. | 11.5 | — | — |

From rest through gears to :

| M.P.H. | sec |
|---|---|
| 30 .. | 4.6 |
| 50 .. | 10.9 |
| 60 .. | 16.9 |
| 70 .. | 23.0 |
| 80 .. | 36.3 |

Standing quarter mile, 20.3 sec.

SPEED ON GEARS :

| Gear | | M.P.H. (normal and max.) | K.P.H. (normal and max.) |
|---|---|---|---|
| Top | (mean) | 84.6 | 136.0 |
| | (best) | 87.0 | 140.0 |
| 2nd | .. .. | 50—62 | 80—100 |
| 1st | .. .. | 22—30 | 35—48 |

TRACTIVE RESISTANCE : 30 lb per ton at 10 M.P.H.

TRACTIVE EFFORT :

| | Pull (lb per ton) | Equivalent Gradient |
|---|---|---|
| Top .. .. | 280 | 1 in 7.9 |
| Second .. .. | 446 | 1 in 5 |

BRAKES :

| Efficiency | Pedal Pressure (lb) |
|---|---|
| 87 per cent | 100 |
| 77 per cent | 70 |
| 55 per cent | 50 |

FUEL CONSUMPTION :

21.6 m.p.g. overall for 600 miles (13.1 litres per 100 km.)
Approximate normal range 20–25 m.p.g. (14.1–11.3 litres per 100 km.)
Fuel, First grade.

WEATHER : Overcast, slight breeze ; damp surface.
Air temperature 46 deg F.
Acceleration figures are the means of several runs in opposite directions.
Tractive effort and resistance obtained by Tapley meter.
Model described in *The Autocar* of August 29, 1952.

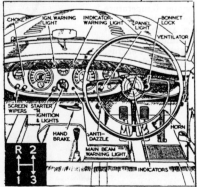

SPEEDOMETER CORRECTION : M.P.H.

| Car speedometer .. .. | 10 | 20 | 30 | 40 | 50 | 60 | 70 | 80 | 90 | 96 |
|---|---|---|---|---|---|---|---|---|---|---|
| True speed .. .. .. | 8 | 17 | 26 | 36 | 46 | 54 | 64 | 72 | 81 | 87 |

Twin fuel tanks are provided with quick action filler caps and the luggage accommodation is generous by sports car standards.

counter, driven from the rear of the dynamo, and oil pressure and water temperature gauges. It is worthy of note that the readings of the latter instruments remained constant throughout the test. The head lamps, the foot-operated dip switch for which is easily reached, give a good spread of light, but the main beam could be more in keeping with the car's performance—criticism which is made all too often these days. Winking direction indicators are supplied, being incorporated in the side and rear lamps, and the horn, which is actuated by a half ring on the steering wheel, gives a useful note. As often applies with horn rings, the driver is divided between regard for its convenience when it is wanted and faint irritation when it is operated unintentionally.

The bonnet is released by pulling a knob in the right-hand facia cubby hole and there is a very large opening with the top raised to its fullest extent. It is difficult to see how one would open the bonnet if the release cable broke or some similar mishap occurred. All under-bonnet auxiliary units are most accessible, and even the major operation of engine removal should not present too great a problem. At the other end of the car the luggage locker has a two-level floor, with the spare wheel and tools occupying the lower level.

## ROAD TEST . . . . . . . . . . . . . continued

adults and a small child may be said to be more comfortable. There is ample leg room on both sides of the gear box cover and the passengers can sit well down in the car, the big windscreen and side curtains giving ample protection.

As with most sports cars, the hood is a necessary evil and visibility becomes somewhat restricted with it erected. A rear window and corner panels of a plastic material are incorporated and are of great assistance when reversing in congested areas. When the hood cover is unfurled the frame folds down behind the seat and the hood itself can be rolled up. At night with the hood and side curtains raised, and the car cruising fast in the easy way it does, it is very pleasant, with the not too bright instrument lighting and the healthy exhaust note heard in the background.

The instruments are well laid out and include a rev

There are 20 points which require lubrication every 500 and 1,000 miles. The locker is lined with a felt material which should prevent damage to suitcases, and the lid, which can be locked, is held open by two struts.

The Palm Beach Allard is a safe and fast road car, which can be used for competition work if the owner desires. It is not a delicate, highly tuned piece of machinery, but its competition background helps to give it the qualification of being able to hold the road well and to produce an average speed of which a more costly and bigger-engined car would not be ashamed. By virtue of its construction, the majority of the spares which might be required are available in most parts of the motoring world and this alone should make it attractive to enthusiasts overseas as well as those in Great Britain.

The Zephyr engine fills most of the space under the bonnet. Starter solenoid, fuses, sparking plugs and fluid reservoir for both brake and clutch operation are readily accessible. Engine intake roar is kept to a minimum by the use of a small air cleaner. The capillary tube for the water temperature gauge leads from a union at the back of the cylinder head, on the right of the engine, through a hole in the bulkhead.

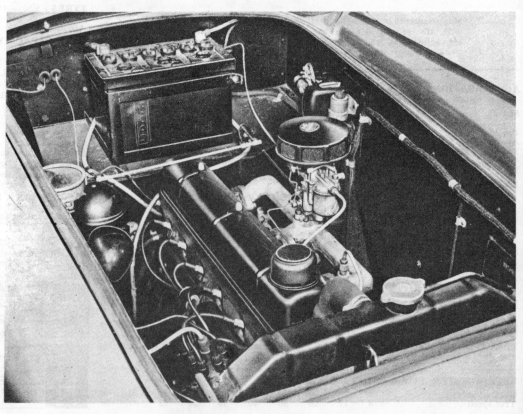

Simplicity of line is the keynote of Allard's entry in the $3000 sports car class.

# Road Testing
# the
# Allard Palm Beach

photographs by

Rolofson

Throwing the Allard into a hard corner (above) produces very little roll. Large, easily read instrumentation is shown at the right.

Not once in our five years of testing sports cars have we had the opportunity to subject an Allard to a full scale road test. Only through the courtesy of a real enthusiast, Mr. Charles Conn of Toluca Lake, California, have we been able to reproduce the attached data, on Allard's entry in the $3000 sport car field, the Ford Zephyr powered Palm Beach.

The Palm Beach is a different breed of cat from the usual run of sports cars. It is one of the most softly suspended sports cars extant, seats three abreast with ease, corners as good as any competition car (with solid rear axle), and cruises along the highway like an old Essex.

With respect to the Allard's suspension, the factory is one of the few firms which give out actual data. Generally we have to describe the ride as being soft, or medium or firm, but the exclusive Allard form of independent front suspension has a ride rate of only 52 lbs/in. Whether you understand this term is not important, but translated into terms of ride motion, the front end frequency is only 65-O.P.M. (oscillations per minute). Re-stated this simply means that the front end has a natural tendency to bounce at this frequency when excited by a bump or bumps. Only a few American cars "bounce" more slowly than 65-O.P.M. In conformance with accepted practice the rear end "bounce-rate" is slightly higher at 92-O.P.M.

How can Allard provide such a "soft" slow-bounce-frequency suspension and still get sports car handling and stability characteristics? Simply because their swinging half-axle front suspension gives a high roll center with accompanying low roll angle in hard cornering work. Are there any disadvantages? Absolutely none that we could determine although the front wheel bump travel is inadequate and the suspension bottoms much too often in average driving. The Palm Beach appears to be especially proficient in sharp right angle turns—it can literally be flung around them, without any noticeable strain, squeal, or excitement. The steering, with 2.6 turns lock to lock, is a little heavy at under 30 mph, but there is no sign of gyroscopic wheel reactions at any speed within the capabilities of the machine.

So we come to the timed top speed average, which in turn brings us back to the earlier reference to the old Essex. At 82.6 mph, the short stroke Ford engine is turning at 5160 rpm, or 1160 rpm past the peak horsepower point. Obviously a car with 40% more wind and rolling resistance than a stock Ford Zephyr 6 and the same gear ratios, isn't going to go any faster than the family sedan—if as fast. Recognizing this fact (rather late) the factory now offers a new axle ratio of 4.11 to 1 and 5.50-15 tires on knock-off type wire wheels. Although this combination will improve the top speed by 4 or 5 mph, the Palm Beach *screams* for want of more useful gear ratios.

Just how unhappy the passenger car gearing becomes, when applied to a sports car can be shown by noting that the maximum speeds in the gears quoted required no less than 6350 rpm from the willing little engine. The fact that the engine stands up to this treatment is a compliment to the engine, but to no one else. However, the choice of gear ratios do give rapid acceleration, as can be seen from our usual acceleration plot. Zero to 60 mph in 14.8 seconds is a very creditable time and the high gear acceleration gives the feeling of a big American car. After our test the owner milled the heads .090, added an American Ford 6 Holley carburetor, a three-branch exhaust header and an M type Jaguar muffler. With these changes he reports a zero to 60 time of 13.0 seconds, using our speedometer corrections.

The speedometer error of 5% is slightly in excess of both common practice and proper decorum, but even less "cricket" was an unusually high tachometer error—plus 4.5% at 4000 rpm. Although there is no excuse for more than 1 or 2% error in a speedometer, the rev-counter optimism is as thoroughly inexcusable as the original factory claim of a timed 100 mph for the Palm Beach.

However, the P.B. is an interesting and comfortable car to drive, both in city traffic and on the highway. It is very easy to drive, requiring no special skill and the controls are well placed and smooth in operation. It starts from a standstill in second gear without sign of strain and can be put into high gear at 10 mph. From that speed it accelerates smoothly and briskly, all the way to its maximum. A comfortable cruising speed on the highway is 60 mph at 3750 rpm. At 70 mph, 4370 rpm, the engine is beginning to "buzz" and the passenger is apt to think the driver has forgotten to shift out of third, or should lift his foot to get overdrive. At all speeds the car has excellent directional stability making it easy to steer and restful on long trips.

Unfortunately for comfort the three-abreast seats have very little padding, in order to keep the seats as close to the propellor shaft tunnel as possible. There is also a need for a folding center arm rest in order to keep the driver properly behind the wheel—tires having notably better adhesion than the seat of one's pants. One peculiarity is the projection of the double tube frame into the floor, running along between the clutch and brake pedals. This proved not objectionable in any way after driving the car for a short while.

Inevitably the Palm Beach will be compared with other sports cars in its price class. Its acceleration performance is approximately midway in the available choice of $3000 cars. Its top speed capabilities are among the slowest, its top gear acceleration is the best of the lot. In our opinion it is the easiest to drive in traffic, ranks the best in low-speed "tight" cornering, and near the top in high speed handling, comfort and stability. The extra width of seat is a feature available in no other sports car, at the price, and one which many prospective buyers will definitely appreciate. Accessibility can be rated very high—the engine in particular being easy to service, with ample room in the large engine compartment.

In brief, the Allard Palm Beach with Ford Zephyr engine must be classified as a touring-sports car. Its good handling qualities are worthy of some of the best competition cars, but its chance of a class win in even a novice road race event are virtually nil. Finally, to answer the obvious question, an overdrive is not available, probably because the propellor-shaft would become shorter, imposing angles too large for the universal joints to accommodate. ●

# ROAD AND TRACK ROAD TEST NO. F-8-54

## ALLARD PALM BEACH (ZEPHYR)

### SPECIFICATIONS

| | |
|---|---|
| List price | $2995 |
| Wheelbase | 96 in. |
| Tread, front | 51 in. |
| rear | 50 in. |
| Tire size | 6.40-13 |
| Curb weight | 2110 lbs |
| distribution | 52/48 |
| Test weight | 2440 lbs |
| Engine | 6 cyl. |
| Valves | ohv |
| Bore & stroke | 3.125 x 3.0 |
| Displacement | 138.3 cu in. |
| | (2262 cc) |
| Compression ratio | 6.80 |
| Horsepower | 68 |
| peaking speed | 4000 |
| equivalent mph | 64 |
| Torque, ft/lbs | 112 |
| peaking speed | 2000 |
| equivalent mph | 32 |
| Mph per 1000 rpm | 16.0 |
| Mph at 2500 fpm | |
| piston speed | 80.0 |
| Gear ratios (overall) | |
| high | 4.44 |
| 2nd | 7.94 |
| 1st | 14.52 |
| R & T perf. factor | 58.0 |

### PERFORMANCE

| | |
|---|---|
| Top speed (avg.) | 82.6 |
| fastest one way | 83.3 |
| Max speeds in gears | |
| 2nd (6350 rpm) | 57 |
| 1st (6350 rpm) | 31 |
| Shift points from— | |
| 2nd | 55 |
| 1st | 30 |
| Mileage | 17/23 mpg |

### ACCELERATION

| | |
|---|---|
| 0-30 mph | 4.5 secs |
| 0-40 mph | 7.5 secs |
| 0-50 mph | 10.7 secs |
| 0-60 mph | 14.8 secs |
| 0-70 mph | 19.8 secs |
| Standing start ¼ mile— | |
| average | 20.70 secs |
| best | 20.60 secs |

### TAPLEY READINGS

| Gear | Lbs/ton | at | Mph |
|---|---|---|---|
| 1st | 585 | at | 22 |
| 2nd | 450 | at | 30 |
| high | 290 | at | 40 |

#### COASTING
(wind and rolling resistance)

| | | |
|---|---|---|
| 125 lbs/ton | at | 60 mph |
| 65 lbs/ton | at | 30 mph |
| 40 lbs/ton | at | 10 mph |

### SPEEDO ERROR

| Indicated | Actual |
|---|---|
| 10 | 12.9 |
| 20 | 21.2 |
| 30 | 29.6 |
| 40 | 38.0 |
| 50 | 47.5 |
| 60 | 57.0 |
| 70 | 66.4 |
| 80 | 74.4 |

Allard Palm Beach (Zephyr)
Acceleration through the gears

ROAD and TRACK

*Road Testing the*

# ALLARD K-3 CONVERTIBLE

Photographs by Rolofson

THREE months ago we carried out a road test on the Allard Palm Beach. This month we move onward and upward with the Allard family and give you our impressions of the K-3 model, the firm's big-car entry in the sports-touring class.

Allard has always kept its competition and sports models separate; the J-2 (competition) and K-2 (sports) were contemporaries, but they were homely looking cars, and more glamorous, eye-catching models were soon in preparation. The K-3 is the product of this evolution, and is undoubtedly the

handsomest car the company has yet built (considering that looks have never been their forte.)

Like the Palm Beach, this car holds a unique spot in the sports car field. It is probably the roomiest of all sports cars. It not only accommodates three comfortably on its single bench-type seat, but the floor, having been raised over the transmission and drive shaft, lies flat, giving the middle passenger clear foot space. The gear-shift lever has been moved to a notch between the driver's seat and the door, even further

uncluttering the spacious interior. Glass windup windows and small, snap-in rear quarter curtains seal against the canvas top for excellent weatherproofing. An unusually large-trunk space, made possible by twin gas tanks in the rear fenders, is one more feature which points to the company's aim of offering the public a practical touring car with sports car performance.

As usual with Allard, no engine is provided by the factory, but the car is set up to take any of the large-displacement, U.S. V-8's. Many of the car's components are re-

A true cosmopolite: English body, American engine, Italian tires, and French headlights.

The spacious interior is simple yet tasteful.

worked Ford parts, and the frame is reinforced chrome-moly tubing. The 3-speed transmission and clutch on our test-car were also Ford, although other makes are sometimes used. The rear-end is de Dion, with coil springs all around and airplane-type shock absorbers.

The first impression of the Allard K-3 is one of smooth, powerful lines, a little box-like, but broad and rugged. The hand-formed aluminum body is almost chrome-free, and the windshield posts and front grille panels are buffed aluminum. Even the dashboard is an aluminum panel with the tasteful, legible instruments grouped in a central cluster.

Driving the car, one is immediately struck with the quick response and brute-like power of the big, high-torque engine—in this case a Chrysler V-8. Although the overall weight of the car if high for a sports car, the weight distribution fore and aft was exactly 50/50, and the car's handling qualities are among the best. The springing in the K-3 is considerably stiffer than the Palm Beach, especially in front, where the bounce frequency is about 100 oscillations per minute (as compared to 65 O.P.M. for the P.B.). Steering is surprisingly light and easy when the car is in motion and is quick enough (2.8 turns lock-to-lock) for all but the competition driver. Unfortunately the front wheels will not turn nearly far enough in either direction, and sharp-angle maneuvering in traffic or parking is virtually impossible. The car is not recommended for Gymkhana work!

The acceleration figures are healthy enough for any car and, in view of the weight involved, are outstanding for the K-3. But just as in the case of the Palm Beach, we felt that the gearing could be improved. The engine winds up too fast too soon, and the acceleration curve begins to flatten out more than it should at 90 mph. Perhaps a 3.27 rear-end would be more desirable than the 3.54. The linkage of the left-hand shift does not permit anything like swift gear changes, and slowed the 0-60 time by perhaps a second. An overdrive might possibly be used to advantage because with differential bolted directly to the frame (in the de Dion set-up), there is no problem of acute angularity between the differential and drive-shaft.

An all-out high speed run could not be

**The Chrysler V-8 fills the engine space neatly.**

# ROAD AND TRACK ROAD TEST NO. F-13-54

## ALLARD K-3 CONVERTIBLE

### SPECIFICATIONS

| | |
|---|---|
| List price | $5370 |
| Wheelbase | 100 in. |
| Tread, front | 56.5 in. |
| rear | 58.5 in. |
| Tire size | 6.00-16 |
| Curb weight | 3150 lbs |
| distribution | 50/50 |
| Test weight | 3490 lbs |
| Engine | Chrysler V-8 |
| Valves | incl. ohv |
| Bore & stroke | 3.81 x 3.62 |
| Displacment | 331 cu in. |
| | (5428 cc) |
| Compression ratio | 7.50 |
| Horsepower | 180 |
| peaking speed | 4000 |
| equivalent mph | 89.0 |
| Torque, ft/lbs | 312 |
| peaking speed | 2000 |
| equivalent mph | 44.5 |
| Mph per 1000 rpm | 22.2 |
| Mph at 2500 fpm | |
| piston speed | 92.0 |
| Gear ratios (overall) | |
| high | 3.54 |
| 2nd | 5.67 |
| 1st | 9.98 |
| R & T perf. factor | 78.4 |

### PERFORMANCE

| | |
|---|---|
| Top Speed | 115 |
| (see text) | |
| Max speeds in gears— | |
| 2nd | 65 |
| 1st | 41 |
| Shift points from— | |
| 2nd | 65 |
| 1st | 37 |
| Mileage | 17/21 mpg |

### ACCELERATION

| | |
|---|---|
| 0-30 mph | 3.2 |
| 0-40 mph | 5.0 |
| 0-50 mph | 6.4 |
| 0-60 mph | 8.6 |
| 0-70 mph | 12.2 |
| 0-80 mph | 16.0 |
| 0-90 mph | 21.2 |
| 0-100 mph | 29.7 |
| Standing start ¼ mile— | |
| average | 16.9 secs |
| best | 16.6 secs |

### TAPLEY READINGS

| Gear | Lbs/ton | | Mph |
|---|---|---|---|
| 1st | off scale — | | |
| 2nd | 580 | at | 40 |
| high | 400 | at | 50 |

#### COASTING

(wind and rolling resistance)

| | | |
|---|---|---|
| 90 lbs/ton | at | 60 mph |
| 40 lbs/ton | at | 30 mph |
| 25 lbs/ton | at | 10 mph |

### SPEEDO ERROR

| Indicated | Actual |
|---|---|
| 30 | 23.0 |
| 40 | 30.6 |
| 50 | 40.5 |
| 60 | 49.5 |
| 70 | 58.7 |
| 80 | 68.1 |
| 90 | 77.5 |
| 100 | 86.5 |

ALLARD K-3 CONVERTIBLE
Acceleration Through the Gears

ROAD and TRACK

**ALLARD ROAD TEST . . .**

made due to the fact that our usual desert testing strip was hot beyond endurance, and a cooler but more congested location had to be used. Our Technical Editor estimated top speed, however, on the basis of experience and a little slide-rule work. Incorrect gearing in the speedometer resulted in an unusually high error.

The test car had traveled almost 12,000 miles, including a gruelling journey to Acapulco, and after we became familiar with the car and talked to the owner, certain shortcomings were noted which were not at first apparent. The flaws which exist in the car are all the more irritating because for the most part they are needless and could easily be corrected by the factory with a little more attention to detail.

The main weak point of the car seems to lie in the clutch and transmission. The process of "marrying" a big, powerful engine to a drive-train is one that should take place at the factory, even if it means shipping the engine to England and then back to the U.S. in the completed car. Although

Foreign Cars, Inc. of Norfolk, Va., did a competent engine-installation job on our test car, (after waiting 3 months for engine delivery), three clutches and two transmissions have been needed in less than ten months of non-competition driving.

The aluminum body's great vulnerability to dents and ripples makes it most impractical for this type of car. Pebbles flying out of the deep Pirelli treads cause external fender pimples from which the paint soon flakes away. The high floor arrangement causes the head of a 6-foot occupant to rise above the windshield level. Result: with the top down, the wind buffets; with the top up, one looks into canvas or develops a crick in the neck. The two gas tanks hold just over six gallons each, limiting the cruising range annoyingly. The doors will not open far enough, and consequently the hinge bar is soon forced against the outer body metal bulging it and again flaking the paint. With the top up and windows down, the car cannot be driven comfortably over 35 mph due to the incredible flopping and shaking of the top. But with the windows closed, the

ventilation (through two hoses leading from the grille) is totally inadequate. By no means the least exasperating fact is that no manual or written information of any kind is supplied to the owner. This means that car maintenance (excluding the engine, of course) depends on pure guesswork and the ingenuity of whatever mechanic may be encountered. With a car as complex and costly as the K-3, this seems inexcusable. Add to these, no tonneau cover; inadequate windshield wipers; no provision for heating and defrosting, no room provided for an air cleaner, etc., and one soon gains the impression that the cars were rushed out of the shop long before they were ready for the public.

If the flaws were corrected, the car's good points would be even more striking, and in spite of the high price, the Allard K-3 might easily fill a demand for a well-behaved, high-speed touring-sports car to a degree that no product now on the market can equal. ●

---

**Performance notes and speeds for a 1953 Allard-Cadillac on the Le Mans course. Map from a color slide courtesy Chevrolet Engineering Department from a paper, "Le Mans and its Meaning to the Automobile Industry," presented in Detroit, Michigan, Oct. 1953 by Zora Arkus-Dontov.**

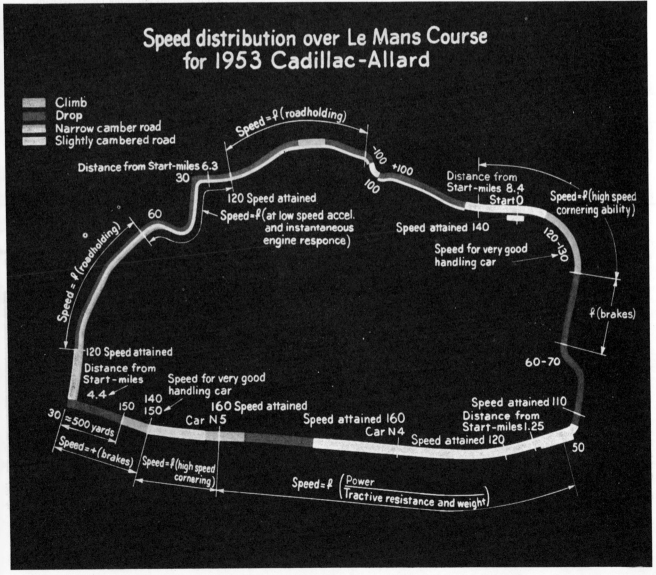

# ALLARD

## *Saloon Model on Palm Beach Chassis*

SALOON coachwork is now offered on the Allard Palm Beach 6-cylinder model, as an alternative to the lower-priced 2/3-seat open sports body which will also be shown at Earls Court.

ONE model is being added to the Allard range for 1954, a closed version of the six-cylinder Palm Beach. Coachbuilt by E. D. Abbott, with aluminium panels over an ash framework, this car offers 2-3-seat accommodation together with ample internal space for luggage.

Strictly in the Allard tradition of sports cars with V-8 engines, the K3 model is an open car providing three-abreast seating, which like other V-8 Allard models is offered in Britain with a British Ford engine, or can be supplied to dollar markets with larger American V-8 engines such as the Dodge, Cadillac or Chrysler as specified by any particular customer. Features of this and all other models include a chassis, each of the two longerons of which is formed by two tubes set one above the other, the use of coil springs and telescopic dampers at both front and rear, and independent front wheel suspension by a divided axle layout which has the minimum number of wearing points. Lockheed hydraulic brakes are used on the V-8 Allard models, of 12-inch size and with two-leading shoes in the front drums.

On a longer chassis, of 9 ft. 4 in. wheelbase, two closed bodies are offered, the Monte Carlo 5-6-seater 2-door saloon, and the Safari estate car which can carry either eight passengers, or six people and a great deal of luggage. All the V-8 Allard models, open and closed, are now built with de Dion-type rear axles for which alternative gear ratios are available.

Smaller sports cars are a more recent addition to the range, the Palm Beach model retaining the Allard principle of using readily serviced Ford components wherever possible (although exclusively Allard suspensions are used, such items as hub bearings and other details liable to need eventual replacement remain of Ford pattern) but using the Dagenham-built 4-cylinder Consul and 6-cylinder Zephyr power units in narrower-track chassis than carry the V-8 engines. Conventional rear axles are used on these models, which normally carry open 2-3-seat bodywork, but the tubular chassis, divided-axle I.F.S., and use of coil springs at front and rear are continued.

# RETURN TO THE CYCLECAR

## *The Allard Clipper—£267 . 15s.*

SIDNEY ALLARD, famous for his sports cars and for winning the Monte Carlo Rally for Britain in the difficult year of 1952, announces that his "years of automotive engineering, racing and track experience are blended in the Allard Clipper."

This new model, which we believe was intended to appear last Easter but is now going into production, is rather startling to those who recall the V8 and V12-engined Allards of J2, K3 and Monte Carlo conception.

The Allard Clipper is a three-wheeler economy car, with single wheel leading, powered by a 346-c.c. Villiers 28B two-stroke engine at the back. Transmission is by belts to a three-speed and reverse Burman gearbox and by chain to the back axle. The engine possesses an electric self-starter, is cooled by a cowled fan, and is claimed to give 60-70 m.p.g., pulling a top-gear ratio of 3.78 to 1.

Interesting features are 7-in. Lockheed brakes on all wheels, a 48-in.-wide bench-seat and a cruciform, channel-section frame. Revolutionary is an all-plastic coupé body by Hordern-Richmond which is self-coloured, in maroon, blue or ivory, and consequently will never require painting. It seats three adults and two children in the dickey—a jolly load for 346 c.c. to pull! The unladen weight is given as 6 cwt. so the reverse gear is in the nature of a luxury. Suspension is by swing-arms and the wheels use Goodyear 4.00 by 8 tyres.

This new Allard Clipper is priced competitively at £267 15s. inclusive of p.t.

It is stated that the Clipper answers the challenge put out by H.R.H. the Duke of Edinburgh when, opening the 1953 Motor Show, he called for a "Comet" of the motoring world. As to that, can we be blamed for preferring to wait and see . . . ?

*ALL PLASTIC EGG.—The new Allard Clipper two-stroke three-wheeler, which sells for less than £268 with purchase-tax paid, has a self-coloured glass-fibre three-seater coupé body, and has a dickey seat for two children.*

# ALLARD

AFTER a venture into the market for 1½-litre and 2¼-litre sports cars, the Allard Motor Company are once again concentrating on the large cars for which they are famous, and the lowest-powered model catalogued for 1956 has a 3½-litre 6-cylinder engine quoted as developing 190 b.h.p. At Earls Court, the cars on show will be a J2R competition 2-seater, a Monte-Carlo 2-door 5-seat saloon, and a Safari estate car, American V-8 engines being fitted to all the exhibits. Also listed is the K3 open 3-seat fast tourer.

Although examples have been raced on many occasions, the J2R competition 2-seater with full-width bodywork has not previously been seen at a Motor Show. Having a wheelbase of only 8 feet, it is powered by a V-8 Cadillac engine of 5.4 litres, which with four twin-choke Solex carburetters and a compression ratio of 9/1 develops 270 b.h.p. at 4,600 r.p.m. This model has been used to develop the suspension system now used throughout the range, I.F.S. being by coil springs and swinging half-axles, rear suspension by coil springs and a tubular " de Dion " axle beam.

### Engines to Choice

Other models in the range can be supplied to order with either a 3½-litre Jaguar XK engine and 4-speed synchromesh gearbox or a 5.4-litre Cadillac engine and Hydra-Matic two-pedal transmission. If required, special engine mountings to accommodate other large power units such as the Lincoln V-8 can be provided, the Allard Motor Company being able to modify the specifications of their hand-made cars to meet special orders.

Especially interesting to overseas buyers will be the Safari estate car which, with high performance, great roominess and a go-anywhere suspension system, is well suited to long-distance motoring in countries with few properly surfaced main roads.

LARGE V-8 engines provide power for the Allard range at Earls Court which includes the sports/racing J2R above and the roomy, rugged Safari below.

---

# ALLARDS TO SPECIAL ORDER

TWO basic models will be produced by the Allard Motor Company for 1957, both to special order only. Production of the Monte Carlo saloon, Safari estate car and the K3 tourer has been terminated. The new version of the Palm Beach (designated Mk. II) can be powered by a 3½-litre Jaguar engine or a 2½-litre Ford Zodiac engine, according to choice. In a somewhat different category the J2R sports car, built to order and mainly for export, is still available and fitted with a tuned version of the 5½-litre Cadillac Vee-eight engine.

The Palm Beach has an entirely new design of front suspension layout and steering; it is the first model produced by the company which has not used the divided front axle type of i.f.s. The new design is a derivative of the original McPherson, as used in the current Ford models. There is a single lower wishbone of triangulated form, and to this is attached a telescopic damper which forms a long hollow king-pin on which the wheels turn. The top end of this suspension strut is attached to the frame, and incorporates a pivot bearing. From the wishbone an operating lever and droplink connects to a group of laminated torsion bars which are placed parallel with each chassis frame side member.

The tubular chassis frame is similar to that of the earlier model. Leading dimensions are: Wheelbase 8ft, track 4ft 3in, overall length 12ft 6in, overall width 5ft 3in, ground clearance 6in. With the Jaguar engine, the dry weight is 21½cwt, and the Zodiac version 20cwt.

Larger brakes have been fitted, and are now 12in diameter by 2½in wide, of Lockheed manufacture. Alternative axle ratios to suit customers' requirements are available. The aluminium bodies, equipped with stowable all-weather equipment, are trimmed to individual preference. Prices are: With Zodiac engine £1,050 basic, £1,576 7s total; with Jaguar engine £1,300 basic, £1,951 7s total.

The new Mark II Palm Beach model

*The new "MARK II PALM BEACH" Allard model with 3½-litre Jaguar engine. (Alternatively the 2½-litre Zodiac engine may be fitted.)*

# NEW PALM BEACH ALLARD

**From GORDON WILKINS**

*Choice of Ford Zodiac or 3½ Litre Jaguar engines in slickly turned out sports car with good road-holding, slashing performance.*

ALLARD Motor Company programme for 1957 provides for two basic models—a new Palm Beach Mark II, and the J2R sports racing car. Production of the Monte Carlo sedan, Safari Estate Car and K3 Tourer has ceased.

The Palm Beach II is an open 2/3-seater sports model offered with a choice of Ford Zodiac 2½-litre, or Jaguar 3½-litre engine. A tubular chassis is fitted with an entirely new front end steering and suspension layout, utilising wishbones and laminated torsion bars. Rear axle is a rigid hypoid unit, with suspension by coil springs, trailing arms and parallel radius rods. Steering is Marles cam and roller, and brakes are Lockheed hydraulic with two leading shoes at the front, drums being 12-inch diameter and 2¼ inches wide.

The body is panelled in aluminium on a steel tube frame welded to the chassis. The hood folds away behind the seats, and details of trim, seating, colour and equipment are to customer's choice. With the two alternative engines, the Allard buyer has his choice of a really fast sports model with four-speed gearbox, or a rapid three-speed sports touring car.

The Ford Zodiac version with six-cylinder engine of 2,553 c.c. develops 90 b.h.p. at 4,400 r.p.m. It has three Zenith carburettors. The single-plate clutch is hydraulically operated, and the gearbox has three speeds with synchromesh second and top; control is by central lever.

On the Jaguar engined car, fitted with two S.U. carburettors, and using an 8 to 1 compression ratio, 190 b.h.p. is available at 5,500 r.p.m. This version has a Jaguar four-speed gearbox, also with central stick shift.

## ALLARD PALM BEACH II SPECIFICATIONS

Engine—*Ford Zodiac*: 6-cyl. o.h.v. 82.5 x 79.5 m.m., 2,553 c.c. Three Zenith carburettors. 7.8 to 1 compression. 90 b.h.p. at 4,400 r.p.m.

*Jaguar* 6-cyl. o.h.c., 83 x 106 m.m. 3,442 c.c. Two S.U. carburettors. 8 to 1 compression. 190 b.h.p. at 5,500 r.p.m.

*Transmission*:—Single plate dry clutch hydraulically operated. *With Ford*, three-speed synchromesh gearbox, central shift. Overall ratios 10.7, 6.18, 3.77 to 1. *With Jaguar*, four-speed gearbox. Overall ratios 10.55, 6.2, 4.28, 3.54 to 1.

*Suspension*:—F r o n t independent wishbones and laminated torsion bars. Rear rigid axle with coil springs, trailing arms, and parallel radius rods.

*Brakes*:—Lockheed with 2 LS front. Drums 12 in. 2¼ in. Wire wheels, with 6.00-15 tyres. Steel disc wheels optional.

Two separate 6-gallon fuel tanks.

*Dimensions*:—Wheelbase 96 in. Track 51 in. Length 150 in. Width 63 in. Height 40 in. Weight (Zodiac.) 2,240 lb., (Jaguar) 2,408 lb.

The Allard J2R model is being built mainly for export, and is usually fitted with a tuned Cadillac V8 engine.

# ALLARD Introduce
## a Gran Turismo Saloon

New for the Motor Show is this Gran Turismo 2/4 seat saloon, based on the Jaguar-powered Palm Beach Mark II chassis. Suspension of the front wheels is independent, by laminated torsion bars linked by long ball-jointed shackles to sliding pillars of which the lower ends are held by transverse radius arms.

NEW model on the Allard stand at Earls Court will be a Gran Turismo 2-4-seater saloon, based upon the Palm Beach Mk. II chassis, of which our artist's impression appears on this page. Like the sports two-seater which will also be exhibited, this car has a 3.4-litre Jaguar engine, alternative power units being a Ford Zodiac engine and gearbox of lower cost and performance, or any of a variety of big overhead-valve V-8 American engines which are available for dollars only. With the Jaguar engine, the basic price of the new model is £1,700, or with purchase tax £2,551 7s.

As illustrated here, the Allard i.f.s. system is now on MacPherson lines, each wheel being located by a telescopic strut and low-mounted transverse radius arm. Use of a laminated torsion bar spring, with the lever arm at its front end which is shackled to the telescopic unit variable in effective length, provides flexibility adjustment to suit varying power unit weights. At the rear, a Salisbury hypoid-geared axle is located by a Panhard rod and pairs of trailing radius arms, supporting the frame through a pair of coil springs; a race-proved de Dion rear axle layout is offered as an alternative at an extra cost of £150.

Based upon an X-braced tubular chassis, the new Gran Turismo body is a sleek two-door saloon built in the Allard works at Clapham; a very comfortable two-seater with a back seat which can accommodate two children. Very slender roof pillars are used to ensure the best possible driving vision, and there are wind-down windows in the doors of both this and the corresponding open-bodied car. Knock-on wire wheels carry 6.00-15 tyres, the hydraulic brakes of 12-in. diameter and 2½-in. width are of Lockheed make, a 20-gallon fuel tank is accommodated in the tail of the body, and the normal top gear ratio of 3.54 : 1 will give 100 m.p.h. at an engine speed of only 4,500 r.p.m.

Each car being built individually the detail specification is variable to special order in respect of equipment and also of major items such as the addition of either a Laycock-de Normanville overdrive or a Borg Warner fully automatic transmission.

With Jaguar engine, the open two-seater is priced at £1,300 (with purchase tax, £1,951 7s.), whilst with the Ford Zodiac power unit its price is reduced to £1,050 (with purchase tax, £1,576 7s.).

## ALLARD

WITH the addition of an extra model to the existing range, now manufactured to special order, the Allard Motor Co., continues a policy of refining and improvement. The new model is a Gran Turismo two-seater similar to the coupé shown above, with a fixed head and large windows at side and rear. Two excellent seats are provided for driver and passenger at the front of the car with an additional seat for two children at the rear. Headroom at the rear is particularly ample. Price of the Gran Turismo model is £1,700 plus purchase tax of £851 7s.—a total of £2,551 7s.

The coupé model shown above is the Palm Beach Mk. II, derived from the J3R racing chassis and it may be equipped with either a three carburetter version of the 2,552 c.c. Ford Zephyr engine producing 90 b.h.p. or a Jaguar 3.4-litre engine. An optional item on both the G.T. car and on the Palm Beach Mk. II, is a de Dion rear end as used in the J3R. The Palm Beach is fitted with a 15-gallon fuel tank, while the Gran Turismo car has a 20-gallon tank.

When fitted with the Ford engine, the Palm Beach model has a three-speed gearbox with a central lever. When the Jaguar engine is specified a four-speed gearbox is provided. In either case a Borg Warner automatic transmission may be specified as an alternative. The Palm Beach with a Ford engine costs £1,576 including purchase tax, while the Jaguar engined version costs £1,951.

The de Dion rear end adds a further £150 to the cost.

In all cases, Allard models are based on the familiar double-tubular chassis in which the side members are spaced by steel plates. Front suspension is an interesting arrangement of vertical pillar, swinging lower link (similar to the Ford front suspension) but with laminated torsion bars as the suspension medium. Brakes are drum type, with 12 in. drums and 2¼ in. wide shoes front and rear. ★

# A TALE OF THREE ALLARDS

ALL-ALLARD STABLE.—Eric Alexander's three Allards photographed outside the Dover House, near Worthing. On the left of the picture is the 1952 Le Mans Cadillac-Allard he uses for sprint racing, in the centre his Cadillac-Allard saloon with Hydramatic transmission, and on the right the hack M-type Allard coupe with tuned Ford V8 engine.

ONE of the most potent Allards in the world and three of the most interesting cars of this make in one stable are the property of Mr. Eric Alexander of Worthing.

The fastest of the trio is a remarkable car, inasmuch as it serves as a shopping runabout, is an extremely fast sports car and competes very successfully in sprint contests, its acceleration matching that of American " dragsters."

This J2X Allard was built for Le Mans. It has a 5,420-c.c. V8 Cadillac engine with Detroit Automotive Company full race equipment, including twin Rochester Quadruple downdraught carburetters, solid tappets, a compression-ratio in the region of 10 to 1 and Buick inner with Cadillac outer valve springs, of 190 lb./sq. in. against the standard engines' 160-lb. valve springs. Ignition is by a Mallory distributor and Mallory " Magspark " high-efficiency coil, and there is food for thought in the ignition advance used— 9 deg. before t.d.c. on the hand setting, which increases to 31 deg. maximum advance when the automatic control takes over !

Power from this bonnetful of potent machinery goes, *via* a Cadillac clutch, to a 3-speed and reverse gearbox with central " stick," the gears being Chevrolet, in an Oldsmobile casing. Thus were a desirable set of close ratios obtained. These can be further varied because the de Dion back axle incorporates an Allard quick-change spur-gear train at the end of the open propeller-shaft. With this there are twelve combinations, giving a range of final-drive ratios from 2.0 to 1 to 4.9 to 1. This range of ratios enable effective use to be made of the power available, which is probably in excess of 300 b.h.p., the engine running up to a remarkable 5,000 r.p.m. when at the top of its form.

For example, at Brighton Alexander uses a 3-to-1 ratio. For a s.s. ¼-mile this is altered to 3.78 to 1, and for a s.s. ½-mile sprint, such as at Thorney Island, when the Allard has thrice in succession made fastest-time-of-the-day against racing-car opposition, a 3.20 to 1 ratio is employed. Up Prescott a 3.45 to 1 ratio is found more suitable, while at Shelsley-Walsh the 3.2 axle ratio enables second gear to be used all the way up and over the line, after stepping off in bottom gear.

MOST POTENT OF THE TRIO.—Miss Hockenhull about to " take off " in the Le Mans Allard, which has three times in succession made f.t.d. at Thorney Island Speed Trials, returning as its best time 21.8 sec. for the s.s. ½-mile, and which is capable of covering a s.s. ¼-mile in well under 15 sec. No easy car for a girl to handle, Miss Hockenhull nonchalantly uses the Allard for shopping as well as for sprints.

After running at Le Mans in 1952, this Allard was modified f[or] sprint work, in which sphere it has certainly collected the silve[r] ware, as a glance at Mr. Alexander's sideboard proves ! Speci[al] 100-ton steel half-shafts were machined for the car and the 40-gall[on] fuel tank was replaced by a 10-gallon tank with its own electric fu[el] pump feeding to the mechanical fuel pump on the engine. F[or] serious sprinting a two-gallon tank, again with its own electric pum[p] is fitted on the bulkhead. Plastic fuel-lines have given bett[er] results than the original copper piping, as has a ring-pipe round th[e] carburetters feeding both float chambers, instead of separate pip[es] to each float chamber.

The body, ugly but suggestive of the latent brute-force of th[is] particular Sydney Allard baby, was built by the Allard Motor Co[.] of 16g. alloy panels. The radiator is normal Allard, the coolin[g] system using a water impeller in the cylinder block, and two 6-vo[lt] batteries live under the seat.

The chassis is the usual boxed-in channel-section J2X with cruc[i-] form bracing, and Lockheed 12 in. by 2¼ in. brakes with twin mast[er] cylinders and ribbed Alfin drums are used, each retaining th[e] external adjuster fitted for the Le Mans race. The linings ar[e] Ferodo VG 95. Suspension is by coil-springs all round, with th[e] divided-beam axle at the front.

The power of the modified Cadillac engine has never bee[n] measured but it was noticeably improved by raising the compressio[n] ratio and particularly by replacing the three exhaust pipes fro[m] each three-port head which merged into a single pipe, with thre[e] separate pipes from each head, these running to D-type Jagua[r] silencers each with twin tail pipes. The Allard now possesses [a] throaty rumble, good to hear, but take-off is rendered exciting by [a] somewhat " sudden " clutch and the great urge unleashed when th[e] throttles are opened.

The car's owner is the first to admit that this Allard is no ligh[t] weight. It scales some 23½ cwt. at the kerbside. Consequently, i[ts] sprint successes are all the more creditable. These include th[e] s.s. ¼-mile against a strong headwind at Eastney in 14.7 sec. (befor[e] later modifications), the Thorney Island s.s. ½-mile in 21.8 sec., an[d] best British time in the semi-wet at Brighton (25.67 sec. for th[e] s.s. kilo). That this is a very potent machine is recalled by a bill f[or] £275 which Alexander received from Brighton Corporation, price [of] a lamp standard he demolished soon after the start of the 1956 Spee[d] Trials. He makes no attempt to excuse this lapse; indeed, a chun[k] of the damaged post, suitably mounted and inscribed, occupies [a] prominent place amongst his trophies. At the top end of the Brighto[n] course, where peak revs. are just about reached in top gear, equivalen[t] to some 140 m.p.h., Alexander admits to apprehension as the ca[r] tries to slide into the seaside kerb. Incidentally, at Le Mans, wit[h] a 2.8-to-1 axle ratio, the car was timed at 148 m.p.h.

Yet the Le Mans Cadillac-Allard is used frequently for shoppin[g] expeditions, both by its owner and his business partner, Miss Ma[r-] garet Hockenhull, who holds members' f.t.d. for Thorney Island, i[n] the excellent time of 23.6 sec.

The car's maxima in the gears are difficult to assess, because th[e] driver has little inclination to line-up the tachometer reading whe[n] driving against the watch, but approximately 60 m.p.h. in firs[t] and 95 m.p.h. in second gear are obtainable. At Brighton in 195[?] before the more recent mods. were made, the last 88 yards [of] the course were covered at a timed 128.6 m.p.h., so that a max[i-] mum in the region of 140 m.p.h. (in sports-car trim, remember[)] seems a reasonable estimate.

The procedure for breaking course records is to keep seven gallo[ns] of fuel in the rear tank to aid rear-wheel adhesion. The centre-loc[k]

CONTINUED ON PAGE 14[?]

# ALLARD

## The Allard Sprint Car

BARE BONES.—*The chassis of the Allard in course of assembly.*

SYDNEY ALLARD'S Steyr-engined "specials" have been a feature of sprints and hill climbs since the war, but the latest in the series promises to be the most exciting of all. It is a twin-engined four-wheel-drive sprint car using two of the well-known Steyr engines.

Back in 1946 Sydney Allard was using a sprint car fitted with a Ford V8 engine, which was not really satisfactory, and his attention was drawn to a German engine originally intended to power lorries. It was a V8 of similar capacity to the Ford but being 100 lb. lighter and giving more power—about 90 b.h.p. at a modest 3,600 r.p.m. It was also air-cooled, thus saving the weight and complication of a cooling system.

Mr. Allard managed to obtain four of these engines together with a spare crankcase and a few spares which have gradually dwindled over the years until his spares' situation is now virtually nil, so that any major damage to an engine will put it completely out of action. One engine is fitted in his sports hill climb car, two in the new car and one as a standby. These interesting engines are 60 deg. V8s having a cast-iron crankcase, with each cylinder being a separate well-finned barrel upon which is fitted the light alloy cylinder head casting carrying two push-rod operated, inclined overhead valves. The crankshaft runs in five plain bearings using the quick-change thin shell type. Above the crankshaft runs the chain-driven camshaft which operates the valves through relatively short push-rods. Ignition is by Scintilla Vertex magneto driven from the nose of the camshaft, while each cylinder is fitted with an Amal carburetter.

The engines have been bored out once since 1947, giving bore and stroke dimensions of 80 by 92 mm. and a capacity of 3.7 litres. Modifications to compression-ratio and carburation have put the maximum power up from its original 91 b.h.p. at 3,600 r.p.m. to over 180 b.h.p. at 5,000 r.p.m. In order to obtain a very low build for the new sprint car two engines have been converted to dry sump lubrication which has meant the fabrication of new sumps only two inches deep. The oil pumps have been adapted to run from the timing gear in front of the engine and the oil tank is situated right at the front of the car.

Turning to the chassis, this is a fairly simple structure being of the ladder type and made from 14-gauge butt-welded channel section mild steel. This chassis virtually forms a base plate because, as can be seen from our photograph, the chassis rails rest on the wooden bench and all mechanical components are above this level. There are three tubular "hoops" welded to the chassis, one in front of the engines, one behind and a half hoop in front of the driver which will serve as a bulkhead and to hold the steering wheel and instruments.

Front suspension is by very large fabricated wishbones, the lower arms pivoting on the chassis side members and the upper arms being pivoted on a tube which runs from the first "hoop" to the housing which locates the rack and pinion steering gear. A transverse leaf spring will be attached to the lower arms of the wishbones and will run through the chassis side members. Damping will be by large telescopic shock-absorber units, but in practice the suspension will be virtually solid. The front differential is a Ford commercial unit as modified for Allard de Dion axles which will drive universally-jointed half-shafts to special Allard-manufactured hubs. A Girling disc brake is mounted sideways behind the differential, *a la* B.R.M.

The rear suspension is simple to describe because there is none. The well-known Allard chassis mounting differential is bolted to the three central chassis tubes with inboard mounted 12 in. by 1¾ in. Lockheed drum brakes. Behind the differential is the housing for the quick-change spur gears to effect rapid alteration of the final-drive ratio. On each outer chassis member a housing has been fabricated which will hold the fully-floating hubs. The driver will sit just in front of the differential to the right, while on the left a petrol tank holding about three gallons of fuel will be fitted. To keep up air pressure a hand pump will be fitted for the driver to operate.

THE STEYR ENGINE, *showing a cylinder head in position.*

THE REAR DIFFERENTIAL *with a Lockheed brake fitted.*

*THE FRONT DIFFERENTIAL, showing oil tank, steering gear and wishbones.*

The engines will be mounted side by side, each one driving through a Ford V8 three-speed gearbox. The right-hand engine will use a gearbox with higher ratios in which the first gear ratio is the same as second gear on the standard left-hand box. These two gearboxes will each drive through short shafts to a housing which holds a series of sprockets. The final drive will then be taken by chain to the propeller shaft. A freewheel will be fitted between the front and

rear propeller shafts, allowing the front-wheel drive to be overridden by the rear.

The use of two engines and gearboxes means the use of two clutch pedals and two gear levers with all its attendant problems, but Mr. Allard has evolved a cockpit drill which he hopes will prove satisfactory. The two gear levers will be mounted side by side to the left of the driver (two Ford Consul column levers used vertically) and on the starting line he will engage both gearboxes in first speed and as soon as possible after he has started he will change the left-hand box into second gear, which has the same ratio as first gear in the right-hand box. The propeller shaft has eight sprockets, each engine driving four chains to these sprockets. Thus when the gearboxes are in the same ratio the power from both engines will be transmitted to the wheels, but when one gearbox is in a higher ratio that engine will be doing most of the work, therefore Mr. Allard hopes to do most of the acceleration in the gears with equal ratios. His next change will be from second to top in the left-hand box and from first to second in the right-hand box. At maximum revs. in these gears the road speed should be about 120 m.p.h. and with the present tyre sizes of 6.00 by 16 at the front and 7.00 by 16 at the rear he calculates that the maximum speed should be 165 m.p.h. at 5,500 r.p.m. using the present 2.8 to 1 top gear ratio.

The car will stand only 2 ft. 6 in. high when completed and no bodywork will be fitted for the time being except for a nosepiece. When bodywork is eventually added the wheels will be exposed. He also hopes to obtain a set of American "slicker" tyres which are used on all the best "dragsters" in the States.

Mr. Allard is going to be a busy man during his runs but his car is certainly something different in the true sprint "special" tradition, and the public are obviously going to appreciate his efforts. We look forward to his first appearance at Brighton on September 5th. —M. L. T.

---

CONTINUED FROM PAGE 140

wire wheels are shod with 6.50 by 16 tyres at the back, 6.00 by 16 at the front, these tyres being Dunlop Racing, all of which are Pneugrippa-ed.

A carburation flat-spot has been cured by using Cleveland Discol petrol. When Allard raced the car Lodge R47 plugs were used but, after experimenting with A.C. 42s, specially imported from the States, Alexander now prefers the softer Champion J6s, sacrificing a set of these, however, after every run. So far as lubricants are concerned, the sump is filled with 50/50 Bardahl and Castrolite, drained after each meeting. Castrol XL with the addition of 25 per cent. Bardahl being used in the gearbox and Castrol Hypoid 90 plus 25 per cent. Bardahl in the back axle.

In spite of its potency this remarkable Allard has been driven some 5,000 miles on the road by its present owner, who gets an excellent 17 m.p.g. when thus commuting. Raced, this rises to around 8 m.p.g., naturally.

Alexander is no newcomer to sprint motoring, for in 1926, riding a 350-c.c. Calthorpe tuned by Fall, he beat the venerable Baragwanarth at Lewes, and subsequently sprinted in the saddles of Brough-Superior, long-stroke Sunbeam and Norton motor-cycles. He then turned his attention to cars, graduating through seven different Austin Sevens, Clynos, Morrises, etc., to the hobby of turning out fine cars to Concours d'Elegance standard. These latter have included Talbot 105, Speed Six Bentley, a beautiful cream drophead 540K Mercedes-Benz (now in America) and his present Allard saloon. He did not return to sprint motoring until recently, with a 1953 T.T. Arden-head Mercury-Allard.

The saloon Allard is another remarkable car, and probably the most expensive ever built by the Allard Company. It was listed at over £2,500. It is a blue P2 1956 Monte Carlo model with another 5.4-litre Cadillac engine under its bonnet. This engine is quite standard (at the time of writing!), with hydraulic tappets and single Carter Quadruple carburetter, and so is the Hydramatic fully automatic transmission. The coil-spring suspension, Lockheed brakes and de Dion back axle (3.5 to 1) are much as on the J2X, but the two-door Allard saloon body is very heavy and this car weighs about 29 cwt. Luxuriously upholstered in leather, this is a fine car, which handles well and is very quiet-running. Naturally, it possesses outstanding acceleration; at M.I.R.A. the Allard Company timed it to do 0 to 60 m.p.h. in 10.2 sec. and the s.s. ¼-mile in 17 sec.

On this occasion there was apparently insufficient space for the car to get into its stride, because the maximum speed of 112 m.p.h. scarcely did it justice. The Hydramatic transmission has an over-ride lever and kick-down, providing two settings, changes into the highest ratio taking place at 30 m.p.h. or at 65/68 m.p.h. according to the driving technique adopted. In view of the appeal of a 5.4-litre fully-automatic Allard it is surprising that this model went out of production. But only six were built. Of these, there

*POWER PACK.—The 5.4-litre Cadillac vee-8 engine of Alexander's Le Mans Allard, which now has modifications in the best American dragster tradition.*

is a Cadillac-engined example with normal Ford gearbox in Ireland, two others, one with Ford, another with Mercury engine, in this country, the others being exported without power units. So Alexander has a unique Allard in this Cadillac Hydramatic saloon. It has run about 20,000 trouble-free miles, doing 17 m.p.g., and looks very smart, with 6.00 by 16 Dunlop Road Speed Whitewall tyres. Miss Hockenhull has exhibited it at the Brighton Concours d'Elegance, and it has won the closed-car class at Thorney Island Speed Trials. Incidentally, Castrolite is used in the engine and appropriate Castrol lubricants for the transmission and back axle of this car.

After buying these cars Alexander craved hack-transport and seems to have decided on an all-Allard stable, because he purchased, from the Allard Company and for no very fabulous sum of money, his third Allard. This is a 1949 M-type coupé with 30-h.p. Ford V8 engine. The late property of a member of the Competition Department of Amal Ltd., it is by no means as ordinary as it looks. The Ford gearbox has a floor gear-lever, which is rare. The engine boasts alloy heads, a compression-ratio of 8.25 to 1, dual Solex carburetters, a three-branch exhaust manifold and a special eight-lobe distributor. This model had the transverse leaf-spring divided-axle front suspension. This particular Allard has a 3.54-to-1 axle ratio and Michelin "X" tyres all round and is a faster conveyance from A to B than you might suppose!—W. B.

The Autocar
ROAD TEST
1735

Allard
Gran Turismo
Coupé

Striking lines are used on the G.T. coupé, enhanced by the stark twin bars which form the bumper. The auxiliary lamps for fog and long range work are standard

FROM about the time the old Ford V8 side-valve engine went out of production—succumbing, after years of successful service in all sorts of vehicles, to the challenge of more efficient o.h.v. units—the Allard marque has been rather less in evidence on the roads than of old. The occasion of a test of the latest, made-to-order, Jaguar-engined Gran Turismo Coupé is timely, therefore, for a quick résumé of the background to this exceptionally individual make.

Founder of the enterprise centred in Clapham, London, is Mr. Sydney Allard, for many years one of this country's best-known trials and hill-climb drivers. His reputation abroad has been enhanced by participation in international rallies and sports car races. The know-how behind the Allard cars includes an outright victory for Sydney Allard in one of his own cars in the 1952 Monte Carlo Rally, and a number of courageous attempts at Le Mans' *Grand Prix d'Endurance*, gaining third place in 1950.

Great strides have been made in Allard development since the trials cars—the slightly primitive but very effective mud-pluggers—reached the pinnacle of their post-war success. The latest G.T. version is an interesting example, for it has an unusual front-suspension layout, a de Dion system at the back, and a power-to-weight ratio contributing towards a standstill-to-100 m.p.h. time well under the half minute—28.3 sec to be exact. That the car tested displayed some touches of sub-standard detail workmanship is a pity, especially now that the model—retailing at a basic ex-works price of £1,700 with orthodox back axle—has entered the bespoke class. With tax the British buyer pays £2,410, exclusive of the de Dion axle, heater and other items of equipment which tend to be taken for granted in this type of high-powered, long-legged carriage.

The car is founded on a stout chassis frame to which the hand-made, light alloy body is attached. The front hub and wheel assemblies are mounted on pillars sliding in cylinders open-ended at the top. At the bottom there are long swinging links which extend fore and aft to pivot on the chassis frame. Laminated torsion bars are used in conjunction with telescopic dampers. An anti-roll bar

also is fitted. The de Dion layout at the rear incorporates brake drums at the inboard ends of the drive shafts. Disc brakes have been made standard at the front, the complete system being by Girling. Servo-assistance is not provided. Knock-off wire wheels are standard.

In this type of car performance accounts for much of the appeal; it certainly proves to be the Allard's outstanding feature. The times taken to reach various speeds from a standstill are really impressive. In addition to the very short elapsed time to a full 100 m.p.h., the car will reach the widely used cruising speed of 80 m.p.h. in 16.6 sec. A standing-start quarter mile can be covered in 17.1 sec. These figures owe much to exceptionally good traction on getaway. The clutch is admirably suited to all forms of normal driving, but is a little slow to engage completely on full-throttle getaways; most cars with such power would suffer far more from wheelspin. The de Dion layout which helps to achieve this standard of traction costs an extra £150 basic (£212 10s to the British buyer).

There is no need to dwell upon the already well-known power unit. The engine in the Allard was all that one could desire in the matter of smoothness throughout the range, and provided town-carriage docility when required. The Allard installation permitted a good deal of noise outside the car, including some impressive crackling sounds on over-run which passed almost unnoticed by the occupants. A rev limit is marked on the counter from 5,500 upwards, and there is no benefit to be obtained from exceeding this figure. Maximum speeds attainable in the lower indirect gears are 39, 70, and 105 m.p.h. on first, second and third respectively. In any context, 105 m.p.h. in third, with two higher gears still in hand, is an exciting figure. The usefulness of 70 m.p.h. in second on overcrowded roads can well be imagined. The vigorous acceleration allows quick, safe overtaking.

In top the G.T. reaches 120 m.p.h. In practice this prospect does not often arise, for such speeds are strictly for motorways, and on these overdrive would normally be used, even though this cruising ratio on the Allard is too high to enable the absolute maximum to be maintained.

Left: The occasional rear seats are suitable for children. Entry is rather easier than it appears here. There is a lot of space on the shelf under the back window

Right: Occupants have separate seats, and are further divided by the transmission tunnel. Gear and brake levers are central, and all the controls are conveniently placed

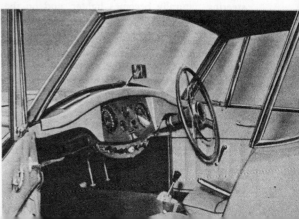

# Allard G.T. . . .

On Jaguars, lower top gearing is installed when overdrive is specified, but the Allard has the standard direct top ratio of 3.54 to 1. Thus it is the true overdrive which many drivers relish. In fast road work it is little used, but may be engaged at the touch of a conveniently placed switch whenever a high speed may be steadily held.

When changing from top into overdrive at maximum speed the m.p.h. drops to 117, although this car cannot be accelerated to this figure in overdrive. The change is smooth into or out of the Laycock overdrive.

Mounted centrally, the gear lever is a little far from the driver. Changes could be made more easily were the knob of a different shape; the action is rather stiff and the synchromesh easily to beat. However, the lever movement is positive and there is never any fear of engaging the wrong gear. In really hard driving on a long run, the fuel consumption is unlikely to fall below 16 m.p.g. and may be appreciably more with quiet driving, when plentiful use can be made of overdrive, due to the engine's tractability.

While the suspension is unusual in design and behaviour, its performance on the road is marred by such stiffness as materially affects average speeds on all but the most smoothly surfaced roads. On typical French roads, for example, which are straight and fast, if narrow and indifferently surfaced, 80 m.p.h. is as much as most drivers will care to hold without conscious effort. Over this speed there is a lessening of contact between wheels and road, and the car wanders. This being so, the exciting fast curves so often encountered have to be approached with some caution lest the car should patter too far outward.

On smooth English roads the driver can be more relaxed; it was found that adhesion was generally much improved and that corners could be taken faster. In these circumstances the tail becomes skittish, but not unpleasantly so, except that it needs to be treated cautiously in the wet. At speed the rear suspension is rather noisy, and reaches its bump stops too readily. Steering is rather heavy at 2¼ turns from lock to lock, and the restricted full lock hampers parking and other low-speed manoeuvres, the turning circle between walls being over 40ft. At speed the steering naturally becomes lighter, and on the open road is responsive and reasonably accurate. There is very little self-centring.

Fast driving shows up the most disappointing feature of an otherwise impressive machine. This concerns the body structure, particularly above the waistline. The car tested is the sole G.T. in the company's use and with some 20,000 miles on "the clock" it has to put up with a good deal of experimental work, the recently introduced disc brakes being an example. Even so, it appeared that to stand up to the vibration at high speed, stronger frames are needed for the large areas of glass. During the test the windscreen became loose in its surround, causing a good deal of noise; the doors were sometimes difficult to open, and there was a number of rattles.

Braking power proved adequate. Maximum retardation of 88 per cent is above average, and although repeated application caused a falling-off in efficiency, this never reached a condition of fade. Pedal pressures are heavy by present-day standards, nearly 100 lb being necessary to obtain maximum effect. The travel is also long. The high pressure might be interpreted as labelling the brakes insensitive, but the pressure required is not difficult to achieve, particularly for a man. At high speed, hard braking called for concentration on the steering to hold the car straight. The characteristic disc brake squeak could be heard sometimes from the front, but otherwise there was no sound. Tyre squeal is confined to emergencies. The long hand-brake lever has its mounting behind the driving seat, and is canted across between the seats. It is of the fly-off type and proved effective.

Care has been taken to see that the cockpit is right for the type of driver whom such a model attracts. The separate driving seat is comfortable, and the rather big wheel adjustable. It is not possible for tall drivers quite to achieve a full arm reach. Instruments comprise two large dials for speed and r.p.m., with total and trip mileage recorders, and smaller dials for fuel and dynamo charging. Also included are a clock, positive petrol reserve with additional warning light, and tell-tale lights also for overdrive, direction indicators, main head lamp beam and, of course, ignition. The indicator switch is on the hub of the three-spoked sprung wheel. The horn ring is sensibly placed about half-way between the rim and the boss. The instruments would be more simply checked at a glance if mounted in front of the driver, instead of in the middle of the facia.

Pedal arrangement permits heel-and-toe changes to be made (in fact, with the side of the foot against the throttle). All the switches are easy to reach, including that for the lamps; the dip switch is near the top of the facia to the driver's right, beside the overdrive control. The driver's window winds down very quickly.

All-round visibility is excellent, with the qualification that the Perspex rear window on the test car was crazed and, therefore, not fully transparent in bright sunshine.

Facia lighting is controlled by a rheostat, and the main lighting proved up to high-speed travel by night. Additionally a long-range driving lamp and a fog lamp are included in the specification. The wipers sweep a large area of glass, but to achieve this one of them extends beyond its nearest windscreen pillar when horizontal. There are no ashtrays.

Entry into this low car is greatly helped by the width of the doors; the lower edges of them are high enough not to touch kerbs. Behind the tip-up front seats are two padded perches that would accommodate small children. Alternatively one small adult might recline across them. The sharp slope of the rear window confines this accommodation to short runs for the grown-ups. This rear compart-

*There is no separate accommodation for luggage, the locker at the rear housing simply the spare wheel and tools. The single exhaust outlet is paired by the reversing lamp. A quick release petrol filler is fitted*

# Allard G.T. . . .

ment is primarily for luggage and, in conjunction with its big shelf at the rear, is very well worth having.

The very high performance of the G.T. Allard has its competition potential reduced by the rather intractable suspension and by the soft clutch. On the other hand, the car falls short of the true luxury *gran turismo* in matters of detail. However, as this is a machine tailor-made to order, the buyer could probably have the specification adjusted in many little ways to suit his requirements. The car is certainly of strikingly purposeful appearance, very fast, and exciting to drive.

## ALLARD GRAN TURISMO COUPÉ

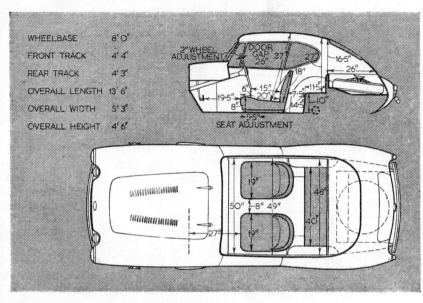

| WHEELBASE | 8' 0" |
|---|---|
| FRONT TRACK | 4' 4" |
| REAR TRACK | 4' 3" |
| OVERALL LENGTH | 13' 6" |
| OVERALL WIDTH | 5' 3" |
| OVERALL HEIGHT | 4' 6" |

*Scale ⅛in to 1ft. Driving seat in central position. Cushions uncompressed.*

## ——— DATA ———

**PRICE** (basic), with coupé body, £1,700.
British purchase tax, £709 10s 0d.
Total (in Great Britain), £2,409 10s.
Extras: de Dion axle £150 (£212 10s with tax). Heater £25 (with tax).

**ENGINE:** Capacity, 3,442 c.c. (210 cu in.).
Number of cylinders, 6.
Bore and stroke, 83 × 106 mm (3.27 × 4.17in).
Valve gear, two overhead camshafts.
Compression ratio, 8 to 1.
B.H.P. 210 (gross) at 5,500 r.p.m. (B.H.P. per ton laden 147.4).
Torque, 213 lb ft at 4,000 r.p.m.
M.P.H. per 1,000 r.p.m. in top gear. 22. in overdrive 29.

**WEIGHT:** (With 5 gals fuel), 25.5 cwt (2,856 lb).
Weight distribution (per cent) F, 52: R, 48.
Laden as tested, 28.5 cwt (3,192lb).
Lb per c.c. (laden), 0.93.

**BRAKES:** Type, Girling; disc front, drum rear without servo-assistance.
Method of operation, hydraulic.
Dimensions: F, 11.7 in diameter. R, 12 in diameter; 2.25in wide.
Swept area, front, 275 sq in., rear, 170 sq in.

**TYRES:** 600—15in Dunlop R.S.4.
Pressures (lb per sq in); F, 22; R, 24 (normal); F, 25; R, 30 (fast driving).

**TANK CAPACITY:** 17.5 Imperial gallons.
Oil sump, 22 pints.
Cooling system, 22 pints (plus 1.5 pints if heater fitted).

**STEERING:** Turning circle:
Between kerbs, R, 42ft 6in; L. 41ft 11in.
Between walls, R, 43ft 10in; L, 43ft 2in.
Turns of steering wheel from lock to lock, 2¼.

**DIMENSIONS:** Wheelbase, 8ft. 0in.
Track: F, 4ft 4in; R, 4ft 3in.
Length (overall), 13ft 6in.
Width, 5ft 3in.
Height, 4ft 6in.
Ground clearance, 6in.

**ELECTRICAL SYSTEM:** 12-volt; 60 ampère-hour battery.
Head lights, Double dip; 36—60 watt bulbs.

**SUSPENSION:** Front, independent, with swinging lower link and sliding pillar; laminated torsion bars and anti-roll bar. Rear, de Dion with coil springs.

## ——— PERFORMANCE ———

### ACCELERATION:

Speed range, Gear Ratios and Time in Sec.

| M.P.H. | 2.71 to 1* | 3.54 to 1 | 4.7 to 1 | 7.05 to 1 | 11.8 to 1 |
|---|---|---|---|---|---|
| 10—30 | — | — | — | 3.8 | 2.4 |
| 20—40 | — | 6.6 | 5.4 | 3.9 | — |
| 30—50 | 9.2 | 6.6 | 5.6 | 4.1 | — |
| 40—60 | 9.6 | 7.2 | 5.9 | 4.3 | — |
| 50—70 | 10.4 | 7.9 | 6.6 | 4.8 | — |
| 60—80 | 12.3 | 9.1 | 7.3 | — | — |
| 70—90 | 15.7 | 10.7 | 8.5 | — | — |
| 80—100 | 21.9 | 13.3 | — | — | — |

*Overdrive.

From rest through gears to:

| M.P.H. | sec. |
|---|---|
| 30 | 3.4 |
| 40 | 5.3 |
| 50 | 7.4 |
| 60 | 9.6 |
| 70 | 12.6 |
| 80 | 16.6 |
| 90 | 21.1 |
| 100 | 28.3 |

**Standing quarter mile, 17.1 sec.**

### MAXIMUM SPEEDS ON GEARS:

| Gear | | | M.P.H. | K.P.H. |
|---|---|---|---|---|
| O.D. | (mean) | | 117 | 188.3 |
| | (best) | | 117 | 188.3 |
| Top | (mean) | | 120 | 193.1 |
| | (best) | | 120 | 193.1 |
| 3rd | | | 105 | 169.0 |
| 2nd | | | 70 | 113.0 |
| 1st | | | 39 | 63.0 |

### TRACTIVE EFFORT:

| | Pull (lb per ton) | Equivalent gradient |
|---|---|---|
| O.D. | 190 | 1 in 11.7 |
| Top | 270 | 1 in 8.2 |
| Third | 340 | 1 in 6.5 |
| Second | 540 | 1 in 4.0 |

### BRAKES: (at 30 m.p.h. in neutral)

| Pedal load in lb | Retardation | Equivalent stopping distance in ft |
|---|---|---|
| 50 | 0.43g | 70 |
| 75 | 0.68g | 44 |
| 95 | 0.88g | 34.2 |

### FUEL CONSUMPTION: Constant speeds.

| M.P.H. | M.P.G. | |
|---|---|---|
| | Direct Top | O.D. Top |
| 30 | 50.0 | 60.2 |
| 40 | 32.5 | 43.8 |
| 50 | 24.0 | 33.1 |
| 60 | 19.8 | 26.6 |
| 70 | 17.3 | 21.9 |
| 80 | 15.6 | 19.0 |
| 90 | 15.0 | 17.1 |
| 100 | 14.1 | 15.5 |

Overall fuel consumption for 1,046 miles, 16.3 m.p.g. (17.34 litres per 100 km).

Approximate normal range, 14—24 m.p.g. (20.2-11.8 litres per 100 km).

Fuel: Premium grade.

### TEST CONDITIONS: Weather Dry, slight cross breeze.

Air temperature, 59 deg. F.

Acceleration figures are the mean of several runs in opposite directions.

Tractive effort obtained by Tapley meter.

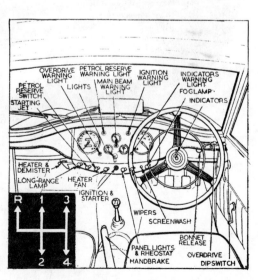

### SPEEDOMETER CORRECTION: M.P.H.

| Car speedometer: | 10 | 20 | 30 | 40 | 50 | 60 | 70 | 80 | 90 | 100 | 110 |
|---|---|---|---|---|---|---|---|---|---|---|---|
| True speed: | 12 | 20 | 30 | 39 | 49 | 57 | 67 | 76 | 85 | 95 | 105 |

The name is a simple one; it stood and still stands for two things: a car that's the image
brute power and performance, and a man with the courage to create it and drive it very, very f

# ALLARD

## by Dennis May

BRUNELL

Allard tries out the driving position on one of his Le Mans machines. He is one of the few constructors who compete in their own products.

It's too late now to buy an Allard, or anyway a new one, but if you ever happen to be knocked down on the streets of London the chances are your ride to the hospital will be cushioned by Allard's interpretation of the de Dion back axle. When Allard car production ceased a while back, temporarily at least, the company's potential was largely switched to the conversion of London County Council ambulances to this classic adjunct to traction and safety, ensuring as far as possible that the halt and the maimed don't become halter and maimeder en route. Allard was the first British make to feature a de Dion rear end on production cars and practically all of its postwar competition successes have been scored with de Dionized posteriors. So if racing doesn't improve *the* breed (or does it?), it could perhaps be claimed it improves the breed of London ambulances.

In relation to Allard's very small output, only amounting to about 2000 cars in a 25-year lease of life, the make's contribution to competition history was formidable, and the fact that Sydney Allard, the man in the title role, himself drove or co-drove the Allards responsible for the firm's three finest achievements, doesn't spike the compliment. On the contrary, it shows he had the courage of the convictions he designed and built into these homely but dynamic bolides. In 1949, after twice consecutively ranking third, Sydney copped his country's most coveted sprinting honor, the British hillclimb championship. The following year, while Erwin Goldschmidt and his Cad-Allard were winning the first Watkins Glen G.P. to make the international calendar, Sydney Allard, with help from Tom Cole, was putting 2101 miles onto *his* Cad-Allard at Le Mans, placing third overall and taking the 8-liter class; this incidentally was the first time any British car had passed the 2000-mile mark at Le Mans . . . not that the part played by its American engine was exactly negligible. In '51, among a host of other conquests on both sides of the ocean, John Fitch with a J2 Allard was first and turned fastest lap at Costanera in the sports car leg of the Argentine's Temporada series. Then, as further and sensational proof of his products' versatility, Sydney won the 1952 Monte Carlo Rally under nightmare conditions, skippering an Allard sedan powered by a flathead V8 Ford engine. Twenty-one years had gone by since the last British win in *Le Rallye*, and the fact that less than half of the 328 starters reached the finish, and a mere fifteen came through the road section unpenalized, showed it was no fluke for the Allard/Warburton/Lush trio.

This, by the way, was one of the few important postwar Allard successes gained without benefit of a de Dion axle. Sydney had sacrificed the feature because he wanted to demonstrate that the basic specification, innocent of the various sophisticated options that were available, was equal to any demands you could make on it. He made his point.

Allard and the late Tom Cole broke their class record at Le Mans in the 1950 race recalled above, and that isn't all they broke. In fact, they were lucky even to start, say nothing of finishing. On Wednesday of race week they cracked a piston. Paris was the nearest source of Cadillac parts, so while the engine was being torn down the least indispensable member of the meager Allard entourage drove hotfoot to the capital, grabbed a piston, hurried back to Le Mans. Inspection then showed the replacement to be oversize, so the relevant cylinder was rebored and everything thrown together again. If anything else was wrong with the car, neither Allard nor Cole caught onto it — or if they did, they didn't mention it — during subsequent training. But in the small hours of the Saturday itself, Sydney, a man whose hunches are usually infallible if occasionally a bit belated, decided he "wasn't happy about the steering." He woke Tom Lush, who was and still is one of the props of the Allard Motor Company and its related firms, and unbosomed his fears. They forthwith "welded and bodged" the arm, completing the job at 1 p.m., three hours before the race was to start. "Should keep us going for three or four hours with luck," philosophized Allard, a man of few words in the presence of actual or potential drama.

It kept them going, as it developed, the full twenty-four hours, but for more than half the race the car only had one *vitesse* left in its nominally three-speed *boite*; the lone survivor, luckily, was top.

This episode amply vindicated Sydney's long-standing fondness for big-displacement American engines. Without the freight-train flexibility that characterizes the type, he and

ABRAHAMSEN

A restored J2X Allard glistens in the sunlight. American road courses on the early '50s rocked to the hoarse bellow of these brutal machines.

Allard's latest motor car is this sprint machine powered by two Steyr engines. Sydney used one of these powerplants in a fast hill-climb car.

Cole assuredly couldn't have maintained enough speed during their fourteen-hour spell in direct drive to produce a race average of 87.8 mph. (The Rosiers, father and son, who won on a 4.5 Talbot, did 89.73 mph overall, a record.)

This wasn't Allard's first bid for the elusive *Grand Prix d'Endurance* and it wouldn't be his last, but it was his most successful one. Consistent winners over short to medium distances, both at home and on U.S. circuits, Allards often lacked the stamina demanded by marathon-lengthers. It's only fair to add, though, that the firm's resources were almost pathetically slender compared with rivals of, for instance, Jaguar's standing. Right through the early and middle phase of the London make's history, moreover, Allard accepted a voluntary handicap by using the maximum of stock Ford chassis components, with the double object of giving owners the advantage of the unrivaled parts and service facilities offered by Ford Motor Company's English offshoot, and keeping car weight and complication down. Generous as their strength factor was in the roles they'd been designed for, the Ford elements could hardly be blamed if they occasionally succumbed to the nonstandard stresses generated by Allard's nonstandard performance. This isn't to say that the bits bearing Allard part numbers didn't fail too from time to time — undoubtedly they did. Somebody once described Sydney Allard as "a conscientious blacksmith with scientific leanings;" and while this perhaps was an uncharitable estimate, he was and is no Chapman, nor an Issigonis either.

Sydney's physical courage, on the other hand, is unbounded, and assorts rather oddly with his mild, almost benign demeanor. During Le Mans practice in '53, Lush recalls, an ominous clonking manifested itself at the back end of the J2 that Allard was to co-drive with Philip Fotheringham-Parker. "Don't go, Guvnor," pleaded Lush, after all efforts to pinpoint the noise had failed (Sydney was always "Guvnor" to his employees and associates, signifying a nice blend of affection and respect). The Guvnor was slated for the first driving stint, so the decision — to go or not to go — was all his. He took it. "I'll go — as fast as I know how until something breaks," he said.

He knew, it transpired, how to go faster than anybody else in the race. At the end of the first lap he was leading, which, the Le Mans tradition of *blitzkreig* openers being what it is, must have taken some doing. But one lap was enough. On the second, with a last *fortissimo* clonk, the differential mounting fractured, severing the pipelines to the rear brakes. Only then, content with his essay in practical, high-speed diagnosis, the Guvnor pulled out.

His left eye is almost sightless — it stopped a slug from an air rifle his brother Denis inadvertently fired at him when the Allards were kids. But the Guvnor's race driving under conditions of bad vision never gave any hint of his disability. In the misty night hours at Le Mans in 1952, I remember, he was passing the ultimately victorious 300SL Mercs on the Mulsanne Straight with perfect *sang froid*. "Well, hell, we can't hang about, can we?" he growled when somebody suggested this seemed an enterprising thing to do.

If it had been in his nature to hang about, he certainly never would have won that murderous Monte in '52, when reliable eye-witnesses counted over fifty wrecks on the roadside where drivers had attempted to maintain the practically

impossible schedule over the final 600 miles through the Massif Central and the Maritime Alps. Tom Lush, who navigated the entry, testifies that Sydney not only remained calm through a recurrent series of hair-raising crises but demonstrated a propensity for "doing calculus in his head," simultaneously. He is, indeed, quite an extraordinary mental mathematician.

As on many other rallies, his wife Eleanor was captaining another Allard on her own account in the 1952 Monte, with her two sisters as crew. In competition, as far as Sydney is concerned, chivalry isn't dead, it's merely in abeyance. Somewhere in the Auvergne foothills, when all concerned were feeling pretty detuned from fatigue and fright, he came across Eleanor's car stationary at the roadside. He slid No. 146 to a standstill, wound his window down, yelled, "You all right?" into the freezing darkness. "*No*," piped three female voices in unison. "Too bad," said Sydney, hurriedly cranking the window back up before all the heat escaped, and departing in a flurry of wheelspin. The girls finally fixed the trouble themselves but later spun out and ditched their car inextricably and didn't make the finish.

Eleanor Allard has been represented by some imaginative writers as a burning enthusiast for motor sport, but she never really cared much for it and only did rallies and stuff because Sydney wanted her to. In Bugatti Owners' Club

XXII<sup>me</sup> RALLYE AUTOMOBILE MONTE-CARLO
JANVIER 1952

Allard and crew receive congratulations from Monte Carlo Rally officials after their hair-raising ride. Sidney's trials experience helped on the last icey stage, which he did mostly sideways.

hillclimbs at Prescott, the Allards, husband and wife, at least once won the team prize jointly. Three cars went to make a team but the rules didn't say anything about three drivers, so Sydney drove his Steyr-engined sprinter and one sports car; Eleanor used a different sports Allard.

Wherever he drives in competition, and also among his employees, Sydney Allard is extremely well-liked. Whenever any Allard company man or woman is down on his or her luck, the Guvnor invariably thinks up some way of playing the benefactor by stealth — it genuinely embarasses him to have anyone know he's personally concerned in these kindly stratagems. Naturally, Allard people tend to stay in Allard employ years, and years. When the car manufacturing side of the business was at its peak, the payroll was somewhere around the 200 mark.

## ALLARD

Sydney's Steyr-powered single-seater, which won him the British hillclimb championship in 1949 and twice placed him third, makes a story in itself. Structurally, the car was simply a sports Allard with its side rails moved closer together, a suitably narrow body fitted and fenders omitted, but the engine was quite a novelty to English eyes. During the war, a batch of these air-cooled V8s had been captured as part of the cargo of a German freighter that surrendered to a Royal Navy interceptor en route from Italy to Rommel's forces in North Africa. Through various channels Allard secured four or five Steyrs at one time or another, the cheapest pair costing him ten dollars' worth of Sterling (this was what he paid for both, not just one). Designed as they were for a variety of mundane purposes (driving trucks, staff cars, generators, etc.), and in the expectation they'd be called upon under war exigencies to run on practically anything that would catch fire, the Steyrs originally had a compression ratio of 4½ to one and developed only 45 bhp from 3.6 liters. Bore and stroke were the same as the side-valve V8 built before and just after the war by the British Ford company, and the bottom end of the unit showed signs of Ford inspiration.

On the other hand, made as it was in aluminum alloy, with no water jacketing or radiator to add weight, the thing was far lighter than its Ford counterpart, and anyway its hemispherical heads and pushrod o.h.v. actuated by a single camshaft suggested latent possibilities to Sydney Allard. These he exploited to the full, in gradual stages spread over a period of years that hasn't finished yet. Among other treatments, he raised the compression progressively to 14 to one, entirely reworked the porting, enlarged the displacement to 5 liters. With the exception of the con-rods, with shanks like chopsticks and a large ominous-looking balancing hole in the already scanty land adjacent to the big end, all the original Steyr parts were as solid and robust as a medieval cathedral; surprisingly enough, the rods have always withstood successive power increments, even including the 200 bhp generated by each of the two engines fitted to Sydney's current sprint car. This one, built primarily for Britain's annual standing kilometer speed trial at Brighton, Sussex, hadn't yet run in public when this was written.

Allard previously held the Brighton course record with his old single-Steyr sprinter, and he should be capable of regaining it with the new twin-engine monster. The dual Steyrs, giving him 400 bhp net, are placed side by side on the front; they drive initially by duplex chains to a central shaft, then through one gearbox to all four wheels. Sixteen motorcycle-type Amal carbs, representing a pretty problem in the art of synchronization, are fitted. The back end, true to tradition, is de Dion,

or perhaps I should say *half* true to tradition, because there aren't any springs.

The complexity of this remarkable vehicle does not, as Sydney says with a short laugh at his own expense, have any practical justification. "I find the older I get the more amusing mechanical complication becomes," he says. "I suppose I could just as well have used one engine with as much power as these two put together, but it wouldn't have been such fun, would it?" Sydney is 50. By the time he's 60, I wonder how many cylinders and carburetors it'll take to satisfy his taste for complication. By then, though, it's likely his son Alan, now 20, will be erasing the last hazy traces of the old man's black wheeltracks on Brighton's Madiera Drive. In fact I think Allard had Alan's future education in mind when he went to work on the two-Steyr wonder.

The reason, oddly enough, why Sydney finally won the hillclimb championship, after several determined but abortive attempts, was that he had had relatively *little* power under his toe. His main rivals back then were Raymond Mays with a 2-liter E.R.A. claimed to develop 330 bhp, and Denis Poore with a 3.8 Alfa rated at 380 horse. Sydney, on the other hand, was only getting 140 from the Steyr at the time. It was of course unblown, unlike the competition.

"That was their trouble: too *much* power, if anything," Allard recalls. "I never had to worry about wheelspin; in fact on a dry surface I couldn't spin wheels if I wanted to, on any gear but bottom." At hill meetings he'd always be accompanied by his whole family: wife, two small daughters, one son, one or both of his brothers (who also drove Allards competitively), usually a few remoter relatives; and this impressive retinue would join in willing it to rain for Sydney's benefit, making traction even more elusive for overpowered E.R.A.s and Alfas, or, if it wasn't going to rain, they'd hope it would be so hot the tar would melt.

The original Allard Special, foundation on which a respected and legitimate make would be built, was the outcome of a merger between two heaps of debris, leftovers from a crashed Ford V8 on the one hand and a G.P. Bugatti on the other. Rolling them up into one took Sydney 20 days and the greater part of 20 nights — this was in 1936. The Ford was the major contributor, providing everything except the body and steering gear. The previous season Allard had used a T.T.-type Ford V8 in the peculiarly English branch of motor sport called trials, with monotonously consistent success. The fruit of the Ford/Bug fusion proved even more disdainful of mud, rocks and gradient, and soon Sydney's friends were begging him to reproduce the species for their benefit. Initially, two more Allard Specials were run up, and their owners, Ken Hutchison and Guy Warburton (the latter was Sydney's co-driver when he won *Le Rallye* 16 years later), ganged with him to form a virtually invincible trials team known as the Tail Waggers.

Describing the Allard Special won't use up much space. It was simply a Ford with minor chassis revisions, a lot of weight lopped off, the engine moved back a piece, Allard's own distinctive body and frontispiece. At least, that about sums up the

earlier samples. Anon, the design acquired the rudimentary but effective form of i.f.s. that was to be one of the Allard hallmarks for many years, right on into postwar times. This consisted of a divided front axle with the inner ends of the halves pivoted cheek by jowl, so to speak, the suspension medium still being a transverse leaf spring, à la contemporary Ford.

Due partly to the far-back engine placement that was to remain one of the simple secrets of the Allard's phenomenal traction, and partly to the extreme vigor with which the Tail Waggers and their later emulators attacked heathenish trials terrain, Allard Specials spent a good deal of their lives with their front ends anything up to a couple of feet off the ground. In this attitude, gravity permitted an enormous downswing by the divided axle, the front wheels assuming angles of perhaps 30 degrees from the vertical.

It was Hutchison's idea, I think, to substitute a V12 Lincoln Zephyr engine for the normal V8, and Allard, complaisant as always, complied. Three of these V12 Allard Specials were built and Hutchison owned two of them. The original one in particular became famous in its day, winning not only a multitude of trials but excelling also in sports car races, hillclimbs and sprints.

Somewhere, and here will do, it's relevant to mention that at no stage of his adult life has Sydney Allard been solely dependent on car manufacture or competitions as a means of livelihood. When he'd finished an adolescent apprenticeship in a South London garage, his father looked around for a business to buy him. He found one and, rather confusingly, it was called Adlards Motors. Sydney, who's often alluded to or addressed by his slighter acquaintances as Mr. Adlard, became managing director and *de facto* proprietor of Adlards back before the first Allard Special was spawned. He still heads this prosperous Ford dealership, located at Clapham, an inner southern suburb of London, sharing premises with one of the Allard Motor Company's branches.

Sydney was on the point of lopping the suffix Special off the Allard label and going into business as a small-scale manufacturer when the war broke out in 1939; this development was postponed until 1946, when he launched a three-car range, types J1, K1 and L, respectively a 100-inch wheelbase competition two-seater, a 106-inch touring two-seater, and a 112-inch touring four-seater — all sharing Ford's then-current flathead V8 engine of 3.6 liters. Best known and most popular of these was the J1, which sold, preponderantly in the States, as fast as Allard's limited facilities and stringent steel rationing allowed. All types retained the divided axle i.f.s. and transverse leaf spring, in conjunction with an obviously indispensible something I forgot to mention earlier: radius arms running back to the side rails from the axle extremities.

Via types M and P, spanning the 1947/49 period — these models didn't humding in any way that's memorable — the Allard alphabet doubled back on itself and, in 1950, came up with the J2. This 100-inch competition two-seater was the first British production car featuring a de Dion back end; coil springs replaced a transverse leaf

(*Continued on page* 180)

# TWO FOR THE QUARTER

Six thousand miles apart two men are working to revolutionize one phase of racing in their respective countries. Both are concerned with building machines to record the lowest elapsed times and highest terminal speeds over quarter-mile courses. Dennis May relates Sydney Allard's efforts to transplant the American dragster to English soil while Griff Borgeson details the exciting plans of Californian Jocko Johnson to produce a new species at home

Allard gives his supercharged dragster a shakedown run on a wet course. Unlike the U.S., England requires full bodywork on the car

## ALLARD

● In developing England's first slingshot dragster, Sydney Allard's objectives have been threefold: 1) To create an indigenous audience for a phenomenon the British have so far merely read about and likely not even envisioned with any accuracy; 2) To encourage the construction in Britain of other cars capable of giving his Allard some realistic competition; 3) To reinforce the American drag racing fraternity's case for FIA recognition for the standing quarter-mile as an international and world record distance.

Designed under Sydney's supervision by Dave Hooper, a long-service Allard engineer, and built at Allard's south London place by John Hume, formerly chief racing mechanic at Cooper Cars, the Allard dragster isn't as close a copy of American originals as it might be because its authors didn't have direct access to U.S. sources of the kind of detailed technical data they needed. Their method was therefore to mug up such relevant facts as could be gleaned from published articles (including this magazine's description and drawing of Chris Karamesines's incredible Chizler, *vide* October, 1960 issue) and interpret it in the light of common sense and their own engineering experience.

Thus in its general configuration and the relative positioning of its main masses the Allard follows the U.S. dragster norm, though both its wheelbase (108 inches) and overall length (162 inches) exceed the aver-

age. Chassis design as exemplified by the Chizler seemed to Allard and his team to border on the crude; so the chassis, for better or worse, takes the form of a simplified space frame with fully duplicated longitudinals—3-inch diameter tubes at sub-hub level, surmounted by an spaced about nine inches from parallel 1½-inch-diameter members. In plan, both pairs of fore/aft tubes run parallel from their rear ends to a point just ahead of the engine, then converge to a junction at the center of the front axle; this is of the usual beam type, much drilled for lightness, and a relic from a Ford truck. Tubular hoops—or more exactly part hoops, for they aren't carried under the car—straddle the chassis immediately behind and in front of the engine bay. Material for these as for all members except the 3-inch lower longerons, is 1½-inch mild steel tube, all joints being welded. The anti-roll cage is much like any other modern dragster's. The rear end is springless, front suspension being by transverse leaf spring with adjustable Armstrong lever type shock absorbers. Front axle locators are tubular radius arms no less than 49 inches long; these were originally back axle ties from a Ford Pilot, the Dagenham factory's early postwar V8 sedan. The car weighs 1460 pounds dry, carries 60% of this on its back wheels in the unladen state, obviously more with the driver aboard. Fuel injection is by Hilborn-Travers system, consumption being around one mile per gallon.

The present GMC-Potvin blower installation driven at engine speed and gives a boost of 20 psi at the 5000 rpm at which the Chrysler develops its 48

The British motoring press was treated to the music of a blown Chrysler mill and screaming slicks biting the asphalt at Silverstone.

hp. Allard Motor Company is a distributor for the British Shorrock compressor, and this eccentric-vane device will likely replace the existing GMC blower when Shorrock has had time to develop a unit big enough to feed the 354 cubic inches.

At the time of writing the car has only made one public appearance, though during a demonstration before a press audience at Silverstone it turned a promising 9.5 seconds for the quarter mile from a walking pace rolling start. This was done sans "bodywork," which can hardly be valueless at a terminal speed of around 160 mph.

Brakes all around being obligatory under British print laws, the Allard's front wheels carry Girling discs, ex Ford Zephyr. All-wheel braking being a practical necessity, as well as a "legal" requirement, on the short courses available in Britain, the front wheels have to be more robust than the wire-spoked motorcycle type used on American dragsters; as you can see, the Allard's front wheels are ex Lotus, crimped magnesium alloy discs. They carry 5.25 x 16 Dunlop road racing tires, the rears being 7.00 x 16 Inglewood Dragmasters with 7½-inch treads remolded onto Indianpolis casings.

Steering gear consists of a Marles reduction box, outrigger shaft, drop arm and dual drag links with a combined length of 84 inches; these are connected amidships by a slave arm. The steering wheel is of eye-glass type, as used by the late Goldie Gardner on his MG record cars.

Originally, the Allard used a Schiefer double-disc clutch unit—another U.S. import, of course; but after two Schiefers had gone up in smoke—which Sydney allows may well have been the fault of his own inexperienced manipulation—they switched to a Borg and Beck clutch of the unique type developed for the 16-cylinder B.R.M. This has five plates and is only 7½ inches in diameter. So far, it's held up.

The back axle is cut-down British Ford, giving a tread of 41 inches, compared with 51 inches at the front. To improve chances of the car staying on course in the event of losing a wheel at speed, a normal differential, devoid of locking devices, is employed. Initial braking from terminal speeds is by triple parachutes packed in the roll cage framing.

In contrast with many traditional British sprint cars, this highly untraditional Allard is meticulously finished, with its chassis sprayed in the shade of blue that Sydney always favors for his street cars, its panelwork blue and white (perhaps as an oblique tribute to the U.S. origin of so many of its constituent parts) and innumerable small components gleamingly chromed. The project has received liberal press and television coverage in Britain, and Allard, smart businessman that he is, isn't giving anyone the chance to fault his firm's product on hygienic grounds.

On the technical side, though, he and his associates are the first to admit they still have more to learn than they've learnt.

—DM

# ALLARD'S DAY AT BRANDS

The Allard Motor Co., Ltd., 24-28 Clapham High Street, S.W.4, have been appointed sole world distributors for Shorrock Superchargers, Ltd., a company associated with the Owen Organization.

In order to celebrate this appointment, the Brands Hatch circuit was taken over for a day, and representative cars were made available for testing by heavy-footed journalists. It is splendid to record that none of these supercharged vehicles succumbed to the harsh treatment which was meted out to them.

Having already performed a full road test on the Shorrock-supercharged Ford Anglia, I took over the new Classic, which had been similarly treated. In standard form, the Classic is an ideal family car, but a bit "dead" for the enthusiastic driver. Supercharged, it becomes an entirely different machine, for not only is the performance vastly increased, but the handling becomes better altogether. There is now enough power for real drifting on the corners, and the supercharged Classic must be regarded as a fast car with exceptional roadholding.

Driven at near-racing velocities, the Classic soon loses its full braking power in spite of the front discs. Some attention to the brakes would certainly be advisable, but no other modification is

*INSTALLATION of the sprint car's supercharged 5¾-litre Chrysler V-8 engine, showing the separate pipe for each cylinder.*

called for, the smoothness and flexibility being enhanced.

A Mini-Minor was also sampled which

*FRONT SUSPENSION and disc brake of the dragster.*

had been given "the treatment". The supercharger installation had been carried out very neatly, and there was no bulge in the bonnet or other external evidence. A rev. counter had been fitted to the test car, and I made my up-changes at 6,500 r.p.m., the little engine being entirely happy at this speed.

The supercharged Mini is no noisier than a standard model, except for a very faint whine from the blower. This note is more pronounced outside the car, but to the driver and passenger it is by no means disturbing. The car has none of the roughness associated with tuned B.M.C. babies, and its shopping manners are even superior to those of the standard production. Because the engine is smooth, the increase in performance is not at first particularly apparent. The improvement is, however, very real, and although accurate measurement is not possible at the Hatch, I would say that about three seconds would be saved in the standing quarter-mile and the maximum speed would be increased by over 10 m.p.h.

The complete outfit costs £69 15s., and there is absolutely no other work to be done on the car. When selling the vehicle, one merely restores the original carburetter and puts the blower on next

year's model. The drive is very simply arranged by a rubber vee-belt from the front of the crankshaft. A small increase in fuel consumption is to be expected, but the appetite for oil of the Shorrock eccentric vane supercharger is strictly moderate.

Also on view at the Hatch was Sidney Allard's new dragster. This is a real monster, which should practically turn the Brighton Speed Trials into a *Grande Epreuve*.

The motive power is a Chrysler V-8 engine of 5¾ litres capacity. It is supercharged by a G.M.C. Rootes-type blower, which gives a boost of 15-20 lbs. The methanol fuel is injected on the Hilborn Travers constant delivery system to the supercharger air intake. A Scintilla Vertex looks after the ignition. As the engine is not intended to run for more than a few seconds, the water in the cylinder jackets suffices for cooling, and there is no radiator. There is a separate short exhaust pipe for each cylinder, and 450-500 b.h.p. will be developed.

The drive is via a Schiefer clutch to a two-speed gearbox of Ford ancestry. This is coupled directly to a quick-change rear axle with a spur-gear drive to the pinion, which is behind the crown wheel. There is no rear suspension and the rear tyres are 8 ins. "slicks" on 16 ins. steel disc wheels.

The frame is a simple tubular structure, and the front axle is on a transverse spring. There are disc brakes, and the Lotus light alloy wheels carry 5.25-15 ins. tyres. A centrally mounted Allard steering box operates an enormously long drag link which is split centrally with a slave arm. The driver sits just behind the differential and is protected by sturdy roll bars. It will be necessary to evolve a fireproof bulkhead and some sort of a body before the monster is presented to the scrutineers.

The performance of this weapon must be immense, but if it rains at Brighton I would advise Sidney not to have a go on the notoriously slippery Madeira Drive. The engine was started at Brands Hatch, and the sheer volume of sound was immense.

JOHN V. BOLSTER.

# put them all together, they spell

T. C. MARCH PHOTO

# ALLARD

BY DOUG BLAIN

No LONGER DO THE familiar lanky, lumpy battleships of track and boulevard roll out from behind those modest double doors in Clapham, London, England. The closest one can get to owning a new Allard today is to settle for one of the celebrated Sydney's current Shorrock-blown 105-E Fords—Allardettes, to modified-motoring *aficionadi*.

One can, if he's inclined, label the Allard the most consistently successful hot rod of all time. "The daddy of the dragsters" is a name that sits equally easily on the brutal J-2-X and its burly, back-ballasted brethren.

Every one of the big V-8 powered sportsters was a direct descendant of instigator Sydney's own self-built backyard record breaker, the original Allard Special of 1934. Two more facts link them with hot rods: the Allard Special Mark One was a weird, willful one-off designed as the answer to Britain's freak power mudplug formula, the demands for which were much the same as for American drag racing today; and its specifications included a modicum of perfectly stock U.S. Ford-built parts. Hot rod, then, is very much the term.

It all began back around 1929. Sydney Allard at 19 was racing a 3-wheeled Super Sports Morgan on Brooklands with little success. He added a fourth wheel—thus producing the very first Allard Special.

The first Ford connections came a year or two later. Henry's old 4-cyl B-models were going cheap in 1932. Allard bought one and installed a nearly new BB four, wildly modified to give a respectable output at nearly twice the original revs. Suitably bodied, it went well enough to sell young Sydney on the idea of an early lightweight Detroit-built frame with perhaps the then new and exciting flathead Ford V-8.

Just such a combination showed up for the Tourist Trophy on Ireland's celebrated Ards circuit in 1934. The land o' the green was ever a prime Ford stronghold: the Ards locals specialized at that time in cunning creations built around Michigan components designed no more with speed or roadholding powers in mind than the original horseless carriage. The area distributor started that year with a pair of shiny new specials that answered Sydney's specification as if he'd ordered the things himself. He bought one on the spot.

Syd Allard really put that special through the mill; races, hillclimbs, rallies, and finally the crazy mudplug "trials" so beloved in England kept both mount and rider busy for nearly two full seasons. But the do-it-yourself demon had a firm grip on Allard.

Work started in the repair shop his father, Arthur Allard, had given him when he finished his mechanic's training back in 1930—a garage called Adlards Motors (*sic*) for no better reason than that Adlard was the name the business had borne when Arthur took over. An ideal point of departure presented itself: a near-new type-48 Ford coupe, conveniently junked not far from the Allard headquarters in Putney, South London. Sydney signed for the wreck Friday and towed it home. Monday he started ripping off the pulped paneling, chopping the frame, replacing the heavy 1935 front suspension with a B-type setup he figured would save some weight, and finally fitting the steering and installing the graceful pointed-tail Grand Prix body, *in toto*, from Lord Howe's venerable Type-51 Bugatti. Saturday the first Allard Special to carry the name was ready.

The cynics covered their eyes when the new car began appearing regularly, with its lowly flathead V-8 grinding away

Allard rolled this early mudplugger.

For the truly determined, the Allard J-2 was an all-weather car.

beneath such hallowed paneling. About the only people who found themselves with little time for laughter were the drivers, with their over-bored ohc PB Midgets, the Cream Crackers *et al.*, who foresaw big trouble after they lost out to Allard in the rugged, end-of-season Lawrence Cup Trial.

The next year, Sydney had suspension engineer Leslie Bellamy design and build a split-axle adaptation using his B-Ford beam. I.f.s., of course, was not the everyday feature in 1936 it has become today; when Allard's 5-day marvel appeared for its second season with a predisposition for flapping its front wheels on a rough surface like a duck with loose wings, the fraternity's derision turned to open scorn. Yet so successfully did Allard start his season that they soon led the rush for replicas.

Thus encouraged, Sydney set about building his cars as a kind of profitable relaxation from running the repair shop. Weekends he would often rumble off in the original, mowing down the field in some rural trial or hillclimb and as likely as not returning with a new sheaf of orders in his pocket.

The Allard Specials—no pre-war car was ever called just Allard—were highly individual competition machines, designed primarily for mudplugging but incidentally very suitable for climbs, sprints (drags) and even road work. The engine could, of course, be varied to suit any customer's ideas, but always the plan was to match its characteristics to those of the chassis. That was the reason every buyer specified a U.S. Ford-built V engine of some kind.

The ultimate in Allard Specials featured Ford's V-12 Lincoln-Zephyr unit, completely stock except for thinner head gaskets. Only three saw daylight, because of the war. With a label that read just 570 pounds sterling, or $1596 at today's rate, a Special so equipped offered the most performance any Englishman could buy within hundreds of dollars of its cost.

Those who swung to Allard Specials built such a reputation for the new marque by 1938 that Sydney started considering serious production. Looking around, he could see Reid Railton already selling 500 of his Hudson Terraplane-powered sedans and cabriolets each year: why not try the same thing with a highway version of the glorious mud-machine?

The war killed that one too. Sydney had his first batch of production Lincoln-Allards, a V-12 roadster and a four-place V-8, all ready for the London Show in 1939. He even had permission from Lincoln to use its title in his name. But the show never materialized, and neither did the Lincoln-Allard.

Instead Sydney found himself first trying to sell a modified Special specification to the UK War Office as a sort of pre-Jeep and, when that failed, turning over his newly acquired floor space to reconditioning war-weary WOT 1, 2, 6 and 8 Ford trucks.

At least it served to keep his Ford relationship alive, which helped a lot when the Allard Motor Company (Almotco, for short) got under way at Clapham in 1945. The first Allards were really just straight developments of the trials car, very like the 1939 Lincoln-Allards in both styling and construction.

Because he was quick to realize that success in steel-starved postwar Britain lay not so much in building hairy, highly specialized sports cars as in using what material he could get his hands on for just cars, period, Syd Allard quickly dropped his early J and came up with a range of longer-wheelbase touring machines christened K, L and M.

The K-1, the most interesting, was just like the J-1 but 6 in. longer all over. Like all but the very first cars in the J series, it had chassis cross-braces as well as side-members stamped specially by Thomsons of Wolverhampton and not made up from Ford bits. The body was little changed except for wider doors: like a blend of BMW's pre-war 328 and the much later XK Jaguar, but with an oddly distinctive wrap-over grille. Its stock engine was the old 3622-cc 90° Ford, now English-built and pushing out 80 bhp at 3600 rpm.

The K's bulkier, uglier but somewhat similar companions, the L and the M, both had wheelbases 6 in. longer again. Both were 4-place softtops—heavy, unattractive cars. The standard Ford V-8 gave them no more than domestic performance.

The next Allard was slower still. Christened the P-type, it appeared in 1949 as a semi-luxury sedan for people who needed transport and who could afford the quantities of state-rationed fuel it demanded. Heavy, lumpy coachwork smothered but failed to nullify the handling qualities inherited from its more sporting forebears—a fact Allard himself was to demonstrate three years later with the famous Monte Carlo win.

The company's efforts in the Monte did lead to the offer, from 1950 on, of Ford's familiar (ex-Lincoln) Mercury V-8, stretched at Clapham to 84 by 98.4 mm and 4375 cc, as a performance alternative throughout the Allard range. Sydney had had the foresight to buy up and convert a big supply of Army surplus units, a move that turned out to be even wiser than it looked at the time.

At about the same time, Allard began to see the need for an economic upshift. He had been getting by, he knew, for the past few years with cars that were neither one thing nor another—cars that came with heavy domestic bodywork on a frame that was basically intended for mud trials! People had

*The M-1 cabriolet was a 4/5 seater of some luxury.*      *A purposeful interior (J-2).*      *A K-2 Allard.*

*Sidney Allard climbs Prescott.*   *Find anything in there, Cedric?*   *Allard in his J-2-R at Le Mans.*

ignored this fundamental incongruity because steel rationing meant everyday automobiles were short. Other builders had been doing the same, and worse: Ford with its Pilot relic, Austin with the unforgivable Sheerline. The idea among all the big firms was not so much to give the public what it wanted as to get the most possible profit from a given quantity of steel, in the certain knowledge that buyers would accept anything. That meant people like Allard could tackle the big boys in a way that would have been impossible in a free market. The trouble was, Sydney suspected, a free market lay just around the corner.

A tour through the U.S. showed him two things: one, that Americans didn't want his existing models; two, that they might go for an updated version of the original J. It didn't take long to arrive at an answer.

The Allard J-2, easily the best-remembered car of the marque and probably the most successful, emerged with the original 100-in. chassis altered to take an all-new suspension. The front split-axle with its neat and simple trailing radius arms stayed on, but with short vertical coil springs in place of the original transverse leaf. At the back, a de Dion setup transplanted from Sydney's successful war surplus Steyr racer incorporated a quick-change center section with integral 12-in. Al-Fin brake drums. Steel arms, working on the center pivot that had served before for the rigid axle, took over as locating members for the coil sprung de Dion tube. Dry weight could run as low as 2000 lb. It never rose above 2600 lb, even with the big Cadillac engine option and the extra 50-gal. fuel tank that ousted the spare from trunk to body side.

The J-2 marked Sydney Allard's first all-out attempt at beating the engine problem. Ford's flathead 8, 18 years old and by then thoroughly uncompetitive internationally, obviously needed either a major revision or scrapping altogether. Britain offered nothing to replace either engine, and government rigidity still made it impossible to import anything for resale within the UK. The only answer was to offer a choice of local ohv V-8s for the U.S. market and to modify the old Mercury at home.

The modification was an ingenious but elaborate and costly overhead-valve conversion then just beginning to gain favor in the United States. Marketed for the normal 4-liter version of Dearborn's ancient Rumbleguts plant by an outfit called Ardun Engine Corporation on Broadway, in New York, it took the form of a formidable twin-head pack complete with manifolding and all essential ancillaries. Allard sent for a fully built-up unit. It looked all right. He went ahead and launched the J-2 with three impressive power options: Allard (alias Ardun) V-8 for Britain and overseas, 5420-cc Cadillac or Chrysler (the dimensions and capacities were identical) for overseas markets only.

Transmission was another perennial Allard headache, and there again Sydney made a big effort for the J-2. He offered two basic choices, the 3-speed British-built Ford or France's famous electric-shift Cotal, as coupled to the current Ford-of-France Comete V-8. To overcome probable objections to the English box's lack of versatility he came up with both the quick-change rear end we've spoken of and an alternative set of ultra-close intermediate ratios. Shift medium was a remote control link-up with a stubby center lever.

Make no mistake, the J-2 was a big performer. With the 160-bhp Cadillac running at only 7.5:1, mounting dual twin-barrel Carters and pulling the close-ratio gears through a 3.27 axle, it would see 60 in 7.4 sec, 80 in 13.1 and 100 in 23.6!

The J's slightly less potent companion, the K-2, appeared a little later the same year. It looked similar, but there were major differences. The chassis was the old 106-in. item with transverse leaf suspension and a solid back axle. The body had the same frontal contours, but with a K-1-style cockpit and back panel (Allard had some old ones left over), and big, flaring front fenders in place of the J's cycle-types. Dry weight was 2464 lb. *Autocar* tested an Ardun version and squeezed 102 mph out of it, with 0-60 in 11.6 and an 80 time of 19.8.

Pretty soon the Ardun engine showed signs of trouble. Allard wrote indignantly to the factory, and Chief Engineer Zora Arkus-Duntov agreed to fly across and take charge of development at Clapham. The Ardun conversion was, in essence, a very fine piece of work. It had a lot of affinities with today's superb Daimler-Jaguar 2.5- and 4.5-liter V-8s: the same alloy heads, hemispherical chambers, crossover pushrods, side-by-side carburetors and vertical spark plug mounts. The trouble was that no one could persuade the thing to operate either reliably or well. In the end Allard dropped it (after selling around 75) along with the expensive Cotal gearbox.

The J-2 in its original form was probably the one car no red-blooded American sportsman could resist. It was incredibly fast, it was good looking in a brutish kind of way, and it was far from costly to buy and maintain. Disadvantages such as lack of either ground clearance or trunk space (3.5 in. and zero, respectively) mattered little in an automobile that appealed primarily as a weekend prestige and fun car. Yet, the model failed as the best-selling sports machine it could most certainly have become—primarily through the tiny factory's sheer inability to meet such an unprecedented demand. Emphasis swung in consequence to its clearcut racing potential; Syd Allard's own achievement in placing a Cadillac-powered J-2 third overall at Le Mans jolted enthusiasts into realizing that here was a production sports car, tough, simple and cheap, that was all but guaranteed able to paste anything in its

*The 5.5-liter Cadillac V-8 powered many Allards.*   *Last of the line: Allard's Gran Turismo coupes.*

# ALLARD

own or any other class, and in every kind of competition short of the full international classics.

From a sales viewpoint, then, it was the J-2's performance that finally clinched its own and Allard's survival. The man who was prepared to order one so he could go out and beat up the local race opposition would hardly cancel out when a factory foul-up held up delivery. For one thing, he had no second choice. Anyway, his interest accounted for Allard's introduction within two years of a far superior sports-racing challenger, the J-2-X. The X-suffix in the type name stood for extended, and the item that grew was the chassis—not the wheelbase, just the chassis. Legroom for a tall driver was a big problem with the J-2: the only answer was to shift the engine forward. That brought trouble with the mounting

## THE ALLARD DECADE—A COMPLETE CHART OF MO

| Type | Other Names | Body Styles | Approx. No. Built | Approx. Years | Chassis Numbers, From | Chassis Type | Suspension Front | Rear | Eng Ava |
|---|---|---|---|---|---|---|---|---|---|
| J-1 | Competition Series | 2-Pass. Roadster | 12 | 1946 to 1947 | 106 | Box Steel | TL, Split Axle | TL, Rigid Axle | Ford (Eng |
| K-1 | | 2-Pass. Roadster | 50 | 1946 to 1950 | 104 | Box Steel | TL, Split Axle | TL, Rigid Axle | Ford (Eng |
| L | | 4-Pass. Convertible | 100 | 1946 to 1950 | 102 | Box Steel | TL, Split Axle | TL, Rigid Axle | Ford (Eng |
| M-1 | | 4–5-Pass. Cabriolet | 500 | 1947 to 1950 | 208 | Box Steel | TL, Split Axle | TL, Rigid Axle | Ford (Eng |
| P-1 | | 5–6-Pass. Sedan | 800 | 1949 to 1952 | 1500 | Box Steel | TL, Split Axle | TL, Rigid Axle | Ford (Eng |
| | Competition Series | '' | '' | 1950 to 1952 | '' | '' | TL, Split Axle | TL, Rigid Axle | Mercury ( |
| | Revised (Stock) Version | '' | '' | 1951 to 1952 | '' | '' | Coil, Split Axle | TL, Rigid Axle | Ford (Eng |
| | High Compression Version | '' | '' | 1951 to 1952 | '' | '' | Coil, Split Axle | TL, Rigid Axle | Ford (Eng |
| | | '' | '' | 1951 to 1952 | '' | '' | Coil, Split Axle | TL, Rigid Axle | Mercury ( |
| J-2 | | 2-Pass. Sports/Racing | 200 | 1950 to 1951 | 1512 | Box Steel | Coil, Split Axle | Coil, de Dion | Mercury ( |
| | | '' | '' | 1950 to 1951 | '' | '' | Coil, Split Axle | Coil, de Dion | Allard-Ar |
| | | '' | '' | 1950 to 1951 | '' | '' | Coil, Split Axle | Coil, de Dion | Cadillac ( |
| | | '' | '' | 1950 to 1951 | '' | '' | Coil, Split Axle | Coil, de Dion | Chrysler ( |
| K-2 | | 2–3-Pass. Roadster | 50 | 1950 to 1953 | 1700 | Box Steel | Coil, Split Axle | TL, Rigid Axle | Ford (Eng |
| | | '' | '' | 1950 to 1953 | '' | '' | Coil, Split Axle | TL, Rigid Axle | Ford (Eng |
| | High Compression Version | '' | '' | 1950 to 1953 | '' | '' | Coil, Split Axle | TL, Rigid Axle | Allard-Ar |
| | Competition Series | '' | '' | 1950 to 1953 | '' | '' | Coil, Split Axle | TL, Rigid Axle | Mercury ( |
| J-2-X | | 2-Pass. Sports/Racing | 100 | 1951 to 1954 | 2191 | Box Steel | Coil, Split Axle | Coil, de Dion | Mercury ( |
| | | '' | '' | 1951 to 1954 | '' | '' | Coil, Split Axle | Coil, de Dion | Allard-Ar |
| | | '' | '' | 1951 to 1954 | '' | '' | Coil, Split Axle | Coil, de Dion | Cadillac ( |
| | | '' | '' | 1951 to 1954 | '' | '' | Coil, Split Axle | Coil, de Dion | Chrysler ( |
| M-2-X | | 4–5 Pass. Cabriolet | 20 | 1951 to 1952 | 2295 | Box Steel | Coil, Split Axle | TL, Rigid Axle | Ford (Eng |
| | | '' | '' | 1951 to 1952 | '' | '' | Coil, Split Axle | TL, Rigid Axle | Ford (Eng |
| | High Compression Version | '' | '' | 1951 to 1952 | '' | '' | Coil, Split Axle | TL, Rigid Axle | Mercury ( |
| P-2 | Monte Carlo | 5–6-Pass. Sedan | 10 | 1952 to 1955 | 4000 | 4-Tube | Coil, Split Axle | Coil, de Dion | Ford (Eng |
| | | '' | '' | 1952 to 1955 | '' | '' | Coil, Split Axle | Coil, de Dion | Mercury ( |
| | | '' | '' | 1952 to 1955 | '' | '' | Coil, Split Axle | Coil, de Dion | Cadillac ( |
| | Safari | 8 Pass. Station Wagon | 10 | 1952 to 1955 | '' | '' | Coil, Split Axle | Coil, de Dion | Ford (Eng |
| | | '' | '' | 1952 to 1955 | '' | '' | Coil, Split Axle | Coil, de Dion | Mercury ( |
| | | '' | '' | 1952 to 1955 | '' | '' | Coil, Split Axle | Coil, de Dion | Cadillac ( |
| 21-C | Palm Beach | 3-Pass. Roadster | 20 | 1952 to 1955 | 5000 | 4-Tube | Coil, Split Axle | Coil, Rigid Axle | Ford (Eng |
| 21-Z | Palm Beach | 3-Pass. Roadster | 180 | 1952 to 1955 | 5000 | 4-Tube | Coil, Split Axle | Coil, Rigid Axle | Ford (Eng |
| | Coachbuilt Saloon | 2-Pass. Coupe | 1 | 1954 Only | '' | '' | Coil, Split Axle | Coil, Rigid Axle | Ford (Eng |
| — | Red Ram | 3-Pass. Roaster | 1 | | 5000 | 4-Tube | Coil, Split Axle | Coil, Rigid Axle | Dodge (U |
| K-3 | | 3-Pass. Roadster | 50 | 1952 to 1954 | | 4-Tube | Coil, Split Axle | Coil, de Dion | Ford (Eng |
| | | '' | '' | 1952 to 1954 | | '' | Coil, Split Axle | Coil, de Dion | Mercury ( |
| | | '' | '' | 1952 to 1954 | | '' | Coil, Split Axle | Coil, de Dion | Jaguar (E |
| | | '' | '' | 1952 to 1954 | | '' | Coil, Split Axle | Coil, de Dion | Chrysler ( |
| J-2-R | | 2-Pass. Sports/Racing | 10 | 1953 to 1955 | 3400 | 4-Tube | Coil, Split Axle | Coil, de Dion | Cadillac ( |
| — | Palm Beach Mark Two | 2-Pass. Roadster | 4 | 1956 to 1958 | 7000 | 4-Tube | Torsion Bar MacPherson Strut | Coil, Rigid Axle | Jaguar (Er |
| | Palm Beach Mark Two | '' | 2 | 1956 to 1958 | '' | '' | Torsion Bar MacPherson Strut | Coil, Rigid Axle | Ford (Eng |
| — | Gran Turismo | 2-Pass. Coupe | 1 | 1957 Only | 7000 | 4-Tube | Torsion Bar MacPherson Strut | Coil, Rigid Axle | Jaguar (Er |
| | Gran Turismo | '' | 1 | 1958 Only | '' | '' | Torsion Bar MacPherson Strut | Coil, de Dion | Chrysler ( |

SPECIAL NOTE—Chassis numbers quoted are no real indication of date or order of construction. Cars were numbered as they left the workshop and not according to ser Quantities quoted for the more numerous types are round figures only.
Key: TL—Transverse Leaf, IL—In-Line.

*An early Allard 4-place tourer of the pre-war days.*

COURTESY ALMOTCO

*An Allard mudplugger of the late 1930s.*

H. PARKER PHOTO

point for the front suspension locating links, so Allard decided to locate his half-axles from in front instead. Consequently, the frame sprouted a 6-in. forward extension to carry the new mounting, the engine moved 7.5 in. nearer the front axle—and handling turned out to be 100% better.

Gearing was still a worry, though. Because some owners felt the 3-speed Ford box and 3.5 axle normally supplied with J-2s gave too little range in 1st and 2nd, the 3.27 ratio became a standard offering all through instead of just on the bigger-engined cars. Meanwhile, Allard set some of his

## SPECIFICATIONS

| Bore x Stroke (mm) | Bhp | Overall Gear Ratios | Remarks | Wb.in. | Tr.in. Fr. | Tr.in. Rr. |
|---|---|---|---|---|---|---|
| 7.79x95.25 | 85 | 4.11/6.59/14.4 | | 100 | 56 | 52 |
| 7.79x95.25 | 85 | 4.11/6.59/14.4 | | 106 | 56 | 52 |
| 7.79x95.25 | 85 | 4.11/6.59/14.4 | | 112 | 56 | 52 |
| 7.79x95.25 | 85 | 4.11/6.59/14.4 | | 112 | 56 | 58 |
| 7.79x95.25 | 85 | 3.78/6.68/11.75 | Introduced for the | 112 | 56 | 58 |
| 84.13x98.42 | 110 | 3.78/6.68/11.75 | Monte Carlo Rally | 112 | 56 | 58 |
| 7.79x95.25 | 85 | 3.78/6.68/11.75 | X-Type Front-End | 112 | 56 | 58 |
| 7.79x95.25 | 90 | 3.78/6.68/11.75 | Special Alloy Heads | 112 | 56 | 58 |
| 84.13x98.42 | 110 | 3.78/6.68/11.75 | | 112 | 56 | 58 |
| 4.13x98.42 | 120 | 3.5/6.19/10.3 OR 3.5/4.53/6.15 | Alternative Final | 100 | 56 | 52 |
| 1.0 x95.25 | 140 | 3.5/6.19/10.3 OR 3.5/4.53/6.15 | Drive Ratios: | 100 | 56 | 52 |
| 6.8 x92.0 | 160 | 3.27/5.75/10.00 OR 3.27/4.3/5.8 | 4.1, 3.78 | 100 | 56 | 52 |
| 6.8 x92.0 | 172 | 3.27/5.75/10.00 OR 3.27/4.3/5.8 | 4-speed Cotal electric-shift gearbox also available | 100 | 56 | 52 |
| 7.79x95.25 | 85 | 3.78/6.68/11.75 | | 106 | 56 | 52 |
| 7.79x95.25 | 90 | 3.78/6.68/11.75 | Alloy Heads, etc. | 106 | 56 | 52 |
| 1.0 x95.25 | 140 | 3.78/6.68/11.75 | | 106 | 56 | 52 |
| 4.13x98.42 | 110 | 3.78/6.68/11.75 | | 106 | 56 | 52 |
| 4.13x98.42 | 120 | 3.27/5.75/10.0 | Alternative Final | 100 | 56 | 52 |
| 1.0 x95.25 | 140 | 3.27/5.75/10.0 | Drive Ratios: | 100 | 56 | 52 |
| 6.8 x92.0 | 200 | 3.27/5.75/10.0 | 3.5, 3.78, 4.11 | 100 | 56 | 52 |
| 6.8 x92.0 | 180 | 3.27/5.75/10.0 | Engine outputs quoted are Average Figures | 100 | 56 | 52 |
| 7.79x95.25 | 85 | 3.78/6.68/11.75 | | 112 | 56 | 58 |
| 7.79x95.25 | 90 | 3.78/6.68/11.75 | Alloy Heads, etc. | 112 | 56 | 58 |
| 4.13x98.42 | 110 | 3.78/6.68/11.75 | | 112 | 56 | 58 |
| 7.79x95.25 | 85 | 3.78/6.68/11.75 | 3442-cc Jaguar-Powered Version | 112 | 56 | 58 |
| 4.13x98.42 | 110 | 3.78/6.68/11.75 | Announced But | 112 | 56 | 58 |
| 6.8 x92.0 | 250 | 2-Range Hydra-Matic | Never Produced | 112 | 56 | 58 |
| 7.79x95.25 | 85 | 3.78/6.68/11.75 | | 112 | 56 | 58 |
| 4.13x98.42 | 110 | 3.78/6.68/11.75 | | 112 | 56 | 58 |
| 6.8 x92.0 | 250 | 2-Range Hydra-Matic | | 112 | 56 | 58 |
| 9.37x76.2 | 47 | 4.11/6.96/13.45 | Overdrive Available | 96 | 51 | 50 |
| 9.37x76.2 | 68 | 4.11/6.96/13.45 | Overdrive Available | 96 | 51 | 50 |
| 9.37x76.2 | 68 | 4.11/6.96/13.45 | Built by Abbott as Production Prototype, but Never Developed | 96 | 51 | 50 |
| | | | | 96 | 51 | 50 |
| 7.79x95.25 | 95 | 3.5/6.19/10.3 | Special Alloy Heads | 100 | 56 | 58 |
| 4.13x98.42 | 120 | 3.5/6.19/10.3 | | 100 | 56 | 58 |
| 3.0 x106.0 | 190 | 4.27/5.16/7.47/12.73 | | 100 | 56 | 58 |
| 6.8 x92.0 | 180 | 3.54/5.67/9.98 | | 100 | 56 | 58 |
| 6.8 x92.0 | 270 | 3.27/4.9/7.85 | Alternative Final Drive Ratios: 3.5, 3.78, 4.11 | 96 | 51 | 51 |
| 3.0 x106.0 | 210 | 3.54/4.28/6.2/10.55 | Overdrive or Borg-Warner Automatic Transmission Available | 96 | 52 | 51 |
| 2.0 x79.5 | 90 | 3.77/6.18/10.7 | | 96 | 52 | 51 |
| 3.0 x106.0 | 210 | 3.54/4.28/6.2/10.55 | Converted to de Dion Suspension in 1958 | 96 | 52 | 51 |

Copyright Doug Blain © 1962

engineers to work on a 4-speed box based on Ford of Britain's Thames truck unit. They managed to concoct four custom conversions for the streamlined Le Mans J-2-X team in early '52, but all suffered from a major design drawback resulting directly from lack of room in the gear case. Apparently it was easy enough to get nice, close first-second and third-top gaps, but to link the two with a short second-third step was impossible because the necessary outsize gear wheels wouldn't fit the casting. Additionally, there was a weight problem: the truck unit was cast iron and very, very heavy.

The all-new, totally fresh domestic line appeared progressively during 1952. It was the greatest gamble in Allard's history, the one mighty effort at sweeping away half a decade's cobwebs, keeping only what competition had shown to be the best of the old features and aiming primarily at export instead of bureau-bound home market sales.

The heavyweights came first: a new frame using parallel double-deck steel tubes linked by welded plates; new J-type de Dion; new X-style split-axle front; new 12-in. inboard rear brakes—plus a truly dazzling choice of engines and transmissions. Two styling alternatives appeared: a shapely 5-place sedan called the P-2 Monte Carlo, with lines like the Tickford Lagonda and an interior that bristled with walnut, hide and thick pile carpet, and a thumping great ash-framed wagon called the Safari. The option list, starting with the big Cadillac V-8 and winding up with the 190-bhp 3.4 Jaguar, looked as impressive as any. Allard even seemed to have laid his transmission specter at last: the choice included Jaguar's 4-speed and GM's ubiquitous Hydra-Matic.

Yet, somehow it all just failed to click. America in 1952 was barely ready for a handbuilt English luxury car just as big and twice as costly as its own domestic product. Besides, Jaguar was already around with the not quite so exotic, but equally sumptuous and far less expensive, Mark VII. In fact, the Jag-powered P-2 never left the ground at all. One or two Cadillac and Chrysler engines found their way into U.S.-destined frames. For the rest it was the ever-older, ever-less-inspiring flathead Ford, still churning out its unwavering 85 bhp and sounding and feeling as bravely inadequate as before.

The parallel small-car line appeared for Earls Court in October '52 with a single roadster body style and a choice of Ford power. The frame was a reduced-scale, 2-in. tube version of the new big one. It carried a lighter LMB front suspension and a stock English Ford rear end, along with trailing links and coil springs. Restriction of Allard's usually unlimited engine choice to just the Ford 79.37 by 76.2 mm range (1508-cc Consul with four such cylinders, 2267-cc Zephyr with six) meant fairly economical production. Even the gearbox was the same in each case—Dagenham's stock medium-weight 3-speed with a special center-shift conversion.

Obviously the Palm Beach, as it was christened, was no blood-and-thunder road burner in either its 21-C or 21-Z version; it wasn't meant to be. Allard had an idea he could sell roadsters, particularly in the States, on a combination performance-with-practicality platform. The notion has since become depressingly familiar, but it was new then. The Palm Beach appeared with untuned single-carburetor engine options in a chassis that would handle and also ride reasonably

...e ill-fated Ardun-Mercury engine as installed in the K-2.

The Cadillac-powered J-2-R at Silverstone; Allard up.

well without complications or servicing hitches—and flopped. The same show Allard used to debut his new runabout saw the Triumph Roadster and Donald Healey's new 100 model both offering far more performance at less cost.

The Palm Beach was the last totally fresh design to come from the Almotco headquarters in London. The models that followed were just expansions, contractions, remakes and combinations of the ideas that had gone into that and the P-2 line. The company was in money trouble because of the enormous outlay involved in the model switch, so any costly development program centered on the newcomers was out of the question for the time. The only steady and potentially lucrative market left for an operator who needed cash quickly was the one for big-inch performance machinery such as Sydney alone knew how to design and build. Or so it seemed. Hence 1953's offerings, the K-3 and the J-2-R.

A lot of enthusiasts think of the K-3 as a kind of upstaged Palm Beach. It looked almost identical, and there was actually one Palm Beach that got a Dodge Red Ram engine, so the confusion is understandable. But there was no mechanical similarity. The K-3 was related to the big P-3 range and not to the 2-series at all. In general, the list of engine options was the same as for the sedan and wagon. As in all K-type cars, the very wide cockpit, complete with roll-up windows, offered room for three abreast in uncommon comfort. The gearshift, when featured, was on the outside of the driver to avoid interference with passengers' legs.

Despite an undoubted ability to stay in front of the traffic —R&T (October 1954) got 0-60 in 8.6 sec, 0-80 in 16.0 and 0-100 in 29.7, with a 115 mph maximum from the Chrysler version—the K-3 was anything but a successful car. Structural worries with the newly adopted tubular frame were part of the trouble, and a lot of other incidental development bugs kept crowding in. That was the last occasion Allard put in any time on his touring sports car concept.

The J-2-R was different. In 1953 there wasn't much that could get near it, as Sydney promptly proved in the Le Mans classic. Amid scenes of open-mouthed *stupore* in all the Italian and several British pits, he came around on lap one with his factory entry well ahead of everything in the race. Only a broken brakeline kept the marque out of the winners' circle that year; a look at the specifications will show why. Four twin-choke Solex carburetors, a special high-lift cam, solid tappets, 9:1 compression and a highly efficient quadruple exhaust system boosted output to 270 bhp at 4600 rpm.

Oddly, the J-2-R was no relation either to its earlier namesakes or even to the other Cadillac-powered Allards of the day. It featured the smaller, lighter 4-tube Palm Beach frame, unaltered dimensionally but modified to take a totally new de Dion layout with twin A-brackets and parallel radius arms in place of the bigger cars' centrally pivoted links. Stock fuel capacity was around 30 gal., but buyers could order an extra detachable tank the same size. Dry weight was 2200 lb.

The J-2-R was Allard's fastest and best model. It was a special production, and the specifications varied accordingly. Most of the 7-car series came to the U.S. and Canada. Many, not surprisingly, are still around. The reason international success never came the J-R's way was that weight was against it, and within a year Ferrari and others were showing it up in the turns as well with their GP-based suspensions. Then came the CSI's capacity limit and death for the big-inch racer.

Perhaps it should be pointed out here that Allards were always strictly hand-built cars, even if not quite to the same extent as the J-2-R. In the years of 1948 through '51 Sydney organized a kind of production line without any real moving machinery. He had three plants then: the original one at

Clapham for frames, plus two others at nearby Fulham.

Abbott, the once-famous Surrey coachbuilder, put together around 600 bodies during the marque's currency, mostly K roadsters. Abbott president R. G. Sutherland also commissioned one of the best-looking Allards of all, a very neat fastback coupe on the first Palm Beach chassis. It appeared at Earls Court in 1954, but only one was ever built.

Production reached a peak of 10 cars a week during 1949, when demand for the P-1 sedan was strongest. Delivery quotes then ran as low as 6 weeks, but the delay was about three months for a U.S. order.

Sydney Allard, always a brave man on the track, showed equal valor in the battle to save his business. Three years after the first Palm Beach appeared he went to Earls Court with a revised version called the Mark Two, the first and only Allard to have specifications that bore no relation at all to the original special of 1936. In fact, the Palm Beach Mark Two shared very little with any other model. True, the chassis owed a lot to the earlier 21-series, but it carried major alterations front and rear to make way for an entirely new suspension. Gone at last were the old swinging half-axles in the nose; instead, the newcomer featured MacPherson pillars with laminated torsion bar springing. At the back a Panhard rod provided side location, and twin parallel trailing arms forward location, for a simple Salisbury rigid axle, again with helical springs and telescopic shocks.

Mark Two buyers could specify either the 2553-cc Ford Zodiac Mark II six or, tantalizingly, Jaguar's full-house, Special Equipment XK-150 plant. The revised car appeared with lines far more delicate than those of the first Palm Beach; the only clumsy touch was around the grille, where a plated tubular A clashed with the simple contours of an otherwise unadorned orifice. Wire wheels were stock. Trim in the simple but tastefully furnished cockpit was leather, with pile carpeting and a full range of instruments.

Given a little more subtlety of design and execution, the Mark Two might have saved Allard. As it was, potential buyers preferred Jaguar's equivalent model (the similarly-priced Special Equipment XK-150 convertible) regardless of a weight penalty as high as 700 lb. Sydney made a big final effort with a handsome GT coupe on the same chassis for Earls Court 1957, but the end was near.

Modifications applied for the GT configuration included disc brakes all around, a neat fastback alloy top and a rectangular outlet (pre-Mercedes) for trapped air in each front fender. The only example built for sale, a fierce Chrysler-powered automatic ordered in America, featured the J-2-R de Dion setup. Allard later had his own car, the only other GT to leave the plant, altered to match. You could say that was the last directly creative act Almotco performed before Sydney Allard hung up his hat as an auto manufacturer.

Sydney, however, is not a sad or bitter man. Tall, robust, loud-voiced, he is married, has three kids and still is only 53. Most of his effort these days goes into Adlards Motors, the big Ford dealership that has grown from that tiny repair shop of 1931. Spare time? His hobby still is self-designed cars.

The latest of four postwar Allard specials carries us right back to where we started, only this time the car in question really is a dragster—a genuine California slingshot, the work of a gifted young London engineer called John Hume, who got the run of Allard's workshops after he'd shown special promise on an earlier project. It gives the British a kick (Sydney included) to watch their national standing-start records tumble. Already, after a poor debut at the '61 Brighton Speed Trials, the crimson and chrome Allard dragster has established Britain's fastest-ever 4-wheeled quarter-mile at 10.84 sec. [Ed. note: American dragsters, after which Allard's machine was patterned, are currently running the "quarter" between 8 and 9 sec. with a few actually under 8 sec.

Some say Allard has run full circle, and that it's logical such a man should find happiness with a dragster: that's what he was headed for all along.

# ALLARD:
## An owner speaks

**BY TONY HOGG**

THE LIFE of the enthusiast who desires something more than the general run of production sports cars can be extremely frustrating. Exotic machinery is expensive and, if purchased after it has depreciated to the point where the price is within the reach of mortal men, the cost of putting it in shape may still be prohibitive, and the fear of an expensive mechanical breakage can seriously detract from the pleasures of driving the car. My personal solution to the problem was the purchase of a 1951 J-2 Allard and, after a year of daily driving, it appears to have been a wise solution. I have derived infinite pleasure from the car and my bankroll, such as it is, has remained intact.

Originally designed with Le Mans in view, the J-2 is basically a clever assembly of readily available production parts from both sides of the Atlantic, enclosed in a very striking aluminum body. For this reason, the car is comparatively simple and cheap to maintain, although the general impression one obtains from a casual acquaintance with it is that the precise engineering normally associated with very high performance cars has, in this case, been replaced by a lot of brute force and bloody ignorance. Admittedly, a lot of brute force is involved, but what might be construed as ignorance is actually the necessity for compromising in the design so that little specialized equipment is used. A case in point is the de Dion rear axle which incorporates inboard rear brakes, and is so designed that practically all the components can be purchased from your friendly neighborhood parts house.

One of the problems of buying a used competition car in America is that it has almost inevitably been butchered by amateur mechanics. However, in this respect I was extremely fortunate, because the car was practically virgin. The two previous owners were older men who hardly ever drove the car, although they appreciated what they had, and spared no expense in providing it with the best professional attention.

Used daily for commuting in the city of San Francisco, the Allard presents no serious problems, provided certain allowances are made for its idiosyncrasies. The Cadillac engine always fires up at the first touch of the starter and idles at a steady 500 rpm. The Cad is practically stock with the exception of a single 4-barrel carburetor and an Iskenderian camshaft of an excellent "commuting grind," and this combination tends to extract more of the potential of the engine without lessening its tractability. Fuel consumption is high, and the combined efforts of a Bendix and an SU fuel pump are required to keep the float bowls full. Nevertheless, the car does give several superb miles to every gallon of gas.

The 3-speed transmission is entirely adequate for all purposes and shifting is very positive, although low is not synchronized. The foot pedals require some practice before they can be operated smoothly because the 11-in. truck clutch is exceptionally heavy in its action, and the accelerator is extremely light with a short and awkward movement. For optimum efficiency, the most satisfactory combination of footwear would be a deep sea diver's boot on the left foot and a ballet slipper on the right. The best compromise I have found is to remove the right shoe altogether, though this makes constant braking rather tiring, because the brake pressure required is considerably higher than normal.

Although all this leg work may be rather exhausting, it does have the advantage of keeping the little woman out of the driver's seat, removing the attendant possibility of damage to the machinery.

On the road, the Allard is potentially the most dangerous car I have ever driven. The massive torque of the engine is transferred most efficiently by the excellent arrangement attributed to Count de Dion, so that wheelspin is reduced to a minimum, although tire wear is high. However, although one knows exactly what the rear end is doing, the same cannot be said for the front. The front axle is a beam which has been chopped in half and pivoted in the center to give a form of independent suspension, with the result that the car has a violent understeering quality, or an equally violent oversteering quality, depending on whether one is accelerating or decelerating. Furthermore, it will not run in a straight line unless the road surface is absolutely smooth. However, a busy driver is a happy driver.

Reverting to the disadvantages of the Allard for daily use, it can never be parked on the street because people seem compelled to touch it, perhaps to make sure they aren't dreaming. The result is a multitude of small dents in the aluminum body. Another hazard is that it tends to stop traffic and distract other drivers, and then there is a certain class of driver, usually a member of the Volkswagen-Sprite set, who feels obliged to pass it, which leads me to believe that there is some truth in the old saying that "If all the cars in America were lined up end to end, somebody in a Volkswagen would try to pass them."

Fortunately for me, San Francisco has a short rainy season, because the Allard is not designed to keep the driver dry in wet weather. It comes with a top which was definitely an afterthought, and also side curtains which screw onto the windshield. However, nothing fits accurately and the problem is compounded by the cycle fenders, which tend to direct additional water back at the driver. One is also vulnerable from below. The floor is made up of a number of different ill-fitting pieces of aluminum, and you can expect to receive a jet of water up the trouser leg from time to time.

The idea of combining a big American engine with a European chassis and body is by no means new, and predates the Allard by many years. An early example was the Railton of the Thirties, which was powered by a 4-liter straight-8 Hudson engine. The best known contemporary application of this idea is the Ford-engined AC Cobra.

Some of the purists may look on the J-2 Allard as nothing more than a form of automotive bestiality. However, for those of us who have Ferrari tastes and Ford incomes, it is a good compromise. Furthermore, when blasting down the freeway with all systems GO, it has the additional advantage of providing fresh air and exercise (as a reflection on the steering, the car has been called "Sydney Allard's rowing-machine") and, in general, can be considered a most stimulating and therapeutic method of going to and from one's daily task. ▼

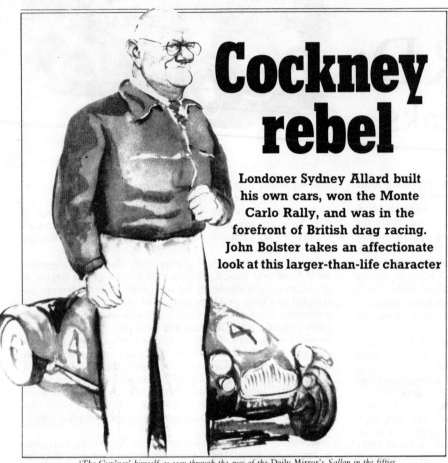

# Cockney rebel

**Londoner Sydney Allard built his own cars, won the Monte Carlo Rally, and was in the forefront of British drag racing. John Bolster takes an affectionate look at this larger-than-life character**

*'The Guv'nor' himself as seen through the eyes of the Daily Mirror's Sallon in the fifties*

Sydney Allard was born in Streatham, South London in 1910, the second son of a family of four boys and one girl. He was educated at Ardingly College and became mad about cars, his first vehicle being an old GP Morgan three-wheeler, later replaced by an Aero of that ilk, with a JAP V-twin engine. His brothers all went into dad's prosperous building business, but Sydney became an apprentice in a garage.

He continued to motor in his tricycle, performing in trials and speed events, culminating in winning the novice's handicap at Brooklands at 84mph in 1929 and later, with an engine tuned by 'Barry' Baragwanath, the Morgan Cup. He then tried to convert the Morgan into a four-wheeler ... but this was a failure, as others have found.

### A confusion of names

In 1930, Sydney's father set him up in a garage business in partnership with Alf Briscoe, who was intended to be a steadying influence. By chance, the premises already carried the name of 'Adlard's', the confusion between Adlard Motors and Allard causing some perplexity later on.

By this time, Sydney had pronounced views on the kind of cars he liked. He had no use for vintage cars, however beautiful, and he admired the construction of cheap American chassis, with steel pressings welded or riveted together. He therefore acquired a Model B Ford open tourer for mud-plugging trials, soon replacing the 14.9hp engine by the alternative 24hp four-cylinder unit.

In 1935, the Model B was replaced by one of the special V8s, built for the previous year's TT, and Sydney broke the class record at Aston Clinton and Brighton, as well as competing in mud-plugging trials, but its weight distribution was not ideal for such goings-on. So, Sydney acquired the then current Model 48 V8 chassis, reduced its wheelbase and track and set back the engine. As Fords had transverse springs, front and rear, he split the front axle on the LMB system, resulting in a pair of swing-axles. The rear part of the body had previously graced a Grand Prix Bugatti, a sacrilege which didn't worry our hero!

This was the very first Allard Special, CLK 5, on which Sydney's fame was founded. Extremely successful in trials, sprints, and races, it is not surprising that there was an instant demand for replicas and Sydney was kept extremely busy from 1937 until the war. In 1938, a trials team was formed called the Tailwaggers, consisting of Sydney, Guy Warburton, and Ken Hutchison, the latter's ca having the Lincoln Zephyr 12-cylinder power unit not a very good engine actually. The Tailwagge carried all before them, but Sydney felt that a muc smaller car could beat the big V8s in trials and he wa busy fabricating such a device, with a Ford I engine, when the war stopped play. How right h was!

During the war, Sydney Allard landed government contract for the repair and servicing army vehicles. This became very big business an extra premises were acquired in Acre Lane, Keswic Road, and particularly a huge factory in Hugo Road, all in South London. Many of the vehicle were of Ford manufacture and at the end of the wa Sydney was offered the option of buying as many the spares as he wished, at knock-down prices. A factories were being re-organised and ste allocations were extremely strict, this was a opportunity that could not be missed.

### The Allard Motor Co is born

Ford's first post-war production car was the Pilo which used up a lot of the 3622cc V8 engines that ha been stock-piled, and incorporated as many W chassis parts as possible. Sydney registered th Allard Motor Company and did likewise, but as h cars were to be lower-built, with the engine mounted much further back, special side-membe were essential, though some Ford cross-membe could be adapted. The side-members came from John Thompsons at Wolverhampton and wer chronically in short supply, the van from Allard frequently making hurried journeys in the nigh when promised consignments failed to turn up. Th same problems with supply applied to such items brakes and radiators, for example.

However, it was infinitely worthwhile to overcom all these problems, for the Allard Motor Co wer actually producing sports cars, with a long queue buyers. Their future rivals were still at the desig stage and if the Allards were on the crude side, the were at least new cars. Just after the war, most of were driving cars that were practically worn out an so a certain lack of refinement passed unnoticed.

The first models were well received, thei unusual styling appealing to the buyers. The M type drophead coupé was in great demand and handled extraordinarily well, perhaps partly becaus the side-valve V8 only developed 85bhp. It was goo value too at £850, plus £233 purchase tax.

So, Sydney Allard was a Motor Manufacturer i his own right and his cars were no longer branded a 'Specials'. His new eminence made not the slightes difference to him and to the chaps who worked fo him he was never 'Sir' or 'Mr Allard' but simply 'th Guv'nor'. He remarked that he had no wish t expand his business greatly for as long as it provide him with the means to go motor racing, and gav employment to the mates who worked for him, h was satisfied.

I saw a good deal of Sydney in those days, becaus we were both competing in speed trials an hillclimbs, and subsequently I knew him when I wa a BBC commentator. He had immense courage and have never known anyone who drove so hard, alway on the very edge of disaster. Some of his cars ha high-speed roadholding that was, shall I say unconventional but, as Freddie Dixon would politel express it, he wrung their bloody necks.

He had a great many accidents – 'Allard's Gap' Prescott commemorates one of them – but I don think that he was ever seriously hurt and nor were th passengers who were riding with him. I remembe one occasion when he and Bill Boddy were flung clea as the car overturned and, in the Experts Trial, th Allard landed upside down right over a convenier gulley, so that Sydney and Eleanor, his wife, coul emerge relatively unscathed. Perhaps it is unfair t mention all these shunts so I will only divulge on more. This was the time, in the British Empir Trophy at the Isle of Man, when Sydney started chain reaction that wrote off six cars, including h own. They finished up in a neat heap, but once agai nobody was seriously hurt. Sydney told me that, he was often driving his sports car against ex-G

*The pre-war 'Tailwaggers' team with the original Allard Special (complete with Bugatti tail) bring up the rear*

ngle-seaters in many of the short and very mixed
ost-war races, he had to take extra risks on the
orners to compensate for his lower speed on the
traights!

Let us return to the car manufacturing business,
owever. Eleanor Allard was the sister of Alan May,
who had re-bodied old Rolls-Royces before the war
ut who did not continue these operations after the
nd of hostilities. The ex-May premises, near
Clapham Common, were therefore taken over by the
Allard Motor Co, with offices and showrooms in
Clapham High Street. The Allard machine shop
onsisted of a lathe and a couple of pillar drills, plus a
orge and hand presses and profile flame cutters.
Accordingly, a lot of work had to be done by outside
irms and many of them were unwilling to take on
elatively small orders, although Allards had a fairly
easonable steel allocation because they had some
rders from the USA. Bodies were built by
Whittingham and Mitchell, Hilton Bros, and
Abbotts of Farnham, but Sydney later regretted
isposing of the very large building at Hugon Road,
which would have given comfortable space for
onstructing bodies 'in house'.

Post war competition was mostly sprints and
ydney did well in the sports classes, notably at
Prescott and Bouley Bay. Trials were re-starting and
new Allard team was formed, called the Candidi
Provocatores and driven by 'Goff' Imhof, Jim
Appleton, and Ken Burgess. Sydney was not in the
eam because he was short of time, but in any case he
was moving away from mud-plugging and
oncentrating on speed events.

## The Steyr-Allard appears

For the 1947 hillclimbs, Sydney built himself a
ngle-seater. At a sale of enemy property, captured
y the Royal Navy, some Steyr air-cooled V8 engines
f about 3.6-litres capacity were sold and, with a
aised compression ratio and one carburettor per
ylinder, they were highly suitable for a hillclimb
pecial. Many standard parts were used in the narrow
hassis, which was shortened and the track reduced
y 4ins. The body was a light tubular structure,
overed with thin sheet aluminium, and coil spring
uspension was adopted at the rear. The transmission
as standard Ford, even including a steering-column
earlever, and twin-tyred rear wheels were used.

Incredibly, at its first appearance, the Steyr broke
he record at Prescott. At Bo'ness, the gear ratios
ere unsuitable and it was sixth, though fastest
nsupercharged car, but at the next Prescott an
ttempt to raise the compression ratio still further
aused trouble, though fastest unblown was still
chieved. At Shelsley it was tenth, again through lack
f ratios in the three-speed 'box but, at Prescott once
ore, poor Sydney was presented with a crash not of
is own making because the steering failed.

Repaired hurriedly but deprived of its twin
wheels, damaged at Prescott, the car was third at
ouley Bay, with a similar placing at Val des Terres.
ydney made the best time at Craigantlet, beating
aymond Mays and George Abecassis, and

*The first post-war Allard Special, here in the hands of Guy Warburton at Bo'ness in 1951 when he broke the sports car record*

*The famous Steyr-engined single seater at Prescott*

concluded the season by being seventh at Poole, sixth
at Prescott, and an also-ran at Shelsley, again due to
gear ratios. As for the sports cars, Sydney put up
several good times with some American ohv
conversion cylinder heads, but reliability was never
attained.

For 1948, the Steyr-Allard had a de Dion axle,
obtained by cutting off the standard Ford axle tubes
and using articulated driveshafts, while an outside
gearlever was mounted on the right. Handling was
greatly improved and a wider-track version of the de
Dion axle was therefore put in hand for the J2 sports
two-seater. Sydney had a most consistent season with
the Steyr, scoring no outright wins but five second

places and various fastest unsupercharged prizes.
Incidentally, I used to regard the unsupercharged
cups as my private property, but Sydney's V8 was too
much for my 2-litre Bloody Mary!

However, the most important event in 1948 was
the first Motor Show after the war, at which the
Allard Motor Company was very properly accepted
as a manufacturer and all models were shown on the
stand. The standard axle ratio had been that of the
Pilot, 4.1:1, which was only tolerable because there
were no motorways, but special crown wheels and
pinions by David Brown then gave a ratio of 3.78:1.
About seven to 12 cars per week were being built,
depending on availability of parts, and some 200
people were employed. Sales at the Show were
tolerable, but there were those who jibbed at buying
a sports car with a side-valve engine and a three-
speed gearbox, inspite of competition results.

## Mercury engines released

In 1949, the War Department released some
Mercury engines, which were slightly larger versions
of the Ford V8, and by boring and stroking them
they could be stretched to 4375cc. They gave 115bhp
and were fine for sprints and short races, but the
exhaust passed through the cylinder block, leading to
overheating and eventual seizure. However, they
were safe for rallies, where you could lift off
occasionally on the straights. Allards made
aluminium cylinder heads and induction manifolds,

*this where 'The Guv'nor' was bitten by the drag-racing bug? Sydney at the Brighton Speed Trials, 1950, in the first J2, registered KXC 170*

which bore a curious resemblance to the Edelbrock bits, but no permits would be granted to import American hot-rod goodies or ohv conversions.

Sydney started his competition season by entering an M-type coupé for the Monte Carlo Rally, taking along Tom Lush and Alan May. They lost no marks on the road but the regularity test foxed them and they finished 24th.

The Steyr-Allard had enlarged Alfin cylinder barrels and eight cylinder heads from the dirt-track JAP engine. This was evidently just what it needed and Sydney made best time at three Prescott meetings, knocking a bit more off the record on each occasion. As he also won at Bouley Bay and Craigantlet and was second to Denis Poore's Alfa Romeo at Bo'ness and Shelsley, he became the 1949 Hillclimb Champion.

Meanwhile, a new J2 sports car, with nothing under the bonnet, was sent out to the States for Tom Cole to fit a proper overhead-valve V8, a 5420cc Cadillac no less. This was just what the Allard had always needed and Tom's impressions were awaited with bated breath. At the Motor Show, the coupé and the saloon appeared with coil spring front suspension, like the J2, but unfortunately still with swing-axles, which Sydney insisting on retaining. The K2 was to follow with similar suspension, early the next year.

In the 1950 Monte Carlo Rally, Sydney and Eleanor had coupés with the enlarged Mercury engines. Sydney was accompanied by Tom Lush and Guy Warburton, while Eleanor had her two sisters, Edna and Hilda. The route after Lyon was covered in ice and there was fog in the Rhone valley. Sydney would have made it but a lead pulled out of the distributor cap on the last stage and he was 2min 23secs late. As there were only five 'clear' and he won the acceleration and braking test, he would have won the event outright if that wire had stayed in place! The girls failed to finish.

## Le Mans in 1950

This was a terrible disappointment, but Sydney was delighted to be invited to drive the J2 at Le Mans with Tom Cole. He had also succeeded in importing his own Cadillac engine 'for experimental purposes', which he proceeded to drop into a J2 and win a couple of short races at Goodwood. He also managed to get a pair of Ardun ohv conversion cylinder heads, which were intended to overcome the Mercury's overheating problems, but they were never really successful in this country, though they evidently performed quite well in the States.

The Le Mans story is soon told. Sydney and Tom were second at 3am, then the usual gearbox failure occurred and they had only top gear left. In spite of that, they soldiered on and finished third, which was the best Le Mans placing that an Allard would ever achieve.

By driving at Le Mans, Sydney missed three vital hillclimbs and he had little chance of being Champion again, though he made the best time at the first Prescott meeting with the Steyr, but the Cadillac-Allard broke the sports car record at Brighton.

In 1951, Sydney was excluded from the Monte Carlo Rally because a silly rule, for one year only, insisted that the car manufacturer must make his own engine. There were complaints about the handling of the J2 – I'm not surprised, it frightened me silly – and the result was the J2X, with the engine moved further forward and some suspension modifications, but still with those swing-axles. There was a new saloon, the P2, with a multi-tubular chassis, and later there was to be a coupé version, the M2X.

For the Tour of Sicily, there was an engine size limit which excluded the Cadillac and Sydney used a 4-litre Ardun-Mercury, in which a piston failed. For the Mille Miglia, the 'Caddy' was back in the J2, but Sydney shot over an embankment down a considerable drop, which did the car no good at all! In the production sports car race at Silverstone, Stirling Moss led six Jaguars in line ahead formation and Sydney was only ninth, with other Cadillac-Allards 11th, 14th and 15th. At Le Mans with Tom Cole, the car again lost all gears except top and the

*The Allard team on their winning way in the 1952 Monte*

*His finest hour – Sydney and trophy, Monte Carlo, 1952*

*What Allards were all about – a Cadillac-powered J2 driven by Mike Graham winning a race at Pebble Beach, 1950*

clutch burnt out at the 13th hour. The story at the Leinster Trophy was similar, with gearbox failure causing retirement. No effective manual gearbox was available for the Cadillac engine because automatic transmissions were universal on the home market.

Sydney was still winning short races at Goodwood and Ibsley, and he took the sports car record at Brighton, where Eleanor won the Ladies' Prize. Sydney also took part in the hillclimb season, the Steyr-Allard having been converted to four-wheel drive. This was not a noticeable improvement, except at Craigantlet where Sydney broke the record. At the Motor Show, Allards were showing the J2X with the big Chrysler engine – still more power to go through the poor little Ford gearbox!

The organisers of the Monte Carlo Rally had again decided to permit proprietary engines and Sydney entered two cars forthwith, for Eleanor and himself. Sydney drove a big P-type saloon and, in appalling conditions, he and his crew, Guy Warburton and Tom Lush, were the only unpenalised finishers from the Glasgow starting point. Seeing 'the Allard Girls' in a ditch after Clermont, Sydney shouted 'are you alright', then accelerated away to finish just in time. In the regularity test, he slid into a wall and buckled a wheel, but finished without loss of marks. At last he had won the Monte Carlo Rally, the first time for 21 years that a Brit had done it, the last one being Donald Healey in the Invicta.

This was Sydney Allard's finest hour and one would have thought that the fortunes of the Allard Motor Company were assured. That was by no means the case and Tom Lush, in his excellent book, *Allard . . . the inside story*, writes that:'. . . it would seem in hindsight that the Company's fortunes began to decline from this point.' It is sad to record the decline and fall, which I shall cover in less detail.

The truth is that, for the first time in many years, we were back to a buyers' market and the manufacturers had at last caught up with the demand. The Allards were too big and heavy on fuel and they lacked the refinement of the new cars of other makes. A new small Allard, the Palm Beach, could be ordered with a Consul or Zephyr engine but I was frankly horrified at its handling and roadholding and it did not compare with the Triumph TR2 and the Healey 100. The last sports racer, the JR, had the compact dimensions of the Palm Beach and that didn't handle either. I believe that a revised version of the Palm Beach actually had a MacPherson-inspired front end, though with laminated torsion bars, but I never drove it.

The production figures tell all: 1952 saw 143 cars built and in 1953 the figure was 121 cars. Come 1954 it was down to 28 cars, and in 1955 to 6 cars – 1957 saw the last Allard stand at the Motor Show.

## Allardettes and dragsters

As for Sydney, he seemed undismayed and in his final Le Mans he led the whole field on the first lap, gladsome sight, but on the second he retired with the back axle adrift. He drove Ford Zephyrs in the big rallies from 1955 to 1960 and then rallied very small Fords, of which he developed a very special and often supercharged version, which he called the Allardette.

His greatest enthusiasm, however, was for dragsters, and he built one himself to introduce the sport into this country, inviting successful American drivers to come over and race against him. Then, his health began to cause concern and he spent some time in hospital but he died at his home in Esher on April 12, 1966. No man ever risked his life so often and it is no disrespect to him to say that nobody expected that he would be spared to die in his bed.

Above all, he was a tremendous enthusiast, and I shall always remember his taking me for a ride in his new saloon. The carburettors spat jets of flame and the huge American V8 seemed to be trying to tear itself free, while a series of terrifying explosions rent the air on the over-run. The doors flapped and tried to escape their latches, while on corners the front wheels performed indescribable antics. It was a stupendous experience, but perhaps one that was not quite what the purchaser of a big luxury car would be expecting . . .

## The thundering classic made modern
## —but not too modern

# Allard J2X2

### by Peter W. Frey
#### PHOTOGRAPHY BY MATT KEEFE

**DRIVING IMPRESSION**

Anyone who has ever felt the mechanokinetic lust of driving an A.C. Cobra at speed owes a debt to Sidney Allard. It was the most famous of his creations—the J2X—that set the stage for Carroll Shelby's aluminum snakes, as well as the flood of musclecars that followed, providing two generations of legend-hungry enthusiasts with machinery that fit the role.

One would think that the time for such

cars is past, but the availability of not one but several A.C. Cobra replicas puts the torch to that idea. And now the Cobra's spiritual progenitor has been resurrected from automotive Valhalla—as a Canadian!

They call it the J2X2, and the principals in this resurrection stress that this is not a replicar. It is the resumed production, after

30 years, of the Allard J2X, altered from the original by as much modern hardware and "civilizing" as could be incorporated without compromising the intended J2X ambiance.

Mel Stein and Arnold Korne are the men who caused production to be resumed, said event occurring with the blessings of the Allard family and the participation of Allan Allard (son of Sidney) as European distributor. Allard, who operates a turbo-charging shop in the west of England, had

# Noise, speed, and wind assault the driver into a state of quivering awareness

been approached half a dozen times over the years by people interested in reviving the company, but nothing came of it until A.H.A. Manufacturing Company Limited—Messrs. Korne, the president, and Stein, the chairman—showed up, expressing the desire and displaying the necessary resources.

A.H.A. (5309 Maingate Drive, Mississagua, Ontario L4W 1G6. Phone: (416) 625-6860) is one of the largest coachbuilding operations in Canada, with a product line that includes limousines, show cars, prototypes, custom one-offs, and convertible Mustangs, Capris, 024s, TC3s, Firebirds, and Camaros.

The seed from which the J2X2 project sprouted was contained in a statment by Korne—a recollection that precisely defines the seemingly undying appeal of such cars. "The Allard always turned my crank as a kid," he said. And turned it so far that later, when resources permitted, he bought an original J2X. The catalyst in the creation of the J2X2—apart from the built-in cult following and a legendary history just waiting to be properly exploited—had to do with what it is like to drive an Allard.

To drive an Allard is to get your crank roundly and soundly turned by a big, gutsy British sports car with an American V-8 engine, a car that embodies a thundering talent for forcibly blending machine, road, and environment into a continuous symphonic crescendo of noise and speed and wind that assaults the driver into a state of quivering awareness. This was the trademark of the original, and the J2X2 has, in a smoother, slightly more civilized way, that same combination of qualities.

But first a bit of history. In 1936 Sidney Allard is said to have created a "Trials Special" (trials being a peculiar British form of off-road race usually conducted in axle-deep mud) by mating a Grand Prix Bugatti body with the remains of a 1934 Ford V-8. Other participants in this odd sport were so impressed with the performance of this Franco-American hybrid that Allard found an immediate market for duplicates.

In 1946 the Allard Motor Company was formed, and offered for sale to the enthusiast public three new Allards—all streetable, all powered by Ford V-8s, and all fitted with a rounder, sleeker style of body work. The standout among these cars was the Cadillac-engined J2X, about which in 1951 the British magazine *The Motor* wrote, "The man who purchases this Allard should not expect luxury travel. What he gets might be best described as the finest sports bicycle on four wheels."

However Spartan the appointments of the J2X might have been, its performance capabilities provided sufficient justification for overlooking them. In road racing competition, Allards ruined the overdog image of many a costlier, more exotic vehicle. While it did so more with brute force than finesse, winning is winning and the distinction became academic.

Allard cars definitely went fast, and quite frequently it was Sidney Allard behind the wheel causing them to do so. Co-driving a Cadillac-powered J2X with American racer Tim Cole, Allard finished third in the 24 Hours of Le Mans in 1950, and in 1952 he was the first British driver in 21 years to win the prestigious Monte Carlo Rallye. In addition to his trials, road racing, and rallying involvements, he became interested in drag racing during a visit to the U.S. in 1963, and returned home to found the British Drag Racing Association. Showing a true promoter's instinct, he even imported 10 top NHRA drivers for Britain's first-ever drag racing festival.

One of the factors that made the Allard cars competitive in so many forms of motorsport was a chassis structure and engine bay designed to permit installation of a variety of engines. Allard was assisted in that design task by a young engineer named Zora Arkus-Duntov, who later went on to achieve some fame of his own with another big-engined sports car. Ford and Cadillac V-8s were the frequent choice of J2X owners, as were Chrysler Hemis; and the tale is told of one gonzo enthusiast who adapted the front end of his Allard to a Lincoln V-12.

The same diversity of customer engine preference that caused Sidney Allard to design-in interchangeability also prompted him to offer cars without an engine or transmission, leaving the choice—and the installation—up to the new owner. In the case of the J2X2, Stein, Korne, and company, adhering to tradition, also make that offer. Should the purchaser of one of the 250 J2X2s that A.H.A. intends to build prefer to take delivery of his car in "turnkey" condition, what his money (anywhere from $38,500 to $41,815, depending on options) will get him is a new car that looks like, drives like, and generates excitement like (but is more comfortable than) a 1952 Allard J2X.

There *have* been changes. Where the body of the J2X was all aluminum, the J2X2's is part aluminum, part glass-reinforced plastic, though the only readily noticeable difference is the energy-absorbing bumper system required by federal regulations. Where the J2X was usually powered by a Cadillac V-8 topped with a 2-bbl Carter carburetor and backed by a 3-speed manual transmission, the J2X2 comes equipped with a 318-cu.-in. Chrysler V-8, a 2-bbl Holley, and a manual 4-speed. Steering that was worm and roller is now

rack and pinion, and the 4-wheel drum brakes have given way to a power-assisted disc/drum arrangement. The J2X's infamous swing-axle front suspension has been replaced with the more conventional, more controllable A-arm configuration. The old "full-length, ladder-type chassis" remains, and the interior, though finished to a higher standard, requires the same ergonomic compromises of taller drivers—and is just as drafty.

The arrangements for keeping most of the rain out are sidecurtains and a non-folding canvas top that has to be removed and stowed, along with the folding support mechanism, behind the seats. The J2X2 comes equipped with Michelin XVS tires, five wire wheels, and a full set of gauges that, unfortunately, look nothing like their handsome predecessors. Optional equipment consists of a second side-mounted

# The J2X2 seems to have been screwed together with more than a casual eye toward quality

re tire ($975), an automatic transmis-
n ($990), leather hood straps ($250),
e-mounted mirrors ($125 each), Brook-
ds windscreens ($380), and the custom-
an even get the steering wheel installed
the right for an additional $470. A com-
ition trim model of the J2X2 is also
ailable without bumpers, and with a
ice of the aforementioned Brooklands
idscreens or a set of full-race Aero
eens.

he car we tested was a pre-production
del driven from Canada to Los Angeles
a man who, given the car's total absence
luggage space, was probably chosen for
job for his ability to travel light. And,
ging from the head-turning, encounter-
erating capabilities the car demon-
ated during our two-day test drive, he
st have had an entertaining time of it,
fun diluted just a bit by a driving posi-

tion that is a little too classically bolt-up-
right, and the Niagara of air that buffets
the cockpit at highway speeds. Another
characteristic that detracts slightly from
the driving pleasures of the J2X2 is rack-
and-pinion steering that, at 4.2 turns lock-
to-lock, is inappropriately slow for a vehicle of such sporting character.

That character exhibits itself in the performance of the Chrysler V-8, which, even
with a 2-bbl carburetor, is capable of moving the Allard's 2180 lb smartly down the
road, all the way to a claimed top end of
140 mph. The combination of acceleration,
muted thunder from the exhausts, the tac-
tile satisfaction of solid-feeling gearbox
linkage—and the wind, of course—this is
what cars like this are for.

The brakes work fine, the handling is
very sports car-like, the suspension faithfully relays all the road surface information

a purist could demand, it feels solid and
stable at speed, and can be serviced by any
Chrysler dealer. And the J2X2 also appears to have been screwed together with
more than a casual eye toward quality in
both materials and assembly. But all that
is secondary to the feeling of joyous power
that accompanies a 3-in. motion of the
driver's right foot.

It is a form of lust that a generation
raised on Honda Civics might not be able
to understand, and might even, on the basis of the J2X2's 14-18-mpg fuel consumption, disapprove of. But their opinions
don't matter to the mature, well-heeled
man who had his "crank turned" as a kid
and now has the opportunity to own the
object of his adolescent affections. Somewhere, Sidney Allard is smiling broadly
about the fact that his investment is still
paying dividends 46 years after the first Allard car thundered through the mud of the
English countryside.                    ⓂⓉ

## ◩ SPECIFICATIONS

### GENERAL

| | |
|---|---|
| Vehicle type | Front-engine, rear-drive, 2-pass. roadster |
| Base price | $38,500 |
| Options on test car | Extra side-mounted spare, twin side-mounted mirrors |
| Price as tested | $39,725 |

### ENGINE

| | |
|---|---|
| Type | V-8, water cooled, cast iron block and heads, 5 main bearings |
| Bore & stroke | 3.91 x 3.31 in. |
| Displacement | 318 cu. in. |
| Compression ratio | 8.5:1 |
| Fuel system | 2-bbl carburetor |
| Recommended fuel | Unleaded |
| Emission control | Federal |
| Valve gear | OHV |
| Horsepower (SAE net) | 165 at 4000 rpm |
| Torque (lb.-ft., SAE net) | 240 at 2000 rpm |
| Power-to-weight ratio | 13.1 lb /hp |

### DRIVETRAIN

| | |
|---|---|
| Transmission | 4-speed manual |

### DIMENSIONS

| | |
|---|---|
| Wheelbase | 100 in. |
| Length | 163 in. |
| Curb weight | 2180 lb |
| Weight distribution (%), F/R | 61/39 |

### CAPACITIES

| | |
|---|---|
| Fuel | 23.8 gals |
| Crankcase | 4.0 qts |
| Cooling system | 15.6 qts |

### SUSPENSION

| | |
|---|---|
| Front | Independent, A-arms, coil springs, telescopic shocks |
| Rear | Live axle, fully adjustable watts link, coil-over telescopic shocks |

### STEERING

| | |
|---|---|
| Type | Rack and pinion |
| Turns lock-to-lock | 4.2 |

### BRAKES

| | |
|---|---|
| Front | Discs, power assist |
| Rear | Discs, power assist |

# The Davis File

— dozens of previously unpublished photographs, letters and other documents, some secret, found in a loft: they relate to the unique British marque of Allard

## by Tony Dron

*So often the car salesman is ignored or derided by the enthusiast, the historian and the journalist, but the late 'Dave' Davis ensured a place in motoring history for himself by hoarding much of his work at home. A war-time bomber pilot with No 9 Squadron, RAF, he survived numerous hair-raising scrapes, once crash-landing after just clearing Beachy Head. He kept two flying log books, one for himself and one for his pet spaniel, Barry, who accompanied him frequently on exciting trips to such places as Hamburg and Cologne in the Wellington.*

*A few years later, many of his customers were to be ex-bomber pilots, particularly American ones including Paul Tibbetts, who flew the first A-bomb to Japan.*

*Davis was appointed to the sales staff of Adlards Motors Ltd, Acre Lane, Brixton, London SW2, on December 3, 1945. Adlards was the successful Ford dealership which Sydney Allard had purchased in the Thirties. Soon after joining, Davis was selling the new Allard cars as well as Fords and on March 30, 1955, he was appointed Allard sales manager, home and export. He was, therefore, deeply involved in the company's commercial activities throughout the entire period of post-war Allard car production, for he stayed on until 1959, only leaving after a bad row with Reg Canham, Sydney Allard's co-director.*

*Davis, whose real Christian names were Herbert Joseph Angelo — the latter chosen by his Swiss mother and the first two by his English father — perhaps understandably insisted on being called David, Dave, or sometimes Davey. He died in December, 1980, after 18 years of happy retirement, but it was not until late last year that an alert T&CC reader, Denis Ivey, stumbled across a box full of photographs, brochures and company correspondence relating to Allard in Mrs Davis's loft. This collection is all the more valuable as virtually all the Allard company records were destroyed by fire in April, 1966.*

*These surviving documents provide a fascinating if sometimes tantalising glimpse into the Allard story, and indeed of social conditions in Britain itself in the immediate post-war years. We hope this article will prompt readers to write in, filling in the odd gap and adding to the story. We are grateful to the Allard Owners Club, Tom Lush, Denis Ivey and Mrs Lilian Davis for their help in making this article a reality. Mrs Davis has kindly offered the entire file to the Allard Owners Club for their archives.*

'DAVE' Davis was quite a character as well as being a very professional sales manager: that much is clear from his correspondence with Allard customers and business contacts. He had the typical appearance of a successful post-war London car salesman with an RAF background, an awkward gait that was the legacy of several war-time flying accidents, a flowery verbosity that was known to some at the time as the gift of the gab, but which Tom Lush recalls used to drive Sydney Allard to the limit of exasperation. "Come to the point, man," Sydney would say to Davis. "What the devil are you talking about?

Some 1900 Allard cars were built between 1946 and 1959, including competition cars, sports cars, tourers, coupés, estate cars, three-wheelers, saloons, GTs and specials. Throughou it all Davis developed close links with many of th customers, some of whom sent gifts to the contact man in South London. It's worth re membering that not only was the Allard compan producing a wide range of road cars but it wa also the only British company manufacturin competition cars for sale for several years.

The company's export record was quite re markable and the Allard name became famous the J2X Le Mans model was featured in *Eagle* the boys' comic, as a colour cutaway drawing o June 13, 1952 (a copy of this is included in th Davis collection), and Sydney Allard's victory wit navigator Tom Lush and co-driver Guy Warburto in the Monte Carlo rally of the same year remain unique in the history of the event: as a construc

**Centre left, below, this unique J2X was prepared for racing by the owner, Harry Steele of Arizona, in 1952 with a new, highly tuned, ohv 5765cc Lincoln V8 with eight carburettors. Due to race on Nov 9 it was 'sabotaged' by rivals, Davis was told.**

**Below, lhd Allard K2 sports two-seaters lined up in the Peckham premises of export packers Evan Cook's Ltd. Part of a US spec J2 can be seen on the right of the picture, which dates from c 1950**

**Right, Mrs Lilian Davis with Allard P1 saloon at Horse Guards Parade in the early Fifties. Of all the Allard cars made, this model was the most successful in terms of sales. A similar car to this, also with the later short radiator grille seen here, was driven to victory in the Monte Carlo rally of 1952 by Sydney Allard himself. Davis bought this car for his own personal use and, together with Mrs Davis, toured Europe in it. Below, Henry Ford II at the wheel of the first Ford ever imported into Belgium (a 1919 model), talking to Davis (right) in Brussels in February, 1948. Ford drove a Ford-powered Allard M-type and said: "I have seen those cars in New York and I would like to buy one, but they are too expensive for me."**

or at the wheel of his own car, Sydney Allard finished first overall, narrowly beating Stirling Moss.

Looking back, it is probably fair to say that this whole Allard and Adlards empire existed mainly to provide Sydney with the opportunities to compete in a wide variety of events, from international rallies and sports car races to mud-plugging trials and, latterly, drag racing — and why not? But Davis had little to do with that side of the business. He was, above all, a salesman and a very good one at that, who knew his own value. His letter of engagement and contract, both signed by the then sales manager H J Wills, on December 3 and 4, 1945, show that although he was employed on a salary of £4 per week, plus a motoring allowance of £2 per week, plus ten per cent of the net profit on each sales deal, these terms were immediately amended in Davis's favour. He actually started work at £6 per week plus the £2 car allowance, and received ten per cent of the gross profit on each sales deal!

His ability was obvious from the start, and Sydney Allard retained a respect for Davis's talents throughout their long and happy working relationship, as was confirmed to me by Tom Lush recently. It seems fairly clear that Davis got down to steady sales work for four years, for the letters file shows nothing until November, 1949, but it opens with something that will be something of a revelation to Allard enthusiasts. Dated November 24, it is from the well-known firm of Abbotts of Farnham, to a Mr L Hurley at Davis's home address in Prince of Wales Mansions, Battersea. Now, the Farnham firm already had a business link with Allard in that they had been under contract to produce ash frames for the Allard K1 bodies  A large number of these frames remained in the Allard stores for some time because of a lack of orders for the K1 of which only about 150 were made between 1946 and 1948. Subsequently they were shifted by the introduction of the K2 sports car of 1950, which although restyled from the original K-series used the same ash frame.

Did Mr Hurley really exist, I wondered, or was Davis making clandestine enquiries on behalf of someone else, using the name Hurley as an alias? This letter had escaped the attention of Mrs Davis, and it startled her a little as she had been Miss L Hurley prior to their marriage in 42!

Top row, centre, US Gen Curtis Le May, head of Strategic Air Command, before a race at Lockburne, Ohio in October, 1953, with his Allard JR. Top right, New York distributor Major R Seddon (bow tie) with J2 and K2 Allards in his workshop

The complete motorist March. 1947.

Right and below, H J A Davis of the Allard Motor Co Ltd. The M-Type shown in snowy London was one of the first made; the 17-bar grille was dropped in favour of an 11-bar design after overheating problems on the earlier cars. The picture is captioned by Davis himself:- 'The complete motorist, March, 1947.' Below, Davis at his desk in 1954

Right, Danish driver Robert Nelleman enjoyed great success with his J2, named C'est si bon after a popular song of the day. In 1951 he won both the Danish Speedway and Hillclimb Championships. Here he leads an XK120 in a race at Helsinki, date not known. His nephew, Jac Nelleman, later became a successful competition driver too

# The Davis File

The letter from Abbott refers to an enquiry about "a special type of sports two-seater body similar to the one supplied with the Allard car", and goes on to quote a price of £230 "finished on the appropriate chassis" or £95 for the "body only panelled up without seats, dashboard, bulkhead, windscreen, trimmings, or painting". Handwritten by Davis at the top of the letter is the note "Midas cars?".

Shortly after this, Davis received a letter from the R M Overseas Motor Sales Co of Dusseldorf, and signed 'Ronnie' with the reference 'MIDAS/JCB' and on R M Overseas notepaper, saying that he had received a cheering reply from Abbott, and wondering "whether Fritz and you could make the necessary representation at their works on this matter". Mrs Davis solved this puzzle for me by explaining that Fritz was none other than Fritz Skatula, a highly talented eastern European and one of Allard's backroom boys. Ronnie or R M, was Ronnie Myhill, and the name Midas was made up from the surnames Myhill, Davis and Skatula. The three of them had planned to go into production in Germany in competition with Allard! No wonder Davis kept that one at home: the project did not have the true Midas touch, however, and it came to nothing.

Modern day motor industry and trade personnel might raise a smile at that story, and also a document dated January 24, 1950, from the British Motor Trade Association of 97, Park Lane, summoning Davis to a meeting of their Price Protection Committee on February 1.

Even more intriguing was Allard's involvement in the 1948 British Exhibition in Copenhagen, which appears to have been a complete disaster. The photographs show an M-Type and a K1 on the Allard stand, which was organised in conjunction with a company known as Brosson. One of the photographs, showing people on the stand, epitomises the atmosphere in Europe in the early post-war years. On the back of this picture, Davis noted in his own hand some highly libellous comments, which we daren't reproduce even now for fear of legal action.

Since seeing this I have discovered that payment for the M-Type, which was offered at the time as first prize in the official Copenhagen lottery, never reached Allard. Both cars disappeared after the Exhibition, though the M-Type was said to have been seen being driven by a Copenhagen docker during the summer of 1949. Another mystery!

## Post-war austerity

Life was so different in those days, as a letter from the New York Allard distributor, R/P Imported Motor Car Company, shows. Dated September 18, 1950, and signed by the proprietor, Major Richard D Seddon, it complains about the state of a Le Mans model and a J2. Seddon warns to his subject and is worth quoting at some length:

"First the Le Mans car:- We installed a new Cadillac motor and took the car out on test. Everything throughout the chassis that could rattle certainly rattled . . .

". . . we had to rewire almost entirely.

"Now on the J2:- The brakes were so tight that they had to be taken down and the drums had to be ground.

"It appears to us that you consider that anything will do for America as long as you can rake in the dollars . . .

"It is this English contempt for the 'foreigner and colonial' that has . . . brought her to her present position in the world.

"What you do with your own people in England, who do not have all the decent living Americans have, is not my concern and I am not

directly interested. I am not going to stand for the British attitude of 'They are only foreigners and anything will do'.

Very truly yours, etc"

While the distributor may have been steamed up, the customers themselves appear to have been very happy with their Allards, and this led many of them to take a far more charitable view of Britain, and 'Dave' in particular. I cannot resist the temptation to publish in full a letter from Davis to one S H Arnott, President of the Arnott Corp Inc, of Warsaw, Indiana, USA. It shows Davis on the peak of his form as the master of flowery prose:

"Dear Mr Arnott,

Please permit me to express my most sincere thanks and appreciation for your unexpected, unsolicited, extremely welcome gift — which incidentally I had the pleasure of sharing with our two directors Mr S H Allard and Mr R J Canham — not that I had to, but simply as a gesture in keeping with your own goodwill on this Seasonal occasion; I would add however in fairness to my conscience, that it would have been criminal (if not High Treason) for me to have taken home for consumption of the Davis *ménage* a HAM of such gigantic proportions representing more than

the annual meat ration of the average Englishman. I shudder at the complications that might have followed such an action — the irate long suffering near vegetarian British public would have written strong letters of protest to their M— the "*Times*" — the Ministry of Food — who knows I might even have been termed a SOCIALIST (perish the thought).

Kindest regards,

H J Davis"

I still cannot quite work out the meaning of that cryptic political comment, but I can just hear Sydney Allard, listening to this kind of verbosity work every day, bellowing: "Get to the point man!" for the umpteenth time. Still, even though Davis may be seen as the unwitting fore-runner of many successful comedians, his style has a certain old-fashioned charm.

He received many food parcels from the States, plus sheath knives from Finland ("Your local craftsmen are to be complimented in respect of the finish of these knives", said Davis in his letter of thanks), and other gifts from around the world. A great fishing enthusiast, Davis was the proud owner of one of the first glass-fibre fishing rods to arrive in the UK, donated by a grateful US customer.

Above, in the early days of Allard production a dispute at the coachbuilder meant that cars were made in chassis form for sale. This led to some interesting styling exercises of which this saloon was one of the more successful examples. Can any readers comment?

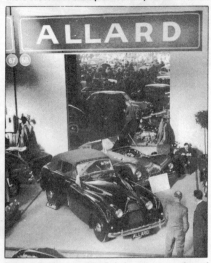

Left, Allard M2 and K2 cars at the Geneva Motor Show in 1951. Above, proposed Allard design of the early Fifties by Ronald Kent (Coach Builders) Ltd of Shepherds Bush. It came to nothing, the photograph being that of a superb model superimposed on an attractive setting

Below left, the Allard P2 Safari estate car under-going testing at MIRA, probably in 1952. Only 11 of these giant eight-seater estates were made. Below right, this 1951 P1 saloon crashed near Kuala Lumpur in October 1954, and the owner obtained an engineer's report blaming Allard for wheel-stud failure. Sydney Allard settled the matter, according to Davis's note on the back, by stating: "(The) accident was due to excessive broadside movement of (the) car — the latter being due to the negligence of the driver"

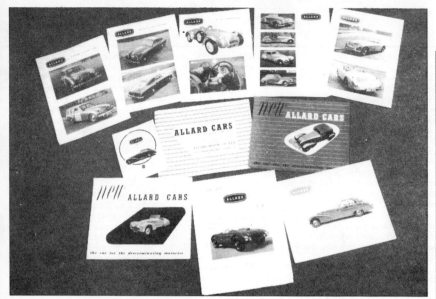

Above, a selection of Allard brochures saved by Davis. The stylish design seen centre, right, was an early example of Godfrey Imhof's work for the company. Imhof, known as Goff, was a successful designer based in London's West End, but he is better known as a keen trials and rally driver, and Allard enthusiast. He helped the company to gain a smart, go-ahead post-war image in the early days of Allard production

When I showed this letter to Tom Lush he recalled that Davis used to keep a small boat on the Thames near Hampton Court, with all his fishing gear on board. One day this began to sink, so Tom took some men out of the works to help retrieve all this valuable equipment. They decided to tow the boat out of the river with a rope on the

back of a car but in a scene worthy of a *Carry On* film the rotten old boat simply broke instantly into a hundred pieces and everything went to the bottom. This reduced Davis's "helpers" to help-less laughter, but to his credit Davis saw the joke and accepted the loss with a grin and a shrug.

The donor of the hunting knives was in fact the Finnish importer of Allard cars, Mr Hietanen of Keskus Auto Oy, who wrote to Davis at Clapham High Street on May 21, 1951, to tell the story of two Allard cars delivered for customers just in time for them to compete in the Finnish Grand Prix. For once, the photographs and letters in the Davis file make a complete story in themselves: an extract from the letter:-

". . . Mr Wallenius and Mr Hallman at the start of the Finnish Grand Prix. It was really a pity that the cars arrived in Finland so late and there was not time enough for driving in the cars and getting them into trim. Nevertheless, Wallenius was quite successful securing the second place, while Hallman got the fourth place . . . Hallman has been rather annoyed that he was not in a position to get his car into a tip-top form and that it did not, accordingly, pull hard enough. We anyhow hope that he will cool down and get pleased with his Allard after having got it into real trim." ⬭

Above, a beautiful brand new Allard J2 crated for export at Evan Crook's Ltd, Peckham, in 1950. These seats were the standard fitting, with buckets optional. Right, Sydney Allard by a J2X at MIRA with the man from *Eagle* in 1952. The intrepid gentleman did some high speed laps on the banked circuit and Allard was banned from MIRA for three months!

Below, the first of the Allard J2 series in chassis form seen at the company's Park Hill, Clapham, premises in 1949. Over the next couple of years 99 J2s were built

Above, new J2s arriving at Helsinki in May, 1951, for customers Hallman and Wallenius to race in the Finnish Grand Prix. Below, the two cars on the grid for that race with Hallman, right. (see text)

Below, in 1953 Davis noted on the back of this artist's impression of the Monte Carlo model that the first car had been built and sold to the order of a Dr Reid Tweedie of Malaya. It was "designed by Ingham"

Below, the famous 'Red Ram', a one-off Dodge V8-powered Palm Beach model. Davis saved this unique photograph, taken in April, 1954, "on the road between Paris and Fontainebleau". The owner, Mr Wolfenson, toured Europe before shipping the car to his home in Argentina

Below, the P2 'Monte Carlo' saloon of 1952, a tubular-framed chassis car with de Dion rear axle of which 21 examples were built. According to Tom Lush, Sydney allowed himself to be talked into this grandiose venture by fellow director, Reg Canham

# Allard v The World

### Plus — we drive the powerful J2X

This month the secret files of Dave Davis, home and export sales manager of the Allard Motor Co Ltd, reveal engine deals for Le Mans, an insight into the Allard production story, more interesting anecdotes and previously unpublished photographs. Tony Dron pieced this concluding story together.

EARLY in 1952 Dave Davis went to a great deal of trouble to woo the Chrysler management on behalf of Allard in order to secure some very powerful racing engines. Engines were always in short supply in those days and that is why so many different types were tried. However, special hopes were vested in the Chrysler, and Davis took the trouble to visit C B Thomas, then president of the Chrysler Corporation's export division, when he was staying at the Savoy Hotel, London in March, 1952. The visit bore fruit.

First, Davis wrote to the technical editor of *Road & Track* in Glendale, California, complimenting him on an article on the Ghia/Chrysler 310 in their February edition, and describing the car as being: 'I believe, in confidence, his own (ie, Thomas's) brainchild'. Davis suggested that *R&T* should send free copies to Thomas. That was on April 1, 1952, and shortly afterwards Davis received the reply he had been looking for from Thomas, who had left London and returned to Detroit. He wrote:

"I want to thank you for sending me the publication *Road & Track*...

"This is the first time I had seen this magazine and I now understand what you meant... I did not know there was such a publication in the United States...

"I have advised our Billing Department to ship the two motors you have on order... and you may be assured it is our pleasure to co-operate*..."

An extract from Davis's reply gives a fascinating insight into those times: after explaining that it would be impossible to show an Allard with a Chrysler engine at the forthcoming Turin motor show, which was only a couple of weeks away, Davis went on:

"It may be coincidental that Briggs Cunningham has followed your lead, even though his coachbuilder in Turin has not the world famous reputation of Ghia — the fact remains however that we like reaping the whirlwind of an American sportscar public who practically overnight have developed a colossal appetite for Italianesque bodies; it appears that we will have to get in the swim, or sink? Fortunately for us we were already working on these lines.... Our problem is to keep our cars in the same price field as Jaguar Cars Ltd and yet satisfy the new demand — we

must admit however that the Chrysler 310/Ghia ($400,000.00) and the Cunningham at $10,000.00 current values, are a slight encouragement to future progress!!"

After that nice joke at Chrysler's expense he went on to request that the engines be shipped as soon as possible as they were destined for the works Allards at Le Mans that year.

A real gem in the Davis collection is a hand-written letter from Briggs Cunningham himself, which Davis received shortly before he made his successful effort with Chrysler. Davis had written trying to obtain Cadillac competition engines, and Cunningham had put him off with such comments as:

"Last year I sent Mr Donald Healey a Cadillac engine for testing in a Healey, and I suggest you contact him about borrowing that engine for Le Mans. I will write to him today, asking him to lend it to you, as I still own it.

"Also could you get Tom Cole in New York to let you have his Cady engine from his Allard? I'm sure this will be OK with Tom, and there again I am part owner of this outfit, and it is OK with me. I am terribly sorry I can't help you with a new engine, but we just don't have any left. We are using the new Chrysler for our Le Mans cars, and I hope it works out as well as the Cady did last year. It will develop a lot more power, but don't know if it will be as reliable."

As we have seen, Davis went straight to the

top of Chrysler immediately, catching the export president himself at the Savoy Hotel.

In the race at Le Mans that year a Cunningham driven by Walters led on the first lap but retired with engine failure at about half-distance. Briggs Cunningham himself (sharing with Spear) had a steady drive to finish fourth. Sydney Allard ran as high as fifth in the early stages, only to retire because of a fuel leak with a mere two hours of the race to run. Mercedes-Benz won the race and took second place too, while Tommy Wisdom and Leslie Johnson brought their Nash-Healey home third.

Later in the year things weren't going well, for despite its promise the Chrysler Firepower engine fitted to some of the production cars was giving problems, "but", Davis wrote to Thomas in August, "we are gradually overcoming the various problems of efficient carburation, ignition, manifolding, etc, and feel confident that we will eventually attain the success which must inevitably result from such a fine combination of American and British engineering skill." He was a salesman to the core.

At the same time, Allard was experimenting with the Hobbs transmission, but as is well known the two companies required greater funds than they could afford to develop the combination of US V8 engines, Allard chassis and the Hobbs gearbox. The correspondence is interesting, though, and no less a person than H F Hobbs

Right, the Allard Palm Beach of 1952-4. Most of these cars were fitted with the Ford Zephyr engine, though a few were Consul-powered: 73 were built in all. The car shown was the first Palm Beach to be shipped to South Africa. Above, one-off prototype Palm Beach Mk II, as seen in November, 1956, with new body fitted to Mk I chassis. This was the actual Earls Court Show car of that year. Below, Palm Beach Mk II production car, with new chassis and vertical pillar front suspension. Only seven were built between 1956 and 1959

himself, the technical director, wrote to Davis: "Since we are designing a special transmission for the Allard, the gears will be such as to provide a four-speed 'box capable of dealing with the powerful engines you mention. As the vehicles may be used for competition work, we will provide ample capacity to deal with considerable periods of operation in the indirect ratios.

"We are of the opinion that the transmission will be attractive in the US, particularly since in either form it eliminates the clutch pedal and gives very smooth operation in traffic."

The penetration into the vast US market of the Allard company, which we must remember was in reality a comparatively tiny South London concern, was incredible. Col Paul Tibbets, the pilot who dropped the atom bomb on Hiroshima was one (and contrary to popular opinion, we must remember was not converted into a religious ascetic by the spectacle of the destruction of that city, nor did he go mad — he simply returned to the States and resumed his interest in sports car racing). Another customer was Philip Schwartz, vice president of Colt's Manufacturing Company, the famous firearms manufacturers established in 1836, who sent Davis a set of historical gun prints. There were many others and the US market was naturally of great importance to Allard, whose home business dwindled away to almost nothing fairly quickly, as the following table compiled by Davis shows:

| Year | No of cars built | No of cars exported | Export percentage |
|------|------------------|---------------------|-------------------|
| 1946 | 6 | 3 | 50% |
| 1947 | 173 | 29 | 17% |
| 1948 | 401 | 36 | 9% |
| 1949 | 267 | 18 | 7% |
| 1950 | 354 | 71 | 20% |
| 1951 | 344 | 128 | 37% |
| 1952 | 132 | 96 | 74% |
| 1953 | 123 | 119 | 99% |
| (to Sep 30) | | | |

This accounts for all but a handful of Allard cars produced in total and probably no more cars were built in 1953 after the end of September.

As I went through these papers, I discovered many things that were completely new to me, particularly relating to the difficulties faced by a small South London company struggling successfully to make a worldwide name for itself out of specialised motor manufacturing. I had no idea, for example, that the SMM&T used to have a permanent office in Argentina until I found a letter to Davis from their South American representative K R Stirling-Wyllie.

He wrote on June 21, 1950, replying to Davis's letters of June 6 and 12. The Allard Motor Co was unhappy at that time with its Argentinian importer and had requested Stirling-Wyllie's help in finding an alternative distributor for that area. The SMM&T's man in Buenos Aires told Davis that the distributor was not wholly to blame, the essence of his lengthy reply being summed up in the following extract:

"The fact is that under the 1948 Anglo-Argentine Trade Agreement permits were issued for only 500 cars and 500 commercial vehicles and under the 1949/50 Agreement only exchange to the value of £500,000 has been promised, but no licences have been issued yet. Three Jaguar XK120 models and three Silverstone Healeys were imported recently for the use of one of the Argentine Motor Racing Clubs, with special permission from the Argentine Central Bank."

The implication is that Allard felt that similar special permission should have been secured for the importation of their own models. It was not only foreign officialdom that seemed in Davis's view, to be obstructive. As can be seen from Davis's carefully kept export statistics, Allard's high proportion of exports was admittedly the result of a decline in home sales rather than an increase in production but it was nevertheless a significant contribution to Britain's balance of payments. The normal system, incidentally, with American market Allard cars was to ship the rolling chassis to the States for US V8 motors to be fitted over there by the official distributors. Despite this impressive business record, Davis was able to write to a regular American correspondent in February, 1954:

"TREASURY! I forgot whether I mentioned my frustrated attempt to persuade them to permit us to import American engines for re-export to non-dollar countries, but my eloquent plea was ada-

Above, only two of these elegant Allard GT models were made. One went to the States, the other being owned by Alan Allard today. Below, the competition J2R of Rupert de Larinaga, May, 1955. Note dual screens.

Above, another one-off body built on to an early Allard chassis, this curious mixture of styles was created by Laystall. Right, Allard K3 as shown at the Los Angeles Motorama, Nov 1953, by West Coast distributor Noel Kirk. Below right, Davis retained this Chrysler picture of the Firepower engine, complete with four carburettors.

## Allard v The World

monthly rejected and the inference implied that it was TOO MUCH to expect from a Government department whose aims should be interpreted as hypothetical never practical."

I would love to have heard that "eloquent plea" but the letter itself shows that Davis was indeed a master of succinct prose when he wanted to be.

Allard had been riding high in 1950 and 1951, and in 1952 his Monte Carlo Rally victory seemed to set the seal on a great future. In November, 1952, Sydney Allard was in New York with a contract in his pocket that he was trying to get signed with the Allard Motor Co Inc of the United States (the president's name is shown as Edgar S De Meyer). It makes unbelievable reading and is possibly the most remarkable of all the papers in the Davis collection.

Had the American agent signed it he would have put his name to the purchase of 500 Palm Beach and 150 K-series or J-series Allard cars in 1953 alone, whereas in that year we now know that only 38 Palm Beach models, 57 K-series and 26 J-series were built. The contract went on to say that in 1954 the Americans would take 750 Palm Beach cars plus 225 Ks or Js. In 1955 the totals rose to 1000 Palm Beach plus 300 Ks or Js.

Sydney Allard had seen the trend of sales for his monster V8-powered cars, and it was down.

He saw the future in smaller-engined Palm Beach models, built in larger numbers and powered by British Ford Zephyr or Consul engines. The contract he devised seems to have had little basis in reality, and it was designed to tie the American importer down. For example, the price of the cars was to be fixed by Allard in London and could be changed at any time, and payment became due the moment the cars left the Allard premises in Fulham. The original copy in front of me as I write was not signed.

Instead of producing all these cars, Sydney allowed himself to be talked into a dead-end venture, the three-wheeler Clipper model of which about 12 were made. If the Palm Beach car seemed a comedown, the Clipper was a desperate shot in the dark. You can see the thinking: big thirsty cars were out, so make smaller more economical sports cars; but then they don't sell. The logical answer was to build the ultimate economy car, hence the Clipper.

I am told that Sydney Allard would stride through the factory, while his employees hid, cheerfully shouting out the virtues of the Clipper. "We need a slogan," he would say. "Put your nipper in a Clipper! That's it!"

One Clipper was actually sold, which seems surprising as most of the batch could hardly be called running prototypes. Tom Lush recalled that one day, to the astonishment of everyone at the works, a small man in a cloth cap came all the way from Perth, Scotland, with the unflinching determination to buy one of these improbable vehicles. "We knew damned well he wouldn't make it," Tom told me, "in fact, he'd have been lucky to reach the start of the Great North Road, but he paid up and set off. And, you know, the remarkable thing is we never heard from him again." Even today, Tom half expects to hear from him, needing parts to help him complete the journey.

I prefer to remember the great Allard days, summed up in this extract from one Jim Thatcher of Columbus, Ohio, who formed the Ecurie Buckeye racing team:

"I have junked the Mercury motor that came with the Allard and picked up a Oldsmobile '88'... I figure with the right gearing I'll be able to dust of most any Jag. This is all I ask out of life... I even have the guy who has the Jagalac in town worried. They damn well better be worried, cause I'm going to suck them all up the tail pipes of that Allard." ▲

**Right, Allard M2X prototype somewhere in the Far East in the early Fifties. Has this car survived? Below, typical early Allard chassis**

**Below, Allard J2X Le Mans car, as prepared for Frank Curtis to race at the Sarthe circuit in 1952**

**Above, left and right, these designs were submitted to Allard by Pierre Kieffer of Belgium in April, 1955, but they were not adopted**

**Left, the Allardette was a conversion of the 1958 Ford Anglia. For £140 customers could have had aluminium cylinder head, two-tone paint, tail fins, wrap around rear window and new frontal treatment. None was sold. Tom Lush says: "It was a one-off by a design consultant who was not consulted again." Below, the equally unattractive Allard Clipper**

# Salon

# 1950 ALLARD J2

*The saga of what is probably the first J2 Allard-Cadillac*

BY TONY HOGG

PHOTOS BY WM. A. MOTTA

THE HISTORY OF most classic cars is usually somewhat confused and often erroneously recorded, and it is therefore interesting to come across a car with a history that is so well documented that no detail of its life, however small, has been lost. The 1950 J2 Allard owned by Paul Pappalardo of Greenwich, Connecticut is such a car, and the story is made even

more interesting because it was probably the first Allard fitted with a Cadillac engine.

The car was bought originally in 1950 by Frederick Gibbs of New York City, who kept it for the rest of his life and it was bought from his estate by Paul in 1979. Gibbs was a vice president of a company called Gibbs & Cox at One Broadway in New York, which is one of the world's leading firms of ships architects, and he appears to have been a most meticulous man because, when Paul acquired the car, with it came a file containing seemingly every letter, receipt and document related to it, plus some incredibly long memos dictated by Gibbs setting down still more information about the car.

The story really begins on April 13, 1950 when Gibbs wrote to the Allard Motor Co in London asking for a quotation for a J2 Allard equipped with a Cadillac engine. However, a few days later (April 17 to be exact), Gibbs talked to Sydney Allard, who was in New York, and was told that the price delivered in New York would be about $3445. But, after further discussions, it was decided that the Cadillac engine should be bought by Gibbs separately, shipped to England and the completed car shipped to. New York.

Gibbs communicated with the Export Division of General

Motors in New York about the Cadillac engine and was put in touch with a Mr A.R. McConnell, who discussed the whole matter with him. During the conversation, the interesting subject of power to weight ratios came up and when it was pointed out that the Cadillac Allard would have about 13 lb of weight per brake horsepower, compared to about 26 lb for a Cadillac, Mr McConnell ventured to say, "You will have to be careful because the car would shoot out from under you." Despite this potential hazard, General Motors agreed to sell Gibbs a complete engine for $595. However, because the engine was shipped without the air cleaner, Gibbs received credit in the amount of $5.50 on June 1, 1950 with a request that he deposit the check as soon as possible, enabling GM to clear its records on the transaction. Uncrated and without a clutch, the engine weighed 667 lb and it was shipped on the *Queen Mary*, which sailed on May 9.

After voluminous correspondence between Gibbs and a Mr

H.J. Davis, who was Allard's Export Manager, the completed car was finally shipped to New York, where it was received by Gibbs at Pier 60 on August 10, 1950. The time was 3:45 p.m. He put 2. gal. of Prestone and about a half-gallon of water in the radiator. For starting purposes he dumped 5 gal. of premium gasoline into the tank with the addition of a pint of Mobil 10W oil, and noted that the tire pressures were about 18 psi and the odometer showed 43 miles. He then started the engine and drove away, presumably without the car shooting out from under him. The complete car cost Gibbs $3402.47, which included 10-percent import duty. This amount also includes a charge of $45.00 for "modifying chassis and fitting client's Cadillac engine—manufacturing special brackets, etc."

Evidently Frederick Gibbs was as meticulous about car maintenance as he was about record keeping and he seems to have been quite fanatical about the necessity for changing oil, although, surprisingly, not particularly interested in driving the car. His first oil change came on November 18, 1950 when the odometer reading was 506 miles and he put in 5 quarts of Mobil 10W. The next time he changed the oil was on June 2, 1951 when the odometer reading was 691 and this time he put in 3 quarts of Mobil 20W and 2 quarts of 10W, "for an average of 16." It appears that in order to derive the maximum enjoyment from changing oil, Gibbs used to do it himself because, on October 25, 1950, he bought "1 only #18 Mechanics Creeper—smash proof" for $7.46. And so it goes on until October 4, 1964 when Gibbs apparently stopped keeping records. At that time the odometer reading was 6531 and he had changed the oil 23 times.

When Gibbs ordered his car, the idea of using a Cadillac engine was almost certainly an original one as far as he was concerned, and it was the first Cadillac installation the Allard factory had carried out. However, what Gibbs almost certainly didn't know was that the Anglo-American enthusiast, Tom Cole, had recently received a J2 in New York without an engine and was in the process of installing a Cadillac himself. However, the Cadillac very soon became the standard power unit for Allards, although later cars were sometimes fitted with the Chrysler hemi engine.

Prior to the use of Cadillacs, Allard had used various V-8s of Ford origin because Sydney Allard (June 5, 1910–April 12, 1966) was a Ford dealer in London and English Ford had built a V-8 for many years, and also Allard had access to American built Ford V-8. However, this availability had been severely cut back following World War II because of restrictions imposed by the British government on the importation of anything that was not vital to the economy of the country. For this reason the Cadillac idea was most beneficial to Allard because it meant that the cars could be shipped to the U.S. without engines, which saved all the work of getting licenses to import engines and then exporting them again.

During the Thirties, Sydney Allard built several Ford-based specials which were successful in various forms of competition. After WWII, during which he ran a repair shop for military vehicles, he went into the business of car manufacturing and he also started racing in earnest. Although short on money, Allard had always been long on ingenuity and, of course, he could obtain Ford components quite cheaply.

When the war started in Europe in 1939, the top of Ford's British line was a sedan with a flathead V-8 engine of 3622 cc developing 85 bhp. During the war, production of this chassis continued but with a pickup truck body, and part of Allard's job was the maintenance of these vehicles. When the war ended he was given the option of buying a lot of the existing components in his shop, which he did. By modifying these chassis quite considerably and rebodying them, he was able to come up with an effective and quite handsome sports car at a time when cars of any kind were virtually impossible to obtain. When English Ford started production of cars after the war, it introduced the V-8 Pilot, which was virtually the same as the prewar car, but with a different body, so Allard was assured of continuity in his supply of components.

In fact, Sydney Allard moved so quickly and ingeniously that on February 1, 1946 (when the dust had hardly settled) he announced a range of four different models. These were a competition 2-seater, a touring 4-seater, a convertible 2-seater, and a 2-door sedan. Not announced, but in the planning stage, was a serious competition car, designated the J1, of which a total of 12 were eventually built.

Meanwhile, believing firmly that competition successes were the best way of selling cars, Allard built another special. Being fascinated by any V-8 engine, he had acquired two aircooled Steyr V-8s of slightly under 4 liters, which had been captured from the Germans. This special was to be a single-seater and it was built by the usual Allard method, which was known as the "soapbox technique." In order to establish the dimensions, the engine was placed on a box the correct height above the ground in the middle of the shop. Next, a bucket seat was placed on a box behind the engine and Sydney, who was a very big man, sat in the seat. A wheel was placed at each corner, pedal positions were established, rough sketches made and construction begun. The Steyr was very successful in competition and it brought Allard a lot of publicity. At one stage Allard converted this car to 4-wheel drive and later he built a sports car using two Steyrs located side by side.

Although the flathead V-8 engine built by English Ford was suitable for the production Allards, it was not particularly competitive in the J1 competition sports cars. However, what was available was an American-built flathead Mercury V-8 of 3917 cc, which had powered a variety of military vehicles during the war and some were still in their shipping crates. Furthermore, these engines could be bored and stroked to give 4375 cc but the flathead design limited the maximum compression ratio to 7.0:1. Unfortunately, because of import restriction, American speed equipment such as that made by Edelbrock for this engine could not be obtained, although Allard did receive an Edelbrock kit consigned to him as a personal gift, thereby bending the regulations rather than breaking them.

The problem with the Mercury engine was that the front and rear exhaust ports were very restricted and any attempt at opening them up resulted in excessive coolant temperature if the engines were held at full throttle for any length of time. Sydney Allard had worked with these engines before WWII and had come up with a design for an overhead valve conversion. This design, which was never built, incorporated hemispherical combustion chambers with valves operated by a single camshaft in each head driven by gears from the crankshaft. The design was resurrected, but the cost was found to be prohibitive.

The man who saved the day was Zora Arkus-Duntov, who had developed the Ardun ohv conversion for the Mercury engine. Zora is a remarkable man, whose main claim to fame is that he fathered the Corvette and, if he had never done anything else, would go down in history as being the man who convinced General Motors' bean counters that the Corvette was not an undignified pursuit for the corporation, and was very worthwhile even if it did not always produce the kind of return on the dollar expected from a GM subsidiary. The Ardun conversion was somewhat similar to the design that Allard had conceived before the war, except that the valves, which were in hemispherical combustion chambers, were operated by pushrods by a single camshaft located in the conventional place. Among Gibbs's papers is a letter from Sydney Allard enclosing the practice times for the production car race at Silverstone on August 25, 1950. Significantly, Sydney Allard in an Ardun-powered car lapped at 80.61 mph and Cuthbert Harrison driving a Cadillac version set fastest lap at 85.24 mph.

The Ardun conversion just about coincided with the introduction of the J2 Allard. Initially, the British Import Control permitted an Ardun engine to be imported and a J2 exported to Ardun to be equipped with an engine. The next step was that the Ardun engine became the standard engine for the J2, although not many Ardun J2s were produced because it was just at the time when Tom Cole and Frederick Gibbs simultaneously hit on the idea of the new ohv Cadillac engine, which made a perfect marriage with the J2. In standard form the Cadillac displaced 5.4 liters and produced a claimed 160 bhp at 3500 rpm and 270 lb-ft of torque at just below 1800 rpm. However, in those days Detroit tended to give horsepower figures that were somewhat inflated and among Gibbs's papers is a letter from Mr A.R. McConnell of General Motors enclosing a bulletin on the subject of "1950 Series Cadillac Engines for Special Purpose Installations," and with the bulletin is a graph showing the horsepower and torque curves. The true horsepower shown is much closer to 135 than 160, but it is noted in the bulletin that the figures were obtained from the engine installed with all accessories, muffler, fan, etc. according to GM test code standards and corrected to 100 degrees Fahrenheit for the carburetor air.

The transmission used in Allards was normally a 1947 Ford 3-speed with Lincoln Zephyr gears to give closer ratios. This was a popular hot rod setup at the time, although it was only marginally strong enough to withstand the torque of the Cadillac. Various documents indicate that the Gibbs car had one of these transmissions and, while waiting delivery of the car, he calculated the speed in the gears with 6.00 x 16 tires. These figured out, using 5000 rpm as the peak, at 121.2 mph in high, 83.9 mph in 2nd and 56.3 in 1st. However, whether or not a stock 1950 Cadillac would go to 5000 rpm is debatable, although it certainly would with solid lifters and perhaps two carburetors. Gibbs does not appear to have modified his engine, probably because he felt it already produced sufficient power for normal road use. After all, 121.2 mph in an Allard is very fast, as anyone who has ever been 121.2 mph in an Allard will testify. Assuming that the engine was capable of turning at 5000 rpm, the car should have been able to reach its maximum speed because of the very advantageous power-to-weight ratio. The shipping weight of the complete car is shown on the bill of lading as 2016 lb, but this would be without any fuel or coolant, and it was probably also an estimate and on the low side.

The J2 Allard was a most ingenious car, and it had to be if it were delivered in New York for $3402.47 including 10-percent import duty. It had a wheelbase of 100.0 in. and the frame was simple box section steel. The front suspension consisted of an I-section Ford beam axle cut in half at the center and pivoted with long radius arms running back to ball joints. Springing was by coils and the shock absorbers were tubular. The weight distribution was just about 50/50 so the car was in effect a mid-engine design with the engine in front of the driver.

The drive from the engine was taken through an 11-in. clutch to a Ford gearbox and then through a torque tube to a De Dion rear axle, which was derived from some experimentation that had been done to Sydney Allard's Steyr-engined special. Apart from being remarkably effective, the De Dion system enabled the axle ratio to be changed relatively quickly. The brakes were outboard in front and inboard in the rear and the drums were of the Alfin type, which meant that they were of aluminum but with steel liners inside. The wheels were steel Fords, but most people bought the optional wires which were fitted to the same hubs as the Jaguar XK120. The body was aluminum.

The Allard records show that a total of 90 J2s were built during

the period 1950-1951 and these were followed by 82 J2Xs. The difference between a J2 and a J2X was primarily in the front suspension. Apparently Sydney Allard had noticed that the front suspension left something to be desired and rearrangement of the steering geometry and weight distribution was considered desirable. Until this time, the location of the engine had been determined by location of the pivot points for the two half beams of the front axle. By altering the position of the pivot points, the steering was not only improved but also it was possible to move the engine forward which further improved the handling. An additional advantage of these arrangements was increased cockpit room. Previously the cockpit had been very cramped although Sydney Allard, who stood 6 ft 3 in., had always professed not to notice this shortcoming.

Sydney Allard raced the J2s and J2Xs extensively in national and international events including four attempts at Le Mans. The

team's best showing at Le Mans was in 1950 when one Cadillac engined J2 was entered for Sydney Allard and Tom Cole. The opposition included five Ferraris and various Aston Martin Talbot-Lagos and Jaguars as well as a Cadillac special and Cadillac sedan entered by Briggs Cunningham.

Sydney Allard was away first and the car was reaching about 145 mph on the Mulsanne Straight, aided in its gearing massive 7.50 x 16 tires on the rear. Unfortunately, soon after 3:0 a.m., transmission trouble delayed the car in the pits for about 2 minutes and it restarted with only high gear. This presented some difficulties but the enormous torque of the Cadillac helped considerably and Cole and Allard drove on through the night. A usual, patches of swirling fog made driving very difficult for Sydney Allard, because he had been virtually blind in his left eye for most of his life, a little known fact. Eventually the car finished 3rd overall, winning its class at a record speed, having covered 2106 miles compared to the 2153 miles of the winning Talbot Lago.

Twenty years ago I bought a Cadillac-powered J2 Allard and wrote about it in *Road & Track* for July 1963. I must admit didn't change the oil as frequently as Gibbs but I did drive more. In fact, I used to commute in it every day. My car was very similar to Gibbs's car, but my engine had an Iskenderian cam and solid lifters, which gave it a bit more performance but left totally reliable and incredibly tractable. I lived in San Francisco at the time, and I used to surprise people by starting at the bottom of one of San Francisco's 20-percent gradients and shifting into high at 50 mph halfway up with the car still pulling strongly.

In the July 1963 story, I described the car as potentially the most dangerous car I had ever driven. This was because the special front axle permitted enormous and almost instantaneous variations in camber and track because of weight transfer during acceleration and deceleration. If you drove along slowly, depressing and releasing the accelerator, it was possible to make the whole front of the car move up and down as the camber and track changed. On the other hand, the De Dion in the rear was super because you could put all the torque of the Cadillac through with a minimum of wheelspin. Of course, the roadholding of cars in those days was much more hit and miss than it is today, and driver had to make the best of a car's virtues instead of lamenting its vices, and one of the virtues of the Allard was its tremendous acceleration. The technique for fast cornering in an Allard was establish the line and the amount of throttle opening and endeavor to hold them until you had the car straightened up. My car never did slide out from under me, but it certainly never stopped trying. One thing I never did find out was the gas tank capacity because the tank tended to slop gas when nearly full, so periodically when the gauge started to go down I would just put in 25 gal. I think the tank held 50 gal.

From the records, it appears that Frederick Gibbs didn't use his car at all after Wednesday, December 10, 1969, when he made the last entry in the log of the car. He spent the morning winterizing the cooling system and making sure that everything was in order. He finished his log by writing, "I was driven Stamford in a Hertz Plymouth by a Gibbs & Cox driver, who was very nice. I returned to Manhattan house about 1:00 p.m. This was a very satisfactory day but I was very tired. The car was really left in good shape for the winter. Prestone had not been changed since November 24, 1962—more than *seven years* ago."

Frederick Gibbs died in 1978 and the car didn't have 700 miles on it when it was acquired from the estate by Paul Pappalardo. In fact, the last time Gibbs drove it was apparently on September 11, 1965 when he took it to Pound Ridge to have inspected and the odometer showed 6544 miles when he got back. However, although he never drove it again, he evidently cared very much for it to the extent that on June 24, 1976 he paid a very considerable amount of money for having it completely stripped and rebuilt, so that it was in perfect and original condition on the day he died, 28 years after he bought it.

AT a drivers' party in Tom Lush's motel room the night before the race, Allard J2 Ardun-Ford driver Dean Butler asked Allard design staffer Dudley Hume what he reckoned Sydney Allard would have thought of such a massed gathering of racing J2s, J2Xs and other Allard models some three decades after their production. Dudley, now 62 and a chassis designer in Ford's top secret design department, considered his Chivas Regal and replied: "He'd have been dead chuffed, I should say."

So he should have been, for this second US Allard Reunion was being held at the Southeast Vintage Racing Association's big meet, the Atlanta Vintage Grand Prix at Road Atlanta, and the Allard club is now strong enough to have been able to persuade the SVRA's president, Ford Heacock, to run an all-Allard race for the first time in history. The race was won by Don Marsh in his stunning BRG J2X and in case you think old car racers in the States just cruise around posing in concours cars, it should be noted that Don also won the 'Race Cars thru 1959' race outright as well, beating off Joe Pendergast's Lister Corvette, a Jaguar D-Type and assorted Aston Martins, Lolas, Lotuses and other sports racing machinery from the Fifties. Marsh was *really going* to achieve this win, getting the jump at the start and powering that wriggling brute of a chassis through the corners. It was not fancy parade: we were treated to a motor race.

Most of the 19 known active Stateside Allards were present at the Reunion and they were supported by Tom Lush, Sydney Allard's righthand man and co-driver on that famous Monte Carlo Rally win in 1952. "Everyone said I was mad to ride with Sydney," recalls Tom, "and I suppose we did go through a few hedges and down the odd ravine. I was always curious to know what he would do next but really I was always happy with his driving. I'll never forget once hitting the cobbles in the wet sideways on a town square on the Mille Miglia. The whole crowd stood up to cheer at this skilled display of ragged edge driving and how were they to know that he'd simply lost it and just happened to fly off out of the square down the right road? Tom Lush is also the author of *Allard — the Inside Story*, published by MRP and already a collector's item in its own right. He was for many years the company's competitions and technical chief.

Then there was Alan Tiley, a great Allard expert who worked as a very young man for the company between 1951 and 1959 and who now owns the fabulous (to use this abused word properly) Steyr-Allard. And Cyril Wick, works driver and another leading light in the British Allard Owners Club today. Cyril hadn't raced anything at all for 29 years until this meeting when, to his delight and that of all around, he got a ride in Bob Lytle's superbly restored 'Nailhead' Buick-powered J2X. After some natural hesitancy he began to move the beast in the approved fashion and displayed his old style — just don't tell his wife that he's started racing again.

Ian Grant, owner of the famous J2X that I tested to back up the Davis File features some two years ago in *T&CC*, was an an enthusiastic spectator and adviser to the already very knowledgeable Americans assembled at Road Atlanta. These famous people were already well known to me and it was a great pleasure to meet Dudley Hume, who joined Allard as a draughtsman/designer at the end of the Forties from Aston Martin. At Astons, he had designed the front suspension for the DB 2/4 over the freezing winter of 1946/7, producing some 100 drawings (without the aid of computerised equipment!) before he arrived at the geometry that he wanted. He was destined to have the odd battle with Sydney Allard and the more senior personnel at the South London works

The world's first all Allard race was held at Road Atlanta, Georgia, last November, and senior Allard factory personnel were on hand to assist competitors! Tony Dron tested two of the cars and here reports

Photography by Art Eastman and Jeff Allison

# Dangerous Games

over such things as the Allard front suspension, and he is still planning his revenge!

Stateside Allard owners tend to be successful well-to-do types and many of them are over 50, yet amazingly keen and youthful in their attitude to life. They restore their cars in order to get out and race them against other Allards: if you have never driven an Allard this may not mean much so perhaps I had better explain what it means at this stage.

Road Atlanta circuit is a bit like three miles of the old Nurburgring, up and down hill with 12 turns and several blinds brows as it sweeps through the evergreens, and there are many places where it would be extremely easy to go off in a big way. An Allard is a heavy sports car with a fairly flexible chassis, most often with de Dion rear suspension, split axle front suspension with bump steer you wouldn't believe and drum brakes that tug the car around the road on those occasions when they condescend to work at all. Put a powerful American V8 (Cadillac, Ford, Chrysler, Chevrolet, Oldsmobile, Buick — any of these) into this package and you end up with a car that makes up in excitement what it lacks in sophistication. A dinosaur in its own time, let alone today, it's the kind of machine that Colin Chapman wanted to release us from by starting Lotus. Its appeal today, as then, is its true sports car style (*macho* man's car if you like) matched with the kind of overpowered beastliness that makes you want to get in there and tame the machine. On the track I drove Syd Silverman's J2X and Pete MacManus's K1 (this car will be familiar to British enthusiasts as Pete has campaigned in HSCC events over here for the past two seasons, but has now returned to the States permanently with the car); they date from 1952 and 1948.

Syd's Chrysler-powered car and Pete's blown Ford example are very similar to drive. You sit up high and exposed behind the aeroscreens, close to the big steering wheel, knees splayed so that your feet can get at the big pedals. So great is the torque that it would be possible to tackle the entire circuit, tight turns, hills and all, in third gear (ie top) without any great detriment to lap times. On the straights, the monsters surge ahead relentlessly. As the corners approach one's sense of self-preservation hits the red light full-alert action stations mode. On the brakes the chassis weaves around; ease off them and you aim the massive massive bulk for the corner's apex and can sense the enormous weight trying hard to take you out. A wrestling match is on as you, the driver, decide to take charge and inform this unruly giant that not only will it accept your orders to stay on the road but it will also succumb to your desire to accelerate away, dammit. Down goes the right foot and the V8 thunder begins all over again. It's all quite daft, really, but it is enormous fun. The fact that it would be absurdly easy to kill yourself seems to add a little something to the experience, too.

With Dudley Hume and Tom Lush to help at various stages of the weekend, I went around the paddock inspecting the cars. First we looked at the J2s: one of these, Bob Valpey's, was the first Cad-Allard to reach the States and was the second J-model that the factory exported. It was delivered in 1949, November, for the late Tom Cole (who was killed at Le Mans) and won the major Bridghampton race in 1950. After that it was used successfully in sprint races and the scuttle-mounted fuel cap was fitted in 1951. Bob, a real estate expert, picked it up as a 'basket case' a year ago and has restored it faithfully to its '51 spec, just as it was for most of its competition history.

One of the J2Xs still under restoration (it needs detail attention and painting) was sold to Alan Patterson as new late in 1951. Alan won

▲ the editor sampling the Allard driving experience at Road Atlanta circuit, Georgia, USA. The car belongs to New York enthusiast, Syd Silverman, and is a 1952 J2X model. Perhaps it was a dinosaur in its day but there are few cars more thrilling to drive

*Left, the massed field of Allards headed by, l to r, Don Marsh's 1952 J2X, Bob Valpey's 1950 J2 and Ted Bernstein's 1952 K2. Seven different Allard models were represented in this remarkable line-up*

*Lower left: Reunion group shows the British contingent, l to r, Cyril Wick, Dudley Hume, Pete McManus (hon Brit for this pic!), Tony Dron, Ian Grant, Tom Lush and Alan Tiley. Tom can also be seen greeting the American Allard owners, while the central black and white pics show Cyril Wick 30 years ago rallying in France with LXY 15 and in 1984 preparing thoughtfully for his first race in 29 years, aboard Bob Lytle's J2X*

## Dangerous Games

many hillclimbs in the car and finished first in class at Watkins Glen in 1953, these exploits for the then college boy being enough to attract the attention of professional teams and he soon had a semi-professional career going, driving for such people as Frank Nicholls of Elva at Sebring. Though the car started out as a Chrysler-powered J2X and has recently been changed to a stock Cadillac from a junk yard, the fact is that all along Alan Patterson has owned it, though it did lie idle for many years, and is still racing it today. He was delighted at Road Atlanta, for after some months of effort he has finally managed to make it work properly again. One of the most interesting cars is Dean Butler's 1950 J2, for it is fitted with the original Allard Ardun-Ford type engine, probably the only car in the world still running with this ohv conversion.

Allard was persuaded to take on the system by Zora *Arkus Dunt*ov and Dudley Hume was given the job of making proper drawings from the reams of rough sketches and notes. It was always unreliable and Dean Butler has had terrible trouble getting it all to work right. There are not really enough head studs on the Ford, the rocker arms are extremely long, and keeping the whole thing together requires considerable expertise and patience, but Dean is rightly proud of the achievement and the car now runs very well. The fact that the plugs are almost impossible to change and that, to get the engine out, the entire front half of the body has to be removed from the chassis is just a minor irritation! Hume describes the car as "a remarkable tribute to Dean Butler's persistence." Duntov, by the way, went on to GM to be a chief engineer on Corvettes.

Syd Silverman, of *Variety* magazine and from New York, has a superb J2X Chrysler which is standard but for its fancy nudge bars and exhaust outlet, but Tom Turner, from Fort Worth in Texas, has a J2 with a curious louvred glassfibre panel on the 'boot' lid. Within the body in this area is located a supplementary radiator for the water cooling, a perennial Allard problem. It is hard to see how the smallbore pipes to the rear, which are connected to the two lower front radiator pipes, actually convey any useful quantity of water but Tom says the car resists overheating well.

Dudley Hume explained that a considerable sum of money was spent on designing a so-called venturi effect for incoming air within the Allard nosecones but few of the cars seem to have the right inner panels today. Everybody has his own answer to the cooling problem. Bob Lytle put in a scoop and an old cooler within the lower panel inside the nose and he says his Buick, a notorious overheater in any application, is now all right. This engine got its name 'Nailhead', by the way, from California hotrodders who spurned it because of its tiny valves which they considered to look like carpenters' nails.

Walking around, Dudley was becoming more and more concerned about this venturi air flow business. Clearly, several of the cars had left the factory with incorrectly shaped cooling air ducting and for a moment I felt he was itching to get back to Clapham to give the blokes a roasting for not making these export cars with the right 'trick' parts in them!

There was a considerable variation in front wheel camber on the cars, too. Sydney Allard had the standard setting fixed at 2½ degrees positive, but they go much better with the wheels decambered to about zero (ie upright). This can be done by carefully bending the split axles or by dropping the centre mounting plate by up to half an inch. It's important, too, to reset the anti-droop straps to severely restrict downward movement of the split axle beams as this reduces the bump steer crucially. On Don Marsh's car, the anti-droop straps are metal and very carefully set just right. Sydney Allard, according to Tom Lush, thought all this made the cars too easy to drive, a point which used to drive Dudley Hume to distraction. He went around the paddock explaining to all the drivers with standard camber that they should set about decambering them, which in my opinion was good advice. No Allard was or is 'too easy' to drive!

It would be easy to dwell on any one of these cars for they all have an interesting history and most are superbly restored. Bob Lytle's car has a drag racing history, for it was once owned by a young man whose father worked in the experimental engine department at Buick. That's why it is Buick-powered today, with a modified 364cu in engine installed that gives about 100bhp more than standard for the old Nailhead.

Don Marsh's winning car is beautifully built and is installed with automatic transmission, of all things, which he regards as "a great spoof." Fred Wacker once raced an automatic Allard successfully, so Don is not the first person to try it. Don's car also has fan-ventilated ducting to the rear brakes and a brake balance adjuster in the cockpit.

Looking at some of the other cars assembled for the Reunion and SVRA races, an interesting machine is the standard unrestored K2 of T&CC's Cross the Pond contributor Jim Donick. This car is one of those with a completely wrongly shaped top panel within the nosecone, but it is obviously original as it left the factory! It needs decambering badly and the front suspension straps should be pulled up a lot. The Ford engine is fitted with the optional Allard cylinder heads which were a near copy of the pre-war designed high-performance Edelbrock heads. Dudley Hume recalls that up to 50 per cent of these alloy Allard heads had to be returned to the Birmingham foundry because of porosity: after a time the sub-contractors got the message and quality was improved.

One of the most interesting cars there was the Chrysler 392cu in-powered Allard GT Coupé, one of two such cars made. Better known to us as the Firepower engine, it was originally built to the special order of a member of the du Pont family, complete with push-button automatic transmission and wild cams that made it idle at 1800rpm, way above the engagement rpm of the drivetrain. When new, it was inadvertently driven into the workshop bench twice (with the wheels spinning). Sydney Allard decreed that only he, Jim Mac and a selected few others could drive it prior to shipping: he took it home one night and hit a truck up the back, necessitating repairs to the front right wing. Jim Mac delivered it to Southampton, a journey he described as 2½ hours of non-stop terror!

Meanwhile the US agent is said to have got greedy and the customer baulked at the mark-up. The car then had a chequered history, reputedly one changing hands in a card game between top Mafia men. Now it belongs to motorcycle accessory manufacturer, Bob Girvin, and it has been tuned to perform more predictably. Girvin bought the car from Bob Valpey and his only modification has been to stiffen the rear Panhard rod, which has improved the handling and cut out rapid and terrifying oversteering oscillations. The car dates from 1958 and its sister was fitted with a Jaguar XK engine, a special deal arranged with Lofty England which might have led to a series of Jaguar-Allards.

A Palm Beach Mk2 with a Jaguar engine did turn up at the Reunion, however. These cars were fitted with a stylish body that was specially designed in the US. The chassis came straight from the racing Allard JR. It had a stiff frame with live rear axle and differed from the JR in that the front end had an interesting

Macpherson strut-type suspension, but with a laminated steel torsion bar.

There was a real JR there too, chassis number 3403, which is Syd Silverman's pet restoration project at present. Nearly complete, the job is being carried out by Chris Butler, who also maintains Don Marsh's cars. The condition of the car was so bad that they had to seek help to establish the right shape for the aluminium nose. It looks rather like a prototype AC sports or Cobra: Dudley Hume was able to go up into his loft, find the original drawings and have them unfolded by a special softening process (simply unrolling them would have cracked them up after all this time), and despatch blueprints.

One of the most beautiful cars in the whole paddock was the red K2 of Ted Bernstein, a neuro-surgeon from Dayton, Ohio, whose interest in old cars has led him to set up a restoration business as a hobby. The car originally belonged to the celebrated Allard enthusiast, General Curtis Le May, and on this occasion it picked up second place overall in a concours event held over the weekend, plus the coveted 'Peoples' Choice Award.' A surprise to all was the unexpected arrival of LYX15, Cyril Wick's own J2X many years ago, which has just been restored by its US owner.

I can't move off the cars without mentioning the two J2Xs of John Harden and William G Lassiter. Harden always won the Allard events until Don Marsh came along, and his Olds-Allard, equipped with the original Hilborn constant flow fuel injection of 1952, is a superb car that its driver pushes right to the limit. Lassiter's car is not pretty but it is driven equally hard by the talented Bill Schmidt, who also prepares it (but to a budget that doesn't quite match some, I have to assume!). At the end of the meeting we all dispersed, Tom Lush joining Bob Lytle on the long haul to California and more Allard business. Perhaps they should set up in business in Clapham again!

My conclusions from the weekend were complex, perhaps. First, it would be great if this American Allard circus could visit the UK as a group and put on a race, say, in the HSCC meeting or some other major event. British enthusiasts might be surprised, to say the least.

But the meeting set me thinking about the future of Historic racing (which the Americans call Vintage racing; don't confuse it with our VSCC term 'Vintage'). Dudley Hume sparked a thought when he said he wanted to build a small batch of Allard JRs today. What category would they fall into, I ask you? Even now, he wants to build the car he designed in the first place, without Sydney Allard having the opportunity to stop him! It would have a glassfibre body, disc brakes, independent rear suspension, and the laminated torsion bar front suspension with struts. As Dudley says: "I'm the only bloke with the right to do it who's still alive." Fair comment. I suppose we could call it the 1956 J4R that might have been and now is! Even the proposed J3R never existed, though.

Like the AC MkIV, which is an AC Cobra in resumed production, the car that I call a J4R has a perfect right to exist. Perhaps we should have a class in Historic races for true originals, as now, though increasingly there are worries about metal fatigue in these cars. Then we could have a class for exact copies, for we must recognise that they exist and it is not fair that they should run alongside genuine and much more valuable originals. And how about another class for such cars as the AC MkIV and Dudley Hume's 'J4R' which we might term 'resumed production cars.' These are just some idle thoughts that might stir up positive action or just plain trouble. All I'll say is it's not my job to lay down the law. The world, as always, will do what it wants, and that's that.

(Continued from page 149)

in front, and the old s.v. Ford V8 engine ceased to be compulsory, except for the home market. British buyers, due to import restrictions, were still stuck with this reliable but pedestrian piece of Dagenham-ware, but J2s shipped to the U.S., which is where most of them went, could have a variety of propellants: Cadillac, Chrysler, Mercury, Dodge, Ardun-Ford.

Just to tantalize the poor benighted British, however, one of their magazines road-tested a Cad-Allard J2 early in 1951, and recorded a standing quarter-mile time of 16.25 seconds. Outstanding as such acceleration was for a reasonably habitable sports two-seater in the year 1951, it represented an improvement of only 0.55 seconds over the Zephyr-powered Allard Special of 1939. The latter, moreover, was a side-valver, over a liter and 55 bhp down on displacement and power compared with the J2. Another unrelated contrast shows in the ground clearance department: the pre-war V12 stood 9½ inches off the ground at its lowest point, whereas the J2's clearance was just 3½ inches.

The Ardun engine, to revert to our list of J2 powerplant options, was basically a Ford V8 but with hemispherical heads and rockerbox o.h.v. devised by the fertile-minded Zora Duntov, renowned for his later development work on Corvettes. Duntov spent about a year at Allard, trying to translate some estimable theory into effective practice, but the Ardun never was a great success. Around 75 Allard-Arduns were built, post-delivery conversions included, and most of them went to U.S. homes.

In late 1951 the J2X Allard, with the same choice of engines, sprang from the loins of the J2, and featured a revised front suspension and added weight to the fore. In 1952 the Le Mans car in which Sydney refused to "hang about" in the 300SLs' company on the Mulsanne straight was a streamline-bodied J2X. With its much-improved aerodynamic shape, this was indeed a very fast car.

It wasn't until 1956 that Allard finally ditched the time-hallowed divided axle i.f.s., switching to a variation on the Mc-Pherson front suspension theme on the Palm Beach Allards that had meanwhile supplanted yesteryear's V8s. These cars, which weren't destined to recapture the glamor of their massive forebears, had rockerbox Ford Consul or Zephyr engines as option, with four and six cylinders respectively. Later again, a lengthened and beefed-up derivative of the Palm Beach's tubular frame was wrapped around a 3.4-liter Jaguar engine to form the GT model. What this one could do, the XK150 could do equally well, and what's more the Jag cost less. So, at the letters GT, the Allard alphabet terminated.

The future? Sydney Allard, busy mainly with Adlard affairs, is noncommittal, but those closest to him say he's privately anxious to keep the name alive; alive, that is, for others besides short-haul travelers in London ambulances. My own guess is that, if and when the renaissance comes, Ford, his old love, will be its mainspring. But tomorrow's Allard, if tomorrow holds an Allard, won't just be something old in a new wrapper. Bet you.  —DM